P9-CMU-404

WILL ROGERS

WILL ROGERS

A BIOGRAPHY

BEN YAGODA

UNIVERSITY OF OKLAHOMA PRESS

NORMAN

All photographs accompanying the chapter openings and appearing in the inserts following pages 80 and 208 are used courtesy of the Will Rogers Memorial and Library, unless otherwise specified.

Grateful acknowledgment is made to the following for permission to reprint previously published material or to print unpublished material: *Constance Morrow Morgan*: Material from the diary of Elisabeth Cutter Morrow, December 1927, Sophie Smith Collection, Smith College. Reprinted by permission. *The New York Times:* F. T. Birchall memorandum to proof room (May 19, 1930); Arthur H. Sulzberger to Adolph Ochs (Jan. 17, 1927); Edwin L. James, letter to reader (Jan. 17, 1933); Ochs telegram to Will Rogers (Jan. 21, 1930); F. T. Birchall memorandum to Ochs (Nov. 18, 1931): unsigned telegram to Will Rogers (Feb. 1, 1933); McCaw to James (undated). Courtesy of the New York Times Company.

Library of Congress Cataloging-in-Publication Data

Yagoda, Ben.
    Will Rogers: a biography / Ben Yagoda.
      p.   cm.
    Originally published: New York : Knopf, 1993.
    Includes bibliographical references and index.
    ISBN 0-8061-3238-8 (pbk. : alk. paper)
    1. Rogers, Will, 1879–1935. 2. Entertainers—United States—Biography. 3. Humorists, American—Biography. I. Title.
PN2287.R74 Y34 2000
792.7'028'092—dc21
[B]   99-056657

The paper in this book meets the guidelines for permanence and durability of the Committee on Production Guidelines for Book Longevity of the Council on Library Resources, Inc.∞

Copyright © 1993 by Ben Yagoda. All rights reserved under International and Pan-American Copyright Conventions.

Published by the University of Oklahoma Press, Norman, Publishing Division of the University. Manufactured in the U.S.A. First printing of the University of Oklahoma Press edition, 2000.

1   2   3   4   5   6   7   8   9   10

FOR WILLIAM VANN ROGERS
AND FOR GIGI

To
Dad
from
Garry

Christmas
2000

CONTENTS

CONTENTS

Illustrations follow pages 80 and 208.

AUTHOR'S NOTE

In 1930, F. T. Birchall, managing editor of *The New York Times,* sent a memo to the newspaper's proofroom concerning the man who at the time was its only signed columnist. He wrote: "Please do not correct Will Rogers's English or spelling. His little pieces are unique because he makes his own English. When you 'improve' it you are taking away part of the personality he is selling to readers."

Rogers's pieces weren't "little"—they're much fresher and sharper today, for example, than any *Times* editorial of the time—but otherwise Birchall was on the money. In quoting from Rogers's letters and unpublished manuscripts, I resisted any urge to clean up grammar and capitalization. Punctuation was a little more complicated, since Rogers, always in a hurry, habitually used commas where periods were meant to be, Here is an example. I generally put the periods in. He typed fast, of course, and made a lot of spelling mistakes. I corrected some obvious typos, left the other errors in, and used "[*sic*]" only in cases of real ambiguity.

Another stylistic note: Readers will observe that I continue to refer to Rogers as "Will" not only in the chapters covering the time before he reaches what a friend of mine calls the age of biographical majority (in most biographies, nineteen or twenty) but throughout the book. I have done so, at the risk of appearing overly familiar toward my subject, because the man himself was so constitutionally opposed to pomp and pretense that writing a whole book about "Rogers" seemed absurd.

HENRY FORD MUSEUM

AMERICAN ICONS: WILL ROGERS, A LINCOLNESQUE ACTOR,
AND HENRY FORD

INTRODUCTION

Will Rogers . . . has a curious national quality. He gives the impression that the country is filled with such sages, wise with years, young in humor and love of life, shrewd yet gentle. He is what Americans think other Americans are like.

— NEW YORK SUN, APRIL 5, 1935

Why not *try* to test Ronald Reagan for the part of Will Rogers? He is droll homely humorous and an all around good actor.

— UNSIGNED MEMORANDUM,
WARNER BROTHERS PICTURES, CA. 1941

AMERICA SURPRISED ITSELF when Will Rogers died, surprised itself by the size and force of its grief. The Associated Press sent out the news a little past 10:00 a.m., eastern time, August 16, 1935: The evening before, Rogers and aviator Wiley Post, whose tour of Alaska the country had been following for the last ten days, had died in an airplane crash near Point Barrow, the northernmost point in U.S. territory. By afternoon, the whole country had seen the banner headlines in the newspaper extras, had heard the radio flashes. On the floor of the Senate, Majority Leader Joe Robinson, a longtime friend of Rogers's, stood up and announced: "Will Rogers, probably the most widely known private citizen and certainly the best beloved, met his death some hours ago in a lonely, far-away place." Another friend, Vice President John Nance Garner, was asked for a reaction by a reporter; overcome with emotion, he simply said, "I cannot talk about it." In a store in Maine, a boy came in from the street and shouted the news. The clerks stopped what they were doing and three or four customers left the store. No one spoke for a full minute. One woman, feeling that her legs were no longer of any use, just sat down on a box. The scene was repeated, with marginal variations, across the country.

Editorials were written, theaters darkened, telegrams sent, and high schools renamed. The magnitude of the reaction, in point of fact, was such as you would expect the passing of a beloved President to engender. Will Rogers, fifty-five years old, had a radio show, wrote a daily newspaper column, acted in the movies. Years earlier he had been a rope-twirling monologist in the *Ziegfeld Follies*, before that a vaudeville gypsy. Yet people had come to depend on his presence—his absence was making them realize—more than that of any politician.

Rogers's ascendancy was puzzling, and is even more so to a later generation that knows him (if at all) for a charitable fund with which he had, and his estate has, no connection whatsoever, and for two slogans that appear to bespeak either disingenuousness or simplemindedness—"I never met a man I didn't like" and "All I know is what I read in the papers." How did it happen? The answer, as far as there is one, lies in the pages that follow. But a few points bear preliminary consideration. The first is that Will Rogers was a Cherokee Indian. He was scarcely more than a quarter Cherokee, to be sure, but in the Indian Territory (where he was born and where he lived for most of the first twenty-three years of his life) that in no way diminished his standing in the tribe. Rogers was just two generations removed from the massive betrayal of the Cherokees and the four other so-called Civilized Tribes by Andrew Jackson and the U.S. government. He lived through a second swindle, and as a result of it his father, a prominent rancher, lost the use of 60,000 acres of prime grazing land. Other than a gag or two, and an occasional barbed reference to Jackson, Will Rogers did not make much of his Cherokee heritage. But the weight of that heritage, the sense that history can turn on you when you least expect it, surely helped forge in him an equanimity that colored everything he wrote or said and that the nation appreciated as wisdom.

Cherokees valued literacy, took "white" names, owned slaves; they were widely considered the most "civilized" of the Civilized Tribes. As such they—especially the mixed-bloods among them—had one foot in each camp, the white and the red. They were mediators. In Rogers's case, this revealed itself in a kind of dual consciousness he displayed all his life: the way he could be a hero to the forces of "decency" and yet be a headliner in the all-but-pornographic *Ziegfeld Follies*, the way he could present himself as a mere comedian and yet be an extremely influential political voice in the country, the way he could take strong stands without, usually, offending those on the opposite side of the issue.

As an entertainer, Will Rogers was a beneficiary of circumstances. He started out as a cowboy vaudevillian at precisely the moment when vaudeville was at its zenith as an entertainment form and when a national vogue for cowboys was in full force. As his career progressed, a dizzying array of new media presented themselves: the radio, the phonograph record, the syndicated newspaper column, the motion picture (silent and talking). Rogers tackled them, one by one, with almost shocking success.

What is more, the message he communicated was perfectly suited to his times. In the 1920s, American society transmogrified itself into something unfamiliar and (for many) a little frightening; in the early 1930s, the bottom fell out of the economy. Rogers was an astute and sagacious observer of politics and other foibles, a purveyor of great good humor, and a decent man who knew how to communicate decency masterfully. But what was probably more important during this period of anxiety was the way his wry, genial, supremely self-effacing, pointed yet never overheated wit and commentary implicitly asserted that maybe things hadn't changed so much after all. He was like Lincoln or Twain, only better. (They did meet people they didn't like, and they couldn't throw a lasso.) He took care not to offend or to challenge core beliefs, and he allowed his listeners to continue to think that common sense and two-syllable words could get to the heart of any problem.

To a country obsessed with self-definition, he was an irresistible personification of America. In a rather uncanny way, he seemed to span the nation's history. Not so many generations before him, as he liked to say, his ancestors had met the *Mayflower*. His father pioneered virgin prairie and fought for the South in the Civil War. In his youth, Will himself rode the plains as a cowboy. (And, as these words are being written, his two sons are alive and well.)

But Rogers participated in the process as well. Part of his paradox was that along with the old-time values, he was opportunistic and prescient enough to embrace as well the brand-new mass-culture media; it was as if someone came along today and became celebrated for generating virtual-reality representations of log-cabin hearths. His message, too, must have been tailored in some measure to what he perceived the needs of his audience to be. Of course the papers weren't his only source of information; of course there were people he couldn't stand. More than one observer has noted that the older and more worldly he got, the more socially at ease he was with senators and tycoons, the worse the grammar and spelling in his columns became.

Yet it's too easy to transpose him into the movie *A Face in the Crowd*, where Andy Griffith's Lonesome Rhodes parlays calculated folksiness into mass success, or into Ronald Reagan, who didn't get to play Will Rogers in the movie biography (Will Rogers, Jr., got the part), but who, with his "Well" 's and shrugs, his just-folks bonhomie, managed a pretty impressive Rogers impersonation in the White House. Rogers's persona *wasn't* an act—or, to the extent that it was, it had been almost totally internalized by the time he reached the height of his success. "He built himself up till he became, both on and off the stage, the Will Rogers the public knew," wrote his friend, scenarist, and biographer, Homer Croy. "The older he grew, and the more successful he became, the more he played this character."

As Croy's comment suggests, Rogers was a hard person to know. He was not given to self-revelation or easy intimacy, and his ready access to the "Will Rogers" character gave him a perfect escape route when things got too personal. As a young man he was just Will Rogers, and in his letters to an Arkansas girl named Betty Blake he let his doubt, his despair, his anger, and his glee pour onto the page. Then he married Betty, and all of a sudden a veil dropped over the inner man. The second puzzle of Will Rogers was how his emotionally erratic, undirected youth was transformed into an adulthood of unmatched stability, drive, and contentment. The evidence suggests that the answer starts with Betty.

For there to be another Will Rogers today, he (or she) would have to combine the separate attributes of Johnny Carson, Roy Rogers, Clark Clifford, Walter Cronkite, Bill Cosby, Bob Hope, Russell Baker, H. Ross Perot, and James Reston. It just can't happen. Which is all the more reason to take a look back to how it once did.

WILL ROGERS

CLEM AND MARY ROGERS

CHAPTER I

INDIAN TERRITORY

WILL ROGERS had to invent himself—no one else would have known what to make of him. He was a Cherokee Indian, and also the son of a Confederate veteran who fancied himself a southern gentleman; the heir to a sizable fortune, and also an itinerant cowboy; a high school dropout, and also, eventually, perhaps the most successful writer in America. He grew up in the Indian Territory (later to become the state of Oklahoma), and as he reached his maturity he found that the land was literally shifting under his feet. From these aggressively indeterminate beginnings, he shaped himself into a figure the likes of which America had never seen before and hasn't seen since.

This capacity for self-creation is one of the few qualities—a devotion to horses, an aversion to formal education, and a remarkable level of achievement are the others—he shared with his father, Clement Vann Rogers. When Clem Rogers died in 1911, his obituary called him "a pioneer who was a statesman and a man. . . . He was a great man from any point you choose to look at it." But, like Will, he had a socially, ethnically, and geographically ambiguous starting point.

Clem Rogers's paternal grandfather was Robert Rogers, a Scotch-Irishman who came to West Virginia around 1800 to trade with Indians; he married Lucy Cordery, one-half Cherokee. Their first son, also named Robert, was born in Georgia in 1815. In 1835, Robert Rogers, Jr., married Sallie Vann, who was probably three-eighths Cherokee. Their son, Clement Vann Rogers, was thus five-sixteenths Cherokee.

The diversity within the Rogers line was nothing remarkable: Among Cherokee Indians in the nineteenth century, particularly female Cherokees, intermarriage was as much rule as exception. The practice resulted in a mixed-blood strain with a striking dual consciousness: people who acted, dressed, thought, and often looked like whites and were almost as prejudiced toward "lesser" tribes and Cherokee full-bloods as whites were, but who at the same time considered themselves—and were considered—no less Cherokee than the purest full-blood, with the same status, rights, and privileges within the tribe. Indeed, mixed-bloods tended to be more likely to amass wealth and occupy positions of leadership.

For both mixed-bloods and full-, the milestones of Cherokee history are two very large broken promises. Clem Rogers was born shortly after the first betrayal, and his life roughly coincided with a onetime window of opportunity, a foreshortened Cherokee version of the American dream of unfettered opportunity. Clem dove through the window and succeeded beyond his dreams. Then came the second betrayal, and it largely wiped his fortune out. That he seemed neither surprised nor particularly resentful shows his understanding of how lucky he had been.

European explorers had found the Cherokees living in mountain areas of what are now the Carolinas, Georgia, Alabama, and Tennessee. More than the other tribes of the Southeast—the Choctaws, Chickasaws, Creeks, and Seminoles—they had always accommodated themselves enthusiastically to white culture. They were a farming people and in their agriculture they followed the practices of the colonists, including the owning of slaves. They placed a strong emphasis on education, establishing their own school system and sending many of its graduates to the best white colleges. (The Cherokee leader Sequoyah [c.1766–1843] created a syllabary, unique among Indian languages, that permitted Cherokee to be written and read, and heightened the value placed on education and self-expression. The tribe established its own newspaper, printed in English and Cherokee, in 1828.) They adopted a republican form of government in 1820 and by 1827 had formulated a constitution and established themselves politically as the Cherokee Nation. Many Cherokees, and nearly all the mixed-bloods, took white names.

But this adaptation bought them no security. Whites began encroaching on their land in the eighteenth century, and in the early nineteenth century the U.S. government began to purchase it in exchange for money and territory west of the Mississippi River. In 1828, the Georgia legislature passed an act that baldly took land away from Cherokees and distributed it to white settlers; it also declared all persons of Indian blood incompetent to serve as witness or party to any suit in which the defendant was a white man. In 1829, Robert Rogers, Jr., his mother, and his two sisters (his father had apparently died), then living in Big Tallapossa, Georgia, were among a small group of Cherokees signing an agreement to relinquish all their territory in the East and remove themselves to the northeast section of what was called the Indian Territory. This was a body of land—bounded on the east by what is now Arkansas, on the north by Kansas, and on the south by the fork formed by the Arkansas and Canadian rivers—from which *other* Indian tribes had been removed. (It constitutes the present-day state of Oklahoma, minus the Panhandle.)

In 1830, Congress, with the strong support of President Andrew Jackson, passed the Indian Removal Act, calling for the resettlement of all eastern tribes in the Indian Territory. By 1832, the Choctaws, Chickasaws, Creeks, and Seminoles had all agreed. The Cherokees, in whom the whites had most successfully instilled their notions of freedom and due process, held out the longest. In 1835, a minority group composed mostly of mixed-bloods, convinced that removal was inevitable, approved the Treaty of New Echota, under which, for the sum of $5 million, they agreed to relinquish their claims to all lands east of the Mississippi. Some two thousand people made the journey to the part of the Indian Territory—the northeast corner—that had been reserved for the Cherokees. Together with the earlier arrivals, like the Rogerses, they became known as the "Old Settlers."

The majority, under the leadership of Chief John Ross, continued to resist. But they were no match for their adversaries, and in 1838 they were forcibly removed from their homes and land and driven west with an army escort. The march—so grueling that an estimated one-quarter of the sixteen thousand participants died along the way—became known as the Trail of Tears.

Robert and Sallie Rogers had built a five-room, two-story house on a high place in the Going-Snake district near the Arkansas border, not far from the present town of Westville, Oklahoma. Overlooking fertile farmlands and hickory valleys and the foothills of the Ozark Mountains, the area was a reasonable approximation of the Georgia home Robert Rogers had left behind. Cherokee law and tradition held that all land was communally held, available to any member who had need of it, and Rogers established a profitable farm and ranch, raising horses and cattle, growing wheat and corn and fruit from his orchards. A daughter, Margaret, was born in 1836. Clem arrived three years later.

Those who had been driven unwillingly from their homes, and had suffered the indignities and deprivations of the Trail of Tears, naturally felt betrayed by the Old Settlers, who had signed away the rights and land of *all* Cherokees, who had had a comfortable passage to the new land, and who were now conspicuously prospering. It was not precisely a question of full-blood versus mixed-blood (Chief Ross, leader of the Trail of Tears group, was only one-eighth Cherokee), but there was a racial component to the conflict which helped make it as bloody as it eventually was. In 1839, three of the men who had spearheaded the Treaty of New Echota were murdered by men loyal to Ross. There followed seven years of internecine bitterness that occasionally threatened to erupt into full-fledged civil war. That never happened, but there were innumerable assaults and assassinations; as one historian put it, among Cherokees, "the ingrained tradition of revenge rose above constitution, acts of union, and laws." Robert Rogers died in the summer of 1842—an especially contentious season—and plausible local tradition has it that he was murdered by a Ross loyalist. Many years later, his granddaughter remembered being told that his last words were a sort of Cherokee legacy to his three-year-old son: "See that Clem always rides his own horse."

Two years later, Sallie Rogers remarried. Her new husband, William Musgrove, was a prosperous jack-of-many-trades. In addition to taking over the Rogers farming and ranching activities, he was a carpenter and blacksmith and part-owner of a factory that processed tobacco into plugs for chewing. According to family folklore, young Clem threw rocks at the buggy when Musgrove and his mother drove off to their wedding. The relations between stepfather and stepson, naturally, had their ups and downs. After one bitter quarrel, Clem rode up to the house with a gun, called Musgrove out, and put a bullet into the rafters above his head. Musgrove brought out his own pistol, but in his anger he cocked the weapon so vigorously that he broke the trigger mechanism.

Clem hated going to school. The first one he attended was a Baptist missionary institution less than a mile from his home. His sister remembered that he would begin his walk there backward, shouting, "Let me stay" as loudly as possible. He went on to the Cherokee Male Seminary at Tahlequah, but he dropped out to take a job as a hand with Joel M. Bryan, who like other farseeing mixed-bloods had begun to raise longhorned cattle on the endless Indian Territory prairies. As a young cowboy, Clem dressed like a man who had found his calling, cutting a striking figure in black-and-red striped shirt, homespun wool pants, and red-topped black leather boots that came up to his knees.

On May 15, 1855, Clem and five other cowboys began escorting some five hundred long-horned steers to market in Kansas City. When they got there they found no demand for the cattle and so continued on to St. Louis, 250 miles away; the final crossing of the Mississippi River was made by ferryboat. The drive took four months and established beyond any doubt the toughness and tenacity of sixteen-year-old Clem.

He was ambitious, too. Inspired after a brief tenure with Bryan to start his own ranching operation, he convinced his mother and step-father to give him twenty-five cows, a bull, four horses, and two slaves, Rabb and Houston, who had belonged to his father. In 1856, when Clem was seventeen, he and his entourage traveled west from Going-Snake. They continued past Bryan's ranch, in Choteau, and settled on a tributary of the Caney River, a short distance west of the present town of Talala, Oklahoma. (The tributary then had no name, but would later come to be known as Rabb's Creek, in honor of the slave who after emancipation made his home there.) Clem built a two-room log house, the rooms connected by an open porch, and opened his ranch and trading post for business.

Originally inhabited by Osage Indians, the western part of the Cherokee Nation was markedly different from the woody and hilly east—rich, rolling prairie land, teeming with wildlife. An early settler cataloged the native population: wild turkey, quail, prairie chicken, wild geese, green parakeet in the Verdigris River bottoms, deer, wolves, prairie owls, and panthers. The human residents tended to be the more adventurous of the Cherokees, mostly mixed-bloods who had no qualms about leaving the familiar territory to the east and staking out a new life. By the late 1850s, the Cherokee Indian agent was noting that more and more of them were beginning to come out "for the purpose of utilizing the open range."

If Clem had been a different type of person, he would have taken a moment to reflect on the name of his new home. At first, this region was merely the vast western part of the Saline district, one of eight in the Cherokee Nation. But by 1856, the year Clem arrived, there were enough settlers there for it to have its own designation—Coo-weescoowee, after the Cherokee name of Chief John Ross, the man indirectly responsible for his father's death. But the young settler did not have a highly developed sense of irony. Any time he did allow himself for meditation was doubtless devoted to the endless bluestem grass, perfect for the feeding of cattle, the many rivers, perfect for watering them, the moderate temperatures, the abundant rainfall.

To these advantages of geography Clem brought formidable personal qualities: He was young, almost frighteningly industrious, a superb horseman. He was also starting with a substantial stake, and his Cherokee citizenship meant that he could have use, free of charge, of as much land as he needed.

It wasn't surprising, then, that by 1858 he should have sufficiently prospered to take a bride. She was Mary America Schrimsher, also nineteen years old, whom he had met while a student at Tahlequah. Mary had roughly the same amount of Cherokee blood as Clem and her family was similarly well-to-do, but in all other respects they were opposites. Mary, with her black hair, narrow cheekbones, and broad face, *looked* Indian; Clem's fair hair, blue eyes, and bushy mustache belied his Cherokee roots. Clem was taciturn and gruff; Mary was vivacious and sweet and funny, an excellent musician and dancer. He couldn't be bothered about religion; she was a devout Methodist. His people were Old Settlers, while hers had come on the Trail of Tears—a distinction that made their union almost like intermarriage.

Despite these differences, or maybe because of them, the marriage was a success. The ranch prospered, too. A daughter, Elizabeth—nine-thirty-seconds Cherokee, like all their children—was born in September 1861.

That, of course, was nearly a year after South Carolina had seceded from the Union and five months after the Confederates fired on Fort Sumter. Among the Cherokees, the Civil War was a tribal catastrophe that decisively ended a fifteen-year period of prosperity and good feeling. It brought to the surface old antagonisms, the Treaty of New Echota group mostly favoring the Confederacy, the Ross men publicly supporting neutrality, but privately siding with the Union. By the late summer of 1861, John Ross, still the chief, realized that neither of these positions was tenable—both because the Cherokees were surrounded by Confederates and because the Confederacy was offering the tribes substantially better terms than the Union was—and he cast his lot with the South.

Clem, like most mixed-bloods, was for the Confederates all along. In 1853, a traveler in the Cherokee Nation observed that some Cherokees "live much in the style of Southern gentlemen of easy circumstances." Clem's circumstances were still hard, but he was already very much of this party—mixed-bloods who not only were slaveholders but who talked, acted, and thought like Southerners. He knew, however, that this stand would involve considerable personal sacrifice: His ranch lay just sixty miles from the border of Kansas, a Union stronghold. Sure enough, early in the hostilities Jayhawkers from the North swooped down and ran off all his stock. It was clear that the family would be in danger if they stayed on the ranch, so Clem sent them southeast to his mother's home. On the trip, Elizabeth became ill and died. Later, as the fighting entered Indian Territory, Mary and some of her relatives took refuge in Texas.

Clem signed up with the regiment of Colonel Stand Watie, a near-mythical figure in Cherokee history. Watie's brother, Elias Boudinot, was one of the Treaty of New Echota men who was murdered in 1839; Watie was pegged for assassination on the same day, but he managed to escape by darting out a back door. Throughout the 1840s and 1850s, he had led the Treaty group in their political and, sometimes, physical battles with the Ross men. Now he had the opportunity to fight an official war. In contrast to most of the Confederate Indians, who were disorganized and ineffectual, the squat, bowlegged Watie was a brilliant soldier, eager for the opportunity to right old wrongs.

With a few notable exceptions, however, it was an inglorious war for Clem Rogers and the other Cherokee Indians. Early in 1862, they took part in the Battle of Pea Ridge, Arkansas, a significant Confederate defeat that ended the rebels' last threat to Missouri and has been credited with saving that state for the Union. Later that year, Chief Ross allowed himself to be "arrested" by federal forces; he spent the rest of the war in Washington (and died there a year after it ended). After his departure, the Indian Territory was essentially ignored by both sides, leaving the pro-North and pro-South Indians to wage viciously destructive guerrilla warfare, mostly against each other. One target of Watie's men was white abolitionist missionaries who had converted many full-bloods to the Union cause. The daughter of one missionary saw her husband killed and her house burned to the ground. "Oh, our God, send deliverance," she wrote in her diary. "Make haste to help us, Oh God, for our salvation."

Watie was also known for his lightning raids against Union forces, most triumphantly at Cabin Creek, Indian Territory, in 1864. In a predawn strike, his men, Clem Rogers among them, captured a federal wagon train valued at $1.5 million and prompted a Confederate general to say, "The brilliancy and completeness of this expedition has not been excelled in the history of the war." By that time, Watie had been promoted to brigadier general (the first Indian to achieve that rank), and Rogers from first lieutenant to captain of his own regiment. Clem had also been elected one of three delegates from Cooweescoowee district to the Cherokee Confederate Convention in 1862, a foretaste of future political activity and a remarkable achievement for a man of twenty-three.

Watie's other notable achievement was single-handedly to delay the final moment of Confederate defeat. It was not until June 23, 1865—more than two months after Lee met Grant at Appomattox—that Watie, the last Confederate general to surrender, rode into Doaksville, in southern Indian Territory, and offered his brigade to federal officers.

In later years, Clem Rogers did not permit himself to transform the horrors he had witnessed and, perhaps, participated in into the stuff of fireside tales. Indeed, his children recalled that even if they begged him, he always refused to talk about the war.

THE CHEROKEES did not fare badly in their treaty with the U.S. government, the significant provisions calling for the abolition of slavery in the Cherokee Nation and the granting of permission for railroads to be constructed across their land. But many had been wiped out by the war, including Clem, who had a new daughter—Sallie, conceived on furlough and born in December 1863—but precious little else. His farm was overgrown, his cattle gone, his slaves free. His heart was still in the Verdigris country, but he knew he would have to bide his time before going back. In 1866, he rented a farm in the eastern part of the Nation, near Fort Gibson, from his sister-in-law, Alabama Schrimsher Adair, and planted a crop of corn. He hired a young man to work the fields and took a job himself as a wagon driver for a merchant and mill owner named Oliver Lipe, who was married to his mother-in-law's sister. Within a couple of years, he had earned enough to go into the cattle business again, buying a herd of Choctaw steers in partnership with Lipe's son, Maj. Dewitt Clinton Lipe. In 1868, he went back to Cooweescoowee, settling on a site on the Verdigris, about seven miles east of his previous ranch. A full-blood named Tom Boot was living in a log cabin there; Clem paid him twenty-five dollars for squatter's rights. The cabin was sixteen feet square, with a small porch held up by cedar posts with nubbed branches that Clem's cowhands hung their coats on. He refurbished and added on to the place, and in the fall of 1870 he brought out his family—which by this time included Robert, born in 1866, and Maud, just a year old.

Clem had chosen the location well. His range—by 1872 he was on his own, his partnership with Lipe dissolved—was in the shape of a V. The eastern and western boundaries were formed by the Caney and Verdigris rivers, which met at a point a few miles east of what would, with the arrival of the St. Louis and San Francisco Railroad in 1882, become the town of Claremore. The rivers provided not only water for the cattle but a natural boundary preventing them from drifting—extremely important in the days before the ranges were fenced. The northern border of the range, about twelve miles north of the rivers' confluence, was patrolled by line riders in Clem's employ, who would turn back any cattle that had drifted north. The size of the range has been estimated at sixty thousand acres. Under Cherokee law, it was rent- and tax-free.

Following the practice of his early employer Joel M. Bryan, Clem's

notion was to bring up herds of longhorn from Texas each spring, fatten
them on the Verdigris bluestem for a year, and then ship them off to
market at St. Louis. Especially considering the fact that there were virtually no expenses, other than labor, the potential for profit was considerable. At the very most, range cattle would run him three to four
dollars a head; and he was able to sell them in St. Louis for ten times
that. The price went up over the years. Someone who'd worked for
Clem as a young cowboy remembered seeing him gesture at a herd of
steers and remark, "These steers are walking fifty-dollar bills." They
were, and he marketed two to four thousand of them a year.

Obviously, the structure of the business was favorable, but Clem was
not content until he had squeezed as much profit out of it as there was.
He was such a tireless worker that he habitually ate his breakfast before
the sun came up and his supper after it went down, so as not to waste
any daylight. And he had a way with horses. "My father was the best
driver I ever saw," his son Will wrote years later. "I have seen papa
hitch 'em up when they was really wild and go where he wanted with
'em, not where they wanted to." "Take it from me," said a former cowboy of his named Ed Sunday, "Clem Rogers was a ranchman any way
you wanted to look at him. He wore tall top cowboy boots with his pant
legs stuffed in them leather chaps, and a western hat of medium size. I
never saw him wearing the big ten-gallon cowboy hat. He was a keen
trader, knew cattle, was one of the best riders I have ever known, and,
get this, he never carried on his cattle business in an easy chair. He was
a hard worker and if he ran one horse down he'd get another. He took
part in the roundups, branding and shipping of steers, and, believe me,
he was boss of the range." Nor was cattle his only interest. He was the
first man to grow wheat in the area, and did so well with the crop that
the local newspaper dubbed him "Wheat King."

Very quickly, Clem became a wealthy man. He needed a house befitting his stature, and by 1875 he had built one that, in frontier terms
at least, could fairly be called palatial. It was a two-story, seven-room
structure, made of logs, plastered on the inside and weatherboarded and
painted white on the outside. There were four open fireplaces, and upstairs and downstairs porches in front, supported by columns that bespoke Clem and Mary's southern heritage. Behind the house, protecting
it on the north, was a rocky hill. It looked out over the Verdigris, three-
quarters of a mile away, and the oaks, elms, pecans, and sycamores on
the opposite bank.

The house was furnished with taste and a kind of frontier
elegance—quite an accomplishment for Mary Rogers, considering that

the nearest place to shop was Coffeyville, Kansas, some forty-four miles away. But she did manage to get her Nottingham lace curtains and her walnut furniture upholstered in rose damask, her lamps and her carpets, and her grand piano. The grace notes, provided by Mary Rogers, were homegrown. On either side of the front walk, she planted circular flower beds and rows of cedars that met in a cool green arch overhead. Inside a white picket fence in front of the house were yellow jonquils and white and lavender hyacinths, area landmarks in the springtime. In the winter, she'd make bouquets of bittersweet from the woods, dried coxcomb and bachelor's buttons from the summer flower garden, and cedar and crystallized grasses.

Another grace note was her own presence, so modest and warm that, in the words of Agnes "Babe" Walker, the daughter of Clem Rogers's old slave Huse, "She was loved by all who knew her." She dressed simply, wearing plain white collars and cuffs that could be taken off and washed. She told Mary Newcomb, the girl who helped her with sewing and housekeeping, to trim her dresses moderately; she was too plain, she said, to wear the beaded collars and ruffles that were in fashion. She had a gently disarming sense of humor. Mary once was showing one of her babies to a cowboy and, noting his silence, said, "I know exactly what you're thinking. You're thinking this is the homeliest baby you ever saw." Another cowboy was constantly playing pranks on Mary Newcomb. Mary Rogers helped her get revenge by serving the fellow, who was known as a lemon-pie lover, a mock pie with browned meringue on top and cotton in the middle. Clem Rogers was not without his own humor, but it tended toward the gruff. In a letter about tribal politics to Dennis Bushyhead, who was married to his wife's sister Elizabeth, Clem closed, "Tell the *Little Giant* Mrs. B. We would like her to pay us a visit this spring. Tell her we can feed her on wild onions and poke leaves."

Given the combination of (comparative) luxury and graciousness, it wasn't surprising that the Rogers home became the social center of Cooweescoowee. People from throughout the district would gather there for dancing, music, and laughter. A frequent visitor remembered: "Aunt Mary [in the Cherokee Nation, elders were always "Aunt" and "Uncle"] always met you at the door with a smile and made everything so nice and pleasant for you. Just being in her presence made you feel comfortable. In those days people visited all day and our family would go in the morning and stay over for a fine country dinner with the Rogerses. Then Aunt Mary would spread quilts all over the upstairs of the house and we'd take naps. Aunt Mary had such an individual way of expressing herself and would say the wittiest things. When we started home she'd take us out to the orchard and make us take home apples, peaches and grapes."

His business and his home established, Clem found and pursued another calling—politics, which in the Cherokee Nation was an exceedingly important pastime, a sort of spectator sport that attracted near-universal interest, along with wide participation. As the Oklahoma historian Angie Debo wrote, "In a political unit so small that it was possible for every voter to have a personal knowledge of candidates and issues, the elections and inaugural ceremonies and deliberations furnished recreation and excitement for the entire populace." Clem's son Will would absorb this ethos into his bones. Half a century later, when he had become the most widely read political columnist in the country, the most distinctive quality of his commentary was just this sense that each of the players, all the way up to the president, was a personal acquaintance of his and all his readers'.

Clem's first run for office came in 1877, when he was thirty-eight. He won election as Cooweescoowee district judge and served for two years. His lack of legal training was not a handicap, the docket being filled mainly with small cases and misdemeanors. The court was sufficiently informal that on hot days Clem would move the entire proceedings out of the one-room, sixteen-foot-square log cabin and take them outside, under the shade of the hickory and oak trees.

In 1879, he was elected to one of Cooweescoowee's two seats in the Cherokee senate, the Nation's upper legislative house, which met in Tahlequah each November, as well as for special sessions. Over the years, he served three additional two-year terms. He was appointed—once by President Cleveland—to several commissions charged with carrying out important tribal business, and in 1907 he capped his political career by being elected a delegate to the convention charged with formulating a constitution for the new state of Oklahoma. Clem's success in politics—he never lost an election for public office—was achieved despite his marked deficiencies in public speaking and pressing the flesh, where his bluntness was a glaring liability. But he was excellent at the political game of currying loyalty and favors, with a particular genius for getting out and winning the black vote. And his diligence, competence, and commitment to the Cherokee people were obvious.

In his entire political career, there was only one stain on Clem's reputation—the result of a bill he wrote and introduced in 1883. The bill concerned the Cherokee Strip, a 6-million-acre rectangular area west of the Cooweescoowee district that had been ceded to the Cherokees in

1828 in return for lands in the Southeast. Settlers were barred from it, but because it was, according to one expert, the finest cattle land in the country, cowmen from Texas and Kansas had been using it to graze their herds for years, free of charge. Clem's bill awarded a lease on the land to the people using it, in return for an annual payment of $100,000. Soon after it passed, persistent rumors sprang up that the bill's supporters had been bribed by the cattlemen, one Cherokee testifying before the U.S. Senate that he had heard that Clem himself had taken four thousand dollars. But no hard evidence of bribery was ever introduced.

With the years came more children. Mary (always called May) arrived in 1873. Zoe was born in 1876 and Homer in 1878; both died in infancy. A year later, on November 4, 1879, Mary delivered another son. He was born in his parents' bedroom, the east room on the first floor of the old home place. After Mary Rogers had gone into labor, Mrs. William Penn Adair got a telegram from her husband, a prominent attorney who had been commander of the Second Cherokee Mounted Volunteers during the Civil War, and who was then in Washington on tribal business. The message read, as she remembered, "Clem's wife is sick, go there and help her. Boy or girl, name it William Penn Adair." Since family names had been more or less exhausted by this point, and since Mary Rogers knew of her husband's reverence for Colonel Adair and his strong feelings about his own service in the Confederate cause, she agreed. (Clem was away, so he had no input.) For a time, the appellation was taken literally: The 1880 Cherokee Census Roll listed the boy as "Col. W. P. Rogers." But the rank was soon dropped, never to return, and he was known by one and all as Willie.

The nickname had a diminutive feel to it, which was apt. It being clear that Willie would be the final Rogers child—Clem and Mary were both forty years old at his birth, and Mary was subject to bouts of illness—he was treasured, not to say spoiled, as only the baby of a large family can be. The tendency to indulgence was heightened by a wrenching event that took place in Willie's fourth year. His brother, Robert, was from all accounts his father's son—quiet, serious, diligent, and devoted to horses and cattle. According to a neighbor whose house he often visited, he liked to get up early on winter mornings and run barefoot in the snow, so as to toughen himself. This cast of mind wasn't the reason why he contracted typhoid, but it probably did lead him to go back to work, branding calves, before he should have. In any case, his body wasn't prepared for the strenuousness of the activity, and on April 13, 1883, just two days before his seventeenth birthday, he died.

Now Willie was the only Rogers son, the pet of three adoring older sisters, an adoring mother, and a father who, while not exactly adoring, was prepared to give him anything he wanted—and forgive him any mischief. One time, Willie decided that the hunting hounds would look better with different colored spots, so he painted them all green. On another occasion, his mother had a pan of yeast on the floor of the kitchen, into which Willie couldn't resist placing his foot. Mrs. Rogers's response was to say, "Willie has a good idea. That'll make it sweeter. It'll be the best bread we ever had."

Like his brother, Willie loved horses. He rode from the time he was three or four, his father assigning a man to put him on and take him off his mount. "Willie would ride about half the day," remembered the cowboy B. T. Hooper, "and then would come in on a fast trot to the headquarters, and I'd help him off the horse, and away he would go to his mother." When he wasn't riding, he'd pretend that he was. In the 1950s, Will Rogers's biographer Homer Croy spoke with the son of Clem Rogers's old slave Rabb, who had grown up with Willie. The son's name was, of all things, Clement Vann Rogers. After the Civil War, the white Clem Rogers's slaves had stayed in the area, working for Clem and taking Rogers as a surname; Rabb had given one of his sons his old master's first and middle names, as well. The young Clem, his brothers and sisters, and other children of freedmen were Willie's first playmates. That they were *not* his equals is well illustrated by the nature of their games.

"We played horse together," Clem, then seventy-eight years old, told Croy. "He used to put a saddle on my back and make me pretend I was a bucking horse and he would ride me, spurrin' with his bare heels. One time he gets mad with me and shoved a branding iron against my behind, but it wasn't very hot, scared me more'n anything else."

It was from his other former slave, Huse Rogers, that Clem bought Willie the greatest gift he would ever receive. Huse owned a five-year-old pony named Comanche, a cream-colored animal with faint black markings. Since he was mainly ridden by Huse's son, Anderson, he'd received an AR brand on his left shoulder. Willie, five or six years old at the time, coveted Comanche, and one day Clem asked Huse how much he wanted for the pony. The response was sixty-five dollars. Clem offered ten dollars plus one of his own horses, and Huse accepted. "I didn't exactly want to swap him off," biographer Harold Keith reported Huse as saying years later, "but Mistah Clem Rogahs kinda took me by surprise. I was out of work and needed a little extra spendin' money anyway, so I let ole Comanche go." Comanche, weighing about a thousand pounds and standing fourteen hands high, was a remarkable horse, extraordinarily fast and intelligent, and for the next twenty years he would be a centerpiece of Willie's life. His cousin Spi Trent described boy and horse as being "almost like Siamese twins." Comanche, he said, was "Will's heart."

Comanche's true expertise, it would later become clear, was as a roping pony. But Willie's passion for roping predated the horse's arrival in his life. To a boy growing up on a ranch, roping was omnipresent— like dribbling basketballs or riding skateboards in other milieus. It was even more deep-seated, because it wasn't just a pastime but a key component of the local economy. Cowboys roped for a simple reason—it was the best way to rein in steers for roundups and calves for branding—and since the range cattle industry had come into its own, in the years following the Civil War, roping techniques adapted from Mexican vaqueros had become, after riding, the most important skill in the trade.

Lariats (from the Spanish *riata*, or rope) were made of forty or fifty feet of braided rawhide strips, horsehair, maguey fiber, or, most commonly, Manila hemp. At one end would be an eye, or "honda," made of metal, leather, or just a knot in the rope itself, through which the other end would be threaded to form a loop. Cowboys carried their coiled-up lariats everywhere and spent a good portion of their leisure time refining their skills—trying out different "throws" or experimenting with a completely useless (for the cattle business) capability of the lasso, the way a loop could be made to spin endlessly and behave in odd ways.

Willie absorbed this ethos before he could walk, and started roping soon afterward. The best roper working for Clem was a black man named Dan Walker, and Willie would watch him throw for hours. By himself, he would practice endlessly on an oak stump in the backyard. Before long, to Willie's absolute delight, Clem let him help rope calves for branding. Huse's son, Anderson, who sometimes slept over at the Rogers's place, remembered that cries of "Catch him! Catch him! Rope him! Don't let him get away!" would emanate from Willie's room at night. "All the time he was sleepin' he was thinkin' about dem ole calves."

At the age of seven, Willie was sent to the Drumgoole School, in Chelsea, about twelve miles from his home. Because of the distance, he lived with his sister Sallie and her husband, Tom McSpadden, who settled in Chelsea after they married in 1886, going back to the ranch every weekend. (McSpadden was the son of a white Methodist circuit rider who had come as a missionary to the Indian Territory in 1869.) He would have to ride the three miles to and from school each day, and, as a parting gift, Clem gave his son a specially made saddle, with WPR stamped on the back.

It was soon obvious that Willie had inherited his father's antipathy to formal education. Sallie later remembered that, after tying his lunch box to his saddle every morning, she'd stand and watch him ride all the way down the lane; otherwise he'd ride off in another direction.

Drumgoole, Will Rogers later wrote, "was a little one-room log cabin. . . . It was all Indian kids went there, and I being part cherokee (had just enough white in me to make my honesty questionable)." The last sentence—indicating that many if not most of the students were full-bloods—may explain why Clem took his son out of Drumgoole after a year. The next year, he went to the Harrell Institute in Muskogee, a Methodist boarding school for girls attended by his sister May. He was allowed to enroll only because the superintendent of the school, the Reverend Theodore Brewer, had a son the same age with whom Willie could room.

While Willie was home on vacation from Harrell, Sallie and Maud came down with typhoid fever, and both Will and Sallie's son, Clem, with measles. Then Mary Rogers fell ill and was put to bed. A messenger was sent to Clem Rogers, away from home at the time, and he drove sixty miles overnight, a lantern attached to his buggy. The family's doctor, A. L. Lane, was in Kansas on vacation, and so Dr. Oliver Bagby of Vinita was wired for. He drove his horse and buggy thirty-six miles in four hours, he later told Harold Keith, splashing across the Verdigris just before sundown. He found Mary Rogers practically pulseless; he diagnosed her condition as amoebic dysentery. The next day, Dr. Lane returned home. "My mother told him what had happened," his daughter remembered. "Father said, 'We will have an early dinner and go over and see how Mrs. Rogers and the girls are.' He found Mrs. Rogers quite sick. She was in the east room upstairs. When he went in, she was lying with her back to the door, but she heard his footsteps and said, 'There's Dr. Lane, but you've come too late. If you had come yesterday I would have been all right.' "

At four o'clock on the morning of May 28, 1890, Mary Rogers died. She was fifty-one.

It would be easier to calculate just how much of a blow the loss of his mother was for Will Rogers if he had spoken about it more than he did. In the millions of words he wrote for publication, there are just two mentions of Mary Rogers. "My own mother died when I was ten years old," he said in a Mother's Day radio broadcast. "My own folks have told me that what little humor I have comes from her. I can't remember her humor but I can remember her love and understanding of me." His wife, Betty, felt that he never got over Mary Rogers's death: "He cried when he told me about it many years later. It left in him a lonely, lost feeling that persisted long after he was successful and famous." But, Betty wrote, his mother also left in him the memory of helping her cover, on winter nights, the seedlings set out on the shelf of an unheated room in the ranch. The image stayed with him, of course, because that was exactly the way she had nurtured him.

WILL AND CHARLEY MCCLELLAN

CHAPTER 2

THE RANCH

... really at heart I love ranching. I have always regretted that I didn't live about 30 or 40 years earlier, and in the same old country, the Indian Territory. I would have liked to got here ahead of the "Nestors," the Bob wire fence, and so called civilization.

—WILL ROGERS

SOON AFTER Mary Rogers died, the shape of the family was further changed by three marriages. In 1891, Willie's sister Maud, who during Mary's illnesses had served as a kind of surrogate mother, married a white druggist from Texas with the unlikely name of Captain Lane Lane. They settled in Chelsea. The next year, Willie's sister May married Matt Yocum. Just a few years before, the household had been full of voices and laughter; now it consisted of a gruff fifty-three-year-old man and a twelve-year-old boy. A third person joined in 1893, when Clem married Mary Bibles, who was half his age; she was officially his housekeeper, but had been something more than that at least since Maud's wedding, when her gift of five dollars was recorded in the Chelsea newspaper. But in all his published and unpublished writing and his surviving correspondence, Will Rogers never once mentions her—a gauge of his feelings toward his stepmother.

There was one positive development for Willie. In 1890, Clem Rogers had bought a few thousand head of cattle and had them shipped up from Texas. When the shipment arrived, it included seventy-five "dogies"—calves that no mother would claim—and Clem gave them to his son, motherless as well. He chose a brand, in the shape of the fireplace andirons at the home place, and over the years his herd increased. As early as 1894, he had his own letterhead:

W . P . R O G E R S
CATTLE DEALER
RANCH BETWEEN C. V. ROGERS AND OOLAGAH

No Cattle Sold except for Shipment. A Liberal Reward will be paid for any Cattle in the Brand found off the Range.

Meanwhile, Willie's education was proceeding. He attended the Presbyterian Mission School at Tahlequah for a year, and then, in the fall of 1892, was sent to Willie Halsell College, in Vinita, a good-sized railroad town forty miles northeast of the ranch. He went as a first-year student in the preparatory department, the equivalent of the seventh grade. Halsell, opened the year before by the Methodist Church, funded largely by the Indian Territory cattleman W. E. Halsell and named for his late daughter, was a coeducational counterpart to Harrell Institute. By this time, it was clear that school was not the most congenial environment for the boy. Although he squeezed onto the honor roll his first term with an average of 90 2/3 (the cutoff point was 90), his heart was with cattle, not books. In the winter, he complained to his best friend, Charley McClellan, who was still enrolled in the Mission School at Tahlequah, that because class would be in session till June 15, "we will miss all the roundups, won't we? . . . Do you have day schoolers down there? I would like to be down there and go to school I am a getting tired of this place."

Gradually, Willie warmed to Halsell. He was popular with the other students, who, in recognition of his speed on foot and his large ears, nicknamed him "Rabbit." He also began to see the merits of coeducation. By March, cheered by the news that he would be home the next month to help brand calves and colts, he was positively enthusiastic. "You ought to be up there," he wrote Charley. "We have boys and girls all board here and we take them to church every sunday night and have dances and do any thing that you want to. I sure have lots of fun up here." He even found a subject he was good at and enjoyed: elocution. ("Careful and thorough training will be given in articulation, vocalization and production of tone, by lessons based on scientific principles," stated the catalogue.) In the program that closed the fall session, the president of the school reported in the local newspaper, "Willie Rogers was inimitable in each of his declamations & never failed to receive a hearty round of applause." By the next year, although he wasn't the winner of the schoolwide elocution contest, he was deemed good enough to receive a duplicate gold medal.

The 1893–1894 school year was even better, principally because Charley McClellan persuaded his parents to let him attend Halsell. For two boys of such similar backgrounds—both quarter-blood Cherokees (although Charley's father was white), born and raised on ranches within five miles of each other, both fond of roping and riding—they presented a remarkable contrast. The bespectacled Charley was studious and serious. Most striking was his attitude to his Indian heritage. Where the clear goal of the other Cooweescoowee mixed-bloods was assimilation, their model the culture of whites, Charley was a militant and very proud Cherokee, like the middle-class black kids of the 1960s who put on dashikis and grew Afros. He wore his black hair in a long braid that fell down his back, and in the summertime he went about the ranch with his face painted, wearing a breechclout, buckskin leggings, and moccasins. Once a train carrying the members of Buffalo Bill's Wild West stopped in Claremore for a rest. Charley was the only one to approach the aloof Sioux Indians of the troupe. His brother and sister said later that the Sioux were so taken with him that they tried to convince him to join them. Another time, away from home on a business trip with his father, he engaged a group of Kaw Indians in a discussion and ended up using most of his train fare home to buy them lunch.

Very likely, Charley was playing out a personal drama animated by his feelings about his father. But his proselytizing had its effects: The young people of the Verdigris began to develop a halting awareness of their heritage. He used to go up to the northeastern corner of the Indian Territory, where the Shawnee Indians had a tiny reservation, and learn the ancient "stomp dance" from them. Back home, he taught the steps to his friends and, with Willie's assistance, put on exhibitions on Saturday nights at a knoll just north of the Oowala School House. Inside a tepee, cider would be served, and the boys and girls would wear headbands, paint themselves like Plains Indians, give out loud war whoops, and do the venerable dance.

Like many assimilating groups before and since, the mixed-blood Cherokees were torn between respect for their heritage and a desire to obliterate it; in keeping with this ambivalence, their acknowledgments of it were facetious, self-conscious, and imprecise. The young women formed a social group called the Pocahontas Club. (At Will's insistence—he was Willie now only to family and old friends—boys were allowed to join, too.) One night, an "Evening with Hiawatha" party was held. "Mr. Will Rogers," reported the Claremore *Weekly Progress,* "appeared in full Indian costume, of war paint, tomahawk & other paraphernalia, & favored the company with several excellent songs, which were highly appreciated."

Will was delighted to have Charley at Halsell. Schoolmates remembered that his favorite pose was to stand leaning against his friend, his elbow on Charley's shoulder and his legs crossed so that everyone could get a view of his fancy stitched boots. In addition to signs of dandyism, he was now showing the tendencies of a class clown. When Charley would make speeches in Cherokee for the benefit of the boys, Will would translate, adding his own comic interpolations. A favorite feature of school programs was Will putting on white gloves, a swallow-tailed coat, and glasses, blackening his face and imitating a black preacher.

His rope was also good for much comic mileage. Always attached to it, he had barely let it leave his hand since the summer of 1893, after his first year at Halsell, when he'd gone to Chicago's World's Columbian Exposition with his father and seen Buffalo Bill's Wild West. The performer who most caught Will's attention was Vincente Oropeza, a Mexican vaquero and part-time matador who introduced trick roping to this country. Oropeza took the utilitarian skill of roping and stretched it wider than any cowboy would have thought possible. Part of his artistry was making fancy and intricate catches of horses and riders; one of his specialties was the "umbrella," where he would throw out a big loop, letting one horse run through it and then catching a second horse with the same loop. And part of it was not catching anything at all but, rather, utilizing a principle that the great roper Chester Byers, who was taught by Will Rogers, described this way: "the centrifugal force of the loop distends it in such a way that it will lie open in midair as long as revolved." The fancy roper would spin his lasso horizontally and vertically, in figure eights and cylinders, over his back and down the other side, jumping in and out of it, until it seemed like a living thing with an irrepressible will of its own.

Back at Halsell, Will roped everything that moved—especially girls. A favorite victim was Oneida Cooper, daughter of the woman who ran the dormitory where forty of the Halsell boys boarded. On her way to school, fearing the inevitable coil, she would drag her feet along the pavement, knowing that she could lift them off the ground only at her own peril. The strategy worked until she came to an intersection. As soon as she stepped off the curb, she was roped.

After three years, Halsell had exhausted its usefulness for Will, and he for it. In the fall of 1895, his father sent him to Scarritt College, in the southwestern corner of Missouri, his fifth school and the first located outside Indian Territory. At his other schools, all the students had been Indian; here there were only three other Cherokee boys. Will was nicknamed "Wild Indian," and for months his only friends were the three other Cherokees. Although he was gradually absorbed into the social mainstream at Scarritt, there's no doubt that some of the shock and hurt of suddenly being different never left him. He once invited a town girl named Maggie Nay to a party. Will and some other boys from the college had scandalized the town by drinking homemade wine at the home of a German family who lived nearby, and Maggie refused him, she later said, because "my mother would not let me go out with this wild Indian boy from the territory who drank wine."

He responded with a letter that almost stained the page with tears of sardonic self-pity. "I know I drink and am a wild and bad boy and all that," he wrote, "but you know that Marvin [his rival for Maggie's affections] is a model boy. He never did anything in his life. I am an outcast I suppose so. Of course I don't do anything that will get you with a *drunkard as I am*." He went on in this vein for an impressive number of paragraphs, concluding, "Well, I suppose you have heard enough of the *Drunkard* that they call Will Rogers, so I will close hoping you all a merry evening." Some of the hurt, no doubt, was rhetorical. Some if it was real.

Roping-related misbehavior continued to be a problem at Scarritt. Two incidents survive. Once Will roped a teacher's horse. Unaccustomed to such treatment, the animal knocked over a picket fence and ran through the backstop of the tennis court. Another time, he roped the arm on a statue of a Grecian goddess and broke it off. His academic record was mediocre, owing partly to his habit of cutting classes and repairing to the railroad stockyards to rope steers. Overall, he did not leave a sterling impression. One of the Scarritt teachers wrote years later that "even the most sanguine could not have predicted that the funny fellow we knew as Will Rogers, would be anything but mediocre, or live anything but an absurdly uneventful life."

In May 1896, Will traveled to Buffalo, New York, for reasons unknown. On the way into a barbershop, he was stopped by a panhandler, who asked him for a dime. As he was fumbling in his pocket, the building with the shop in it collapsed, killing a barber, a cashier, and two customers.

Will returned to Scarritt for a second year, but was called home in early December because of a family catastrophe: the assassination of Matt Yocum, his sister May's husband. Yocum was just getting into bed one evening, the Vinita *Chieftain* reported, "when the first shot struck him and [he] cried out to his wife, 'Oh, May, help me! Help me!' Mrs. Yocum thought a lamp had exploded and drew down under her bed clothes, holding her child. Tracks at the window indicate that the assassin had stood there some time waiting for commission of the crime." Within days, a man named Sharp Rogers—no relation to Will and apparently black—was arrested. "In addition to being seen at Oologah shortly before the murder it is said there are several other incidents which cast suspicion upon him," the newspaper reported. The charges against him were eventually dropped, however.

Six months later, May was involved in another murder. She went to a show with William Cheatam, a young man who worked in an Oologah livery stable. He walked her to her house, about a mile and a quarter from town, and on his way back he was shot with a number-twelve shotgun, "the charge taking effect in his head, neck and breast." He was found with a revolver in his hand, and the story circulated that May had warned him not to return the way he had come. As in the Yocum murder, a man was arrested for the crime, one W. E. Milstead, then discharged. In reporting the latter development, the *Chieftain* provocatively intoned that "there is a clue in existence which if followed out will result in the capture of not only the murderer of Cheatam, but of Matt Yocum also. We are not at liberty at present to state all that is known of this mysterious affair, but whenever it will be proper to do so it will be one of the most remarkable and thrilling episodes that ever transpired in this country. It is a passage in human life that represents the perfidy of man and the inconstancy of woman in a remarkable degree."

This was the last mention of the "clue." But before Milstead was released, an unsigned article in the Kansas City *Journal* quoted him as saying that he had been hired to commit the Cheatam murder by none other than C. V. Rogers, and that "Rogers' son, Bill Rogers, was with him when the shooting occurred." Clem was also accused of being behind the Yocum murder, although no motive was known, other than "that Yocum had betrayed his daughter and was only prevailed on to marry her by her father paying him a large amount of money." The article went on to predict that May would be implicated as an accessory in the murder of her husband, having on the night of the crime, contrary to her custom, pinned up the corner of the curtain of the window through which he was shot. She was said to have cast suspicion on Clem by lamenting that "her 'father's money had killed her husband and now had killed the only man she loved.' "

On the publication of this story, Clem immediately went to Kansas City to learn the name of the person who had written it. He sued the man, Tom A. Latta, for criminal libel, but the charges against him eventually were "continued generally." The criminal (or criminals) was never found, and there was no more talk of any Rogers family involvement. A year later, May—now and hereafter referred to by her sisters, in Homeric formula, as "poor May"—married Matt Yocum's first cousin, Frank Stine. And Will, in the remaining thirty-seven years of his life, never publicly referred to either murder.

CLEM DIDN'T SEND Will back to Scarritt for the second term. He opted instead for what many parents have seen as a remedy for unruly, apparently unmotivated boys—military school. He sent Will to Kansas City with a herd of steers and instructions to sell them and use the proceeds to pay his tuition to the Kemper Military School. Kemper, located in the central Missouri town of Boonville, had a family connection, being the alma mater of Maud's husband, Cap Lane; a year or two later, Sallie's son Clem McSpadden would enroll. It also had social cachet—when Will was there, other students included the sons of a judge on the Missouri Supreme Court and the presidents of the Santa Fe and the Mexican and Central railroads. Will arrived on January 13, 1897, wearing a cowboy hat with a braided horse-hair cord around the brim, a flannel shirt, a red bandanna around his neck, a brightly colored vest, and his trousers tucked into high-heeled red-top boots with spurs. The ensemble, striking in any setting, made even more of an impression in a group of boys wearing gray uniforms.

Will's record at Kemper was true to form. His first report card—he was now up to the sophomore year of high school—showed grades ranging from 62 (algebra) to 100 (U.S. history). He had also accumulated fifty demerits, each one requiring that the offender walk a beat for an hour. This is not surprising: Will Rogers and military school made one of the poorer matches in the history of pedagogy. He was chronically late, his uniform was unkempt, his room was a mess, he hated to clean his rifle, and he was so inept at handling it that, when he was showing his parade moves to a friend during his first summer at home, the gun accidentally went off and the bullet grazed his temple, causing a permanent scar. At Kemper, Will was unable to resist making wisecracks in inappropriate settings and playing pranks involving alarm clocks, fire hoses, and, of course, his lariat. A favorite game was paying other boys twenty-five cents an hour to get on their hands and knees and moo like calves as Will roped their feet. At one point, weary of having the teachers confiscate lariat after lariat, he wrapped one around his torso and put his shirt on over it. But the teacher noticed the protuberance on his stomach. One less rope. One more demerit.

Will was good-natured about it all. He participated in school life, playing end on the football team, and, judging by the number of humorous remarks he made about Kemper in his later years, he seems to have retained a good feeling about his time there. He even made the most of guard duty by marching past the kitchen and convincing the cooks to pass him food. After his death in 1935, a Kemper teacher compiling a pamphlet about Will's time there was able to unearth only three incidents where he lost his equanimity. Two sprang from the sensitivity of Will—whose nickname at the school was "Swarthy"—to slights against Indians.

> Once a classmate referred to a certain Indian chief as a thoroughbred. Will's voice rose to a high pitch in resentment as he explained that "fullblood" was the proper term and that it spoiled his whole afternoon to hear someone call a fine Indian a thoroughbred. Again in a "bull session" a cadet inadvertently or perhaps purposefully remarked that Indians and Negroes were very much alike. Will lost no time in challenging the remark. With much heat and no humor he argued that the two races were wholly different in origin, ideals, characteristics and possibilities.

By February 1898, Will, three months past his eighteenth birthday, was in his third term at Kemper. To graduate, he would have to stay until the following May. It seemed far too long, especially now that the smell of spring was in the air and Will's thoughts were turning to colts and calves. Going back to Oologah was not an option, for the simple reason that, as Will wrote later, "I was leary of going home to my dad." A Texas classmate of his, Billy Johnson, also from cattle country and sympathetic to his longings, told Will about the Ewing Ranch, in the eastern Panhandle town of Higgins, where he had heard jobs were available. That settled it. Will wrote separate letters to his sisters Sallie and Maud, asking for ten dollars. They compared notes, as he should have realized they would; typically, they sent him the money anyway. (When they bought a money order at the post office, Sallie remembered, "Even the postmaster disapproved. 'Will gets too many money orders already. His father sends him more money than he ought to have.' ") Will used the funds for train fare to Higgins. When he left Boonville under cover of darkness, he had 150 hours of demerits to his name.

• • •

WILL PROBABLY expected to step off the train in Higgins and onto the Ewing Ranch. It turned out, however, that the ranch was actually across the border, in Oklahoma Territory, ten miles or so outside of town, and there was no way to get to it other than on foot. But he looked up Perry Ewing's daughter, who lived in town; she agreed not only to send word that Will Rogers had arrived but to put the boy up until someone came to fetch him. Within a few days, Ewing drove his buggy into Higgins and found Will Rogers, eighteen years old, wearing a black-and-red-striped Kemper football sweater. The Billy Johnson connection was put forward; it was deemed sufficient, at least, for Ewing to take Will back to the ranch, a thirteen-thousand-acre spread bordered on the southwest by the Canadian River. On arrival, Ewing immediately wrote to Clem, advising him of Will's whereabouts. "Will's father was thoroughly miffed at Will's desertion of school," Perry's son Frank remembered, "and wrote back for him to keep him and that if he could get any work out of Will it would be better than he'd ever done."

So he had a job as a ranch hand. Frank Ewing reported that he was actually an excellent worker. Such was his joy at being released from classrooms and demerits that when Perry Ewing tried to pay him his thirty-dollar salary after a month, Will turned it down, saying that he hadn't been working—he was just "visiting."

Things got even better. Early in May, Ewing needed to have four hundred head of cattle driven to Medicine Lodge, Kansas, about one hundred and sixty miles northeast, where he planned to fatten them on a pasture he'd leased before selling them in the Kansas City market. Frank, Will, four other hands, a cook named Aaron, and a remuda of about thirty-five horses made the drive. They quickly settled into a routine. In the morning, the cattle would be thrown off the bedding ground and grazed, all the while advancing a mile or two, then bunched and driven a similar distance. They would be rested and watered until three o'clock, then gathered and driven another three miles or so until sundown. One difficulty was the paucity of freshwater creeks; sometimes the cowboys had to open a can of tomatoes to quench their thirst. But the food was plentiful and good. "I'll never forget how Will could eat," Frank Ewing said. "He never got enough. Aaron was a good cook and when we tumbled out at daybreak for breakfast, he'd have black coffee, sow belly, molasses and sour dough biscuits baked in a Dutch oven all hot and ready for us. Sometimes we'd buy loose boxes of dried blackberries. They'd be wormy, but we'd sort out the worst and cook the rest.

"Once in a while we'd pass a little ranch and buy butter, milk, and eggs and have us a feast. There was lots of wild plums in those days, and we'd gather 'em in our hats while horseback, or just eat 'em off the bushes. Once in a while the cook might gather 'em in a dishpan and make us a cobbler in the Dutch oven."

Balancing Aaron's chuck-wagon prowess was his nasty temper; supposedly he had killed two men in knife fights. Near the end of the drive, when tempers were short, he falsely accused Will of committing a misdeed against him. Will stood up to him, saying (according to Harold Keith's rendition of Frank Ewing's account of the incident), "They tell me you're a killer, but you're not. You're just a plain murderer. You haven't got nerve enough to fight. If you have, come on out here." He motioned to the prairie around him. Aaron backed down.

They made excellent time, covering five or six miles a day, until they hit the Salt Fork of the Arkansas River, just southwest of Medicine Lodge. There, a sudden and violent prairie storm hit, raising the possibility of a stampede. The cattle were kept calm, but the storm flooded the creek, and at first they declined to swim across. The next day, they reconsidered, and the drive was completed in six weeks, without the loss of a single animal.

Like his father forty-three years before, Will Rogers became a man on a cattle drive. The experience was such a transcendent one for him that barely a week after he got back to Higgins he secured a horse and set out for Amarillo, eighty miles to the west, where he heard he could get on another drive. When he arrived after an eventful journey—he'd been surprised by a violent storm while sleeping out on the range and nearly lost his horse—he had a sudden change of plans. In late April, the Spanish-American war had broken out, and in cattle country recruiting was heavy for Theodore Roosevelt's voluntary cavalry regiment. (The fighting at San Juan Hill took place July 1.) Will, possibly thinking that his Kemper military schooling could finally be put to use, was inspired to enlist. But he was turned down—too young.

He got a job with an outfit driving a much larger herd—2,500 head—to the town of Liberal, Kansas. When that was completed, he was hired by the Mashed-O Ranch, in Muleshoe, Texas. The Mashed-O, roughly 250,000 acres, had been part of the mammoth XIT Ranch, 3 million acres that occupied a substantial part of the western Panhandle. It was owned by W. E. Halsell, benefactor and namesake of Will's old school and a man with significant holdings in the Indian Territory as well. After some time there, he moved on to work on other ranches. In the fall, having successfully avoided the start of a new school year, he returned to the Indian Territory.

Will Rogers was a Texas cowboy for little more than half a year. By the time he got there, he was already participating in something of an anachronism. The great days of the range cattle industry, with its long drives and unfenced limitless spaces, were over—one authority pinpoints 1887 as the year of demise—a victim of railroads, barbed wire, homesteaders, severe winters, and low beef prices. Despite this, or maybe because of it, the experience affected him profoundly. He referred to it again and again over the years, he repeatedly tried to re-create it in unlikely ways, and it became for him a kind of edenic model of how sweet, simple, and comradely life could be. In 1934, revisiting the Panhandle, as he did whenever he had the chance, he wrote:

> We was driving over a Country where 36 years before as a boy 18 years old I had helped drive a bunch of cattle from that very place to Western Kansas, and there wasent a house or a chicken in a whole county. That plains was the prettiest country I ever saw in my life, as flat as a beauty contest winner's stomach, and prairie lakes scattered all over it. And mirages! You could see anything in the world—just ahead of you—I eat out of a chuck wagon, and slept on the ground all that spring and summer of '98.

IN THE TWELVE YEARS that had passed since Will had last lived at home full-time, the Indian Territory, the Cherokee Nation, the Cooweescoowee district, and the Clem Rogers ranch had undergone cataclysmic changes. The most visible alteration was the Missouri Pacific Railroad, which opened in 1889, running from Van Buren, Arkansas, to Coffeyville, Kansas, in the process vertically bisecting Clem's range. In some ways, the railroad was a boon. For one thing, it eliminated the need for cattle drives—the stock could be shipped up from Texas, and then, when they were ready to market, sent on to Coffeyville and thence to points east. Typically, Clem realized this advantage at once. The first year the Missouri Pacific was in place, he went to Texas and bought 3,500 cows to stock his range. Also welcome were the towns that sprang up where the train stopped, towns with real stores, post offices, and mayors; now people didn't have to travel great distances to buy supplies or socialize, to mail a letter or get married. The closest stop to Clem's ranch, about six miles southwest of headquarters, was dubbed Oologah (sometimes called Oolagah)—a Cherokee word meaning "dark clouds" or "cloudy weather." For the first time, the Rogers family had a hometown.

But there were more ominous portents. For a quarter of a century after the end of the Civil War, the Cherokees had enjoyed peace and affluence; to a rather astonishing degree, they had been left alone. Clem, more than most, had prospered. The 1890 Cherokee census listed him as owning three dwellings and seven other structures, plus improvements valued at fifteen thousand dollars. Only two other men in the Cooweescoowee district reported higher figures. But the Missouri Pacific—along with the Frisco, and the Missouri, Kansas and Texas line, which had opened in 1872, both of which ran through the Cherokee Nation—signaled the beginning of the end of the isolation and freedom from interference that had permitted his and others' success. It was in the interest of the railroad companies to bring as many settlers in as possible. At the same time, the Indian Territory was bordered on the north and east by Kansas and Arkansas, both filled to the bursting point with anxious white men eyeing the empty land over the border. As early as 1870, groups of "intruders," as they were called, were spilling over the Kansas border and establishing themselves in Cooweescoowee and the Cherokee Outlet. At first, the federal government forcibly evicted them. But many managed to stay, legally and otherwise, and more would inevitably follow, making the "open range" a misnomer.

As well as he could, Clem adapted. In 1891, anticipating the changes that would come, he constructed, out of barbed wire, the first range fence in the Verdigris country. His stock in trade had always been longhorned cattle, which fed on the bluestem grasses for up to four years before they were ready to market. Now, because of the closing of the open range, and changes in the market for cattle as well, he began to make the switch to shorthorns, which could be fed and contained in fenced pastures. By 1897, he was marketing only four hundred head for the season (and getting a modest $37.51 per head).

Even more prescient was his large-scale move into wheat farming. The Verdigris country, with moist falls and springs, moderately cold winters, hot, dry harvests, and excellent soil, was perfectly suited to winter wheat. Clem was the first in the area to foresee this, planting his first big crop of Red Turkey wheat, a Russian hard variety, in 1891. By the middle of the decade, he was planting three to five hundred acres a year, harvesting forty bushels an acre. In July 1895, the Claremore *Weekly Progress,* aware that he had not run for the senate in some time, reported, "C. V. Rogers, the Oologah wheat king, has threshed his crop which turned out 11,000 bushels. No wonder Clem does not want any office."

But even wheat needed land, and land was now becoming a precarious commodity. The intruders had begun to swarm into Indian Territory. Some were there legitimately, as employees or renters of Indians, but others came surreptitiously and squatted, or married Indian women for the express purpose of taking control of Indian land. And there was a significant outlaw population, wanted criminals who had crossed the border to escape arrest. At one time or other, the James, Younger, and Dalton gangs all took refuge in the Cherokee Nation.

Clem, always foresighted, was extremely worried about the intruders. His outrage over the liberties they had taken, and the failure of Cherokee or U.S. officials to take any action against them, moved him to uncharacteristic eloquence in an 1885 letter to his brother-in-law Chief Dennis Bushyhead:

> Are we powerless to enforce our own laws? Are we to submit to such great wrongs by white men not citizens? Dennis Bushyhead, there is not a single law in this country enforced. Men are hauling cattle in this country in open violation of the law, and the sheriff and solicitor both know it, white men are putting up hay all along the line in the nation, and a few days ago the sheriff went up and collected a tax on the hay. Where is the law authorizing such act? Timber plank and logs are conveyed all the while to which the sheriff and solicitors well know. How in the world can we hold up a nation when our officers don't respect the law, as the oath they have taken? We are *fast fast* drifting into the hands of the white men. Hoping you will not get offended at this letter, will close. Give my respect to your wife, my wife is sick.
>
> From your personal friend but not political.
>   C. V. Rogers.

The 1890 census showed 29,199 whites in the Cherokee territory, 5,127 blacks and only 22,015 Indians, or 39.1 percent of the total. The whites kept arriving. In an 1894 letter, Clem noted with dismay and something close to panic, "The Intruders are coming into the Country nearly every day."

In 1893, for the price of $8.6 million, the Cherokees sold the Outlet to the U.S. government, which two years later opened it up to homesteaders—the greatest land run in American history. (After the proceeds were divided up, each Cherokee citizen, man, woman, and child, including the Rogerses, received the sum of $365.70.) And so there were more whites surrounding the Cherokees, and thus more pressure to open up their own lands. Additional pressure came from the railroads, which lobbied relentlessly for the opening of the Indian

Territory, and, beginning in the 1890s, from the U.S. Congress. In 1893, the Senate formed a commission, headed by and named after Henry L. Dawes, Republican of Massachusetts, to figure out what to do with the Five Civilized Tribes. From the beginning, it was clear that the eventual aim was to end the tribes' autonomy, to make the Indian Territory into an American territory, and to absorb its residents into the United States.

The rationale for this stance was humanitarian. In hearings in Washington, the point was made again and again—and not without justification—that the Indian Territory was a lawless country, terrorized by armed criminals, that needed the official protection of the U.S. government. The point was made—again, not without justification—that a fatal flaw in the current system was that a small number of residents, most of them mixed-bloods or intermarried whites, controlled a disproportionate amount of the land and wealth. A study presented to Congress in 1896 showed that just twenty-three individuals controlled 174,000 acres, an estimated one-seventh of the arable land in the Nation. The largest such "monopolist" was none other than W. E. Halsell, the benefactor of Will Rogers's former school and his future employer, with twenty thousand acres. (He was disdainfully described by Senator Archibald McKennon of the Dawes Commission as "a white man who married an Indian woman, who died, and he then married a white woman, as I am informed.") Also on the list was C. V. Rogers, credited with five thousand acres.

But much of the rhetoric of the Dawes Commission and other white "friends of the Indian" focused on ideology rather than welfare. Increasingly, offense was taken that this group of people, surrounded by capitalist, private-property America, lived within a land system that in a later era would be called Communistic. Henry Dawes admitted as much in a speech he gave in 1885. The Cherokees were prosperous, he reported: "The head chief told us that there was not a family in that whole nation that had not a home of its own. There was not a pauper in that nation, and the nation did not owe a dollar." But somehow this was not good enough:

> . . . the defect of the system was apparent. They have got as far
> as they can go, because they own their land in common. It is
> Henry George's system, and under that there is no enterprise to
> make your home any better than that of your neighbors. There
> is no selfishness, which is at the bottom of civilization. Till this
> people will consent to give up their lands, and divide them

among the citizens so that each can own the land he cultivates, they will not make much more progress.

Clem saw the future earlier than most. In 1896, he was named to a delegation of five Cherokees to meet with the Dawes Commission regarding the eventual fate of the Nation. Clem felt that his people's only chance of obtaining reasonable terms from the government was to take a strong negotiating stance with the Commission, and he was exasperated with the delegation's inability to reach a consensus on what their position should be. "We can settle a great many things with the Dawes Commission that, if Congress takes it in hand, will never be looked after," he warned. He pointed out that he, more than most, would suffer from a change in the communal land policy, but there were no alternatives: ". . . if any man will suggest anything, I will donate $1,000 a year for every year this Nation can stand just as it is, because I am getting more benefit from this public domain than any man on it, and I want it to stand." There were no suggestions.

On June 28, 1898, Congress passed the Curtis Act, abolishing tribal law and mandating allotment—the policy of dividing up all the land in the territory equally among the members of the tribe. The Cherokee Nation and the U.S. government would not agree on terms for another four years, but Clem knew it was only a matter of time. He sold his cattle, traded his horses for a hotel, rented out his farmland to a family from Illinois, and, on August 20, 1898, moved to a two-story frame house in Claremore, a burgeoning town a dozen miles southwest of Oologah, at the intersection of the Missouri Pacific and the Frisco railroads. A year later, he would become a director and vice president of the new Claremore National Bank. (His partners were the ubiquitous W. E. Halsell and Jim Hall, another big rancher.) In 1902 he started a livery stable in Claremore. He would never live on the old home place again.

SUCH WAS the situation Will found when he came home from his Texas hegira in the fall of 1898. His father had an offer for him: If he would agree to live out on the ranch and manage it, he could have a herd of cattle for his own. Better yet, he would never have to go back to school. Will agreed and dubbed the operation Dog Iron Ranch, after his old brand. At first, he lived in the home place, along with the Illinois family, but he found their company uncongenial; a special problem was the wife's insistence on serving toast for breakfast, when Will preferred country fare—biscuits, cream gravy, and navy beans. Possibly the memories of happier days were too strong as well. In any case, with the assistance of his cousin Isparschecher "Spi" Trent and a black man named Hayward, he built a one-room, twelve-foot-square log cabin on a· hill, looking down on a spring, about a mile away from the ranch. In all the excitement of construction, they forgot about windows, so they punched holes in the mud daubing for air and put up with the wet when it rained. Will certainly got to eat as much biscuits, gravy, and navy beans as he wanted. Spi, who was in charge of the cooking, reported of the last item that "we had em 3 times a day, week days, an 3 times on Sundays an anytime you rode in on us you would always find the big ole iron kittle full to overflowin with em."

However diligent Will was about his managerial duties initially, his enthusiasm quickly waned. By this point, the operation was more farm than ranch. It was necessary to cut and stack hay to sustain the cattle over the winter, to plow up the pastures and grow corn, wheat, and alfalfa. That wasn't Will's idea of the cowboy's life. Even more irksome was the way the cattle—and the prairie itself—were fenced in. "He wasn't used to getting off his pony every few minutes to open a gate, or to working cattle in a fence corner," said his nephew Herb McSpadden, who was born in 1893 and idolized Will.

But he bore with it. The ranch didn't require an inordinate amount of work, and it was still a profitable concern. Whenever he was in need of a little quick cash, he could sell a steer or two. Consciously or not, Will recognized that this was the end of an era—allotment, and the permanent breakup of the property, were due to come at any time—and he devoted himself to reaping its benefits while they were there. In a word, he had fun. Train service was such that, on a whim, he could travel to Missouri, Texas, or Arkansas, and he often did. Once, he took Spi Trent's brother Dick all the way to New York.

For nearer jaunts, he bought a rubber-tired buggy, the first in the area. And he socialized. As if in mute recognition of the upcoming changes, of the need to go out with a bang, a disproportionate number of the young people of the Verdigris had put off marriage, and this carefree cohort enjoyed a steady stream of hayrides, roping contests, softball games, swimming expeditions, and all manner of parties. Will, in his trademark hat—a small, derbylike affair, not a ten-gallon Stetson—and, if the occasion demanded, a flowing bow tie, could always be counted on to be there. For dances, he had a wooden platform built out at the ranch. Because of his frequent cattle-selling trips to Kansas City— famous as a place where everything was up-to-date—he took responsibility for keeping his friends apprised of the current crazes. He introduced them with special delight to so-called "coon songs"* and the cakewalk. The former, popularized by the vaudeville team of Williams and Walker, were syncopated numbers, anticipating ragtime, sung in the persona and supposed dialect of blacks; the latter was a high-stepping dance competition, for the prize of a cake, supposedly originated by slaves in plantation days. The newspapers reported that Will took home a ginger cake at one affair, and at another "a large iced pyramid cake." He warmed up for the cakewalk at that party by soloing on a few coon songs and performing "some excellent dialect yarns."

Obviously, Will had some maturing to do; he still hadn't quite grown out of the role of rich man's indulged son, or lost his swollen sense of entitlement. At one point, smallpox broke out in Oologah and the town was quarantined. Signs were posted on all the incoming roads, and a marshal from out of town was posted at the city limits to prevent anyone from entering. Will, coming into town with his friend Gordon Lane to pick up his mail, blithely ignored the signs and galloped his horse around the marshal, who furiously complained to Oologah's sheriff, Buck Sunday, Ed Sunday's son. "Thinking I'd get rid of him, I said, 'You arrest him and I'll fine him,' " Sunday remembered. "The next evening the marshal came by and said, 'I've got your man.' I went up the street from my store where Will was standing with a lariat in his hand and he asked, 'Well, Judge, what are you going to do with me?'. . . I told Will I'd have to fine him and the standard price was $19.85, and I'd also have to fine Gordon Lane. Will asked if I'd take his check and wrote me out a check for both fines using his saddle as a table."

He could be reckless, too. One day in October 1900, he wanted to

---

*It has been estimated that more than six hundred "coon songs" were published in the 1890s, the most popular selling several million copies. The "coon," as the lyrics defined him, was a dice-throwing, razor-wielding, fried-chicken-eating, watermelon-stealing savage. The collective portrait was so shockingly virulent because (in the view of one student of the phenomenon) "the coon song craze in its full frenzy was a manifestation of a peculiar form of the will to believe—to believe in the signified 'coon' as represented in the songs—as a necessary sociopsychological mechanism for justifying segregation and subordination." It is worth noting that many of the most successful writers and performers of coon songs were black. One of them was Bert Williams (later a *Ziegfeld Follies* co-star of Will Rogers) whose "The Coon's Trade Mark," written with his partner George Walker, contained these lyrics:

> As certain and sure as Holy Writ,
> And not a coon's exempt from it,
> Four things you'll always find together,
> Regardless of condition of sun and moon—
> A watermelon, a razor, a chicken and a coon!

go to Claremore, but the Verdigris was up and there was no way across
except the railroad bridge. He put his rope around his horse's neck—not
Comanche—and started to walk across the bridge by the foot planks,
leading the swimming horse below. "About mid-stream," said Ed Sunday, "the horse got a little bit strangled and surged back against the
rope. Will pulled and the horse was ducked and began to fight and before Will could do anything the horse drowned."

What prevented Will from being insufferable was a level of
goodheartedness that no bratty behavior could obscure, and his sense of
humor. Not that the latter was notably sophisticated. His notion of the
height of hilarity was to name his dogs "Did He Bite You" and "You
Know," so as to engineer repeated occurrences of this exchange:

"What's the dog's name?"

"Did He Bite You."

"No—I just want to know his name."

"You Know."

Will was a chatterbox—"He was vaccinated with a gramophone
needle," said Jim Hopkins, a Texas cowboy who worked on Verdigris
ranches in the late 1890s and became Will's roping mentor and lifelong
friend—throwing out dozens of quips and snappers, hoping that two or
three of them would hit. "You never knew what he would say next," said
Will's contemporary Gazelle "Scrap" Lane. She remembered a swimming party where a tall girl named Linda Foreman got into the water
first. Will asked her how deep it was and she motioned to her shoulder.
"My Lord, it would drown the rest of us," he said, getting off a good
one. The swimming over, he went behind a bush to get dressed and
when he emerged called out to the girls, "You can look now. I have my
hat on."

Will's humor was rarely cruel or coarse—surprising, since those
qualities were hallmarks of the all-male cowboy domain he had spent so
much time in. When he did do something hurtful, he immediately tried
to make up for it. Once he was at Scrap Lane's place and decided he
would try roping a turkey. The result was a turkey with a broken neck—
that night's supper. Will made sure to buy the family a nice carving set
on his next trip to Kansas City. He and his friends, great practical jok-
ers, executed a classic at a dance at Vinita. While the festivities were going on, they alighted on one of the buggies outside, took the harness off
the horse, put it on backward, turned the horse around so its head faced
the buggy, reversed all the wheels, and hid nearby to watch the reaction
to their handiwork. When the victim came out, he recalled, "a laugh
greeted me from the darkness. . . . But then one in the crowd took pity

on me, and he helped get the rig righted." Needless to say, this was Will Rogers.

Will didn't carry a gun, didn't like to hunt or fish, and participated in only one recorded fight (with a cowboy named Leonard Trainor—decades later, Will's motion-picture double). Afterward, he did something else that was uncharacteristic—he started to drink. "It was the only time I ever saw him drunk," said Jim Hopkins. "He got roar-eyed. He didn't do anything, just cried all the time."

In his late teens and early twenties, Will cut a handsome figure. He was slim and dark, with high cheekbones and soulful eyes that bespoke his Cherokee heritage. His sweetheart was thought to be one of the daughters of the Oologah hotel keeper, Mrs. Ellis—either Kate, a schoolteacher, or her younger sister Lil. There were others, too, including Linda Foreman's sister Ada. Will was shy but capable of considerable charm and, according to Hopkins, "the greatest ladies man you ever saw."

He had occasion to exercise all his romantic skills late in 1899, when a new girl came to town. She was the sister of the wife of the Missouri Pacific station agent at Oologah; she was twenty years old—the same as Will; she was white; she came from the town of Rogers in the northwest corner of Arkansas; she had brown hair and blue eyes; and her name was Betty Blake. After an attack of typhoid fever, her mother thought a change would do her good, and so she had repaired to the Indian Territory. She met Will when he came into the station to pick up a banjo he had ordered from Kansas City. He left without uttering a word, either from shyness or in shock at the sight of her hair, which because of her illness was shorn close to the scalp.

He had more to say a couple of nights later, when the Ellis family invited him and Betty for dinner at the hotel. Will was silent during the meal, but afterward he warmed up. He took out a roll of sheet music and began singing coon songs a capella in his muscular tenor. The evening was striking in its coziness—after the singing everyone popped corn and rolled taffy—and when it was over Will said to Betty that if she could learn the songs on her sister's piano, he'd like to hear them. The night he came over, he brought his banjo; Betty, a talented musician, impressed him by playing both it and the piano. Soon it was clear that the attraction was mutual; over the following weeks they spent a lot of time together. He said Betty should come out to the ranch, and one day she and her brother-in-law drove out unannounced, only to find that Will wasn't home. They were met by the tenant farmer's wife. "The house was cold, ill-kept and bare of furniture," Betty wrote in the biog-

raphy of Will she published in 1941. "As I remember, the whole place
was run down and neglected, and I knew it had little resemblance to the
hospitable home where the Rogers family had been born and raised."

Betty went back home to Arkansas for Christmas. In the middle of
January, there came a letter from Will. It proved that his schooling had
at least provided him with some prowess in vocabulary and rhetoric (if
not in spelling). "My Dear Friend," he wrote, "No doubt you will be
madly surprised on receipt of this *Epistle*. But never the less I could not
resist the temptation and I hope if you cannot do me the *great* favor of
droping me a few lines you will at least excuse me for I *can't help* it." He
continued in this vein, inviting her out for another visit ("we were just
getting acquainted good when you left") but making sure to let her know
he was having a gay holiday season ("have not been at home three night
in a month") and that "Lil [Ellis] is just the *cutest* girl I know and I am
as silly about her as ever." Although Will was wealthier than Betty—her
mother was a widow who had had to raise seven girls and two boys—
and at least as well educated, emanating from the letter is a strong sense
of social and racial defensiveness. "I know you are having a great time
after being among the 'Wild Tribe,' so long," he wrote; after asking for
her picture, he remarked, "Now isnt that a 'mamoth inducement for
you' to have your pictures in lovely 'indian Wigwam.' " He signed the
letter "your True Friend and Injun Cowboy, WP Rogers."

She wrote back—although not until a suitable time had elapsed, for
Will's next letter to her was dated 14 March. In it, he opened his heart.

> My Dear Betty,
>   For me to express my delight for your sweet letter would be
> uterly impossible so will just put it mildly and say I was *very very*
> much pleased. I was also surprised for I thought you had forgot-
> ten your Cowboy (for I am yours as far as I am concerned). . . .
> I ought not to have gotten so broke up over you. But I could not
> help it so if you do not see fit to answer this please do not say
> a word about it to anyone for the sake of a broken hearted
> Cherokee Cowboy. . . .
>   I am yours with love,
>   Will Rogers.

There was no next letter from Will, suggesting that Betty was too
overwhelmed by this expression of ardor to write back. They saw each
other that September at a roping competition in Springfield, Missouri,
not far from Betty's home. Will joined her in the grandstand, but he was
intimidated by her friends and didn't say much. (Charley McClellan

went to the same contest, the Vinita *Leader* reporting that when he passed through town on his way there, "he was in his war paint.") In the fall, Will and Betty separately attended a street fair in Fort Smith, Arkansas; throughout the week, they kept missing each other. Betty wrote that on the last night, "I kept looking for him all during the evening, and finally, as I danced by a window, I saw him wandering around among the people outside on the cool green lawn. He was watching the dancers and sometimes glancing in my direction. But he did not come in and I did not go out."

THERE WERE OTHER reasons for his discomfiture besides shyness. It had been clear for some time that the arrangement at the ranch was not working out. Will would pack a bag and leave on a moment's notice, staying away for longer and longer periods of time. On a couple of occasions, he hopped a train and went back to Texas to visit the Ewings. These wanderings were not looked on with favor by his father. Spi Trent described Clem Rogers's reaction to one of the Higgins trips: "Willie aint never goin to amount to nothin—all hes good for is to buy up these expensive hosses and fool round ropin contests—huhhh! Hes fixin to ruin us, do you know that?"

Clem had even less patience for his son than usual because something else was then weighing heavily on his mind. Mary Bibles was ill, and she would die in January 1900—almost precisely ten years after Mary Rogers's passing. It naturally was a blow to him, and not only because, now sixty-one and alone, he had lost the woman he'd expected to be his companion for the rest of his life. He also honestly cared for her. A letter he wrote to her brother, Eulson Bibles, is the only surviving documentary evidence that Clem Rogers was capable of tenderness. He assured Bibles that he and his family would not lose their eventual stake in Rogers's estate. "The Love I had for your dear Sister, who is now gone, I will always have the Same for you all," he wrote. "Any time I can assist your little family I will willingly do." Clem was living at a hotel, he told Bibles, "& Am getting very tired off [*sic*] it. But my lovely companions are now gone & am happy to say that she is gone to the House of love."

On February 17, 1900, the Claremore *Weekly Progress* reported that Clem would leave that night for Roswell, New Mexico, "where he goes with a view of locating a ranch for his son, Will." The destination makes sense: his father knew that Will liked the wide open spaces, and in New Mexico the farmers, barbed wire, and railroads had not yet done much to close them up. Clem apparently did not find any land to his liking.

But in the fall of the year—probably soon after he saw but did not speak to Betty Blake at the Fort Gibson Fair—Will left for New Mexico and points west. While there, he and a cowboy named Billy Connell got a job shipping a trainload of cattle to the Hearst ranch in San Luis Obispo, California. They thought about asking for work there but couldn't communicate with the Spanish-speaking foreman, so they went to San Francisco to see the sights. The first night there, Will had his third brush with death. He went to sleep in their hotel room while his friend was still out on the town, and woke up in the hospital. He had been overcome by gas inhalation. Although both denied doing it, it's likely that Will or Connell, used to kerosene illumination, had blown the lamp out and let the gas stream into the room. Whatever happened, it took the doctors nine hours to revive Will. "That was just bull luck," he later wrote. "The main doctors gave me up but a lot of young medical students and just by practicing on me they happened to light on some nut remedy (that no regular doctor would ever think of) and I came alive." When he got back to Oologah, the ranch hand sent to meet the train found Will so weak that he had to help him into the buggy. On the way back to the ranch, he sat with his eyes half-closed, hardly speaking a word. Clem sent him to Hot Springs, Arkansas, and he stayed there until the middle of March, trying to get the gas out of his system.

His health was soon all the way back to normal—two weeks after coming home, he won a cakewalk—but, after being away for so long, there was no longer even a pretense of his taking an active role in running the ranch. By this time, his sister May and her second husband, Frank Stine, were living at the home place and managing the operation. Will still had his herd, but he was now less interested in actual ranching than in what was a kind of metaphor for the cowboy life, a pastime that had emerged in mute and melancholy recognition of the fact that the days of the open range were over. Informal cowboy competitions had been held as early as 1847, when a visitor to Santa Fe noted how the cowhands "contest with each other for the best roping and throwing." But it wasn't until the 1880s and 1890s, when the great days of the cowboy were over, that the contests began to spread through the West. The first commercial rodeo—Frontier Days—was held in 1893 in Lander, Wyoming, but nearly every town in cattle country had a contest of some kind.

Even Claremore. On July 4, 1899, a steer-roping contest was held there as part of the Independence Day festivities, and Will Rogers, riding Comanche, won the first prize of $18.50. The victory was not inscribed in the annals of the sport. His time was a fairly leisurely fifty-two seconds, and in fact he had to beat out only one other contestant. The other eight, the Claremore *Progress* reported, "had bad luck of one kind or another and failed to get in the race."

Steer-roping was an enterprise that required considerable strength, agility, coordination, and practice. It involved sending a steer out of a one-hundred-foot chute into the roping area, where the roper was waiting on horseback. When the animal crossed a line, an umpire shouted "Go!" and the stopwatch started. It was then the roper's task to approach the galloping steer, throw a rope over its horns, and then ride away from the animal until the rope—secured to his saddle—had tightened and, ideally, pulled the steer to the ground. (Less than ideal results included the rope breaking, the saddle breaking, and the horse being pulled to the ground.) At that point—while, in the words of a contemporary newspaper account, "with almost human intelligence the faithful pony digs his hoof into the ground and pulls at his end of the lariat"— the roper would run to the steer and tie one of its hind legs and one of its front legs together with a separate rope. The watch would be stopped, and if the steer remained secured for a predetermined number of minutes—sometimes five, sometimes ten—the time would be recorded. (The pastime was dangerous for the roper, but even more so for the steer, whose neck was sometimes broken, and over the next few decades steer-roping was banned in most states and replaced in rodeos by calf-roping.)

Flushed with his success in Claremore, Will signed up for a roping contest at the St. Louis Fair in October. Because the event was staged by the general livestock agent for the San Francisco Railroad, one "Colonel" Zack Mulhall, a man who would occupy a position of some importance in Will's life, Will and Comanche traveled free of charge on the Frisco. The steers, at around one thousand pounds, were bigger than what either Will or the relatively diminutive Comanche was used to, and both man and horse were thrown to the ground. But, as Will later wrote, "that gave me a touch of 'Show business' in a way, so that meant I was ruined for life as far as actual employment was concerned." He entered more ropings the next year—at the nearby town of Pryor, at Springfield, Missouri (where he saw Betty Blake), and at Oklahoma City, where Teddy Roosevelt's Rough Riders were holding a reunion, and Mulhall was engaged to provide entertainment and put on the cowboy contests. Roosevelt, then running for Vice President on William McKinley's ticket, attended; Spi Trent claimed that both he and Will shook the candidate's hand. Mulhall, who was in the process of casting his lot with show business at the expense of his railroad career, made even more of the Roosevelt connection. In many a subsequent newspaper interview and promotional pamphlet, he claimed that the two men formed a fast and deep friendship, and that the future President was so impressed by the roping and riding skills of Mulhall's daughter Lucille, who was not yet fifteen, that he urged the colonel to take her on tour so that the rest of America could marvel at her.

So far, Will still hadn't repeated his initial success in roping. But in 1901, after he'd recovered from the gas incident, he threw himself into the sport. He practiced assiduously, building on the attributes he already had—his roping skill and his natural quickness. ("He was active as a cat," Jim Hopkins said. "I once saw him rope a steer, then the steer got out and ran towards him. Will jumped right back in the saddle with two feet.") From Jim Rider, a cowboy on the Jim Hall ranch, he learned the "Johnny Blocker," a very effective throw where a big loop is sent over the steer's back and turned over so that it ties its front feet, not its horns. Comanche, meanwhile, was proving to be an exceptional roping pony, "so speedy," in Spi Trent's words, "that he could turn on a dime and give you back the change" and "so smart that if you had a secret to keep you couldn't even spell it in front of him." Will added to his stable whenever he saw a promising horse. From a cowboy named Hick Miller, he bought a bald-faced sorrel horse named Robin for $125, and from his friend Dick Parris he bought a black horse he named Monte, named after a girl he had met while the family was vacationing in Eureka Springs, Arkansas.

Briefly, Will even became a promoter. Early in May, he went to Memphis, where a big Confederate veterans' reunion was to be held later in the month, and, in partnership with Zack Mulhall and some others, arranged to put on a roping contest. Will went to Kansas City and bought steers, shipped them to Memphis, and had chutes constructed. On May 10, he and some forty other cowboys left Claremore in their own railroad car; a big banner that ran the length of the car announced who they were. The boys were primed for high jinks. During the trip, whenever someone passed through their car on the way to the dining car, he would discover himself roped.

The Memphis affair was no standard roping. Will had even budgeted money for advertising, and on May 29 this notice appeared in the Memphis *Commercial Appeal:*

Montgomery Park
Cowboys and Indians
Grand Roping Contests and Indian Parades and War Dances

Miss Lucille Mulhall, the Daring Broncho [*sic*] Rider,
Will Appear Daily and Rope the Wildest Texas Steers
40 Indians and Cowboys
Contests Daily at 3 P.M.

Following the distinction the ad poses, Will and the other part-
Cherokee participants he'd brought with him from Indian Territory (including Charley McClellan, whom the *Commercial Appeal* described in an
article about the event as "among the most daring and skillfull ropers")
were "cowboys," not "Indians." There is no record of what the man
who had signed himself "your Injun Cowboy" thought about this irony,
or even whether he was aware of it. It would come up again.

The event was not a financial success. The promoters could pocket
all gate receipts and could camp for free, but other expenses, particularly
shipping, were high. And attendance was lower than hoped for because
Montgomery Park was a considerable distance from downtown Memphis, where the Confederate festivities took place. Jim Hopkins reckoned
that Will and his partners broke even. But it was by no means a waste
of time. For one thing, Hopkins, riding Comanche, set a world's record
for steer roping, with an amazing time of eighteen and a half seconds.
For another, Will, who wasn't entered in the roping, had a chance to exercise his show-business aptitude in front of an audience for the first
time. Acting as master of ceremonies, he paraded back and forth on his
horse, giving the ropers humorous introductions through a megaphone
and commenting on points of general interest.

After Memphis, Will stuck to roping. On July 4, in Vinita, he took
third place in one competition, with a time of sixty-one seconds, and
second place in another. He did even better at an Elks' convention in
Springfield in September, finishing second in a strong field with a time
of fifty seconds. Hopkins won at forty-five. Will let another cowboy use
Comanche, and the horse showed his mettle. The steer was thrown, but,
as the cowboy was running toward him, it got up and charged him. At
that, said Hopkins, Comanche "turned off and busted the steer all alone.
The cowboy didn't lose over three seconds time." A wealthy New
Yorker hunted up Will and offered him five hundred dollars for Comanche; the answer was no.

The Springfield roping was put on by Zack Mulhall, and it was here
that he and Will became more closely acquainted. Mulhall, born in
1847, was orphaned at the age of eight and raised by an aunt and uncle
in St. Louis. He was a lifelong railroad man—the "Colonel" was an
honorific commonly bestowed on notables in Oklahoma Territory, a sec-

tion of land that was originally part of Indian Territory but that had
never been assigned to any tribe. In 1889, this land was opened for
white settlement in the first of the great land runs. Mulhall participated,
settling in a town that would take his name. He was a good-hearted man
but prone to impulsive and insensitive behavior. During his railroad
days, he adopted a girl named Georgia; in time she became his mistress
and bore him a son and a daughter, Charley and Mildred. They were
sent to the Mulhall ranch and raised as if they were the son and daughter of Zack's wife, Mary Agnes, who is universally deemed a saint.

In 1899, Mulhall put to use his railroad connection, his access to
livestock, and his measure of show-business genius by starting to stage
roping and riding contests. These soon developed into a new class of entertainment. The Wild West show had been around for twenty years,
but in the hands of Buffalo Bill and his imitators it was an exercise fatally lacking in realism, filled with fake Indian battles and assorted hokum. Mulhall—and such followers as the Miller Brothers 101 Ranch
Show, based near Ponca City, in the former Cherokee Outlet—replaced
this with demonstrations of and competitions in real cowboy skills. As he
had printed on the bottom of one handbill, "The contestants in this carnival are in no case professional show people, but on the other hand
represent the best of their class as found in each instance pursuing their
vocations."

Still, the colonel was no stranger to show-business hype. His shows
included performances by the Frisco Cowboy Band, named for and sub-
sidized by the railroad. Through the Roosevelt connection, the band
had been invited to play at President McKinley's inauguration in Washington the previous winter, and its fame had spread. The sixty-odd musicians wore ten-gallon hats, chaps, boots, and spurs, and Mulhall
advertised a prize of a thousand dollars if anyone could rope and tie a
steer faster than one of them. The key point was which one. Since
the instrumentalists could no more rope a steer than butcher one, he
cannily arranged for assorted ringers, including Will Rogers, to travel
with the band and compete against any challengers. When Will joined
up, he was given a trombone and told to mime playing it between
ropings.

In October, Will participated in a roping contest Mulhall put on at
a Des Moines fair called SEMI-OM-SED (Des Moines spelled roughly
backward). According to the Vinita *Leader,* Mulhall told the seventy-one
cowboys and musicians in attendance that "their money was 'no good'
and paid all their bills until they came home." There was one problem.
Iowa being a considerable distance from the plains and Iowans being

unfamiliar with ranch life, a Des Moines newspaper found it necessary to assure readers, "There is positively nothing about this wild west show that is repulsive or brutal or would offend women viewers." Nevertheless, on the second day of the roping, the local Humane Society succeeded in stopping the steer-throwing competition. At that, the troupe packed up and traveled to St. Louis, where Mulhall put on a "Big Western Show" at the Delmar Race Track.

From there, Will and Jim Hopkins went on to the San Antonio State Fair, with its first prize of fifteen hundred dollars and its reputation as the premier roping competition in the country. It was a heady experience. The famous John Blocker, originator of the throw Jim Rider had taught Will, was the judge of the roping competition, and Jim Hopkins introduced his friend to celebrated Texas cowboys such as Joe Gardner, Clay McGonigle, and Johnny Murrah. At the end of the first day of competition, a cowboy named Charles Tomkins was sitting in a chair outside the Southern Hotel as darkness fell. Will came by, spotted an empty chair, and straddled down on it. "He was small and a wiry-looking fellow, dark hair, and I knew at once that he had some Indian blood in him," Tomkins recalled five decades later. "His first words were, 'Gee you sure did make good time on that steer. . . . I hope I do half as well tomorrow.' I then asked, 'Are you roping tomorrow?' thinking at the same time you are pretty light to tackle those big wild steers."

Tomkins's assessment was on the mark. Will finished eleventh in a field of nineteen in the second day's roping, missing his steer with three loops until he finally roped and tied him in a minute and thirty-six seconds. "I . . . had a little Pony," he wrote later, referring to Comanche, "and got it jerked down so many times they wanted me to tie the horse's feet instead of the steer's."

It was clear that Will couldn't really make a living as a roper. Opportunities were limited, and, he now realized, he and Comanche were both too slight of stature to reach the top echelon of the sport. Going back to the ranch wasn't really an option, not only because of his lack of interest in the work but because, with allotment only months away, the ranch was soon to be a thing of the past. That winter, he thought a lot about what he wanted to do, and he emerged with a scheme that, even for Will Rogers, sounded outlandish. He would go to Argentina and work cattle. There was no barbed wire on the pampas, no farms or railroads, and the cattle fed on native grasses. It would be like going back in time fifty years.

For $3,000, he sold back to his father the cattle that Clem had given him as a foundation for the ranch three years before, and he sold an additional twenty-five range steers to a friend for $625. He sold all his horses except for Comanche, which he left with his friend John Lipe. From Jim Rider, in exchange for his own saddle, a few Navaho blankets, and fifty dollars, he bought a beautiful oak-tanned leather saddle, hand-stamped with little raised flowers. He told Dick Parris, a quick-witted roping buddy from Tahlequah, that he would pay his way if he came along. He signed up for a twenty-year life-insurance policy that required a $140 yearly premium. He packed his bags, and he left.

THE CHEROKEE KID WITH THE WIRTH BROTHERS CIRCUS, 1903

CHAPTER 3

ABROAD

I am going to learn things . . . that will enable me to make my living
in the world without making it by day labor.

—WILL ROGERS TO C. V. ROGERS,

DECEMBER 28, 1902

THE TRIP BEGAN badly and quickly got worse. Will and Dick were
unsure of the best way to get to Argentina, but, knowing it was south of
the Indian Territory, they set out in that direction by train on February 19. On arrival in New Orleans, they discovered that the only
Argentina-bound ships departed from New York. So—after Will picked
up thirteen hundred dollars his father had wired him—they backtracked
to Galveston, Texas, and took a small steamer across the Gulf and up
the Atlantic coast. On arrival they were disappointed again: No ship
would leave for Argentina for another three weeks. They could, however, get to Buenos Aires sooner and for roughly the same price by going to England and sailing from there. That option made sense, and
they took it, but the fact remained that they were spending more and
more money, consuming more and more time, and getting farther
and farther away from their destination.

Their ship, the SS *Philadelphia*, sailed March 25, and Will immediately absorbed another unpleasant fact: He was greatly prone to seasickness. They landed in Southampton after eight days at sea, at which
point "Our baggage was searched for tobacco and spirits; they did not
find any in mine for I don't chew and my spirits had all left me on that
boat if I had any at all I contributed them to the briny deep."

This last intelligence was contained in a letter Will wrote home from

Southampton and posted on April 4. His sisters were so taken with it that they cleaned up the grammar, punctuation, and vocabulary, eliminated a few personal references, and gave it to the editor of the Chelsea *Reporter,* who put it in the paper. Clem Rogers, meanwhile, took Will's subsequent letters to him to the Claremore *Progress.* By this process, a couple of dozen dispatches from the wandering son were published over the next two years. They are the first published writings of Will Rogers, and they show that the high school dropout had a previously undisplayed literary aptitude. (Will knew it. When he found out that the letters were being reprinted, he wrote, with transparent disingenuousness, "I had no idea they would ever come into print. . . . I'm not especially proud of them and am obliged to pen them under very severe difficulties.")

The two travelers from the Cherokee Nation spent nine days in England. They visited London, then in the midst of preparations for the coronation of Edward VII, and took in an impressive roster of sights: the Houses of Parliament, Buckingham Palace, the Tower of London, and Westminster Abbey. "There is no end of theaters in London," he reported, with all the worldliness he could muster, "but they are not up to the Americans in either tragedy or comedy. The only advantage I have seen over our American cities, is that here they have large parks or play grounds all through the city for the children, and you see thousands of them playing all the time."

Will's comments on English money and speech showed the marks of a budding humorist. "Every time We eat or get any thing they speal [*sic*] out what its worth," he wrote his sisters. "I just hand them a pound, that is all I know, which is about a five spot over there, and trust to the lord that they will take pity on me and do me half right. Anyway they'll hand me back a double hand full of something and strut off. I have got enough money in *bulk* to start in some kind of business. But when I count it (or if some one else did) there would not be enough there to make the first payment on a soda cracker."

And the way the people talked! "Our English must be a kind of slow process. I went up to a Man for some information yesterday and he throwed open the throttle and broke out on one of those chained lightning speeches and I flagged him at the first quarter and asked him (in my speediest tones, which by the way he seemed tire [*sic*] of before I got done) that I was perfectly willing to pay him for his over time if he would kindly relate it over agin as though he were speaking of some of his poor or dead relation [*sic*]."

Will and Dick sailed April 14 on the *Danube,* a royal mail steamer that made numerous stops: Rupert, France; Vigo, Spain; Lisbon; São

Vicente, one of the Cape Verde Islands ("oh, what a horrible place that was, it was so hot and all the people were negroes and didn't wear enough clothes to cover a postage stamp"); Pernambuco and Bahia, in Brazil; Rio de Janeiro; Montevideo; and, finally, Sanata, Argentina. After a two-day quarantine on the ship, they took a thirty-five-mile train ride to Buenos Aires. The trip from England had taken twenty-four days; it was now more than two months since the boys had left home.

Will liked Buenos Aires, a cosmopolitan city underwritten by cattle, whose climate was roughly equivalent to Oologah's. He found a hotel called the Phoenix where English was spoken, and, he reported, "the street cars, trains and almost everything else is on the American plan. Much more like it than England." But his bubble was soon burst. Two days after arriving, he had a talk with the United States consul, a Mr. Newbrey, who had some sobering news. There was money to be made in the cattle business, to be sure. Up until the last few years, the United States had been the principal supplier of beef to Great Britain—whose demand was even greater now that it had to feed its troops fighting in South Africa in the Boer War—but the expansion of the internal market had limited how much the United States had to export. Argentina, recently equipped with beef-freezing technology, had stepped in to fill the gap, and the cattle industry was booming. Moreover, the value of land was doubling every year. But the minimum investment necessary was in the neighborhood of ten thousand dollars, and, unless you already owned land, credit was impossible to come by. "The government will give you about fifteen hundred acres if you will become a citizen of the country," Will wrote in a twelve-hundred-word dispatch sent directly to the *Progress*, which titled it "Ranch Life in Argentina," "but it will be away back where you can't get a way out with what you raise and they will tax you to death. You will have to serve in the army and fight in case of war."

So buying land was out. The next option was finding a job on a ranch, or *estancia*, to which end Will and Dick ventured some five hundred miles into the interior of the country. Again the news was bad. The only job that paid a decent wage, about $25 a month, was as head man, but these positions were all filled by Englishmen. Working as a hand (*peon* was apparently the favored term, rather than *gaucho*) was not an option. "We can't begin to compete with the natives here," Will wrote persuasively, "for we can't speak Spanish, we don't know the country, we can't live on their diet, we can't endure the hardships nor work for from $5 to $8 per month in our American money."

His disappointment clearly colored his dismissive characterization of

Argentine ranching procedures. Too many men and horses were used to round up and drive cattle. The cattle were driven in a run ("I asked the boss if it did not run too much of the fat off, and he gave me the horse laugh and said, 'Why they fill right up again.' ") There were no chuck wagons. And the level of roping skill was rudimentary: "They all use a rawhide rope and are doing well to catch one out of three."* Shorn of his expectations, homesick, cold (the Argentine winter was about to reach its solstice), and soon to be broke, Will also indulged in some ethnic calumny of which, under happier circumstances, he would probably have thought better. "All the Americans I have met here are only living to get back to America," he wrote his father. "Any part of the states is better for a man without lots of money, than this place, and the beauty of it is you are among 'people,' and not a lot of 'dagoes' from all over the world and all having a different Lingo."

Things got worse before they got better. Dick had almost immediately lost his enthusiasm, not to mention his sense of humor, and Will agreed to pay his way home. He sailed on May 24, taking with him plentiful gifts from Will, including Brazilian lace collars for his sisters. Letters from home began to arrive, and, if they had been calculated to make him miserable, they could not have done a better job. "Willie, I wish you and Dick was hear [*sic*] the 4th of July . . . they are going to have a roping contest," a pal wrote. "I think you could make it warm for the boys." A girl named Pearl Yocum (probably related to May's late husband) hit even closer to home. "Old Comanche is just as fat as he can be," she reported. "He comes up every night and I think he is looking for you but dont see you. I go out to the fence and rub him and kill horse flies off of him and Pet him a little. . . . We miss you Very much. We are canning Blackberries and when you come home I will make you a Cobler."

Will made a second trip into the interior, with no better luck. Now

---

*He would later give a more generous assessment of the Argentines' roping abilities. "I consider them the best ropers and riders in the world," he said in an interview a half dozen years later. ". . . the champion holders in America use a rope only some twenty-four feet in length. Now down there in South America these punchers will throw a rope seventy-five or eighty feet long, and put the loop just where they want it to go." As for riding, he described a game where a speeding horse carrying a rider was roped. "The noose catches the horse, closing over his fore feet, and down goes Mr. Horse, turning a somersault or two. Now then, if the rider fails to light on his feet, or if he falls down after he has lit on his feet, he loses his drinks. That sort of stunt is commonly done for the drinks. It's pretty hard on the horse, but I never saw a man get hurt."

"Did you ever try it?" the interviewer asked him.

"Not me. I'm reasonably sane."

he was down and out in Buenos Aires, without a job, his assets speedily dwindling. A solitary bit of good fortune was the presence in port of a U.S. battleship. Will wrote home that he almost lived on board for two weeks, teaching all the latest coon songs to the sailors, who had been at sea for two years. He also casually mentioned that he had sung in the English-speaking concert hall.

But he was spinning his wheels. Clearly, it was time to come home. Unfortunately, at this point he didn't even have enough money to stay in a hotel, and he took to sleeping in the park. Too embarrassed by the fiasco to make a direct request to his father for money, he merely wrote, "I don't think there is much use of my staying here, and I may start home anytime," knowing Clem would know he couldn't very well "start home" without any money. He closed the letter, "with all my love to my dear father. I am your loving son, Willie." But Clem didn't bite. His letters stuck to pleasantries on the order of "Good crops on my old Home Place. Wheat corn & oats." Spi Trent reported that he intervened personally on the home front, pleading with Uncle Clem to send Will money. "He says, I dident ask Will to go an if he wants to come home he will have to come without an invitation."

Stung by the paternal silence, with all its disapproving resonance, Will sent back a brief in support of his ways, a declaration that alternated fierce self-defense with unmistakable self-doubt. He was well aware that he had dissipated several thousand dollars in five months, that he was stranded with no prospects, on the other side of the world. But:

> I never cared for money, only for what pleasure it was to spend it, and I am not afraid of work, and so as I am now I feel better than I ever did in my life, and am in good health, so don't you all worry about me because I am not making money. For if I did I would spend it and as long as I dont I cant.
>
> I have spent a world of money in my time but I am satisfied as some one else has got the good of some of it. It has not been all on myself and if you will only give me credit for just spending my own, as I think I have, I will be as happy as if I had a million.
>
> All that worries me is people there all say, "Oh, he is no account. He blows in all his father's money," and all that kind of stuff. Which is not so. I am more than willing to admit that you have done everything in the world for me and tried to make something more than I am out of me (which is not your fault)

but as to our financial dealings, I think I paid you all up and everyone else.

I only write these things so we may better understand each other.

I cannot help it because my nature is not like other people, to make money, and I dont want you all to think I am no good simply because I dont keep my money. I have less money than lots of you and I dare say I enjoy life better than any of you, and that is my policy. I have always delt honestly with everyone and think the world and all of you and all the folks, and will be among you soon as happy as any one in the world, as then I can work and show the people I am only spending what I make.

By the time he wrote the letter, Will could afford to be judiciously defiant. He had a job—helping to tend a shipload of three hundred cattle, six to seven hundred mules, two thousand sheep, and fifty thoroughbred horses that was to sail for South Africa the first week of August. (A Buenos Aires newspaper termed it "by far the most valuable consignment of livestock that has ever left the country.") What's more, the owner of the stock, an Irishman named Piccione, had promised him work at his form and racing stable on their arrival. The journey, on the *Kelvinside*, was predictably unpleasant: "I soon found I couldn't rassle with a bale of hay and a dose of seasickness at the same time and they couldn't fire me, so I was appointed the nightwatchman on the deck with the cows." When he finally did get his sea stomach, he came up with an ingenious scheme, reminiscent of a ploy he'd used at Kemper, to improve the quality of his rations. He managed to get a pint of milk out of the cows, which he then traded with the delighted cook for some decent food. A month after his arrival, he summed up the dismal voyage: "I will mail you a special edition of my drama '25 days on a floating dunghill, or Where did he kick you?' "

Will often said in interviews that his first job on arriving in Durban was breaking horses for the British army, but that was an invention; the ship landed about September 1 and the treaty ending the Boer War had been signed the previous May. In truth, he worked for Piccione in Mooi River Station, in the mountains about 150 miles inland—doing "more different kinds of odd jobs than I thought there were," he wrote home in early October, in a long, amusing letter. He spent most of his time feeding, caring for, and exercising the thoroughbred horses Piccione was offering for three thousand dollars apiece and up; in his spare time, he helped out the veterinarian or the blacksmith. Will was also one of two hands called on to demonstrate horses to prospective purchasers. "When any buyers come here," he wrote, "his Nibs sings out, 'Yank' (as that is all I am known by), 'Bring out such a horse.' Well I walk him out, he will start me in a run with the scoundrel, around and around, him hollering at you all the time for he is the only man that I ever saw that could holler louder and more at a person than Popa. Then he will pump that man with more lies in a minute than you could think of in a year." Will also supplied a vivid description of his appearance: "One of the boys here cut my hair off right short with a pair of horse clippers and when I get up on one of those long thoroughbreds with a little saddle and stirrups I look like a monkey up a stick." He closed the letter: "Tell Jim [Rider] he can rope on Old Comanche next Fourth."

Five weeks after his arrival, Will still didn't know what his salary was; he had been too timid to ask. But it didn't really matter. He was being fed well, he was using his skills productively, and he was around people who spoke English. For amusement—if his later claims are to be believed—he roped zebras on the veldt. In the evenings, he would wander over to the main house, sit on a fence, and eavesdrop through the window as Piccione's daughter—"a damsel of some twenty winters (Which by the way must of been a bit hard)"—gave her rendition of songs that the expatriate coon-song connoisseur scorned as hopelessly old-fashioned: "After the Ball," "The Fatal Wedding," "Sweet Rosie O'Grady," and "The Girl I Loved in Sunny Tennessee." One night, however, Piccione's secretary started in on "All Coons Look Alike to Me." Will was so flabbergasted at this nod to the up-to-date that he fell off the fence.

He quit after about two months and secured the job of transporting some mules to the town of Ladysmith, about 250 miles inland. And then he got a relapse of bad luck: While he was taking the train to Durban, where he was to pick up the herd, someone walked away with his trunk, spurs, leggings, bridle, and the saddle he had bought from Jim Rider. He was left only with a small grip containing, he wrote home, "thirteen collars, one shirt—all soiled—one unmarried sock and a clothes brush."

But what happened in Ladysmith more than made up for the loss. Will saw a sign advertising the appearance of something called Texas Jack's Wild West Show, and he wandered over to the dusty square where the show was to take place. He thought perhaps he might get a job, something along the lines of driving tent stakes. Texas Jack—who in fact was a Texan, a handsome man of forty or so with a firmly set jaw and flowing dark locks—was there, and he and Will got to talking. The subject of roping came up. Jack asked whether Will knew how to throw the "Big Whirl," also known as the crinoline, a stunt in which an entire rope of as much as eighty feet is let out into a loop and twirled in a great horizontal circle. Will said he did and proceeded to demonstrate. At that, Texas Jack offered him a job in the show at twenty dollars a week. Only later did Will find out that Jack had a standing offer to pay fifty pounds to anyone who could successfully attempt a crinoline. Employees, needless to say, were not eligible for the prize.

Will's new employer was the namesake of a more famous Texas Jack, born John B. Omohundro, a frontier scout and guide who served with William Cody in the range wars of the 1860s and 1870s and toured with Cody—now known as Buffalo Bill—in shoot-'em-up melodramas that capitalized on their fame. Shortly after the end of the Civil War, Texas Jack came upon a five-year-old boy whose parents had been killed by Indians. Jack provided for the lad, who, not knowing his last name, called himself Texas Jack, Jr. Texas Jack, Sr., died in 1880, but his protégé kept the flame alive by going into show business himself, as a roughrider and sharpshooter; before finding his way to South Africa, he had performed—or so he claimed—in San Francisco, Honolulu, Australia, New Zealand, Java, India, Egypt, Paris, London, and New York. In 1899, he toured England with a show called Savage South Africa. Returning to Africa two years later, he put on horse-against-cyclist races of one, ten, and twenty-five miles, then started his own "Wild West Show & Circus." This, as the name implied, was a versatile entertainment that, in addition to roping, riding, and shooting exhibitions, included a trapeze act, an Italian tambourine dance, clowns, a turn by "Azodi, the Flexible Marvel," and a "Realistic Western Drama" entitled "Prairie Life."

Jack told Will he wanted him to wait until the arrival of a new tent, without the encumbrance of a center pole, before making his debut as a roper. In the meantime, the Cherokee Kid—as Jack immediately dubbed his troupe's newest member—rode bucking horses, at which he was not expert. Jack told him just to stay on the horse, no matter what. The first night, possibly as a kind of hazing initiation, Will was given an extremely high-spirited mount that immediately ran into the main tent pole, to which the lights were attached. The tent became dark; the audience panicked. Some of the company came up to Will and tried to help him off the horse, but, remembering Jack's instructions, he refused. When the lights came back on, he was still mounted. Mixed in with the embarrassment and fear was a new and beguiling sensation. The audience, wonder of wonders, was laughing.

Touring South Africa, itself a bewildering and shifting conglomeration of blacks and Kaffirs, Englishmen and Afrikaners, and East Indians (including Mohandas Gandhi, who was living in Johannesburg in 1903), Texas Jack's Wild West Show & Circus offered a bizarre cultural and ethnic tableau: English circus performers pretending to be cowboys, white Americans pretending to be West Indians. Then there was the Cherokee Kid. In some of the dramatic pieces, which he described to the folks at home as "blood-curdling scenes of western life in America, showing encounters with Indians and robbers," he portrayed an Indian. In others, he put burnt cork on his face and played a black man, which gave him an opportunity to sing coon songs and dance the cakewalk. "My appearance amused the natives and Kaffirs greatly," he said in an interview half a dozen years later, "as they had never seen the makeup of a colored performer before."

The new tent presently arrived, and Will started to rope. He'd never done trick roping in front of crowds before, but he knew enough—from his memories of seeing Vincente Oropeza with Buffalo Bill, and from the untold hours he'd spent idly practicing with Dan Walker and by himself—to make a hit in front of South Africans; at his first performance, he had two encores. As he wrote home, "They dont use Ropes here to catch things and it is all a mystery to them to see it." He learned some new tricks, too, notably a stunt where he threw two ropes at once, one with each hand, catching a horse and its rider simultaneously. He got a five-dollar raise and started to attract the attention of newspapers, such as the Pretoria *News*, which termed his feats "astounding." Within a couple of months, he was taking his duties seriously enough to ask his father to send some better equipment: "I want about 100 feet of the best kind of hard twist rope you can get. . . . Any of the boys will show you what I used to use. . . . I cant get a thing here. . . . Some nights I rope with old tie ropes or any old thing."

Will was in something like heaven. The show—thirty-five performers and twenty-three horses—toured the country, spending two nights to three weeks in a city, and thus, like the Texas cattle drives that had made such a deep impression on him, satisfied his taste for controlled fraternal nomadism. He was making enough money to send his insurance payments back to his father and to begin planning his homeward voyage. He was eating regularly, too: One recipient of some photos he sent home remarked on the fullness of his cheeks. He even found his saddle, bridle, leggings, and spurs; they had been raffled off, and he was

able to locate the new owner. His first Christmas away from home
wasn't as painful as it might have been, either. After coming upon a
group of Canadian soldiers playing baseball, of all things, he took supper
in their camp and sang them coon songs all evening long.

Best of all, Will, known to one and all as "Kid," was immediately
accepted, not least by Texas Jack himself. In his first letter home after
joining the show, he wrote, "Jack is the finest old boy I ever met, and
he seems to think a great deal of me. . . . It isnt a wild mob like them
at home for he dont drink a drop or smoke or gamble and likes his men
to be the same." The bond became quickly and surprisingly strong: Jack
saw something of himself in Will, and the younger man's thirst for paternal approval was far from being quenched. Before long, Will would
don a wig and play Jack's parts in the shows. (Buffalo Bill had established the tradition: Wild West show heroes had to have long hair.)
Eventually, Jack began talking of the day when the Kid would take over
the whole operation, capital to be supplied by Jack. In all likelihood,
Will didn't take that prospect seriously. But he was serious about the
new idea, exemplified by Jack, that show business could be a vocation.
"I am going to learn things while with him," he wrote home, "that will
enable me to make my living in the world without making it by day
labor."

This new resolve helped him resist the entreaties to return home he
began receiving with a regularity that could have been orchestrated. Jim
Rider tried flattery: "I would give anything if you was here. . . . It dont
seem like there is anything doing if you aint along. These boys get to
bragging on some button prick being an awful fast tie. I tell all of them,
there ain't no body can catch any quicker from his horse or tie up half
as quick as Rogers." His sister Sallie took another tack, confiding, "You
can certainly have your pick of any of these girls when you come home."
Maud pulled out all the stops: "I think you know enough now to find
work of some kind at home," she wrote.

> If you work at so many different kinds of things there surely one
> of them would make you a living here at home. We are all well
> and are all to eat this Thanksgiving dinner here with me. How
> we will miss you. I have Baked my fruitcake and plum pudding,
> salted pecans and Almons. . . . How I do wish I could send you
> some of each. Willie some times I think that prehaps [sic] you
> havent money enough to bring you home. If that is the case
> please let me know and Cap and I will send you what you want.
> I saw Miss Kate [Ellis] last week in Claremore. . . . Miss Kate

looked so well in a white silk waist and the black silk collar you
sent May. . . .*

Miss Kate herself weighed in with a coquettish missive. She'd received his letter on Valentine's Day, she said. "Quite a nice Valentine,
wasn't it? It found me still living in Oolagah and signing myself Kate
Ellis—spinster—tho' many times I've vowed I'd not live longer in single blessedness—but soon get over it—when I look at some married
people."

It was only Clem Rogers who declined to beseech the wanderer to
return. No, he would stick to the noncommittal news of the day. Will's
tenants had paid their rent, he informed his son; his insurance payments
were up to date. "Your 2 Poneys are doing real well," he went on. "Your
Buggy Horse have grown quite a good deal. No one have used either of
them." And, finally, a sad note: "There is not a Cow, Hog, Chicken or
Turkey on the old Home place."

Will later received another piece of distressing news: His great friend
Charley McClellan had died. Charley, carrying through the academic
promise he'd shown at Halsell, had enrolled at Cumberland College in
Tennessee. He hadn't lost his Indian obsession, or his braid. When William Jennings Bryan visited the college, Charley performed the stomp
dance in full regalia; according to family tradition, the Great Commoner
told the lad, "I am proud to meet a true American." On Thanksgiving
Day 1902, six months before he was to graduate, he was stricken with
typhoid fever. He died the day before Christmas.

If the home folks thought Will was living a monastic life abroad,
they were wrong. He had a brief romantic encounter with a resident of
Graaf Reinet, apparently when the show appeared in that town. On its
departure, she wrote him a letter that began, "My Dearest loving boy,
Only these few words to let you know that I do love you so much I
really dont know what to do when you are going to leave me. My heart
will break all over you. . . ." There was a more significant affair with a
woman named Mamie, last initial S.; judging by the undated notes she
wrote to "Kiddie," she was associated with the show. Once she wrote to
him suggesting a "proposition": "Let us both us try & save as much
money as we can, & if you think it advisable send to your people and
get some money & then we also have saved a bit then we could go
away. . . . We need not be intamate [*sic*]. We could just make out as ev-

---

*Romantic attention was focused on Kate Ellis, rather than Lil, because the latter was
pregnant. She would later be abandoned by the father.

ery thing is over between us. Dont you think it is a good plan? . . . Darling, I love you so much that it seems to me I should die if you leave me." Unnerved by this intensity, Will stood her up at an appointed meeting. "You seem to have cut me since last night," she wrote the next day, "and I heard you remark this morning about looking for a boat. Well, darling, if you wish to cut loose frome [*sic*] me come to night & tell me so. Even if it is a great blow to me, any thing would be better than for you to look at me as you did this morning."

Late in May, Will wrote to his father that he would probably stay with the show another four or five months: "I am getting homesick, but don't know what I would do there more than make a living. As it is, I am off here bothering and worrying no one, and getting along first rate." Then, on August 2, Will wrote home that Jack was planning a trip to America to recruit some new talent, during which time he, Will, would stay with the show and take the Texas Jack roles. But just a week later, he got on a ship and set out for Australia. The suddenness of the departure—and Mamie's having heard Will say he was "looking for a boat"—suggests that it was prompted by a desire to disentangle romantically.

He went east instead of west, he explained to his sister Sallie with dubious geographic logic, because Australia was actually closer to America than Africa was. Probably nearer to the truth was a brief phrase in a letter to his father: "I must see a bit more." Jack, who had performed in Sydney, provided a glowing letter of recommendation in case Will should want to find work: "I have very great pleasure in recommending Mr. W. P. Rogers ('The Cherokee Kid') to circus proprietors. He has performed with me during my present South African tour and I consider him to be the Champion Trick Roughrider and Lasso Thrower of the World. He is sober, industrious, hard-working at all times and is always to be relied on."*

The journey was rough, of course, and extremely long. The ship went beyond Australia, landing in Wellington, New Zealand, after twenty-five days at sea. Then there was a boat to Auckland, and finally a four-and-a-half-day jaunt back to Sydney. Will's first order of business was to play the tourist. He attended the Australian Derby and marveled at the way all forty-four horses stuck close together for the entire race, the horse in last place finishing not fifteen feet behind the winner: "It was the greatest sight I ever saw." He observed boomerangs and kangaroos. He visited Melbourne, and spent some time with a friend on a ranch in the interior.

---

*Texas Jack never saw Will again. He died in Kroonstad, South Africa, in 1905.

By now he had been gone nearly two years, and the pull of home was becoming stronger. "I see by your letter that Papa still has my young horse, but you don't mention old Comanche," he wrote Sallie in November. "You don't mean to say there is no Comanche, or that he is dead. If so, I will never come home, for it would not be home if he was not there."

He also felt, with his globe-trotting soon to be over, the stirrings of a nascent national consciousness. He tried it on for literary size in a letter to his father, crafting a set piece that strikingly anticipated his future style. It showed a knack for mixing sardonic observations with a serious point or two, poking some fun at himself, and getting out without offending anyone.

> It is very amusing in all these countries, any thing new or what they havent had before will be called American. You hear electric street cars called American Tram Cars. All the refreshment places are advertised in box car letters, 'American Cold Drinks. American Soda Fountain.' The bars will serve up drinks mixed on the American plan, the barbers will advertise 'American Barber Chair.' You see, if it is one of their kind it will be a strait old chair where you set up strait as if you were in church and they will shave you and that shave is something chronic. I was always proud in America to own that I was a Cherokee and I find on leaving there that I am equally as proud to own that I am an American, for if there is any nation earning a rep abroad it is America. I have had arguments with every nationality of man under the sun in regard to the merits of our people and country, from prize fights to the greatest international questions of which I knew all about. For you are not American if you dont know.

Will initially intended to remain in Australia only a month or so, writing his family that he would be home by December 1. However, his stay was inadvertently prolonged. Away from Texas Jack's steadying influence, he succumbed to temptation, joined a card game, withdrew his savings from a money belt, and lost it all.

Fortunately, he had Texas Jack's letter, and he used it to secure an engagement with the Wirth Brothers Circus, an Australian institution of long standing that was about to begin a tour of New Zealand. It was structured more like a touring vaudeville show than a circus, with fifteen acts following each other in swift succession. The Cherokee Kid fit in nicely with the contortionist, the weightlifter, the various animal acts, and May Wirth, daughter of George Wirth, who juggled on horseback

and would later move to America and become known as the greatest female bareback rider in the world. Will—whom the program inexplicably
described as "America's Champion Mexican Cowboy" and who wore a
tight-fitting gold-embroidered red velvet suit—sent home a clipping in
which he was singled out as "a gentleman from America with a large
American accent and a splendid skill with the lasso." Someone offered
him an engagement with a show that played the coast towns of India,
and went on to China. Will was interested, he later wrote, until he found
out that he would perform only one day out of three; the rest of the time
he would be on a boat.

Early in March, it was time for the troupe to return to Australia, but
Will now had enough money for a third-class ticket home. Besides, as he
wrote later, "I couldn't see any luck having another boat ride going further away from home again." So he would finally go back to America.
He would take an overnight boat to Auckland, and from there catch a
ship to San Francisco. He decided that he might fare better on the first
leg if he went to bed as soon as he got on board. The strategy didn't
work: He was violently sick.

"Well, this had been going on for some distance," Will wrote later—
describing the effects of what he called "a big mess of imagination"—
"when some old wool said to another one, 'I wonder what's the matter?
Ain't this thing going to go?'"

WITH THE MULHALL COWBOY SHOW IN
ST. LOUIS, 1904

CHAPTER 4

MEET ME
IN ST. LOUIS

THE CLAREMORE *Progress* of April 16, 1904, noted that Will Rogers had come home. The very next edition, dated April 23, reported that he was about to leave to spend the summer at the Louisiana Purchase Exposition in St. Louis, set to open on the thirtieth of the month. The brevity of his stay is not surprising. Will was unquestionably happy to see his father, his sisters, his nieces and nephews (with the birth of Mattie Stine the year before, there were now eleven of them), to swap yarns with his friends, to sleep in his own bed, to be on familiar and steady turf. But he wasn't happy enough to stay in Oologah. "Now I am making my own way," he wrote in a letter not long afterward, "and dont feel like staying at home for people would say that I was living off my Father."

Making the decision easier was the sad fact that the edenic Verdigris country of his boyhood and youth was now finally and irrevocably gone. In 1902, the Cherokee senate had agreed to accept the end of tribal government and of the communal land system. Each Cherokee citizen would receive a homestead, not to exceed 110 acres, equal in value to 40 acres of the average land, and such additional land as would make for a total value of $325.60. Will sent his father power of attorney from South Africa, and when the allotments were made early in 1903, Clem took 78.84 acres, including the old home place on the Verdigris, for his son, and an adjacent 69.93 acres for himself. He persuaded friends, relatives, and neighbors to take their allotments next to his so that he could purchase them, but this was only a matter of a hundred more acres. No, the ranch of Will's childhood, 60,000 acres and seemingly endless, was no more. Now the family property was thousands of small and unprepossessing farms.*

*As part of the allotment process, Cherokee citizens were required to "enroll," stating their degree of Cherokee blood. Clem gave the accurate rounding off of one-quarter for

What allowed Will to make his own way was a job offer from Zack Mulhall, who, through horse-trading with Clem Rogers the year before, had heard of Will's exploits abroad. Over the past two years, Mulhall's show—now termed the Mulhall Congress of Rough Riders and Ropers—had toured steadily, moving up the ladder of show-business prominence. Now Mulhall had arranged to put on a cowboy show in St. Louis to run concurrently with the exposition, a world's fair marking the centenary of the Louisiana Purchase of 1803. (The spectacle was of such magnitude that the opening had to be delayed a year.) Will accepted a job as a rider and trick roper and immediately departed for the Mulhall ranch, about sixty-five miles west of Claremore.

There was rehearsing to do, but the lure of the ranch went beyond that. The Mulhalls were a warm, if unconventionally configured, family—it comprised the Colonel and his wife, their two daughters, and his two children by his "daughter" Georgia (she remained in the Colonel's other home, in St. Louis)—and Will found in them the sense of an intact clan he'd missed since the death of his mother. He was a special favorite of Mrs. Mulhall, whom he called "Mother Mulhall." (It's impossible to imagine his ever addressing Mary Bibles that way.) A quarter of a century later, he wrote that she'd "always be remembered by me as just about as fine a character as I have ever known. . . . She had many trials and hardships, but she stood up under them like a Saint." The Colonel, meanwhile, was a kind of fantasy father figure, flamboyant and headstrong and generous. Like Will, he was besotted with show business. Best of all, he carried with him none of Clem's expectations or habitual disappointment.

There was also the matter of Lucille Mulhall, now nineteen years old, who, in the words of a newspaper reporter, had "big, blue-gray eyes that look straight at you, a tanned smooth skin that shows the marks of the sun in sundry small freckles; a small mouth and teeth that are as white as a wolf's; a determined chin, and a forehead in which perception and reflection are both well-marked." Even more impressive, as far as Will was concerned, she was a superlative rider and roper: "the only Girl," he wrote, "that ever rode a horse exactly like a man, (I mean a real Hand)." She was unquestionably the star of the show, and the year before, at Denison, Texas, she had set what was deemed a world's—not just a ladies'—steer-roping record. (True, her time, thirty seconds, was

himself and Will, but Sallie and Maud both gave theirs as one-sixteenth. This may have been due to snobbery, but may also have had to do with restrictions, proportional to the degree of blood, on selling allotted land.

more than Jim Hopkins's eighteen and a half at Memphis, but roping records were not kept with the precision to which baseball statistics have accustomed us.)

Hard evidence of any romantic attraction between Will and Lucille is limited. Spi Trent thought his cousin had a crush on her and so did some of the hands on the Mulhall ranch. Will did preserve in his scrapbook a suspiciously large number of photographs of the cowgirl. In one she stands triumphantly over a roped steer, in another she is riding a bucking horse, and in a third she stands next to Will, as his "wedding ring" of rope encircles them both. She is smiling a delighted smile at the camera; he is grinning capaciously at her. The symbolism is hard to resist. Finally, the clarity with which Will remembered her in the article he wrote at the Colonel's death in 1931—the image he carried with him of an elegant propriety (always a touchstone in his view of women)—attests to a feeling somewhere beyond friendship. "Lucille never dressed like the Cowgirl you know today," he wrote in 1932, "no loud colors, no short leather skirts, and great big hat, no sir, her skirt was divided, but long, away down over her pattent [sic] leather boot tops, a whip cord grey, or grey broadcloth, small stiff brim hat, and always white silk shirt waist."

However high the level of Will's admiration, it did not result in action. Somehow his lengthy trip abroad had caused a kind of emotional regression: He now felt an adolescent awkwardness around women. "I haven't had a girl since I left on that trip," he wrote in a letter late in 1904, conveniently omitting Mamie S. "When I come back I felt so out of place and behind the times I was ashamed and they will tell you at home now I am a girl hater."

But the interlude at the ranch offered other compensations. One of them was camaraderie of the hands, including his old buddy Jim Hopkins, who had been working steadily for Mulhall while Will was abroad. He also became close to a dark, lantern-jawed fellow named Tom Mix. Born in 1880 no farther west than central Pennsylvania, Mix had enlisted in the army in 1898, during the Spanish-American War. He deserted four years later, a fact conveniently omitted from the accounts of his life that appeared after he became a cowboy movie star, but convincingly established in a biography by the grandson of his first cousin. With his wife, he more or less fled to Guthrie, Indian Territory, where he worked as a bartender and taught a physical-education class. Joe Miller of the 101 Ranch in Ponca City saw him and gave him a job not as a working cowboy but as a kind of host for the "dudes" who came to stay at the ranch. Eventually, Mix did develop some riding and roping skills, and Mulhall hired him for his show.

For Will, actual ranch work was no longer part of the equation. He could generally be found indoors, Lucille Mulhall recalled, "sitting at the piano most of the time, picking out tunes and playing them until my dear mother would nearly go crazy and tell Dad to take him out of the house. Will never did any driving of cattle when he was here but would spend hours roping at everything that was in sight from stumps to fence posts. I recall a tune Will used to play entitled, 'I May Be Crazy, But I Ain't No Fool,' but at times we thought he was when we found difficulty in convincing him that he would never master the ivory keys of the piano."

THE LOUISIANA PURCHASE EXPOSITION was to the county fairs Will was used to what an ocean liner is to a canoe. It cost $42.5 million to construct (not including individual exhibitions), and the grounds covered 1,240 acres on the western outskirts of the city—making it the largest such enterprise in the history of the world, almost double the size of Chicago's World's Columbian Exposition of 1893, which had started the trend of these mammoth educational, nationalistic extravaganzas. (In the intervening eleven years, there had been expositions in New Orleans, Atlanta, Nashville, Omaha, and Buffalo.) In the seven months of its run, its turnstiles would record nearly 20 million admissions—an amazing figure given that the population of the entire country was only about four times that.

There was plentiful amusement to be had at the fair, whose theme song was "Meet Me in St. Louis": It was the birthplace of the ice cream cone and iced tea and the site of the largest Ferris wheel ever constructed, and it was famous for its spectacular waterfalls and colored-lights displays, its gondolas, miniature railways, and elephant rides. But it was no theme park. The implicit admonition was that one was there primarily to learn something and only secondarily to have fun. This pedagogical imperative, combined with the vast scale of the exposition—and the fact that the summer of 1904 was hot and humid—exacted a severe toll on visitors. A St. Louis professor of neurology wrote an article warning colleagues that if neurasthenic patients were permitted to visit the fair, they would almost certainly collapse. A British visitor wrote, "The fatigue entailed in seeing the Exhibition was simply enormous, and the glare of the buildings made smoked glasses a necessity." The novelist Kate Chopin, a St. Louis resident, collapsed and died after a day of sight-seeing.

Zack Mulhall's original plan was to put on a show running concurrently with the fair, without any official connection; the site was to be the grounds of the St. Louis Fair Association, where county fairs were customarily held. Ever the publicist, the Colonel managed to get some ink in the local papers, telling reporters that he expected his old companion Theodore Roosevelt, now President of the United States, to attend the show. (There is no evidence that he did.) Somehow, though, he managed to attach himself to the exposition. Frederick Cummins had the concession to produce an Indian show just outside the fairgrounds, with an entrance on the Pike, the amusement strip of the fair, and it was arranged that the Mulhall cowboys would be a part of this extravaganza. In keeping with the instructional character of the exposition, in the words of a fair official, the Pike was "not a jumble of nonsense. It has meaning just as definite as the high motive which inspired the exposition. It mirrors the lighter moods of all countries." Thus "Cummins' Spectacular Indian Congress and Life on the Plains" was not your typical Wild West show. Described in the program as a "HISTORIC, ABORIGINAL, EDUCATIONAL, ETHNOLOGICAL, INDUSTRIAL EXHIBITION," it featured the display of 750 Indians, "including bucks, squaws and papooses."

The most famous participant was Geronimo, the Apache chief who, despite being a prisoner of the U.S. government at Fort Sill, Indian Territory, since 1886, was from time to time permitted to be "borrowed" by Wild West show organizers and other entrepreneurs. At the fair, between appearances with Cummins, he lived in the "Apache Village," where he made bows and arrows and sold them, along with his autograph and picture, and sang and danced when the mood struck him. He briefly mentioned the Cummins show in his memoirs, saying, "There were many other Indian tribes there, and"—an admittedly oblique reference to Mulhall's cowboys—"strange people of whom I had never heard."

Will, once again, was a "cowboy," not an "Indian." In a simulation of Custer's Last Stand, he was the last soldier to die, holding out, Jim Hopkins recalled, until "suddenly he would fall across his pony, and the Indians would give a big war dance over our dead bodies." One day, thinking his gun wasn't loaded, an Indian stuck his gun inches away from Will's head and pulled the trigger, whereupon Will's horse jumped up in the air and stampeded out. "Will could never get his pony to play dead any more after that," Hopkins wrote. "The dead men got so nervous that Will had to keep him out of the act."

Although Will also did trick roping in the show, he was not mentioned in the program at first (Hopkins was). But he quickly began to attract attention. His skills weren't spectacular, in Hopkins's opinion, but his experience with Texas Jack and the Wirth Brothers had turned him into a show-business pro. And there was an indefinable star quality about him: "He had somethin' the rest of us didn't have, no matter who was around. Everybody was always lookin' at Will." The unfamiliar and heady sound of applause from his own countrymen did good things for his self-esteem. In the letters he wrote to his father from the fair—he was living at Mulhall's St. Louis residence—there is no defensiveness, no special pleading, rather a straightforward and comfortable discourse from one adult to another. One thing adults do is trade horses, and Will offered to sell Clem a bay horse and a buggy for $350. ("If you want him this is your chance for he is cheap at that. I give $300.00 for him when he was a colt.") When Clem didn't leap at the offer, Will wrote him, with possibly disingenuous charity, "I wont sell him to any one else at any price for you like him and I wont take him away from you. Now if he is worth only $250.00 or $300.00 to you, why only give me that and if you wont buy him, why I will give him to you. I wont sell him away from you." There was also the matter of some land that had come up for sale back home. Clem wondered whether Will was interested in buying it; Will wrote back that his father should take the opportunity. He himself didn't have enough cash "and I am not going to borrow the money to do it for I am out of debt and going to stay as long as I can."

The Mulhall troupe would have continued on the Pike until the fair ended in December, but for one small problem. On June 18, the Colonel shot three men and almost killed one of them.

Trouble had been brewing for some time between Mulhall and Frank Reed, who was in charge of horses for the Cummins show. An account in the Mulhall *Enterprise* (which, because of previous contretemps, was not inclined to portray the Colonel in a favorable light) stated that Mulhall had had Reed arrested on the charge of disturbing the peace; Reed, in turn, had accused Mulhall of trying to "run things." On the afternoon of the eighteenth, the *Enterprise* reported that they had clashed over the issue of Reed's unauthorized use of a horse and a cowboy to round up some strays, and Mulhall had pulled a gun on him. After the show that night, the two men confronted each other on the crowded Pike. According to the *Enterprise*, only Mulhall drew his revolver, but, according to Jim Hopkins, who was just about to take a walk down the Pike with Will, "Both jerked their guns. Johnny Murrah [the Texas roper, now one of Mulhall's cowboys] grabbed both their guns." Then the shooting started. When it was over, Murrah had been shot in the abdomen, Reed in the arm and the side of the neck, and an eighteen-year-old St. Louis resident named Ernest Morgan, who'd been standing one hundred feet away, in the abdomen. He was initially thought to be fatally wounded, but he pulled through. Will missed it all: It had rained that day, and when the shots were fired he was leaning over a hydrant, washing the mud off his boots. The incident made the front page of *The New York Times* in an article whose headline, PRESIDENT'S FRIEND SLAYS, contained at least one and possibly two errors of fact.

Arrested and taken to the police station, Mulhall "did not seem a bit perturbed over the affair," a St. Louis newspaper reported, "and called through the window to [Lucille] to be a good girl and say her prayers before she went to bed." He was released on twenty-thousand-dollars bond, pending trial. Three days later, exposition authorities barred him from the fair. This would seem a sensible, indeed unavoidable, action, but, an account in the Claremore *Progress* implied, it was taken only after "an indignation meeting" held by the Indians at the Cummins show, presided over by Chief Geronimo and Chief Blue Horse. "After the meeting, they notified the management, that in the event of Mulhall's return, vengeance would be meted out."

The shooting did not lower Will's admiration for the Colonel. "If he had only hit the fellow [Reed] it would have been all right," he wrote to his father, rather coldheartedly. "The other fellow was no good. . . . They can say what they please about Mulhall but he has done more for us boys than any man on earth. . . ." Will briefly bolted the Cummins show to work for a smaller Wild West show operated by his San Antonio acquaintance Charles Tomkins. While there, he had his own brush with the law. He was at a trolley stop one night, on his way to visit a girlfriend downtown, when he got into an argument with a policeman. Before he knew it, he was in a paddy wagon, going directly to jail. He was released the next afternoon.

Before long, he was reunited with Zack Mulhall, who as his case was awaiting trial had arranged to put on a cowboy show every Sunday at 3:00 p.m. at the grounds of a St. Louis racetrack. Here Will was featured as "the most expert Fancy Roper in America." He also participated in the steer-roping contests, and one Sunday, in front of a crowd of ten thousand people, he achieved a time of thirty seconds. The fact that this was the same time Lucille had clocked the year before in Texas did not stop a newspaper—doubtless prompted by the Colonel—from terming it a new world's record.

Geronimo, apparently having risen above his indignation over Mulhall's shoot-out, participated as well, the program soberly remarking that "this great and desperate war chief still has his hate for the white man." Despite his advanced years, he acquitted himself well in the steer-roping. "After circling around, the old Chieftain whirled the lasso and made the throw," a newspaper reported. "The rope settled around the steer's neck on the first attempt. In an instant the roper was off his horse and with all the speed of his youth, proceeded to tie the animal fast and sound." Inspired by the exposition's anthropological bent, the Colonel one Sunday arranged for a group of African pygmies to put on a war dance. "As a reward they were given a huge watermelon," said a newspaper, "which they ate to the delight of the large audience."

Will was involved in another venture, something that had been planted as the seed of an idea by Texas Jack. Back in South Africa, Jack, an astute student of show business, had suggested to the Cherokee Kid that he might want to consider taking a roping act onto the vaudeville stage. Will had been considering it ever since. Now it was time to act. He arranged to appear in a burlesque show at the Standard Theatre in St. Louis, and did well enough to elicit a letter from the theater's management, dated July 24, 1904:

> To Whom It May Concern.
> I take great pleasure in recommending Mr. Will Rogers in his Specialty. I played him at the Standard Theatre, and he proved a decided novelty. He will make good on any bill, and can follow any "head liner."

The recommendation helped get Will a week's engagement at the Chicago Opera House for a salary of thirty dollars. His was a "dumb act," a category of vaudeville performers who had developed a skill amazing enough to hold an audience's attention for ten or twelve minutes without the need for any patter, declamation, or song from the stage. Dumb acts included jugglers, club swingers, hoop rollers, boomerang throwers, whip crackers, sharpshooters, contortionists, posing acts, bicycle acts, acrobats, bag punchers, and weightlifters; they were usually called on either to open or to close the show. Will's rope-twirling fitted nicely into the genre, being palpably a product of years of practice and having a kind of formal beauty besides, with the added attraction of providing Wild West color. But he had an idea about how to make the act even better, and something that happened during a second Chicago engagement convinced him it would work. During one show, one member of a dog act happened to run across the stage. Will, naturally, roped him. The audience's enthusiastic response got him to thinking: "Instead of trying to keep on with this single roping act I decided people wanted to see me catch something. So I went back home and marked me a place of ground about as big as a stage and started to work on the horse act. . . ."

The idea for the "horse act" was this: A man would ride a horse onto the stage, Will would rope them, and then the procedure would be repeated, with different styles of roping. It was the kind of thing he had done, without much difficulty, for Texas Jack and the Wirth Brothers. But managing it on a small vaudeville stage would be very complicated indeed. Will knew that getting the right horse was critical, and he knew the pony he wanted. It was one of Mulhall's, a dark bay with a black mane and tale. He borrowed Teddy (named after the President, of course) from the Colonel and commenced practicing.

WILL HAD something else on his mind in the autumn of 1904—or, rather, someone: Betty Blake. He had not seen her since their encounter four and a half years before, and likely had ceased to think about her except as a bittersweet episode from a time long gone. But in St. Louis, one Sunday in September, she suddenly reentered his life. Visiting the fair with one of her sisters and a friend, she overheard a girl saying she had just seen Will Rogers perform. The sound of this name from the past spurred Betty to action. She took it upon herself to find out Will's address, then sent him a note wondering whether he would be interested in seeing her. This was a move of singular boldness, possibly inspired by the giddiness of three young women out for a fine time, but more likely made even more courageous by the attitudes of Betty's sister and friend. "The girls . . . made no secret of the fact that they thought the occupation an undignified one for a young man with Will's advantages," Betty wrote in her biography of Will. "Though I wanted to see Will very much, I had a wide streak of conventionality in me, and I was not particularly thrilled about Will's profession. But I hid my misgivings and tried not to hear the teasing and joking."

Will answered Betty's note five minutes after getting it. "Dear old Pal," he started, "I sho was glad to hear from you and it is only a Rumor that I dont want to see you right now." He invited her to that afternoon's show at the racetrack. She attended with her sister and friend, but her streak of conventionality was to come to the fore again. To her horror, when he entered the arena for his roping act, he was wearing the tight-fitting gold-braided red velvet suit he'd been issued in Australia, where he was billed as the "Mexican Rope Artist." He had chosen it for her special benefit, but he miscalculated. "He looked so funny," Betty wrote, "and I was so embarrassed when my sister and Mary gave me

sidelong glances and smiled at the costume, that I didn't hear the applause or find much joy in Will's expertness with the rope." She must
have made her feelings on the point clear, because he never wore the
suit again.

After the show, finally free of Betty's companions, she and Will had
dinner and heard the tenor John McCormack—later to be a friend and
colleague of Will's—sing at the Irish Pavilion. There wasn't much time
for talk. Although Will didn't find out Betty's address, or, beyond the
fact that she was still unmarried, anything about her personal life, the
evening was enough of a success that they made a date to see each other
again the next morning. But Will had to cancel it—to go back to
Claremore and pick up a horse, no less. He at least had the sense to be
embarrassed, and he scribbled an apologetic note asking Betty to write
to him.

Despite the indignity of being stood up in favor of a four-legged animal, Betty did write Will. The letter was forwarded to him in Chicago,
where he was in the middle of his vaudeville experiment. Will didn't
keep it or any of her other letters to him (odd, considering that he did
preserve every scrap of newspaper copy that mentioned his name), but
she kept all of his to her—and he would write quite a few over the next
four years, charting his achievements and frustrations, his occasional ela-
tion and the depths of his despair. This first full letter of their
reacquaintance is a remarkable document, its emotional directness and
force obscured only by Will's insistence on using slang terms and catch-
phrases that are unintelligible to the contemporary reader (and very
likely were to Betty as well). After some preliminary pleasantries ("I dont
like it much up here. I am doing all O.K.") and another apology for
breaking their date ("We would of had some fun that day 'and not get
Loaded either' "), he got directly to the point:

> Oh, but things are on the Bum down home. I dident do a
> thing down there this trip, only see the folks. I will be there
> Christmas and I would like to see you some old time then. But
> say I am Goatinskying here just as though I knew all about you
> and had things all fixed. And I only see you a minute and then
> only found out you were not married, that is about all. Lord
> knows how near it may be for I know about how you would
> stand with all those Rail Road Gisables and you know according
> to form we both should have matrimonied long ago. It wouldent
> do for this youth gang to look at our teeth you know.
>
> Now what I want to skoke to you is this. If you are con-

tracted for or have a steady fellow, why please put me down and out in the 1st round. But if not then please file my application Out of paper kindly take a back track. . . .

I could just love a girl about your caliber, see. You know I was always kinder headstrong about you anyway. But I always thought that a cowboy dident come up to your Ideal. But I am plum Blue up here and kneed consolation and havent a soul that I can confide in. Now for Good luck hard luck and no luck at all Experiences I am the limit. . . .

Now I must reluctantly draw this Long distance interview to a close hoping some of these broad minded views of mine (especially the one pertaining to said application) have met with your kind approbation I am yours

any old time
Bill that's me
By the way
Subject this penmanship to a rigid treatment of guessing. Then serve.

This looks very much like a proposal, but Betty chose to respond to, and take offense at, Will's remark about their ages. He was quick to apologize in his next letter, his attempt at formal language dissolving into slang in the course of a sentence: "I am deeply grieved to think that I was so unthoughtful as to refer to something that you could in the least get offended at but it was a joke meaning we both should of married each other by now sabe." The letters continued through November and December. Will made certain to put himself forward as matrimonial material ("I still own the old home place and farm and am even with the world and am as happy as can be"), sing Betty's praises ("You are my style through and through"), and, once, try to provoke a little jealousy. "Oh that Ball," he wrote of a Thanksgiving celebration, "it was the kind we used to make long ago. Oh, there was a lot of the old gang there on the square. I had more good old fun than I have had for some distance." None of it was able to loosen Betty's cordial stiffness. "See here Betty Blake," Will closed one letter, "a longer letter from you next one and take care it is not one I will have to take to my overcoat to read for the other was on the chilly side."

They saw each other soon after Christmas, when Betty visited her sister in Nowata, a town a few miles north of Claremore. They had a long talk one night, and Will made his case once again. She turned him down flat: They could be friends but nothing more than that. Will was hurt, so much so that he didn't write to her again for five months. When he finally did make contact, her words were still smarting. "I just sized you up that night," he wrote, "and thought, no, she dont give a d——— only to be a good old pal and honest it hurt me and I said I wont even write to her for your letters are no encouragement to me. I wish to G——— that I could look at it as you do but I cant. I know you might laugh and say, old Bill is just handing out his line as he always does but It aint so, I swear. You know I have had some experience and have been some to the flirt talk with lots of them but this has been maturing for years. I got to love someone and it dont take me many guesses to tell who it is."

Betty obviously felt an attraction for Will. As he had pointed out, moreover, at twenty-five (she had been born two months before he was) she was at an age when the unenviable state referred to as spinsterhood was becoming an uncomfortably real possibility. And, frankly, marriage would be a financial boon. The Rogers landholdings were not what they had been, but there was still the old home place and Clem's various other assets, all of which Will could one day soon hope to inherit. Betty's circumstances were not so favorable. Her father, James Blake, had owned a saw- and gristmill in the town of Silver Springs, Arkansas, but he died in 1882, leaving his widow, Amelia, with two sons and six daughters to support. Betty, born on September 9, 1879, was the second youngest. Amelia would briefly remarry, the only result of the union being yet another daughter, Zulika.*

After her husband's death, Amelia moved to a large white frame house on East Walnut Street in Rogers, a town northwest of Silver Springs that had risen around the tracks of the St. Louis and San Francisco Railroad, which arrived in 1881. To supplement what rent there was from the mill—and, later, the proceeds from its sale—she worked as a seamstress. And, when the girls got old enough, they took either husbands or jobs. Betty at various times clerked for the railroad and in a local dry-goods store, and intermittently worked as a typesetter for the local newspaper; on two separate occasions she enrolled in courses at the commercial college in Fort Smith. (The 1900 census gave her occupation as "printer," her mother's as "servant," and listed the husbands of three of her sisters as living with the family. It also stated that the house was mortgaged.) But there could never have been an abundance of money.

*A coincidence of some magnitude: James Blake and Clem Rogers had both fought in the Battle of Pea Ridge. The experience made such an impression on Blake that he named one of his daughters Waite, in honor of Stand Watie.

Still, it's not altogether surprising that Betty would initially have spurned Will's advances. There was her wide streak of conventionality to consider, and the incontrovertible fact that Will was an Indian. The Blakes, financially pinched though they may have been, were part of the town gentility—Amelia Blake once served as an officer in the local chapter of the United Daughters of the Confederacy—and marriage to an Indian, even a wealthy and presentable quarter-blood Cherokee, couldn't be seen as anything other than a social step down.

Nor was Betty desperate to marry, as others in her situation might have been. This was due partly to her own independence and good sense and partly to the circumstances of her life. The Blakes were known throughout Rogers as a large, happy, and loving clan, a kind of consanguineous sorority. The girls were all musical, and they used to like to take their banjos and guitars, sit out on the porch, and sing. Homer Croy interviewed a resident who said of the big house on East Walnut, "If you passed there on Sunday you'd hear laughter and see young people havin' a good time. Sometimes they'd overflow out into the yard, there was so many of them."

Like Will a couple of hundred miles to the west, Betty lived a life that seemed to be dedicated to the pursuit of fun. They even engaged in the same activities: The Rogers *Democrat* announced one day in May 1898 that she had won a cakewalk competition. Over the years, the paper chronicled her various musical activities on the guitar, violin, and mandolin, her performances in town theatricals, her extensive travels to neighboring states and the Indian Territory. (Numerous Blakes worked for the railroad, including the older son, John, who died in a train accident in 1889.) A girlhood friend recalled that she "liked to eat better than anyone I ever knew and didn't worry about being overweight." Betty had a vigorous, sometimes wicked, sense of humor. Once, during a banquet, she and some other young women were so busy talking that they didn't realize they were being served consommé in coffee cups, and they flavored it with cream and sugar. When the error was pointed out, Betty drank up anyway, insisting with mock seriousness that she always took her soup that way. A few weeks later during a talent show, the *Democrat* reported, "The two vaudeville actresses, Miss Bettie Blake and Mrs. C. D. Short, brought down the house with their performance. Their song telling of 'consomme with sugar on the side' was the biggest hit of the evening."

Erwin Funk, the longtime editor of the *Democrat,* called her humor "perverse," recalling the times when "she would be working in the back room on a dry goods circular, and I would have a very precise, correct lady visitor in the front office. From Betty would come a clarion call: 'Erwin, this corset [or some other unmentionable] is too small [or perhaps too big]. What do I do now?' "

For some reason, humor seemed to course through the air in Rogers. One of Betty's friends was a man named Tom P. Morgan, who actually made a living selling jokes, captions, and comic sketches to such publications as *Judge, Puck,* and *Country Gentleman.* (Example, from *Puck:* Below a drawing of a man staring through an open door at a violent storm, Morgan's caption read, " 'This is funny—in a modest sort o' way!' philosarcastically commented the Old Codger, as he gazed out the door at the rain. 'The weather clerk has made a grave mistake *this* time; this ain't the day of the picnic.' ") One day in 1907 the *Democrat* announced that Rogersians Tony LeBlanc and Ben Felker had formed a corporation. "The company proposes, as their prospectus points out, to buy a controlling interest in the 'possum dog now owned by Messrs. LeBlanc and Felker and to employ the same in acquiring 'possum hides for the St. Louis and Kansas City Markets. . . . Miss Bettie Blake was presented with one share to keep the dog and Tom P. Morgan was treated to like liberality not to knock the enterprise."

Years later, Will wrote that Morgan (who had been on the stage in his youth and "kept up on show business") was an ally in courtship: "When he would see some little mention in the theatrical papers about me (and it would be mighty little too) why he would send or take them up to Betty. He was kinder my booster. I had a good deal of outside opposition from some local and Semi local talent and needed some aid that was constantly on the ground." The last sentence was no exaggeration. Betty was "the most attractive girl in the group," according to her younger sister Virginia, and there was a long parade of suitors, including a railroad man from Fort Smith who would take an overnight train ride every week just to see her, a young surveyor from the University of Arkansas, a Rogers lad named Yock Oakley, and, most intriguingly, Tom Harvey. Tom's father, William Hope "Coin" Harvey, was one of the odder minor figures in American history. A lawyer by trade, he was a fervent proselytizer for the cause of free silver, and in 1893 had published a tract called *Coin's Financial School* that sold a million copies, supplied him with a nickname, and won him a position as an adviser to William Jennings Bryan. After Bryan's unsuccessful campaign for the presidency in 1896, Harvey was named chairman of the Democratic party's Ways and Means Committee. Three years later, when the party dropped the free-silver platform, he resigned his position and moved to Betty Blake's birthplace, Silver Springs, whose name he promptly

WILLIE'S OLDER SISTERS—
AND SURROGATE MOTHERS—
SALLIE (LEFT), MAUD (ABOVE),
AND MAY.

Above: WILLIE RIDES A BIKE—DOUBTLESS THE FIRST IN
COOWEESCOOWEE DISTRICT—OUTSIDE THE HOME PLACE, CA. 1891.
Below: THE SCARRITT COLLEGE FOOTBALL TEAM. WILL IS SEATED
THIRD FROM LEFT. AT SCARRITT (REALLY A SECONDARY SCHOOL),
THE FOURTH OF WILL'S FIVE SCHOOLS, HE DID NOT DISTINGUISH
HIMSELF ON THE GRIDIRON OR ANYWHERE ELSE. ONE OF HIS
TEACHERS WROTE YEARS LATER, "EVEN THE MOST SANGUINE
COULD NOT HAVE PREDICTED THAT THE FUNNY FELLOW WE KNEW
AS WILL ROGERS, WOULD BE ANYTHING BUT MEDIOCRE."

Above: KEMPER HORSEPLAY.
Below: WILL AND HIS COUSIN SPI TRENT
(AT RIGHT) DO SOME COURTING.

Left: ALONE AMONG
THE YOUNG CHEROKEE MIXED-
BLOODS, WILLIE'S GREAT FRIEND
CHARLEY MCCLELLAN TOOK HIS
INDIAN HERITAGE SERIOUSLY. ONE
WAY HE SHOWED IT WAS BY
WEARING HIS HAIR IN A LONG
SINGLE BRAID. *Below:* WILL ROGERS
AT TWENTY—"THE GREATEST
LADIES' MAN YOU EVER SAW."

AT THE AGE OF TWENTY-ONE, WILL DECIDED HE WANTED TO SEE
NIAGARA FALLS—PREFIGURING LONGER JOURNEYS TO COME.

Above: **BETTY BLAKE AT EIGHTEEN.**
Below: **THE BLAKE SISTERS OF ROGERS, ARKANSAS.**
BETTY IS THIRD FROM THE BOTTOM.

SACRIFICING HER CURLS IN
A SIGHT GAG, ON A DOUBLE
DATE WITH HER SISTER
THEDA, AND SITTING ATOP
A HUMAN PYRAMID AT AN
INDOOR SWIMMING POOL:
LIKE WILL A COUPLE OF
HUNDRED MILES TO THE
WEST, BETTY LIVED A LIFE
THAT SEEMED DEDICATED TO
THE PURSUIT OF FUN.

Above: TEXAS JACK (LEFT) WAS THE FIRST OF WILL'S SURROGATE
FATHERS. "JACK IS THE FINEST OLD BOY I EVER MET," "THE
CHEROKEE KID" WROTE HOME FROM SOUTH AFRICA, "AND HE SEEMS TO
THINK A GREAT DEAL OF ME." *Below:* IN 1898–99, CLEM ROGERS
(STANDING, FAR LEFT) WAS PART OF A CHEROKEE DELEGATION
THAT MET WITH THE DAWES COMMISSION.

FELLOW RANCHHAND TOM MIX THOUGHT WILL HAD A CRUSH ON PIONEER
COWGIRL LUCILLE MULHALL. THIS PHOTO SEEMS TO BACK HIM UP.

COLONEL ZACK MULHALL (FOREGROUND, WITH HIS ARM AROUND
LUCILLE) AND HIS BAND OF COWBOYS IN ST. LOUIS, IN 1899. WILL IS
FOUR ROWS BEHIND THE COLONEL, IN A WHITE SHIRT, HIS HANDS ON
THE SHOULDERS OF THE MEN IN FRONT OF HIM.

First day to [illegible] ith
Madison Square Garden

Me

O. Where I [illegible] the
steer

Above: THE MULHALL COWBOY CARNIVAL IN MADISON SQUARE GARDEN.
THE X, WILL WROTE ON THE PHOTO, IS "ME"; O MARKS "WHERE I
ROPED THE STEER." *Below:* ROPING BUCK MCKEE AND (WHAT
APPEARS TO BE) A STUFFED HORSE.

Throwing two ropes at once.

The Greatest Catch in Vaudeville

Manipulating 90 ft of Rope.

Above: **WILL'S BUSINESS CARD AND A HORSE-BLANKET/BILLBOARD— EARLY EFFORTS AT MARKETING.**
Right: **WITH EDDIE CANTOR—LATER A FOLLIES COSTAR—IN WINNIPEG, 1912.**

Above: FROM THE START, WILL SAVED ALL HIS CLIPPINGS.
Below: WILL ON TEDDY, CA. 1909, DOING A BASEBALL CRINOLINE. ON THE
ROAD, HE BECAME A FANATICAL FOLLOWER OF THE NATIONAL PASTIME.

Above: BETTY (AT FAR LEFT, HAND ON CHIN) VISITED
WILL IN CLAREMORE IN 1906. SHE LATER WROTE, "HE
NEVER LOOKED IN MY DIRECTION." (FARTHEST LEFT,
WITH CIGAR, IS DICK PARRIS, WILL'S ERSTWHILE
TRAVELING COMPANION IN SOUTH AMERICA.)
Below: A CRUCIAL LETTER.

January 6 *Cook P.H. Rochester. N.Y.*	July 6 *Orpheum. Vancouver B.C*
13 *Bennetts. Montreal. Canada*	13 *Grand. Tacoma. Wash.*
20 " *Hamilton* "	20 *Grand. Portland. Ore.*
27 *Gaity Toronto. Can*	27 *T R A V E L*
Febr. 3 *Poli's Worcester. Mass.*	August 3 *Grand. Sacramento. Cal.*
10 *Orpheum Brooklyn. N.Y.*	10 *National. San Francisco.* "
17 *Poli's Springfield. Mass.*	17 *Bell. Oakland. Cal.*
24 *Poli's Hartford. Conn.*	24 *Wigwam. San Francisco. Ca*
March 2 *Poli's New Haven.*	31 *T R A V E L*
9 *closed as the 1st night*	Sept. 7 *Temple - Detroit. Mich*
16 *to go home*	14 *Cooks. O.H. Rochester. N.Y.*
23 *Open. Sick*	21 *Grand. O.H. Pittsburg. Pa.*
30 *home*	28 *Armory - Binghampton. N.Y.*
April 6 "	Octob. 5 *Grand O.H. Syracuse.* "
13 "	12 *Princess Theatre. Montreal.*
20 "	19 *Grand. Auburn. N.Y.*
27 *Poli's. Bridgeport. Conn.*	26 *Poli's Wilkesbarre. Pa.*
May 4 *Open.*	Nov 2 *Open*
11 *open*	9 *Travel HOME.—*
18 *Travel.*	16 *home*
25 *Bijou. Winnipeg. Canada*	23 *GETTING MARRIED.*
June 1 *Bijou. Duluth. Minn.*	30 *Proctors. Newark. N.J.*
8 *Travel.— Yellowstone Park.*	Dec. 7 *Open*
15 *Grand. Butte. Montana*	14 *Colonial New York*
22 *Washing up. Spokane. Wash*	21 *Travel Home*
29 *Star. Seattle.* "	28 *American. St. Louis. Mo*

Above: HIS BOOKINGS DIARY SHOWS THAT 1908 WAS A
BUSY—AND ULTIMATELY JOYOUS—YEAR FOR WILL.
Below: WILL AND BETTY, SNAPPED IN ATLANTIC CITY
SOON AFTER THEIR WEDDING.

"ANDREW" IS JUST ABOUT
TO IMPOSE A LIBRARY
ON SOME POOR TOWN

Above: HIS PARENTS WERE ALWAYS DRESSING YOUNG BILL UP, AT RIGHT
AS A JUNIOR ANDREW CARNEGIE (THE WRITING IS WILL'S), AND IN THE
MORE CUSTOMARY COWBOY GETUP. *Below:* THE ROGERS KIDS
WERE PUT ON HORSES BEFORE THEY COULD WALK. FROM LEFT,
MARY, BILL, AND JIMMY.

changed to Monte Ne (*Monte* being Spanish for "mountain," *Ne* being the Omaha Indian word for "water"). He built a lavish resort there, complete with a golf course, an indoor swimming pool, a lagoon, and gondolas, imported from Italy, that met trains coming in on the special railroad spur he had built.

The entire Blake family spent the summer of 1903 in Monte Ne. This was probably the time when young Robert Halliday "Hal" Harvey began seeing Zulika Blake, and Tom, who planned to become a lawyer, took up with Betty. The couple shared a taste for a good laugh. Once, Virginia Blake Quisenberry remembered, Betty and Tom climbed up in the apple tree in the Blakes' yard. "An old hammock made of barrel staves and laced with rope stretched under it. Later on my sister Anna and her husband-to-be, Lee Adamson, came to sit in the hammock and make a little love. Betty and her young man listened to them for a while, then started throwing apples down on them."*

Betty, then, had more than enough reasons not to rush into marriage with Will. Maybe the strongest of them was Will himself. She was used to beaux who were prospective lawyers, or at the least railroad men. Will was . . . what? A cowboy who wasn't really a cowboy, a twenty-five-year-old who hadn't accomplished much beyond circling the globe and obtaining a red Mexican cowboy's outfit, the scion of a respectable family who was not even a vaudeville entertainer but an *aspiring* vaudeville entertainer.

For that was Will's plan. He had been a success in Chicago; afterward he went back to St. Louis, where, for Will's performance at a fairwide show, exposition director David Francis had presented him with a first-prize blue ribbon. ("I am kinder foolish about my little ribbon," he admitted to Betty.) Buoyed by these triumphs, he intended to go to New York after Christmas and try his luck in the capital of vaudeville. He had to delay the trip because his father had taken ill and there was no one else to care for him. But Will was set on trying his luck. In the winter of 1904–1905, he bided his time, practicing his roping and stewing about Betty Blake. (The Claremore *Progress* noted two trips by Will to the Mulhall Ranch, so he may have been keeping another option in play.)

In March, he got an opportunity to hone his skills before live audiences. The Commercial Club of Tulsa invited him to join a ten-day rail

---

*Coin Harvey's resort went belly-up before long—today it is covered by the man-made Beaver Lake—but Harvey stayed around. In 1932, at the age of eighty-one, he ran for President on the Liberty party ticket. He finished sixth, with 53,434 votes. He died in 1936.

tour of Missouri, Illinois, Indiana, Iowa, and Kansas the next month. One hundred Tulsans, including a sixteen-piece band, made the trip, which was designed to alert Midwesterners to the city's prospects, especially attractive now that it looked as though Indian Territory would become a state. Their presentations gave new meaning to the word *boosterism.* "Before the speakers were through," said a St. Louis newspaper, "the audience was convinced that Tulsa possessed everything worth having, from the climate of California to the golden grain of Kansas: not to speak of the oil, gas and coal of other sections of the country, with the culture of Boston and the effete East coming fast." The entourage traveled on a special train with four cars, one of them a mobile print shop that produced a special newspaper at each stop. And Will got another clipping to add to his scrapbook. "Tom [*sic*] Rogers, a championship lariat thrower, amazed the spectators with his wonderful dexterity in handling the rope," said an Indianapolis paper. "At the conclusion of his performance he was cheered to the echo."

Not long after the tour, Will had his chance to go east. The opportunity was provided, once again, by Zack Mulhall. In January, Mulhall's trial for the St. Louis shooting was completed; he had been found guilty of assault with intent to kill and sentenced to a three-year prison term. But he appealed the verdict and apparently won, because in April he contracted to take a troupe of cowboys to participate in the New York Horse Fair at Madison Square Garden. On the urging of Mother Mulhall, Will was invited. He and Jim Minnick, who had performed in another Wild West show at the St. Louis fair and was also to appear in New York, traveled by way of Washington, D.C. An article in the Washington *Times* described Will as "perhaps the finest ropeman in the world" and reported that "the two Westerners, attired in their cowboy boots and hats, went to the White House, and did some tricks for the entertainment of the children of the President. Rogers showed the children how a cowboy 'jumps the rope.' " Unfortunately, the President was out of town, but Will and Jim palled around with eighteen-year-old Theodore Roosevelt, Jr.

The New York Horse Fair, in its second year, was an outgrowth of the more genteel New York Horse Show; in addition to the traditional equestrian exhibitions, there were trotting races, band concerts, and Mulhall's "Cowboy Carnival," a nine-act spectacle, with thirteen horses and eighteen riders, that lasted a little over an hour. One of the cowboys was listed in the program as "Tom Mixco, cow runner, from Old Mexico." Years later, Mix explained that this assonant fabrication was courtesy of Will: With the colonel's blessing, the two cowboys used to collaborate on the programs. Mix returned the favor with a program entry for Will that, in just two sentences, included five outright untruths: "Rogers is a full blood Cherokee Indian [1], born on the Cherokee Strip [2], and educated at Notre Dame [3] and Carlisle, Pa [4]. His father is now chief of the Cherokee Indians [5]."

Pranks like that were only the mildest of the fun. Zack Miller, from the Miller Brothers 101 Ranch, was along, and the account he gave to author Fred Gipson makes it sound like a week-long fraternity party: "Nights, after the show, they'd all booze up . . . and they'd ride [an automobile] up and down the streets, whooping and yelling like prairie wolves at a kill. . . . They took in all the leg shows, drank everything in sight, and prized up hell in general whenever the notion struck them." According to Miller, Will was a willing—if not particularly proficient— participant in the hell-raising. One day, he tried to break a Madison Square Garden rule against bringing liquor into dressing rooms by hiding five quart bottles of beer in his leather chaps. Unfortunately, on his way up the stairs, they fell out and broke. The Mulhall cowboys also played (and lost) a game of polo against a local riding academy, Will's first taste of what was to be his favorite sport.

The colonel was having a good time, too, and Will and Mix (who shared a room at the Putnam House hotel) had some concern that he was using their salaries to buy drinks for friends and strangers alike every night at the hotel bar. One night, while Mulhall was standing at the bar, they edged up on either side of him and waited for the moment when he paid his tab. They were delighted to see him pull out a twenty-dollar bill: The moment the bartender put down the change, they grabbed it all and ran out the door.

Not surprisingly, the cowboys were seized on by the New York press, which portrayed them as exotic emissaries from the wilderness. One article told of a Mulhall man (unnamed) who won eighteen hundred dollars at the racetrack.

> He was distributing real two-dollar bills to the newsboys when a young woman who evidently had been on Broadway before came along with an escort.
>
> "Darling, you are just about what the doctor ordered," she exclaimed as she left her escort and put her arms about the cowboy. "You certainly are the goods."
>
> The man with her resented this transfer of affection and was

promptly knocked down by the cowboy. Then the young woman who had placed her brand upon him carried him across the street to a rathskeller.

On Easter, the troupe paraded up and down Fifth Avenue. Naturally, the newspapers were there. An article entitled COWGIRLS JOIN IN FASHION'S THRONG played up the contrast between "the open-air flowers of the West" and "the hot-house plants of the East."

The Mulhall girls, the article declared, were:

> ... clear-eyed, sunburned, fearless and yet very curious. What cared they for the upturned noses, the pitying smiles, and the gawkish laughter?
>
> "Did you ever see such complexions?" remarked Cowgirl Lucille Mulhall, a handsome blonde, to Cowboy Bill Rogers as the cavalcade turned into Central Park at Fifty-ninth Street.
>
> "Umph!" replied the favorite son of the chief of the Cherokee Nation, a white man, "these New York gals need a bit of God's sunshine."

The papers liked the show itself, too. New York had been used to Wild West exhibitions from the days of Buffalo Bill; this one, in its emphasis on authenticity and skill, was a little different. After the troupe presented itself ("with pistols cracking and the cowboy yells making the ring like a frontier camp"), the Mulhall girls and their cowboy partners danced the Virginia reel. Then came an exhibition of wild-horse riding, a re-creation of the pony express, Will's lariat exhibition, and Lucille's segment, featuring her trick horse, Governor. There followed more roughriding, an Indian war dance, and some miscellaneous "Cowboy Sports." Lucille was clearly the star of the show, but Will got some good notices, too, one newspaper singling him out for his two-rope throw.

Something that happened during a subsequent show dampened Will's high spirits, at least temporarily. "Bill came to me," Tom Mix recalled to biographer David Milsten, "and said, 'Tom, there are some keen-looking girls out in the boxes and I am going to throw my rope toward 'em to see if I can't get a play out of 'em.' That was Bill's idea of making a play with the girls. We went ahead with the show and that night when Bill came into the room where we were bunked, I noticed he was looking low in spirits. I can see him now as he walked toward me, kicking the floor, his head down, his hat well back on his head, and that familiar strand of hair in a V-shape pointing to his nose. I asked him if anything was wrong, and he replied, 'I heard those girls say they was strong for me till they read on the program that I was an Indian, and one of 'em said she could stand being entertained by the darkest inhabitants of Africa, but an Indian went against her nature.' "

It was a reminder that for some people Will's education, his father's money, his mixed-blood Cherokee pedigree, meant nothing. To them he might as well have been a full-blood Apache warrior, ready for battle. An Indian was an Indian.

During an afternoon performance on the sixth day of the show, Lucille was about to attempt to rope a steer when the animal jumped over a gate and ran up the stairs of Madison Square Garden, making it all the way into the balcony, where it disappeared into a corridor behind some boxes. "Women screamed and men shouted" (said the New York *World*), and the Seventh Regiment Band, present to provide musical entertainment, "abandoned horns of all sizes and fled." Accounts of what happened next vary wildly. The origin of the traditionally recounted version is the front page story in the *World*, a sensationalistic daily owned by Joseph Pulitzer. It reported that "the Indian Will Rogers" ran up another stairway and headed off the steer ("a dun-colored animal, weighing 800 pounds, with horns that spread five feet"), roped it, and "swerved it down the steps" back into the ring, where it was promptly brought down by the other cowboys.

However, the New York *Herald* described things differently. It said that after Will roped the steer, it dragged him "over seats and down the stairs" and he let go, whereupon the steer went back into the arena of its own accord. (The *Herald* also said that " 'Jim' Mixco, a celebrated rope thrower . . . missed [the steer] with his lasso and caught an usher by the leg, bringing him down with a thump on the stairs.") Yet another newspaper agreed that the steer returned to the arena on its own, but said that it was roped there by Will and Tom Mix. Mildred Mulhall, interviewed by Homer Croy, said that Will, Tom, and Jim Minnick "ran" the steer back into the arena. Minnick gave his own account to Cal Tinney in a 1930 interview: When a policeman started to follow the steer up to the balcony, "Will asked the officer, 'What are you going to do with it when you catch it?' Rogers knew the steer would come around to the back side, and it did."

Will's own account was somewhat vague on the details. In a letter to his father, he enclosed a note for the editor of the Claremore *Progress:* "I never did get to write you but here is a clipping or two. I made the biggest hit I ever dreamed of in my Roping Act and finished my good luck by catching the wild steer that went clear up into the dress circles of the garden among the people. I will stay here to do more theatre work for a while." He also sent a clipping to Betty Blake. Not surprisingly, he chose the one from the *World*. He (mis)labeled it "N.Y. Times," put it in an envelope, and mailed it off to her. There was no accompanying letter.

"I WILL stay here to do more theatre work for a while." Just how committed to the new venture Will was is seen by his willingness to alienate Zack Mulhall (who wanted him to stay with the troupe) and to sell Comanche (who was too heavy for stage work). He used $100 of the $250 he received to buy Teddy from the colonel. When the Mulhall troupe packed up and left, Will remained at the Putnam House at Fourth Avenue and Twenty-Sixth Street, right next to Madison Square Garden ("single rooms $.50 and up").*

Will's notion of mounting the stage was not an unreasonable one. In 1905, vaudeville was at the midpoint and close to the peak popularity of its fifty-year reign as the country's preeminent vehicle for live entertainment, and it was a prodigious consumer of talent. There were about forty theaters in New York alone, each requiring eight to twelve acts a week, and hundreds more in the rest of the country. As noted, Will's dumb act fitted nicely into a category for which there was a steady demand, and his notion of roping a horse on the stage was clearly a novelty. Vaudeville liked novelty. It liked celebrity even better, and Will momentarily had some, as a result of his Madison Square Garden heroics. What's more, during the Mulhall run, he'd gone on the stage of a Manhattan burlesque house called Shanley's and won the audience over with just his rope, so he knew that New Yorkers were capable of responding to him on a stage.

And so, armed with his letter of recommendation from St. Louis and his New York newspaper clippings, he presented himself to the United Booking Office in Union Square, which arranged bookings for the entire vaudeville industry. The response was disappointing. There'd be no room to rope a horse onstage, he was told—come back with a better idea. After a week of rejection, his resolve was a little shaky. "I will stay here a week or so yet," he wrote to his father, ". . . but I might be there [Indian Territory] any time."

---

*"I sold Comanche to a man in New York," Will wrote to his sister Sallie in June, "and Mulhall sneakingly bought him when he found out I was going to stay east. He thought I would follow him as he was mad because I quit him." It took five years, but Will finally got his boon companion back from Mulhall (for a price unknown—probably a good deal more than $250), along with a handwritten receipt: "On this day I give and deliver to Willie Rogers his old Pal Commanche [*sic*]."

But Will stuck at it. Every day he, Teddy, and Jim Minnick—who'd also stayed behind when the Mulhalls left and had agreed temporarily to serve as the rider in Will's act—rehearsed on some open land in New Jersey. They were able to make a little money by appearing at the three-day Orange Horse Show in East Orange, New Jersey. Will was a hit there, and he also engaged in some clowning, a tendency not noted in any of the accounts of his work at the Mulhall shows. During one performance, he lassoed a dog that accidentally got into the ring; another time, he was galloping around the ring when he suddenly roped one of the horse show's judges.

After nearly a month of persistent application, he finally got his chance in New York. One of the bookers, Dan Hennessy, took a liking to Will, and convinced the manager of Keith's Union Square, one of the most prominent theaters in town, to give him a tryout. It was to take place at the "supper show," a kind of no-man's land between the matinee and evening performances. Far from the most glorious slot, it was poorly attended (for the obvious reason that most people were home eating supper) and was referred to by a contemporary commentator as "the undivided middle."

Will described what happened:

> Well about 6:30 on a hot afternoon, they flashed an X on the side of that stage, which means here comes another victim. Well I guess I would have been scared if there had been anybody out there to get scared of. Well these 10 or 12 that was out there seemed to think, well this fool is a long way from home, so don't seem to know what he's doing floundering around there. But that's such a nice little pony and seems to be the only one that knows what he is doing, and if we dont help him out he will get rode plain back to Oklahoma. So for the ponys sake, they laid their papers down. . . .

Keith's manager was suitably impressed, and he signed Will to play three shows a day at the theater the week of June 12. The headline act was a farce called "Mr. and Mrs. Nagg," put on by Henry V. Donnelly and his company; the singing team of Egbert Van Alstyne and Louise Henry got second billing. Will came on fifth. He was mentioned in at least one review, and, while it could not be classified as a rave, the two sentences made it clear he had not mounted the stage on false pretenses: "Will Rogers made his debut at the house, being billed as 'The World Champion Lasso Manipulator.' To even the layman it was apparent that he had some right to his claim, and the audience marveled at his skill."

EARLY PUBLICITY SHOTS

CHAPTER 5

IN VAUDEVILLE

I wish there was a vaudeville like there was in those old days. No branch of entertainment was ever so satisfying to work in. Never was there such independence. It was your act. And you could do it like you wanted to, and it was your ingenuity that made it.

—WILL ROGERS, 1934

you see it is the way I do my work is what takes with them and a few funny things I say.

—WILL ROGERS, 1905

WILL WAS PAID seventy-five dollars for his week's engagement at Keith's. It was more money than he had ever got before, but for big-time vaudeville it was minimum wage. Will didn't even take home the full seventy-five, for it was the policy of the Keith organization, which owned the largest chain of theaters in vaudeville, to deduct a 5 percent commission from performers' salaries for the service of having booked them. Out of the remaining $71.25, Will had to pay Jim Minnick's salary and house and feed Teddy.

But Will's reception was favorable enough that he very quickly got a raise. He opened at Keith's Union Square on Monday. That Wednesday, the organization signed him to engagements at its theaters in Boston and Philadelphia, commencing June 26 and July 3, at a salary of $140 a week. The contract called for him to play three shows a day—matinee, evening, and the dreaded supper show. On hearing this schedule, he wrote later, he "puffed up there like a poached egg." He was used to Wild West shows, "where the fellow that could get in and do the most work was the most valuable man . . . it took a lot of time for those acts to beat it into my head [that it was better to work two shows a day] cause I thought they was only jealous cause the manager wouldn't let them work three times."

Word spread quickly that this was an act that played. That same Wednesday, June 14, 1905, Will signed another contract. This one was with Keith's principal competitor in Manhattan, Oscar Hammerstein, to play the week of June 19 at Hammerstein's Victoria Theatre on Forty-second Street and Broadway. The engagement—also paying $140—was a coup. In a letter he wrote a year later, Will described Hammerstein's as "the leading Vaudeville Theatre of the World and all performers are tickled to death to get to play it."

The hyperbole is evident, but the Victoria was without doubt the prime showplace of New York. This was largely due to the efforts of Oscar Hammerstein's son, Willie, who had managed the theater since it opened the year before and who, for his unmatched combination of talent-spotting and promotional instincts, is generally acknowledged as the greatest showman in vaudeville history. Willie Hammerstein—whose son, Oscar II, was the Broadway lyricist—ran the Victoria until his death in 1914. He is most remembered as the principal proponent of the "freak act." A typical Hammerstein sensation was Unthan the Armless Wonder, who fired a rifle and played the violin with his feet. Temporary celebrities made good freak acts, too. After two young women caused a sensation by shooting a socialite in the leg, Hammerstein posted their bail, billed them as the "Shooting Stars," and engaged a monologist to describe their exploits while they stood mutely on the stage. He was also known for introducing exotic dances from Europe, most notably the "Salome Dance," which depicted the reaction of the title character to the beheading of John the Baptist and ended with a frenzied gyration around the decapitated apostle. Hammerstein arranged for the dancer to be arrested for violating decency laws and for a police officer to be conspicuously posted on the stage, ensuring compliance.

In this company, a cowboy throwing a rope around a horse and rider was tame stuff. But the fact that Hammerstein signed Will just two days after his New York debut supports his reputation as an extremely canny judge of talent. So does his response to Will's initial apprehension that the stage at Hammerstein's was too small. That, Willie said, would only make the act go over better.

One of Hammerstein's innovations was the "Roof Garden," a separate enclosed stage constructed on top of the Victoria Theatre. In the summer months, the matinee performance would be played downstairs and the evening show on the roof. The irreversibly upward migration of heat would have sunk a lesser impresario, but it was barely an annoyance to Willie. He heated the elevator carrying customers up to the roof, so that when they emerged the air would seem delightfully cool. The arrangement proved a problem on the first day of Will's engagement. Teddy refused to board the elevator, agreeing to do so only after a long conversation with Willie Hammerstein. (That, anyway, is the account given in a newspaper clipping in Will's scrapbook. The source is unidentified, but it bears the mark of one of the press agents of whom Hammerstein was a pioneer utilizer.) Again, the act was a hit. Among the adjectives the newspapers applied to it that week were "remarkable," "remarkably expert," "novel," "effective," and "surprising."

In the early days, that act followed a simple program. Will, wearing a red shirt and buckskin trousers, entered the stage twirling his lasso, to an orchestral accompaniment. He would do a few fancy loops with a soft cotton rope, then switch to a heavier, stiffer rope and shout, "Right!" This signaled Buck McKee (a former sheriff from Oklahoma who replaced Jim Minnick) to ride onto the stage from the wing atop Teddy. Before they could reach the footlights, Will would rope Teddy by all four feet. (To prevent slippage, the horse wore felt-bottom boots. This generally did the job, but once Will followed a comic-barber act, and Teddy slipped on the lather and fell, pinning Buck's leg under him and dangling over the orchestra pit. Will roped him and lifted him with one hand, freed Buck with the other, and prevented a panic by calmly telling the audience that what they had seen had all been planned.)

Will would twirl the rope into different kinds of knots and nooses. Then came his trademark—the trick where he threw two lassos at once, roping man with one and horse with another. After that, he did some cowboy dances, jumping in and out of his spinning rope. For a finale, he had an usher carry a rope down the aisle to let the audience digest its full eighty-foot length. Will mounted Teddy and started twirling the rope, until it was a giant crinoline spinning and hissing just over the heads of the patrons.

It was, in vaudeville parlance, a wow finish, but initially Will didn't know how to make the most of it. After his first performance, he just walked off the stage and was on his way to his dressing room when Ernest Hogan, a black comedian and singer, grabbed him and rushed him out in front of the curtain. "As I come off he said, Boy dont overlook any of them. They aint bows, he says, thems curtain calls, and there is damned few of them."

Will's was a striking act, carried off with panache. What made it

more unusual, almost from the beginning, was the way it broke free of
the traditional notion of a "dumb act." From the late teens on, every account of Will Rogers's life—biographical, autobiographical, journalistic,
or cinematic—has paid substantial attention to the momentous occasion
when he first talked onstage. It's an essential element of the Will Rogers
myth, usually presented as something akin to the day the thought struck
Charles Lindbergh that he might like to try flying an airplane, or when
the New York Yankees decided to put Babe Ruth in the outfield. Among
those who have been given (or have taken) credit for convincing Will to
open his mouth were Florenz Ziegfeld, Gene Buck (Ziegfeld's principal
writer), Blanche Ring (a vaudeville star with whom he appeared in a
1912 musical), and Max Hart (Will's agent for a time). What is generally
agreed is that for his first few years on the stage, he hardly talked at all.
Eddie Cantor, to cite just one example, wrote of being on a bill with
Will in 1912, at which point "he didn't talk on stage, he was still a little
nervous to try that."

The fact is that he spoke—and was praised for speaking—in the first
weeks of his vaudeville career. After his week at Hammerstein's, he went
to Keith's in Philadelphia. One reviewer there admiringly singled him as
"a character with lots of character" and (in what was probably the first
of the thousands of dismal attempts to reproduce Will's speech on paper)
quoted him as saying, "I'll do it ef I hev luck," before attempting to
throw his lasso over Buck's head, so as to rope Teddy by all four feet.

> The most difficult feat followed—throwing two lassoes,
> catching the man on the horse with one lasso, and the horse
> with another lasso, using a lasso in each hand. Rogers declared
> that this was a new trick which he had kept from the "boys" on
> the plains. His first try was a miss, when he observed, in his
> characteristic manner: "I'm handicapped up h'yar, as the man-
> ager won't let me swear when I miss!"

This last comment—which got a big laugh—was a knowing refer-
ence to the policies of the Keith organization, called "the Sunday School
Circuit" by performers for its near-puritanical insistence on propriety.
The review closed by noting that Will got three curtain calls; obviously,
Ernest Hogan's lesson had sunk in.

But Will had talked onstage even before this. The simple reason was
that his tricks, being unfamiliar, required some explanation; otherwise,
the audience wouldn't know how hard they were. During his very first
engagement, he recalled in an unpublished reminiscence, the other acts
encouraged him to make a kind of introduction. When he did so, he got

a surprising and—to him—disturbing reaction: The audience laughed. "I couldn't see where they come in to laugh at me," Will wrote. "I hadn't said anything funny. I wanted to quit right there. And [the other performers] kept after me to keep that in, and gradually, very gradually, sayings would come to me that they would laugh at, but I didn't like the idea for a *long time.*" (The italics, present in the original, indicate that even at this early date, there were misconceptions about his initial utterance.)

Will's surprise at the laughter is credible, but someone who knew more about the vaudeville stage could have predicted it. The atmosphere in the typical house was palpably jocular; audiences were hungry for humor, ready to laugh at anything. As one contemporary observer remarked, "The most serious thing about the [vaudeville] program is that seriousness is barred, with some melancholy results. From the artist who balances a set of parlor furniture on his nose to the academic baboon, there is one concentrated, strenuous struggle for a laugh. . . . It hangs like a solemn and awful obligation over everything."

Even Will's own account minimized how quickly, enthusiastically, and successfully he embraced comedy. Very nearly from the start, whatever the level of his own nervousness, he was able at least to simulate comfort as he chatted onstage, to pretend to himself that he was at a Claremore cakewalk. From Philadelphia he went to Boston, and there again his speaking was commented on, the *Globe* writing that "his plainsman 'talk' is real comedy of the sort that is seldom heard on the stage." The following week, he was back in New York at Proctor's 23rd Street, and a review noted that "Rogers himself is a good deal of an actor, and his byplay and aside speeches make a great hit with the audience, although his neat work is enough to carry almost any act to a successful conclusion." The next week, he played Hammerstein's again, and the *Sunday Telegraph* wrote that his "personal magnetism, quite apart from the good work which he does with the ropes, has made him a popular roof garden headliner." A few months later, a Providence reviewer wrote, "He laughs and talks wittily throughout his entire act, making the audience enjoy watching his own enjoyment quite as much as his work itself."

From the start, there was something interesting about Will's "sayings." "I'll do it ef I hev luck," he had remarked, and then, "the manager won't let me swear when I miss." Once he was preceded on a bill by a "William Tell act," the archer announcing in Teutonic tones, "Understand, I nefer make meestake." Will's first words when he came out were, "Sometime I make meestake." Even when he was a vaudeville veteran, a striking number of his comments addressed the likelihood that he would muff a trick, or the fact that he had just done so. Among his papers are two sheets of stationery from the Saratoga Hotel in Chicago, headed, in Will's handwriting, "Gags for missing the [horse's] nose," a reference to a tough trick he developed in his first years on the stage. The undated notes may have been written in 1907, when Will appeared in the city; in any case, the self-deprecation evident in them is sufficiently studied to suggest that Will had at least a couple of years of experience under his belt. The gags are:

1. Think I will turn him around and see if I cant throw one on his tail easier
2. If I dont put one on soon will have to give out rain checks
3. Ha you jasper I think I will see if I cant get just one on your nose if it dont make no difference to you mob out there
4. If I have a whole bunch of good luck I will get this on about the 13th throw if this salary wing or whip dont give out on me
5. I should have sprinkled a little Mucilage or rosin on his nose this thing might hang on.
6. What did old [illegible] say, "There is hope." Well we are all chock full of hope—if there was a little better Roping and less hoping we would get out of here early tonight.
7. That's one thing I must say for that ferocious animal he was never much for sticking his neck into things
8. Now this is much easier to do on a blind horse—those dont see the Rope coming.

In some ways, it is completely unremarkable that Will should have taken such care to provide himself with verbal defenses against failure. His tricks were hard, so much so that inevitably they didn't come off a fair percentage of the time; anyone could see that genially acknowledging the misses was a better strategy than pretending they didn't happen. Indeed, there was an honorable vaudeville tradition of such deflection. A juggler named La Dent had a screen on the stage labeled SWEARING ROOM; every time he dropped a ball, he'd repair behind it for a few seconds. But no one took this strategy as far as Will did. He would eventually concoct so many jokes about missing—and get such a good reaction with them—that he began to muff certain tricks on purpose. It went beyond that. When Will Rogers became, first, a show business and, subsequently, a national figure, the element of his persona that was most striking—and, it could be argued, did the most to bring about his enormous popularity—was his profound modesty. It permeated everything he did—his habit of staring at the floor onstage and in the movies, only occasionally lifting a shy gaze, the "kinders" and "sorters" with which he modified nearly every declarative sentence he spoke or wrote, his absolute refusal in the millions of words he spoke and wrote to bring any glory upon himself. Even his slogan "All I know is what I read in the papers" was, after all, a declaration of intellectual modesty.

And so he had said, in 1905, "I'll do it ef I hev luck." And why shouldn't he have? If you looked at it a certain way, his father's way, his whole life up until then had been one misstep after another; he'd absorbed failure into his bones. It was little wonder that he should have embraced it as his comic credo.

THE ODD thing was that now, finally, he was a success. He worked nonstop throughout the summer, and, in early August, a burlesque impresario named Sam Scribner asked him to make a five-week circuit of his theaters in Brooklyn, New York, Buffalo, Cleveland, and Pittsburgh. Although burlesque did not then have quite the salacious connotations it later acquired, it was still a less desirable showcase than vaudeville, the acts being merely "olio," or a way to fill time between the appearances of the girls. Will had been planning to go back home for a visit as well, so, thinking that he'd be turned down, he told Scribner that he'd need $250 a week—nearly double his previous rate. The answer was yes. "Next week," Will wrote home to Clem, with studied casualness, "I get quite a bit more Salary."

In the course of a couple of months, he had become an established and sought-after performer. He was booked through the fall and winter, appearing—and getting excellent notices—in Toledo, Detroit, Rochester, Washington, Worcester, Boston, Providence, Lowell, Syracuse, and Philadelphia. "You see the good part," he wrote his sister Maud in October, "is that I havent lost a single week since I started. Now some acts think they do well to work one week and lay off for one, for you know cant always find people to play you at these houses. But that will make 32 straight even if I cant get any more." As unusual as his full calendar was the fact that he never had to play the second-tier "small-time" circuit in which almost all acts started and in which some remained their whole careers. He was big-time from the start. In some cities, he even got top billing.

Will was not your typical vaudevillian. Most of his fellow performers were first- or second-generation ethnics, or else the offspring of show-business families; almost all of them came from the city streets. Vaudeville culture was fast, facetious, profane. For its humor it relied heavily on winking double entendre, and on stereotyped conceptions of the Jew, the German, the Irishman, the black. But Will took to this new world quickly, almost hungrily. He certainly wasted no time romantically, plunging into a relationship (of some eventual seriousness) with Louise Henry, a singer on the bill his first week at Keith's Union Square. He had done his time in Kansas City, after all; if he could survive Buenos Aires, he could survive New York. And now, as if in recognition of the new world he was essaying, his new friends called him by a jaunty new nickname—Bill.

It was essential, however, that he not completely transform himself into a Broadway song-and-dance man, for, no less than his ability, a key to Will's success was his cowboy persona. A vogue in realms eastern for things western had been brewing for some years, contributed to by such diverse factors as the Wild West shows and frontier melodramas of Bill Cody, (the original) Texas Jack and their imitators, dime novels featuring the likes of Deadeye Dick, and the historian Frederick Jackson Turner, whose famed frontier thesis, first put forth in 1893, celebrated the western wilderness for the personality traits ("that coarseness and strength combined with acuteness and inquisitiveness . . . and withal that buoyancy and exuberance which comes with freedom") it engendered. The fad intensified in the years following the turn of the century, and climbed to a higher realm of culture. New York native Frederic Remington's paintings and sculptures glorifying the West were immensely popular, as was the 1902 novel *The Virginian,* by Philadelphia native and Harvard graduate Owen Wister. It included the first "walkdown" duel in American literature, as well as the line, "When you call me that, smile," and spawned a series of cowboy plays—at least three of which were presented on Broadway in 1905. The first movie to have a plot—*The Great Train Robbery,* produced in 1903 by New Jerseyite Thomas Edison—was a Western. The artist N. C. Wyeth, a Pennsylvanian, got his start illustrating romanticized accounts of cowboy life that appeared in the leading monthlies in 1905 and 1906. What made the cultural climate particularly hospitable to these manifestations was the unavoidable presence of Theodore Roosevelt, President since 1901, to whom *The Virginian* was dedicated. He had been a Dakota rancher in the 1880s and was a habitual idealizer of cowboys, who, he once wrote, are "as hardy and self-reliant as any men who ever breathed—with bronzed, set faces and keen eyes that look all the world in the face without flinching as they flash out from under the broad-brimmed hats." Of special significance to Will was that in the cowboy iconography that developed, the lariat was surpassed in prominence only by the six-shooter and, possibly, the "broad-brimmed hat."

Reviewers, unfamiliar with his Indian Territory pedigree, often wondered in print whether he was the genuine article or merely a dude who wore buckskins and dropped his *g*'s. "He talks and he acts like a lad to the manner born," wrote the Rochester *Herald*, "as though he had thrown the lariat in the way of his everyday occupation out on the plain. If it is acting it is good acting and worthy of praise as art; if it is nature it is worthy of praise as the genuine article." Reporters who came backstage, of course, could satisfy the question of authenticity for themselves. "To meet Rogers and talk with him is as good as reading half a dozen chapters of Owen Wister's 'Virginian,' " one of them wrote in Lowell, Massachusetts.* By November, Will had the ultimate proof of accomplishment: imitation. "The success of Rogers has reached the Indian Territory," noted a New York paper, "and the vaudeville market is flooded with an influx of cowpunchers."

Nothing came of an offer by William Morris, the biggest theatrical agent in the country, to appear in a dramatic production, but Will acquired an agent of his own, a young man named Mort Shea. His fee was established as a flat $250 a week, so that even after expenses he was able to save a good deal of money. Each week, he would send cash home to Clem—fifty dollars, one hundred dollars, sometimes more. By the end of the year, by his reckoning, he had accumulated more than two thousand dollars.

As the months went by, Will continued his education in the ways of showmanship. While his jokes usually got a good response, his understated manner was such that sometimes the audience didn't realize he was being funny. So when he was in New York, he arranged for an employee of Jim Minnick's named Fred Tejan to sit in the audience and laugh loudly at the appropriate times. He would experiment with the act, too, adding new stunts and seeing whether they worked. He put in

---

*Another reporter asked Will whether he was familiar with the Wister novel. "Yep, I read it—leastwise part of it," he said. "We wuz all sitting out on the ranch one night in the summer soon after that book came out. There must have been thirty of us there all together and there was men that had rode all over the West a-punching cattle, and we were mightily interested in this yere [*sic*] story until we got to the part where that main guy—that Virginian, with his black hair and brown eyes—catches his pal cattle rustlin' and hangs him. Say, that was too much. . . . Why if this pal had been a murderer it would have been different, but even that wasn't no hanging affair; but think of stringin' your pal for a few measly calves what wasn't worth hardly anything at all." He concluded, "There ain't no such West as them fellows that wrote say there are."

a three-rope catch, a figure eight, and a tail catch so difficult he never ceased practicing it. He had his own musical score made up, a medley of western tunes featuring "Pony Boy" and "Cheyenne." One night, he addressed the audience: "Now, I'll show you how we land a tenderfoot who comes out our way. It's about as easy landing a tenderfoot with a lasso as it is to eat cold chicken." He thereupon threw the rope around Buck and, with a flick of his wrist, sent a knot traveling through the rope all the way to Buck's neck. Very early on, on an impulse, he roped a fellow performer standing in the wings and dragged him onstage. The audience, always delighted to be let in on something out of the ordinary, went wild, and the move became one of Will's trademarks.

He was also learning something about promoting himself. He got Teddy a blue blanket with a gold border and the name WILL ROGERS written in gold letters. He was trained to follow Buck McKee, and, on arriving in any new city, Buck would walk from the railroad station to the theater, preferably down the main thoroughfare. Behind him would be Teddy and behind the horse would be a parade of kids—an effective and inexpensive way to get attention.

Oddly, he tended to avoid another form of free publicity—newspaper interviews. By now relatively comfortable in front of a theater full of people, he was still too shy to want to talk about himself face-to-face with reporters. He didn't like the liberties they took with his quotes, either; "they ask you a few questions and then put it down to suit themselves," he complained to Maud. But he was induced to speak for publication a few times and, given the striking success he had achieved, what he had to say was surprising. He was planning to give up the stage. "I don't care for this vaudeville life," he said to one newspaperman in early December. "I don't have to do it and I'm not going to do it much after Christmas. . . .

"No, sir: This stage business was never built for me. A feller will have an off day and there ain't no reason for it and it shouldn't be. But it is. Out on the plains, among fellers of your own kind, if you is why you can try it over again and there's nothing said. But plumb up in front of an audience when you miss they think you're no good and it rattles the best feller the Lord ever allowed to rope a steer."

So the pressure was getting to him. To another reporter, he made a different complaint: "Like this theater work? Not much. There's too much sameness about the game. You know just what you're going to do this week, next week, the week after that and every week right through the season. Out on the ranch when you get up in the morning you can never tell what will happen before night."

In fact, true to his habitual inability to stay at any endeavor for very long, Will had been talking about giving up vaudeville from almost the very beginning. Early in August, he was already affecting weariness: "Well its the same old thing. Out twice a day and do a little bum Roping, hear them holler and applaud, bow and then do it the next day," he wrote in a letter. In October, he wrote, "I dont know how long I will stay at this. I might leave at any day and go back to the ranch. I have made a success and thats all I wanted to do."

The recipient of these confidences was none other than Betty Blake. Will had reinitiated their correspondence on June 3. Not coincidentally, this was the day Keith's had engaged him for his first week of vaudeville. After expressing the disappointment and hurt he still felt over her rejection of him as a suitor, he outlined his prospects ("I think I can make good. I am on a fair road to success in my line") and closed with a plea: ". . . truthfully tell me that you could some time learn to love me just a little and I bet there will be a cowboy doing a 100% better act and feeling fine.

"Now Listen, Bettie, I am honest in this and if you dont like me a little bit, Bettie, dont even write me for it would make me all the worse."

She wrote, but the message was the same. They would never be more than friends. It didn't matter. There was finally something in his life for which Will was willing to show commitment, persistence, and dedication, and he kept at it. In August, he took a shot in the dark—a direct marriage proposal. "This might sound like a joke but its certainly so," he said. Again the answer was no. Again Will refused to drop the matter.

"I know it is foolish for me to write to you," he admitted in October, "but I just cant help it and some time when you dont ever hear from old Bill it wont be because he is mad or is fascinated with some other but only because he is at last able to abide by his own judgement.

"You know Betty old pal I have always had about what I wanted and it breaks my heart when I think I'll never get it. I am ordinarily a good loser but my nerve is fooling me this trip."

At Christmastime, he sent her a present and a rather fanciful tale. He said he had bought the enclosed handkerchief in South America from an "old Indian Lady" who asked whether he was married. On hearing he wasn't, "she said then give it to the wife when you do marry. I have kept it, carried it all through Africa at times when I dident have a cent and was actually hungry, then to Australia most of the time in an envelope in my pocket, then back home, and on all my travels I did intend to do as the old woman said. But I guess theres nothing doing for me. I will just give it to you as I kinder pride it and you might do the same." It was a nice try, but it didn't work.

American entertainers had begun to perform in Europe with increasing frequency, the influx being such that in 1906 *Variety* announced that it could be purchased in all European capitals. The astute Mort Shea arranged for Will to play the entire month of April 1906 at Berlin's celebrated Winter Garden for a fee of 3,700 marks. Before sailing from New York, Will was able to visit home for the first time in a year. The rest was well needed: Since June he had worked every week, without a break.

From an engagement in Philadelphia he took a thirty-six-hour train ride to St. Louis and then an overnight train to Rogers, Arkansas, where Betty had agreed to let him spend the day. From there, he went on to the Indian Territory for six days. He spent the entire time with his sisters in Chelsea, only venturing into Claremore once, to be initiated into the Masons. Otherwise, his schedule consisted of socializing, feasting, and sleeping. There was undoubtedly a little gloating as well. At the time of his last homecoming, two years before, he had been without funds or prospects. Now he was in possession of large contracts and rave clippings and sharp clothes. As even Clem had to admit, the boy had in some not quite definable way made good.

He sailed on Saturday, March 17, and the first few days of the voyage were predictably rocky. On Wednesday, happily, he "got a bite to eat down that by some miracle that couldent find its way up again and I done pretty fair the rest of the way." He had intended to stop first in London, before traveling on to Berlin, but some acquaintances he made on ship persuaded him to come to Paris by way of Cherbourg. And, to judge by the way he described the city to Betty, he could not have been happier with the decision. "Polly vue Francaise," he began the letter, firmly ensconced in the jaunty slang mode he found attractive in moments of confidence:

Wee Wee yah, yah. I dont know a darne word anybody's saying. But Pal of Mine I sho do know I am in Paree and old hand she is certainly the Goods. All I regret is you are not here. If we wouldent go the pace that kills.

... Sunday is the day of days. Oh I never seen such a mass of people as are out on the Boulevards on a Sunday. I have been about some but you got to hand it to Paris for a wide open place. There seems to be no laws and especially of morality. When they kinder jar me they are going some but I must admit they kinder did, but then its all to be expected here. Thats Paris. Stage Women aint one two 11 with these for paint and make up. Oh how they do strut. . . .

But say the Grub. It might be because I pay for it that it is so good but . . . it is the best cooked stuff I ever eat, when you can find a guy that can savee enough to know what you want. Oh it has made an offul hit with me. . . .

He left for Berlin on the twenty-seventh and was reunited with Buck and Teddy, who had sailed straight from the States to Hamburg. He found a city that, if possible, was even swifter than his last stop. "It seems that it is a fact here that people dont sleep," he advised Betty. "Why I never get in till 8 or 9 or 10 in the morning and everything is . . . open all night and we just go from one cafe to another and all over town and then in a Cab and drive awhile and then out and drink and its that day and Night. There is quite a bunch of English girls and a few of us boys and I dident think it was possible to go such a clip oh we do have some great old times. . . ."

You would have thought that, by now, Will would have realized that this kind of thing didn't help his cause with Betty.

At the Winter Garden—where he shared the bill with the likes of Professor Thereses, described in the program as a "Komisch-Hyp-notischer Act," and Marguerite Broadfoote, an "Englische Sänger-in"—he was a hit, the utter novelty of how he looked and what he did, and the romance of the Wild West he brought with him, making up for the language barrier. One newspaper, stretching things a bit, described Teddy as "a fiery mustang." When Will roped horse and rider, the review went on, "you might compare it with a brilliant summation of a Buffalo Bill story. . . . That Will Rogers is an unusual fellow and one sees at first glance that he is a true son of the wild west. He, as well as his assistant Buck McKee, are like two figures out of Cooper's Indian stories."

Three incidents survive from Will's month in Germany. Every afternoon, he would exercise Teddy in Berlin's Tiergarten, and on several occasions he encountered a military man also out for a ride. Will's western outfit was noticeable, to say the least, and the two equestrians developed a nodding acquaintance. Will eventually found out that the man was Kaiser Wilhelm. "He always salutes as he gallops past," Will wrote Betty. "Oh he is a dandy good fellow."

A second memorable occurrence took place onstage and taught Will that his casually irreverent style of humor did not necessarily cross national boundaries. He had noticed that an unsmiling fireman was always standing in the wings. For some reason—maybe it was the ax he imperiously wore—the fellow annoyed Will, and he decided to rope him and bring him out before the footlights. Neither the civil servant nor the audience was amused. Indeed, the joke nearly engendered an international incident. The theater manager—after explaining to the audience that Will's rope had slipped—had to spend much of the night trying to convince local authorities that the impudent American should not be arrested. "In Germany they have cultivated everything they got but a sense of humor," Will said when he recounted the story years later.

This impression was heightened by an incident described years later by a friend of Will's from South Africa who visited him in Germany. At the end of the Winter Garden engagement, Will was hired to perform at a circus at Leipzig. He was at the Berlin train station, his trunk being weighed, when a porter took it off the scale, pointed out that part of a shirt was sticking out, and said that the luggage could not be booked through unless the offending article was tucked in. This so infuriated Will that he canceled the engagement.

Instead, he went to England, a country much more in tune with his sensibility. Alfred Butt (later to be knighted), manager of London's Palace Theatre, was aware of Will's great success in Berlin and engaged him for a week. He was such a hit that Butt signed him for four more weeks, increased his stage time from ten minutes to thirteen, and moved him to the featured spot on the bill. The English papers were enthusiastic, although Will's utter foreignness (one critic asserted that he learned roping while "training polo-ponies on a far Western ranch") was such as to leave them in a state of charmed bewilderment. "It is a surprising and very beautiful performance and the audience rose at it," wrote the *Morning Post* about Will's roping. "It made one feel that it is a mistake when tying up a refractory parcel to stand over one's work. One should retire to the other end of the room and make casts at it."

The *Tribune*'s man was especially voluble, in a Bertie Wooster–like way:

> Mr. Rogers, I imagine, hails from America, or, if he does not, he ought to. . . . The lassoist has an accent and a manner of speaking which I believe it is correct to describe as "redolent of the plains." The odd thing, too, is that they sound natural, and not like the acquired intonations of the young women who figure as American heiresses in modern comedies. He does not

show you a new trick, but puts up another "stunt." This is a new word to me, but I like Mr. Rogers's "stunts." The one I like most is when he shows you how to catch and tie up a "bad man" who happens to be riding by while you are lounging around with a rope. In a flash you have a tightening coil round his neck or shoulders (you or I wouldn't, but Mr. Rogers would), and there you have him hooked. You notice then that his arms are free. In tones which brook no denial you accordingly tell him to "put up those flappers," and two arms are held out in to-ken of surrender. Standing twenty or thirty feet away ("it don't do you no good to get too near a bad man," Mr. Rogers will tell you), you give your rope a couple of quick jerks, and the man's arms are caught and bound together; another rapid motion runs along the cord, and the arms are lashed securely to the saddle. You can complete the picture, if you like, by binding the poor wretch to the horse, and then, without ever having gone near your victim, you can drag him off to the police station. It pre-supposes a blind quiescence on the part of the quarry, but I daresay a bad man knows when he is "downed."

Will was the toast of the same town in which he and Dick Parris had been prospectless sightseers just four years before. Word of his skill trav-eled socially upward, and one afternoon he was invited to give an exhi-bition at the exclusive Ranelagh Club. In the audience was King Edward VII. Twenty years later, Will Rogers would play polo at Ranelagh as an honored guest.

He came home by way of Austria and Italy, spending a week in Rome and Naples, and arrived in New York on the Fourth of July. He immediately departed for Indian Territory, where he would finally have a lengthy rest. It was a memorable summer, highlighted by a series of parties given in honor of the Oologah boy who had become a vaudeville star. Will's sister Maud arranged a whole weekend in his honor at her big place in Chelsea, inviting a houseful of young people. One of them was Betty Blake. She took the train from Arkansas—or, rather, trains. The first one left at 4:30 a.m., and there would be two changes before she was due to arrive at two in the afternoon. By the time she reached Vinita, a half hour away from Chelsea, she was hot, tired, and bored, and therefore happy to see the familiar figure of Will Rogers walk into the coach; he had traveled down to accompany her on the last leg. But his shyness outweighed both his gallantry and his ardor. The seat next to Betty was occupied, and, rather than ask the occupant to move, Will shook hands with Betty and deposited himself at the far end of the car, where he rode the rest of the way in silence.

The pattern continued for the whole weekend. While Betty was immediately comfortable with Will's people and they treated her like an old friend, playing amiable practical jokes and teasing her about her suitor, Will himself was unaccountably cool. On all the activities— horseback rides, dinners, parties—"he never looked in my direction or singled me out," Betty wrote. "We all went together in a crowd and came home the same way. Even on our moonlight horseback rides, we both rode up in front with the rest of the riders. He never came around where I was unless we were playing and singing at the piano. I just could not understand him." During the weekend, thirteen of the guests arranged themselves on a wagon, adopted somewhat forced expressions of merriment, and directed their attention to a photographer. Will is on the far left side, his chin on his left hand; Betty is on the far right side, her chin on her left hand. Separated by inclination and space, they were still somehow together.

Will was more forthright when he visited Betty in Rogers a few weeks later. He pressed his proposal again, but with no better luck. Spurred by his success abroad, and a full fall and winter's worth of bookings, Will had cast aside his doubts about making a career in vaudeville. And—at least according to Betty's account in her book—this was now the sticking point: ". . . from my point of view, show business was not a very stable occupation. . . . I simply could not see a life of trouping the country in vaudeville."

Trouping the country in vaudeville is precisely what Will proceeded to do. It's not surprising that he would have taken to the life, for it offered two things that had always attracted him: traveling and unofficial families. The traveling, at least in its concentration and incessantness, surpassed anything he had experienced before. He'd generally get on a train Sunday morning—or, if it was a particularly long jump, right after his show on Saturday night. He would not have the comfort of a sleeping car: too expensive. (In large part because they had to pay their own expenses, vaudevillians, a contemporary observer remarked, "are the best paid and the frugalest [sic], thriftiest workers in the world, I suppose.") On arrival, he would have to arrange for Teddy's boarding and then find lodging for himself. This was not in the most luxurious establishments: He thought he was splurging when he paid $1.50 a night.

He would play two shows a day, Monday to Saturday. Meals would be taken in cheap beaneries; fortunately, Will had a passion for chili. He would generally wake up around eleven and go to the theater to practice, for up to three hours. Then came the afternoon show. Before the evening show, there was time for a nap; afterward he would try to find a café that was still open and wasn't too expensive, and have a sandwich and a couple of beers, or maybe just some pie and milk. He would return to his hotel at two in the morning—"the lonesome time," he called it—and read, play solitaire, or work on a letter to Betty. At the end of a week, he would leave for a new town and the routine would start again.

The life certainly had its grim side, and Will sometimes was tempted to succumb to despair. But he was resilient. As he wrote to Betty, "You must not worry about me cause I am always all right and get by some way cause I have knocked around so much that I just take it as it comes." And in some ways, it wasn't disagreeable at all. In what other profession could one make good money, sleep late in the morning, get a chance to see the country, wear the clothes in which one was most comfortable, and be presented twice a day with a theater full of cheering, laughing people? As for the long train rides, the hotel-room waits, at least they offered an opportunity for reading—which Will for the first time in his life found himself enjoying. He had developed into a passionate consumer of newspapers, and in the course of his travels he mailed copies of six novels to Betty with his recommendations.

The books—*The Devil Together, A Little Brother of the Rich, The Round-Up, Richard the Brazen, Lure of the Dim Trails,* and *Paid in Full*—do not appear to have been chosen at random. They share a view of social class and excessive concern for propriety as barriers to happiness and love. This is a characteristic of popular literature of the period, a time of great social upheaval in American society, but it also had personal resonance for Betty and Will. Three of the books had western themes, including *Richard the Brazen,* about a New York society girl who, while visiting Texas, is saved from a cattle stampede by a mysterious cowboy. The fellow, who turns out to be a graduate of the University of Texas, follows her to New York, where he rescues her from her shallow, petty society crowd. Betty chose not to take this kind of bait, responding instead to the melodramatic cast of the tales. Will wrote back: "yes, dear, these books do show a lot of heartache and misfortune and it makes me sad to read them but it is just all what you make it, as you say, and God and Love is all there is after all."

Another pastime was baseball, for which Will developed a passion. The vaudevillian and the ball player had several similarities: Both were city-to-city nomads, in the business of entertaining the urban masses, frequenting the same cafés and hotels. Many were country boys, like Will, and he became friendly with a number of them. In big-league cities, he would attend games when the local nine was at home, and ball players often came to the theater at night, where he would kid them from the stage. One year, a vaudeville promoter briefly tried the experiment of putting on shows in the ballparks themselves (this was thirty years before the advent of night baseball), and the players hung around to watch. In some cities, the teams let Will come to their morning practice, where he would put on a uniform and shag flies in the outfield. "He was a good ballplayer for an amateur," Detroit Tigers third baseman George Moriarity said years later. "We kidded a lot with him, but he chased those flies like a veteran." From the ball players, Will picked up what would become one of his trademarks—gum chewing. Sometimes the vaudevillians would organize their own games, playing against troupes from other theaters; one newspaper account of such a game noted that Will "played a good game at first and threw the ball hard."

He didn't engage in very much sight-seeing, but, given that he was stopping in towns such as Lowell, Massachusetts, and Altoona, Pennsylvania, it's hard to blame him. There were exceptions. In Louisville, he went to Churchill Downs at dawn, met the owner of the horse that would win the Kentucky Derby the following week, and "had a fine breakfast right in the stables." And he had a memorable visit to Yellowstone National Park during a one-week layover between Duluth and Butte. He arrived one night before the official opening of the hotel at the park's Grand Canyon and for a day had the entire place to himself: "They even had the Orchestra to play while I was in a big dining room that would seat 300. All alone but them." He marveled at the geysers, and he had a chance to remake the acquaintance of Charles M. Russell, a western artist he had gotten to know in Manhattan, who in later years would become a treasured friend. He mailed to Betty eight postcards of Russell's work—jocular western scenes, a self-portrait, and a reproduction of Russell's famous painting *Waiting for a Chinook*, on which Will scribbled, "The original of this is worth thousands of dollars. It is certainly real."*

In a way, vaudeville reproduced the footloose male camaraderie that he had known in his cowboy days and that, one way or another, he tried to reproduce for the rest of his life. There was the additional element of

---

*One of the cards showed a party of well-dressed motorists trying to fix a broken-down car while an Indian family sauntered by on horseback. Will's handwritten caption was: "Me and my Squaw giving you and your swell bunch the horse laugh."

female companionship. Single performers on the road had virtually unlimited opportunity for amorous activities, and on more than one occasion Will took advantage of it. His romance with Louise Henry was serious, at least as far as she was concerned, and once he was imprudent
enough to forward to Betty a note from an actress named Nina (possibly
Nina Morris, with whom he shared a bill in Boston in 1905), who, he
wrote, "got a bit stuck on me." The letter itself was innocuous—"Am
very glad you wrote to me as you did it was just what I needed to restore
to me what little common sense I ever had," Nina confided. ". . . The
girl that wins your love may consider herself very fortunate, only wish
the average man were more like you." But it placed on the table a whole
subject that was better left unmentioned, and probably set his cause with
Betty back a year.

Vaudevillians saw themselves as comrades-in-arms, and there was a
great deal of sharing—of clothing, advice about stage business, intelligence about the peculiarities of theaters or hotels. Will saved as memen-
tos a business card upon which Joe Keaton, father of Buster and
proprietor of a celebrated knockabout act, had scrawled, "Dear Carl,
Give This Boy the Room you have—hes my friend," as well as a crude
cartoon entitled "The Western Circuit—Dope Sheet" he had evidently
found tacked up backstage somewhere. It listed seventeen pieces of mock
advice, including, "If 'your act' went big in the East, tell the piano
player"; "If 'your act' don't go the first show it's because they are coming in. If it don't go the second it's a sign you got 'em going"; and "If
it don't go at all, it's over their heads."

Another aspect of vaudevillians' solidarity concerned their status as
workers in an industry characterized by monopoly, unfair labor practices, and the blackballing of performers who took exception to any of
it. A labor organization called the White Rats was founded in 1900 and
on occasion displayed some militance, calling strikes in 1901 and 1916,
before succumbing to what one historian has called "the Keith-Albee oc-
topus" in the late teens. Although Will belonged to the Rats, he was not
an active member, in part because, unlike most vaudevillians, he came
from a part of the country where the concept of labor struggle was
unfamiliar, not to say incomprehensible. Nor was his nature confron-
tational. On one occasion, when an engagement was canceled at the last
minute, he didn't demand his salary, as was his right, because he didn't
want to "lose out in the long run." Only once did he stand up against
shoddy treatment, refusing to accept any salary at all when managers in
San Francisco decreed that all performers should have their pay reduced
for some no doubt arbitrary reason. The players at another theater

wrote a grateful letter to him: "You are truly worthy of being Captain
. . . you were the only one to refuse your salary, being surrounded as you
were by white rats of professed high standing."

"Vaudeville wasn't just a career or living," wrote the entertainer
June Havoc. "It was a way of life. It was home, it was school." She
might have added that it was a culture, with its own customs, values,
fashions, and superstitions. Will took to these quickly. He always
knocked wood before he walked onstage (a habit he carried with him
when he started making movies), and he absorbed the conventional wisdom of the trade—if you were a big hit in one city, you would flop in
the next; passing another performer on the stairs meant disaster; the
smaller theaters were often the best, and so on. He still did his act in
cowboy regalia, but his offstage dress quickly lost its rural quality. Other
performers thought of him as a fashion plate, and a reporter who interviewed him in 1907 commented on his patent-leather shoes and gold cuff
links. Another vaudeville tradition was the accumulation of diamonds—
they were simultaneously an advertisement of success, a repository for
savings, and a potential source of collateral. Will had a large ring
("slightly yellow," Betty remembered), horseshoe- and cluster-shaped
scarf pins, as well as a smaller one, and cuff buttons and two rings given
him by a woman friend.

A more conventional form of investment favored by vaudevillians
was real estate, and Will, always receptive to the notion of putting something safely away, participated enthusiastically. In December 1906, a pair
of vaudeville performers turned realtors sold him two lots in Nassau
County, Long Island, for six hundred dollars each—sixty dollars down,
and payments of thirty dollars a month. He didn't bother to inspect the
lots until one Saturday in June 1909, when he decided he should see
what they looked like. He found one in the middle of a farmer's corn-
field. He couldn't locate the other.

Less frivolous were his investments back home. As the years passed,
he accumulated more and more property, in anticipation of the day
when he would retire from the stage and go home to ranch. In 1906, he
wrote to Clem about land adjoining the old home place: "buy anything
you see there that looks cheap and borrow the money for me." Three
years later, he was still insistent: "I want to get all that land around there
if you can buy it for me. I think now is the time—it wont be any
cheaper. I want all that north pasture as I dont own the creek at all yet."
By 1910, he estimated that he had six hundred acres, rental houses on
the property that brought him twenty-five dollars a month, and three
thousand dollars in the First National Bank of Claremore. "I own every-

thing I've got outright," he bragged to a reporter. "I reckon if you sold me out tomorrow I'd have something like $100,000, more or less."

That Will was able to invest and save as much as he did is impressive, considering that he still had not hit the really big money in vaudeville. His initial rise had been rapid, and he was always a favorite with audiences and reviewers, but he found it hard to get to the highest level of the trade—headliner. This was a magical plateau that involved more than getting top billing. Being a headliner meant being a star. Will's roping skill, great as it was—and the fact that his act required a horse, an assistant, and a rope—worked against him, pegging him as a "specialty act," as opposed to the singers and monologists, the royalty of the business, who worked completely alone. But he had nowhere near the confidence necessary to strike out on his own. Indeed, he went in the other direction, surrounding himself with even more of a supporting cast. In April 1907, on the spur of the moment, he went to England with a kind of mini Wild West show: three horses and two riders, in addition to himself. The act was well received, but the expense of mounting it was too great. In a postcard to Clem, Will tersely summed the situation up: "No Money to be made here." He was forced to go on a tour of the provinces with just Teddy and Buck to make enough money to ship the whole troupe home.

One good thing did come out of his second English trip, however. Will arrived in London ahead of the horses and men, and Alfred Butt at the Palace engaged him to perform alone. He undoubtedly had some trepidations about going onstage without any props other than his rope, but he didn't have to worry. "Having no horses and no assistants at hand," said one newspaper, "Rogers was obliged to extemporise an entertainment, which none the less engaged the Palace audiences just as completely as ever." It was a piece of information that would before long prove useful.

Sailing to New York on the S.S. *Homeric* that spring was Rouben Mamoulian, a native of Russia and later to be a celebrated theater and film director, who was coming to America to direct operas in Rochester. On the night of the traditional ship's concert, he remembered years later, "A real American cowboy stepped up. This was the first cowboy I ever saw. He had a lariat, and he was chewing gum and doing rope tricks, and talking while he did it. He was so witty and so wise, so intelligent, that my heart fell, because I said, 'Where am I going, if a cowboy is like this? If this is a sample of a cowboy, I should go there to learn. How am I to teach anybody anything?'

"It really gave me a tremendous inferiority complex. In fact, one of

the things this cowboy said I still remember. He said, 'I always wondered why the British drink so much tea. Now I know, because I've
tasted their coffee.'

"You know, it took me seven or eight months to find out that the
cowboy's name was Will Rogers."

BACK IN THE United States, Will was stuck in a sort of rut. Especially galling was his inability to get an engagement with Martin Beck,
whose Orpheum Circuit controlled big-time theaters west of Chicago,
and who possibly felt that people who had some familiarity with cattle
and cowboys wouldn't be as impressed with Will's roping and patter as
Easterners had been. "It seems that I cant get west at all," he wrote
Betty. "They keep playing me over and over around here." When he finally did get west, it was on the less prestigious Sullivan and Considine
circuit.

Will couldn't even profit by a bidding war that sprang up late in
1907. Marc Klaw and A. L. Erlanger, who owned a chain of legitimate
theaters, had decided to try to break B. F. Keith's vaudeville monopoly
with something they called "Advanced Vaudeville." To lure performers
they were paying unprecedented salaries—as much as one thousand
dollars a week. The minimum they paid was three hundred dollars—
exactly the salary Will Rogers had been promised in the twenty-five-
week contract he signed on June 7.

In the middle of August, as Will was playing two weeks in Chicago,
a musical comedy called *The Girl Rangers* was in rehearsal in the city.
Since the show had a western motif, the producers had the sensible idea
of hiring Will to appear between scenes and perform his specialty. He
got enthusiastic reviews. One critic was impressed enough to recom-
mend that a speaking part be written in for him: "The man has temperament . . . and magnetism and every word he says, every glance of his
keen eye, every swift curve of his magic rope comes over the footlights
with a flash of power. It would be too bad to spoil a good vaudeville act,
but Rogers should be in a play. He is a show himself."

The producers didn't take up this suggestion, and, after a run of several weeks, Will was back in New York. On his birthday, November 4,
he clipped out a horoscope saying, "The man [whose birthdate this is]
will have an uneventful business year, not much different than the one
just gone." The horoscope was right.

Personally, however, the year was eventful in the extreme. He
lodged a final, full-scale, frontal assault on Betty Blake. Not much more
than twelve months later, she was his wife.

From the time that Betty had refused Will's proposal in the summer of 1906, their correspondence had followed a familiar pattern. He had continued to press his case. More often than not, he opened by complaining about the infrequency of her letters, often in a whining tone that cannot have helped his cause. Betty, for her part, was alternately coolly cordial and maddeningly coy. At one point, she asked Will what his "plans" were. His response was swift: "Kid, I havent any plans. My plans are in your hands. Shape them to suit yourself." To his annoyance, she refused to tell him her age. Periodically, she tried to make him conform to a more conventional model of suitor, scolding him for the unseemliness of talking too much about his business affairs, reminding him not to drink or gamble, and, as many editors would ache to do in the years to come, correcting his grammar and spelling. Once, annoyed by her lack of correspondence, he wrote, "Well I wont write so 'offul' (note spelling) much now." But in general, he tried to squeeze himself into Betty's model of what a proper beau should be, going so far as to parenthetically ask whether he had used the correct tense. "Honest Kid," he told her, "I am trying (and doing it) to be as I think you would like me to be. I have friends that I jolly around with and go around and have a drink (only beer) with but only to kill time and be friendly."

Every now and then, she dropped her emotional guard, and it was such moments that kept Will going. "Now listen Kid," he once wrote, "I dident like your last letter I got just now. You said you wanted to consider me your best friend. Now dont be silly. You know what you are to me and dont say those things. Oh one littel letter you wrote said 'I will be happy if you love me.' No I sho do keep that letter with me for I like it and if that will constitute your happiness you are the happy Kid. . . ."

But Betty was terminally ambivalent. In September 1907, when the Rogers *Democrat* asked a number of locals to describe their ideal wife or husband, Betty's playful response was so aggressively vague that it seemed she had given up on Will. "My Ideal Husband must be a man not too dark, and not too fair, not too fat, not too slim, not too old or not too young, not too lazy or not too energetic to be out of place in Arkansas." She concluded: "After long and painful waiting I've come to the conclusion that the Ideal man is the one who says, 'let's marry.' Then you may shake him or wed him as you may choose—or both, I'm told."

Early in 1908, the correspondence took on a new urgency. Betty—probably still peeved over the letter from Nina that Will had sent her a year before—not so casually mentioned Tom Harvey, referring to him as her "dearest friend." There was more to tell, she said, but it would

take too long to write it down; she would wait until she saw Will. Predictably, this sent Will into a frenzy of sarcasm. "By the way," he wrote,
"how are you doing with your lawyer? Well its even for I have fell in
love with an actorine and gone plum nutty." Betty took the bait and
wrote a hurtful letter of her own. In Will's response, written from New
Haven, he put petulance aside and declared his love with a new and almost inspiring eloquence, dignity, and force. The letter deserves quoting
at some length:

> *My Dearest* (and that goes)
> Well Betty I received your crazy letter and honest it knocked
> me a twister. You could not of been your same dear old self
> when you wrote it. . . .
> Now in the first place if you remember *rightly* this *coolness* of
> which I fully admit started when you refused to tell me of that
> T.H. [Tom Harvey] thing. Now you know that and I have al-
> ways treated you cooly since. Not because I felt like it but be-
> cause I just felt that I was *getting back* at you and I done the
> whole thing purposely and intended to do it in a way till you did
> tell me. For I honestly felt and do feel that it was *due* me. . . .
> Now *secondly* as to any other girl it is foolish to think of them
> ever in the same breath with you. . . .
> Yes, I got a lot of girls not one as you say but several *on* and
> *off* the stage. I dont mean this as *sarcasm* or conceit its just to put
> you right. Several *girls not sweethearts* or girls that when it comes
> to settling down I would consider for a minute. I kinder always
> thought I knew about where my love and affection lay, and I
> gave you credit for not being a jealous girl and take a thing that
> was put in a letter just for a little *sting* the same as you had put
> in mine several times the last in regard to the Lawyer. Now I am
> the jealous one of the two, and yet I took it as it was meant and
> come back at you with the actor gal one. But no, you size it all
> up wrong and write that offul letter
> You say I spoke of it as a mistake. Yes, so they were *lots* of
> them. I have done nothing all year but the wrong thing and
> then you say *thank goodness* it was discovered in time. You speak
> as if I had a dark plot to deceive you and you *(old sleuth)* had dis-
> covered it. . . .
> You say—("I was idescreet [*sic*] and for that you have never
> thought well of me, or at least have never believed me and when

I refer to other boys you invariably grow suspiciously *sarcastic and throw unpleasant insinuations.*"—

Now Betty plainly, *thats not so* and its the worst thing you could say. For of all the things I admire and Love you for its for you being *good* and *pure* and not silly and *spooney.*

Now I never in all my life insinuated a wrong thing in regard to other boys. It would be the last thing on earth. Why I would fight any one that would insinuate as much to me as that you acted the least bit unladylike at any time. *Why girl* thats why I *love* you. Thats why you are different from the rest. . . .

You size me up cause I showed you a silly letter once. . . . To show her how I knew her to be only fooling she was *mixed* up with to my own knowledge three fellows perhaps writing worse ones to them. No I know these girls in this business a *little.* And I think there is a little difference between you and them.

Now as you have said you would love to tell me that little story why then I know you will when I see you and for the first time in a long time I feel that you are dealing as square with me as I am with you. I came very near closing and coming out there but it would of been very foolish for I would of got in bad here as I have this time to play.

Now Betty I want you to cut out all this foolish talk for when I tell you you are the only girl for me I mean it regardless of how I act sometimes. Now I think I will see you some time soon and oh wont we have a jolly time and oh wont it be great.

Must go do my show now and mail this. Write at once
your same old boy
Billy*

The letter clearly had an effect. Will came home in April because his father was ill. He had a warm visit with Betty, and he left for the road with a good feeling about his prospects. There was just one relapse. In September, he and Betty had a dispute, again about a woman, and it sent Will into a state of fevered despair and self-admonishment. It was a side of himself that he had never displayed before and would never display again. "You are right when you say that I have not treated you square," he wrote.

*Tom Harvey would eventually move to West Virginia (birthplace of his father), marry, and maintain a good enough relationship with both Betty and Will to be invited to opening night of the *Ziegfeld Follies* in 1916. In 1942, at the age of 60, he committed suicide.

No I have not Betty. It seems that I havent treated anyone square. I have *lived* a *lie* and now I am reaping the harvest of it. Please make a little allowance for me dear. I am not myself now and seem to have no mind of my own. I am *scared* and dont know what to do.

Betty this is all what comes of doing wrong. I done the greatest wrong that any one could do and I have wished and prayed a thousand times since that I have not done it.

No I am no man. I am the weakest child you ever saw. If you knew me better I am easily led and can be pulled into almost anything. I have no mind of my own. I just drift and drift. God knows where too. Now listen dont you think of deserting me in all this. I need you and I will be my own self again. . . ."

It may be that Will's despair was like a cleansing downpour, washing away the accumulated detritus of the relationship and allowing him and Betty to start anew. It may be that his self-flagellation struck a chord somewhere deep in Betty; certainly, in the light of the shape their relationship eventually took, his declaration that he was "the weakest child you ever saw" appears significant. In her book, she gives a simpler explanation: that Will had once again become disenchanted with the stage and talked of returning to Oklahoma, that at last he was coming around to her way of thinking. In any case, their odd and protracted courtship very soon was over. Early in November, Will went home again. Not accidentally, he had cleared his calendar until the thirtieth, when he was to open at Proctor's in Newark. On the tenth, without any advance notice, he dropped in on Betty and asked a familiar question. But now, as she remembered the conversation, he promised that, after finishing a tour he had signed to do, he would return to Claremore. This time, the answer was yes. They set the date for November 25, the day before Thanksgiving.

Will was overjoyed. "Oh Betty," he wrote from Chelsea, where he went to tell his family and make preparations, "I am so happy and so glad that it is so soon now, aint you? Cause I just could not wait long for you the way I want and love you now. My folks are so well pleased and just think it fine and love you and think you are grand. They have always been kinder afraid I would grab on to some old show girl or some bum and now that they know it is you they are tickled to death." This was an accurate assessment. A few days after Will broke the news, his brother-in-law Cap Lane—evidently the card of the family—sent

Betty a warmly facetious letter "warning" her of her fiancé's "irrational" behavior:

> I cannot remain silent when I see a girl, trusting her future hap-
> piness into the hands of one who at times is mentally incapa-
> ble. . . . he sits around in a deep study for a few minutes, then
> jumps up, singing and dancing at other times he seems to be in
> an ecstatic condition of mind paying no attention to anyone and
> seems to me like some one walking in his sleep, you know how
> it is. Again, as you know, he has a weakness for beans, the other
> day at dinner he helped himself four times, and then reached for
> the dish and eat all of the beans, topping this all off with a sauce
> of onions.

Cap, of course, was just an in-law. Betty knew that the approval of
Sallie, Maud, and May—who would always think of "Willie" as their
cherished little brother—would be harder won. And so she was doubtless gratified to receive Maud's touching note: "I am sure you are the
only woman for my dear boy, you see I think I love him just a little
more than the other girls for I cared for him when he was a dear baby."

On the day of the wedding, Will, Clem, Maud, and May were to arrive in Rogers on the 11:30 a.m. train. (One of Sallie's children had scar-
let fever, and so she and her family were quarantined.) There was a
momentary scare when the 11:30 arrived and the party was not on it.
But it turned out that the train was in two sections that day, and Will
and his family were on the second one. They obtained a marriage license, Will accurately giving his age as twenty-nine, Betty subtracting a
year to arrive at twenty-eight. The ceremony was at Betty's house at one
o'clock, a Congregationalist minister presiding. Will wore "a dark traveling suit," Betty a blue-and-white silk dress. Afterward, Betty's old
friend and employer Erwin Funk wrote in the Rogers *Democrat,* "Mr.
Rogers and bride left on the northbound evening train for New York
City, where the groom is a prominent figure on the vaudeville stage. We
understand they will make a trip to Europe before the groom returns to
Oklahoma next spring, where he owns a large farm and where they will
make their future home.

"The bride was born in Rogers and has grown to womanhood here.
She has always taken a prominent part in the social functions of the city
and is one of the best known young ladies of Northwest Arkansas. Her
attractive personal qualities have made her a general favorite and she
will be missed by an unusually large circle of friends."

CLOWNING AT A PICNIC

CHAPTER 6

TOGETHER

FROM ROGERS the couple took a train to the town of Monett, Missouri, fifty miles away, where Will had reserved a stateroom through to St. Louis. Suddenly, they were in his world, a world of porters and waiters and railroad coaches. Betty was a spectator, slightly awed but not, she found, uncomfortable. "It was nice," she wrote, "to be reminded that he was an experienced traveler and a man of the world."

Both a year short of thirty, Betty and Will wanted to make up for lost time, to pack as much experience into their first year of marriage as it would hold. The activity started the next day, Thanksgiving, when they went to see a football game in St. Louis between the Carlisle Indian School and Washington University. In the evening, they had Thanksgiving dinner in their hotel room, Betty partaking of champagne for the first time and drinking more than she should have. Afterward, they had tickets for *What Every Woman Knows,* a J. M. Barrie play with the celebrated actress Maude Adams that had opened in New York earlier in the year and was now on national tour. Shortly after the curtain went up, the effects of the alcohol kicked in, and Will had to take Betty back to the hotel.

Then it was on to New York. On their arrival at Pennsylvania Station, Will, in his eagerness to impress his bride, wouldn't settle for one of the hansom cabs cruising up and down the avenue. He insisted that she sit down and wait while he searched out one of the brand-new automobile cabs just beginning to operate. It drove them about a mile down Broadway to a small hotel on a side street just off Union Square. On the way, Will pointed out Madison Square Garden, scene of his first New York triumph.

They found the days weren't long enough for all the things they wanted to do. Will took Betty to Chinatown and the Bowery and Wall Street, to the Statue of Liberty and the top of the forty-seven-story Singer Building, at that time the tallest building in the world. He showed her the hotel near the Battery where he and Dick Parris had stayed on their way to Argentina. "We heard the bells of Old Trinity ring in the New Year and out the Old," Betty wrote. "Will took me to the Bronx Zoo and we had horseback rides in the arena at Durland's Riding Academy, and on nice days in Central Park. And although it made Will utterly miserable, we went many times to grand opera."

The last comment, played for laughs by Betty, suggests some slight tension that still colored the relationship. While her wide streak of conventionality had narrowed a little bit, it was still there—indeed, it was one of the attractions she held for Will. But he had never had much personal concern for propriety, and three years on the road had added a patina of show-business slickness over his cowboy coarseness. Accustomed to the middle-class gentility of small-town Arkansas, Betty was suddenly living in a theatrical hotel in New York with a diamond-ringed vaudevillian. A sharp reminder of the life (and a beau) she had left behind was delivered soon after they came to town, when Tom Harvey's mother and his sister Annette arrived in New York on a visit. "I remember Mrs. Harvey's shocked expression," Betty wrote, "when she discovered that Will had taken Annette and me to dinner at the Metropole Cafe. This was a rendezvous for newspapermen, gamblers, sportsmen and actors. Battling Nelson stopped at our table and Will had introduced us. Mrs. Harvey said, 'Betty, what will your mother think of you meeting a prizefighter?'"

Whatever trepidations she may have felt were not assuaged when she finally witnessed Will's act. She hadn't seen him perform since the St. Louis World's Fair, four years earlier, and—being the recipient of so many glowing notices clipped from newspapers—may well have expected a grand and theatrical turn. However, when she sat in the audience at Proctor's Theater in Newark and saw him do the routine, she was singularly unimpressed.

But none of these disappointments was substantial enough for her to entertain any serious doubts about the rightness of her choice. The same went for Will. And the same would go for both of them for twenty-seven years.

A happy marriage is like a sphere—no rough edges to grab on to, almost dizzying in its regularity, ultimately impenetrable. The opaqueness is intensified when husband and wife are as militantly private as Will and Betty Rogers were (a privateness not contradicted by the unprecedented publicness of Will's career). There is, in other words, no cryptographical archaeology sophisticated enough to decode the precise calculus of mutual attraction, private negotiation, and subtle adjustment that made their union such a resounding success.

But they left clues along the way. The first was the alacrity with which they put the emotional turmoil of their courtship behind them. The transformation from painful and protracted ambivalence to near-placid stability would not have been so sudden if both Betty and Will hadn't—whether they realized it or not—deeply yearned for marriage. Each came from a family that had been dealt a blow (more seriously in Will's case) by the premature death of an opposite-sex parent, and of all the happy discoveries of their first months of marriage, the happiest was surely the blessed ease with which they found that long-forgotten sense of wholeness could be recaptured.

After just a few weeks of engagements in and around New York, they headed west. Will had finally been hired by the Orpheum Circuit, and the tour was to be their real honeymoon. It was a wonderful trip, though a little frenzied in its nonstop activity; it seemed as though, in the space of a few months, Will wanted to show Betty everything he had learned and done in three years on the road, and to reveal the aspects of himself a courtship correspondence could not accommodate. "His life had been full," she wrote, "and he wanted me to know all about it—the bad along with the good—every little thing as far back as he could remember. Although Will and I had been friends for a good many years, we had not been together a great deal, and actually I had known little about the boy I married." To the relief of them both, she liked what she found out. There were more pleasant revelations. The theatrical way of life was by no means as bad as she had feared. Indeed, traveling the country with a trunk, away from the constrictions of Arkansas life, was liberating.

Having an adoring husband was nice, too. "I never see Bill. He sticks to her day and night," Will's assistant, Buck McKee, wrote to his wife in February. "They seem to be very devoted to each other."*

The low point of the tour came in Butte, Montana. Following a savings plan practiced by Will's sister Maud, the couple had put a dollar a day into a big metal box that they carried in their trunk. The day they arrived in Butte, they went out—to go ice skating, Betty remembered; to attend the performance at the Orpheum, reported the local newspapers. In any case, they left both the door to one of their rooms and their trunk unlocked. In their absence, someone came into the room and took the

---

*Buck also reported passing on to Will a letter from "Louise" (Henry, presumably). "She says she is sick of her bargain. She dont like her 'rich Jew doctor.' Bill just laughed & tore her letter up. He said 'well poor girl I cant do anything for you now.' He did not answer her letter."

box, which contained not only two hundred dollars in cash, but other items valued at five hundred dollars: "a gentleman's gold watch, lady's chatelain watch, a locket in the shape of a horseshoe set with chipped diamonds, another locket set with solitaire diamond settings, a stickpin consisting of a gold piece, pair of opera glasses, and a number of fancy handkerchiefs." The two lockets Betty had had made from Will's scarf pins. Will's large diamond is conspicuous in its absence from this list; possibly it was in hock at the time of the theft.

They had planned to return to Oklahoma soon after the end of the tour. But when they got to New York, there was an offer from Percy Williams, a vaudeville impresario known for his generous salaries. Even Betty agreed it was too good to pass up. And so the return was postponed.

It would be postponed quite a few more times in the years that followed. Will's ambivalence about going home was to be expected. And as each month passed, Betty was more and more accepting of the theatrical life. She had taken up the task of writing to Clem, and her letters bubbled with the pleasure she was beginning to feel. "We have had such a good time here that we sorter hate to leave," she wrote from Atlantic City in the middle of July. "We have been going in the water every day and its great. Im not afraid now and I go out and swim with Billy. He has taught me how to float and swim on my back. Oh, we have had some great times and are both as black as niggers." "I feel so well all the time," she wrote another time. "I have real nice rooms and so enjoy housekeeping. We sure have lots of good things to eat. Im a pretty good cook." She raved about local landmarks they saw on their travels and sent him souvenirs, as well as a packet of "good newspaper articles about Billy." And she served as a kind of emotional conduit between father and son, firming up connections that had always been tenuous at best, telling Clem the things Will couldn't. "Your letters have been such a comfort to Billy," she wrote after the death of Will's sister May Stine, after a sudden illness, in July. "He loves you and admires you so much. He reads your letters over and over."

By this time, Clem's long career in public life was over. It had climaxed in 1906 and 1907, when he had served as a delegate to the convention called to write a constitution for the proposed state of Oklahoma. He was the oldest delegate, but his presence was far from honorary. Noting his shrewd and not necessarily proper appropriation of some additional land for the county formed from Cooweescoowee district, a newspaper remarked that he had "displayed more activity and generalship in one way than any man in the convention." Toward the end of the convention, on Clem's sixty-eighth birthday, a Chelsea delegate moved that the county be called Rogers, in his honor. The motion passed unanimously; the legacy of John Ross was finally defeated. Clem made a characteristically ungracious speech, noting that residents of the county had been clamoring for such a name change. He closed by saying, "I congratulate you gentlemen on giving me this honor." In November 1907, the voters accepted the constitution, and Oklahoma became the forty-sixth state.

Will's vocational success had not immediately resolved the tension between father and son. In the early vaudeville days, the money Will sent home ("this will make me $1250.00 in all wont it," he wrote in one accompanying letter) was a weekly declaration he had made good—in the only language he thought his father understood. Clem withheld his enthusiasm, however, to the point where Will repeatedly had to ask him if he even had received the funds. At Christmas 1905, Will mailed his father an overcoat, and Clem returned it as unsuitable. Will could not hide his hurt: "I got the coat allright and cant imagine why it did not suit you. I am keeping it to wear myself and I gave mine to a friend. It was not as fine as some for lots of them cost 3 and 4 hundred dollars and I could not afford a fine one but I thought it would do."

Gradually, however, as he began to comprehend just how successful Will was, Clem had come to accept his son's career. William "Alfalfa Bill" Murray, who presided over the constitutional convention and was later governor of Oklahoma, remembered that during the convention Clem received a five-hundred-dollar check from Will. "Uncle Clem in a very serious tone asked me, 'Bill, do you suppose Will is making all that money honestly?'" His doubts on this score were removed when he, Sallie, and Maud traveled to Washington, D.C., not long afterward and saw Will perform. Back at the hotel, he started asking questions about ticket prices and theater capacity. Then, as Will remembered it, he turned to Maud and said, "I used to think they paid Willie a pretty good salary, but you know, now I figure it out, the managers must make an awful lot of money out of Willie." He eventually became a kind of prairie press agent for his son, cornering friends on the streets of Claremore and insisting that they read a sheaf of battered clippings he would pull out from his wallet.

Early in 1911, Will was thinking of making a European tour. No doubt aware that his father didn't have many years left, he wanted him, Sallie, and Maud to go along: "we will just all go over and have one big time." The trip fell through, but perhaps the invitation was the important thing. And Clem probably was not too disappointed. His life had settled into a comfortable routine. He lived in a small suite of rooms above the bank, where he continued to work on an informal basis. He took his meals in a hotel across the street; for amusement, he liked to have a high-stepping horse called Roger K drive him around town. Each Saturday, he would take the train to Chelsea and follow the same routine. Maud would meet him and take him to her house for supper. He would stay overnight there, go to church, then spend Sunday night at Sallie's house. After the noon meal on Monday, he would go back to Claremore.

He was an honored citizen, and the seventy-second birthday party his daughters gave him on January 11, 1911, was a major local event. The Chelsea *Reporter* covered the affair in great detail, noting that a telegram from Will and Betty was read, and that "Quite a number of friends from town called during the afternoon to offer their congratulations to Mr. Rogers on having passed his 72nd mile stone and still retaining the erect carriage, health and vigor of early middle life."

There were more good tidings a few months later. Betty announced that she was expecting a baby: "Billy wants a boy of course, but I do not care which it is. If it is a boy I am going to name it after Billy. I would name it for you but there are so many Clems in the family I'm afraid they would get mixed up." In October, with the baby due soon, Clem picked up the pace of his letters, writing once a week, sometimes more often than that. "I may go around to some of the Fairs if the weather dont get to bad," he wrote. "I dont want to expose myself if I can avoid it. A Man my age ought to be careful how I look after the Health and care of myself." He seemed to feel the need to write even when there wasn't much to say: "Today is Thursday," he reported on the nineteenth, "and a real nice day the Sun shines so very nice." Previously, he had always ended his letters with the words *Your Pa* and his signature. For this letter, he closed differently: "Love to Both."

The next day saw the birth of William Vann Rogers. So the Rogers name would continue. As soon as Clem heard the news, he bought a pair of beaded moccasins and two pairs of stockings and sent them to the boy by registered letter. His next letter, dated 25 October, was addressed, "Dear Willie & Bettie & William," and had about it an air of measured finality. He and Buck Sunday had, he reported, reassembled a substantial portion of the old property: "Now Willie dont Fret about the Old Home Place as it is in good Shape and if we can find Rosa Patterson [who owned ten acres he still wanted] we then can have the Tittle all perfect & you will have one of the best farms in this state. I still hold to my Rock Barn and what few houses I have here in Claremore. My rent amounts to about $114.00 per month."

The following Sunday, Maud Lane's daughter Estelle went upstairs to wake her grandfather up and found him dead. The funeral was set for Tuesday at 3:00 p.m., and the mayor of Claremore issued a proclamation asking every business in town to close its doors at that hour. Clem was, according to an obituary, "a pioneer who was a statesman and a man. He was a standing refutation of the theory that the Indian cannot take care of himself. . . . He was a great man from any point you choose to look at it and his going away is like the extinguishment of a great light."

WILL IMMEDIATELY traveled to Oklahoma after his father's death. But, as soon as his grieving was done, he went back to New York, where his family was ensconced in their first real apartment, at 551 West 113th Street, near Riverside Drive. Talk of leaving show business had stopped. Now, Will was concentrating on finding some way to transcend the status of midlevel vaudeville act. Late in 1909, he had attempted a replay of his English disaster of a few years earlier, again trying to mount his own Wild West show. The main gimmick was to be the oddity of putting on such a show inside a theater; a secondary gimmick was that all the trick riders and ropers were female. The act was popular but too expensive—the payroll alone was $367 a week, Will figured out on a piece of scratch paper—and unwieldy to produce. Over the next few months, he gradually pruned the troupe until he was back to his old act.

This time, Teddy was not a part of it. The year before, Will had put the now-elderly pony out to pasture at the ranch. One day, the fence broke and Teddy and another horse wandered off. Desperate to get him back, Will asked his father to put a notice in the paper offering a $125 reward for his return, no questions asked. "Do this," he wrote. "I dont want that old pony to be out all winter." Soon afterward, he was home for a visit and went to the Chelsea Fair with his nephew Herb McSpadden, who took care of the ranch. "He and I passed a fortune teller's booth—25c," McSpadden recalled more than six decades later. "He said, 'Let's go in here and maybe we can find out something about our horses.' The gypsy took his hand and began to tell him what his palms read. He said, 'Oh I don't care anything about that. We've lost some horses.' She turned about half around and looked up at a little hole in the top of the tent about a minute and finally said, 'Your horses were not stolen but have wandered away. You'll get them back.' 'When and where do we look?' She looked at the hole again, there was a little streak of sunlight showing through. Finally she said, 'That's all I can tell you.' " The fortune-teller was right. A year and a half later, McSpadden found out that Teddy had been taken up as a stray in the next county over; a sharecropper had bought him for twenty-five dollars at a sheriff's sale. He bought the pony back for fifty dollars, and from then until his death in 1917, Teddy led a peaceful and uneventful existence.

After just a year or so with a new horse, Will finally made the inevitable decision. Yes, roping a horse was a novelty; yet for years audiences had responded more to what Will said than to his tricks. His fee had plateaued at three hundred dollars, an amount that could go incalculably farther if it didn't have to support an assistant and a large animal. He engaged a more aggressive agent, Max Hart, who placed a large ad in the newspapers, announcing, with forgivable redundancy, the change in format: "WILL ROGERS, The Droll Oklahoma Cowboy, IN HIS NEW SINGLE OFFERING, ALL ALONE, NO HORSE."*

Betty attributed the idea to a Philadelphia theater manager who commented to her when they were standing in the wings that he much preferred Will Rogers alone than in the company of horses. But some credit should also go to Fred Stone. Stone, best—if at all—remembered today as the father of Katharine Hepburn in the film *Alice Adams,* was one of the major stars of the day. Born in 1874, the son of an itinerant Kansas barber, he joined the circus as a high-wire walker at the age of ten. Later, he and Dave Montgomery formed a very successful blackface song-and-dance act. But because of their participation in the White Rats—both were founding members—they were blackballed by Albee and Keith. So they went into musical comedy, starring in a string of hits—*The Girl from Up There; The Wizard of Oz,* where Stone was a sensation as the Scarecrow; *The Red Mill,* which Will saw on a layoff in New York in 1906, and *The Old Town.*

Stone was an "eccentric" dancer, more like Ray Bolger than Fred Astaire, specializing in acrobatic knockabout routines with a premium on novelty. In *The Red Mill,* he made his entrance by falling down an eighteen-foot ladder. In another scene in the show, he swung down a moving wing of a windmill with a girl in his arms. There was also a boxing dance, put together with the help of former heavyweight champ

---

*"Will Rogers sold a couple of ponies last week," *Variety* reported on May 27, 1911. "He needs them no longer in vaudeville, where Rogers is now appearing as a 'single turn,' assisted by a few lariats and some talk. Johnny Collins and Geo. McKay are the boys who think they picked up a bargain in the bronchos. They are now negotiating for the saddles, not having previously thought of it."

"Gentleman Jim" Corbett, a pal of Stone's. While in Louisville on tour with the show, he happened to catch a play that featured a young man named Black Chambers spinning a rope. Always on the lookout for novelties, Stone immediately grasped that this could be a stunt for his next show, *The Old Town,* and he engaged Chambers to instruct him in the art.

Chambers was a native of Claremore, and he advised Stone to look up Will Rogers. One day, when the course of instruction was almost finished, Chambers, while attempting the very difficult trick of turning a flip-flop through a loop, burst a blood vessel in his throat. He went back to Oklahoma and died soon afterward. By this time, rehearsals for *The Old Town* had begun. "I was sitting out at the stage door when a fellow wearing a blue suit, no vest, and a straw hat, came up, whipping his leg with a newspaper," Stone wrote in his autobiography.

" 'Fred Stone in there?' he asked the stage doorman, who glanced at me and said, 'I don't know. Who wants to see him?'

" 'Will Rogers.'

"I jumped up. 'Hello, Will Rogers. I'm Fred Stone.' "

That was the beginning of the best—possibly the only—close friendship of Will's adult life. Much more accomplished in show business than Will, Stone was another father figure, but more of a contemporary than the likes of Texas Jack, Zack Mulhall, or Willie Hammerstein. Indeed, a characteristic he and Will shared—and that doubtless contributed to their intimacy—was an exuberant boyishness. They exercised this fully a few summers after their meeting, when Will rented a house in Amityville, Long Island, across the street from the Stones'. "Every morning," Stone's daughter Dorothy told interviewer Bryan Sterling, "Will would come over with his little rope whistling under Daddy's window. Now Daddy was to sleep till noon, because he was working so hard at night. Mother would stick her head out the window and she would say softly, 'Will Rogers, you go away and come back at 12 o'clock! Fred's asleep.' Then Daddy would stick his head out and say, 'I'll be right down!' And the two would ride and rope all day." They would swim, too, in a saltwater creek in the back of Stone's house. One day, Will, whose experience in the Verdigris gave him no knowledge of the vicissitudes of tides, took a running start and dove into the creek when the tide was low. His right arm was temporarily paralyzed, which obviously meant he couldn't rope. Unwilling to give up his bookings, he laboriously taught himself to twirl the lasso left-handed.

In 1911, when Will decided to make a go of it as a single, he did so with Fred Stone's encouragement. In return for Will's finishing up the course of instruction that Black Chambers had started, Stone taught him some steps. And a feature of the new act was dancing, notably an imitation of the rope dance he himself had helped teach Stone. In addition, Will gave his impression of how the dance would be done by George M. Cohan (to the tune of "You're a Grand Old Flag"), Eddie Foy, and what he termed a "Yiddisher cowboy." (Thankfully, no description of the last routine survives.)

That wasn't all. Will had decided, probably correctly, that with the horse and rider gone, his act needed some new features. So he roped while rolling a cigarette with one hand. He roped on a unicycle and on a stepladder. He seems to have briefly experimented with imitating the sound of orchestra instruments. For a time, he even sang, in the nasal tenor he liked to pull out periodically. Coon songs were now passé, but in 1912 there was a vogue for something called the "Houn' Dawg" song, a moaning Ozarks lament (and possibly the ancestor of Elvis Presley's hit of four and a half decades later). Its refrain was:

> Every time I come to town
> The boys keep a-kickin' my dawg aroun';
> Makes no difference if he is a houn'
> They gotta quit kickin' my dog aroun'.

Dozens of parodies were printed in the newspapers, and the Democrats adopted it as an unofficial anthem for the presidential campaign. One night in Springfield, Massachusetts, Will handed a newspaper clipping of the song to the leader of the house orchestra "and after listening to the few bars of it [Will] said he guessed he could sing it, as 'rotten as that,' or words to that effect. Rogers probably hasn't acquired the true Ozark moan as yet, but he made a hit because of the fun he injected in to the song."

Will's first appearance as a single was at Chicago's Majestic Theatre in June 1911. To what must have been his great surprise and relief, none of the critics missed Teddy. Indeed, none of them seemed to notice his absence. Will was such a hit at the Majestic that he was held over for another week, only the second time—according to an advertisement placed by Max Hart—that had occurred in the history of that theater.

Will's dance routines and other bits of business went over. But the real appeal of the new act was the talk, which was like nothing else on the vaudeville stage. True, the vaudeville monologists—George Fuller Golden, Charlie Case, James J. Thornton, and Fred Niblo were among the most prominent—stood on the stage and spoke, just as he was doing, but there the similarity ended. Some told lengthy stories of debatable humor in carefully constructed personas—the shrewd Yankee, the lazy darky, the cornball rube. Others specialized in gags that featured risqué puns and winking, orally italicized punch lines.* The effect was self-consciously facetious. Will—self-effacing and understated—was always himself, or something very close to it, and he almost never delivered a joke of the traditional kind. What he resembled, more than his vaudeville peers, was the stand-up comedians who set a new model for show-business humor decades later.

Similarly ahead of its time was the sense of spontaneity Will exuded. Unlike the studied humor of the monologists, his remarks appeared insistently extemporaneous, almost improvisational. No one knew quite how to take him. In a Columbus, Ohio, paper, he was featured in a color cartoon with the heading, "The peculiar thing about the cowboy act at Keith's last week was that you couldn't make out whether he was in earnest or just 'kidding.' " One critic wrote that he "stands alone and unique in his ability to take liberties with his audience and any and all artists on the stage." Once he shared a bill with an act called the Cherry Sisters—whose distinction was their complete lack of talent but who were blissfully unaware of that fact. Will remarked that the act must have been named before lemons were discovered—whereupon, according to a newspaper account, the older sister had him arrested. Will didn't merely kid members of the audience and other acts on the bill: He would stop a lasso trick in the middle and literally rope them onto the stage, where he would conduct a mock interview. It was an oddly appropriate gesture, for, on a metaphorical level, his off-the-cuff asides and gentle barbs roped in his audience: They were subtly inclusive, inviting his listeners to join him in shared laughter.

But Will's ad-libs were not precisely what they seemed. This fact was discerned by a perceptive Milwaukee critic who, while he enjoyed the act, contended that Will's "apparently ingenuous manner is not ingenu-

---

*One example: A 1907 jokebook used widely by vaudeville performers included this gem: "Last winter I met a charming gentleman, a southern planter. He was an undertaker from New Orleans."

And here is a portion of one of Thornton's monologues from around 1900: "While coming to the theater tonight, I got on a car, the car was full, so was I; every seat was taken, so was my watch, the man alongside of me had a mouth full of sailor's delight. He was endeavoring to expectorate on the ceiling, not having the necessary five hundred for doing it on the floor, the unexpected expectoration of the expectorator, in the opening of the man's map hit the conductor a wallop in the eye. I beg your pardon, says he. My fault says the conductor, I had no right getting in front of a hose."

ous at all, and his running fire of comment, which he reels off, as it were, on the spur of the moment, is simply a manifestation of a good memory. His jokes are always the same, even to his relieving himself of the cud-let of Yucatan [i.e., chewing gum] as 'excess baggage' when he trips over the lariat at exactly the same place."

Proof of these assertions is provided by a typewritten undated document, entitled "Old Vaudeville Act," that Will left in his papers when he died. It is a rough verbatim account of his act (judging from internal evidence, circa 1915), and it leaves no doubt that much of what passed for spontaneity was something quite different.

Here—with spelling and punctuation, but not grammar, cleaned up—is how it went.

After coming out onstage, he climbed a stepladder, from which he threw a crinoline. Just before the rope was all the way out, it fell to the ground. "Gee, I crabbed it," he said. "Had it pretty near all out. Well, there aint much use doing it all over again just for that much.

"My act is getting too big for this circuit anyway.

"It's a pretty good trick when I do it good.

"I got it good the other night. You should have been here then."

He dismounted. "I don't hardly know what to do next. There is not a great deal of intelligence about this act anyway. I keep putting in a lot of stuff and most of it turns out to be rotten and I have to cut it out and I forget where I cut it out at."

By this time, Will was using a little political material, characteristically presenting it in a kind of thesis-antithesis-synthesis sequence. "You notice the act kinder drags right along here," he said. "Well, I used to tell a joke right in here and it got so it did not go so I cut it out. I used to tell a joke about Roosevelt, but I don't tell it anymore. I wonder what become of him." Pause. "Well, he was a good fellow when he had it." Longer pause. "Well, sometimes they come back, but not often."

What's striking is not so much that Will planned his comments in advance, as that almost all of those comments referred to what he had just done and said, and thus relied for their effect on the *appearance* of being unplanned. Since the beginning, he had prepared jokes about missing his tricks; now he prepared jokes about his jokes falling flat.

"You know it's hard to get ahold of a good joke nowadays," he said. "I been on the bill with some of the best acts in vaudeville and have not had a good one yet. I thought I would get a good one here tonight but I have not heard one yet. That French gal knows a lot of good ones but they won't let me tell them."

Then Will moved his position on the stage. "I'll get back here a little so a lot of actresses here can see this. I won't call any names but that blonde that was just out here better go slip a kimono on or she will catch cold."

Will did his unicycle stunt ("I got one pretty good trick on this egg beater here—I could do better if I had something to lean against"), then his Eddie Foy imitation ("another great comedian—there is only a few of us left"), then a new, unspecified, trick. "I got a new one here I been working on for some distance. I tried it last week and spilled it all over the place." At this point, by prearrangement, the orchestra started to play. Will affected annoyance. "Wait a minute. I haven't got to it yet. You horned in with that music too soon."

Referring to a vogue of the day, he said, "I am going to get a moving picture of this trick and just stand and tell about it."

Will closed with a crack he'd been using for ten years: "You know, I am a little bit handicapped up here. The manager don't even let a fellow to cuss a little when he misses."

But he made provisions for an encore. "Had no business coming back here," he said on his return to the stage. "Should of let well enough alone. That's the way with an old country boy: brag on him a little bit and he will work his fool head off."

His encore finale was his Yiddisher cowboy bit, which he topped off with a joke. "I know that will sound strange, talking about a Yiddisher cowboy, 'cause cowboys don't get that much money. Well, this fellow is not doing so bad. That was three years ago and he owns the ranch now. It was a big hog ranch."

"You can tell that's a new one," Will said. "Every time the orchestra laughs."

EARLY IN 1912, while Will was playing in Texas, in his audience one night was the singing star Blanche Ring, a forty-one-year-old veteran of vaudeville and the stage who was best known for the song "I've Got Rings on My Fingers." She decided he would fit perfectly in the second act of a new musical called *The Wall Street Girl* she was preparing for Broadway. As in *The Girl Rangers*, Will wouldn't have a part as such, merely appear during a scenery change and do his regular act. Still, playing in a Broadway show was a new career pinnacle, and Will was nervous on opening night. Characteristically, he admitted it onstage. Referring to the respective ticket prices charged in vaudeville and on Broadway, he said, "I knew it was all right at fifty cents, but I was a little afraid of it at two dollars." Nor were conditions ideal. During the performance, word came through that the *Titanic* had sunk, and Will was given the terrible task of announcing the news. Some of the audience left; others went out during the intermission and returned with newspapers. More than four decades later, Blanche Ring still remembered the sound of the pages rustling.

Despite it all, the show was a modest success. And Will was a palpable hit. He got so many rave reviews that Max Hart took out a half-page newspaper ad to excerpt them. The *Tribune* said he "produced the only real humor" in the show; the *Times* said he "undoubtedly scored the success of the evening." Acton Davies of the *Sun* had lost his program and didn't remember Will's name but wrote, "There was a poet with his lariat who had come out of the West and inserted himself in the middle of the play just when 'The Wall Street Girl' was beginning to die hardest. . . ." On Will's instructions, the last eleven words were not included in the ad.

The show took a break for the summer, Betty and the baby repairing to Rogers, which would be their home base for the next two years, and Will playing vaudeville dates. In September, *The Wall Street Girl* embarked on a seven-month national tour. Now Will had top billing after Blanche Ring, a speaking part, and two musical numbers—another milestone.

The tour ended on April 26, 1913, in Evansville, Indiana. On May 18, Will was playing a vaudeville date in Houston when his second child, Mary Amelia Rogers, was born in Arkansas. With his family growing, he felt that even though he was doing well—a review' would soon refer to him as "the most popular entertainer on the vaudeville stage to-day"—he needed something that offered more money and stability. A Broadway career would be nice, but there were no offers to follow up *The Wall Street Girl.* So he threw himself back into vaudeville, with a fervor that bordered on the obsessive. In one week the following January, he did two shows a day at each of three different theaters in New York—the Alhambra, the Victoria, and the Union Square, where he had started his vaudeville career eight years before. In addition, he gave a performance for a motion picture—probably his first, it does not survive—and some tricks for an organization called the Comedy Club, making a total of forty-four shows for the week. His fee had risen to $350, so the combined paycheck was impressive.

No one could keep up such a pace. Besides, there were now unsettling portents in the air. Will was actually the final act ever to appear on the stage at Keith's Union Square: the following week, the theater dropped vaudeville and began to show motion pictures exclusively. As a newspaper noted, "The change in policy is significant of the trend of the times." Later that year, his old patron Willie Hammerstein died of tuberculosis, and soon afterward Hammerstein's closed its doors. There would be no more publicity stunts or freak acts. The acts on the last week's show were billed as "Willie's Old Favorites." Under Will's name in the program were the words, "He Always Made Willie Laugh—On Stage and Off." In his scrapbook copy, Will underlined the sentence.

In the summer of 1914, more or less on the spur of the moment, Will took Betty, who had never been abroad, to London. On their arrival, his old patron, now Sir Alfred Butt, offered him a part in a revue called *The Merry-Go-Round.* He had fifth billing (Nora Bayes was the star), but was once more taken up by the British papers, one of them remarking that "there is a perfectly delightful person, a genius at rope-throwing and as laughable a patterer as we have seen, whose name we take to be Will Rogers." Will had to stay with the show—it ran for a month—but Betty took a sight-seeing trip to Paris with the wife of the comedian Frank Tinney.

On their return to America, Will hit the road again. By the spring of 1915, Betty was pregnant, and Will was getting discouraged. He played Arkansas in April, and a newspaper reported, "Will Rogers may be playing his 'farewell engagement' here, for the young ranchman is feeling the call of the prairies and states that in one year more he will have enough money to leave the limelight and devote himself to his Oklahoma ranch." That summer, Will, Betty, Billy, Mary, and James Blake Rogers—born on July 15—lived in Amityville, across the road from Fred Stone. Stone counseled his friend not to accept any more offers on the road: He should stay in New York, waiting for a part in a show. Will followed the advice, but it was at considerable financial sacrifice. Until that part came, there simply weren't enough big-time vaudeville dates in and around New York to support the brood, a stable of horses, and the new Overland automobile he'd just bought. There were small-time theaters, but for "Will Rogers" to appear in them would be humiliating. So he'd play the houses under an assumed name, for as little as seventy-five dollars a week.

He finally got a call in July. J. J. and Lee Shubert, probably the most prominent producers on Broadway, were preparing a new musical called *Hands Up.* There was a spot near the finale that needed brightening, and on J. J.'s suggestion Will was hired—the decision being made so close to the opening that his name was not even included in the program. But he was a hit. He did so well on opening night that he continued to perform beyond the number of minutes allotted to him. At one point, handicapped by the shallow space between the footlights and the drop, he muffed his rope dance three times in a row. J. J. Shubert, standing in the wings, ordered that the lights be blacked out.

It was the wrong decision. Fred Stone was in the audience, and he was outraged that this indignity had been committed against his friend. He leapt to his feet and began chanting, "We want Rogers! We want Rogers!" The audience picked it up. The critic Burns Mantle wrote that the "other actors tried to go on with whatever they were using for a plot, but the crowd would not hear of it." Shubert himself had to go to Will's dressing room and apologetically ask him to return for an encore.

Will was only in *Hands Up* for two weeks, but the lights-out incident had the same galvanizing effect as the loose bull in Madison Square Garden ten years before. When the summer was over, Will committed himself to staying in New York, leasing a small house in Forest Hills, Queens, twenty minutes from Manhattan. Homer Croy—later to be Will's scenarist, biographer, and friend, but then a not very successful young writer—also lived in Forest Hills at the time, and he remembered seeing this odd cowboy practice his roping and exercise his horses every day on the vacant lot across the street from Croy's house.*

In August, after he left the show, Will was contacted by Gene Buck, the principal writer of the *Ziegfeld Follies,* a New York summer fixture since 1907. The year before, Buck had started something called the *Midnight Frolic.* It transpired each night after the conclusion of the *Follies,* on the roof of the New Amsterdam Theatre. Patrons sat at tables, ordered drinks, danced, and were entertained by a variety of musical and dance numbers. Buck had the intuition that a drawling cowboy roper would provide a perfect contrast to the show's general air of pulchritude, and offered him a job doing his regular vaudeville act, plus a rope dance with a chorine named Sybil Carmen. Will took it even though the salary was only $175 a week, far below his vaudeville pay. As Buck pointed out, there were no traveling expenses, and, because the only performance was after midnight, he could accept other jobs, too.

He got one in late September. The noted director Ned Wayburn was putting together a show called *Town Topics,* a revue the likes of which had never before been seen, featuring ninety-six chorus girls, twenty-four chorus boys, twenty-four principals, six hundred costumes, and a revolving stage. According to *The New York Times,* it was to be an "all-the-year-around Follies." Will was hired not just as a fill-in but as a

---

*"One peculiar repercussion came from his roping," Croy wrote. "The children in the neighborhood were fascinated, and Will began to teach them. Almost every day, there they would be roping, or trying. The clothesline loss was appalling."

featured performer, a kind of master of ceremonies who also had four musical numbers. (In an early version of the script, he had a sizable speaking part as a cowboy from Oklahoma who was disappointed by the tameness of New York: "I called a lot of guys on Fifth Avenue every name I could think of, and not one of 'em tried to get me.") He wore evening clothes in the show. When he took off his top hat, a rope was revealed on top of his head.

As usual, he got glowing reviews, at least four critics pronouncing him the hit of the show. "Best of all," wrote the *Times*, "is the engaging Mr. Rogers, who is so genuinely amusing and likable that he has carried off the first honors at all the first nights he has enlivened since spring." The Brooklyn *Eagle* suggested just why he was so likable—his "foolish, self-conscious laugh and an extemporizing way of discussing the rehearsals and other things about the show that makes the audience feel that it is being let into the inner secrets."

But *Town Topics* was not a smash, and Will left the show even before it closed because he was asked to take a 50 percent pay cut. At about the same time, the great Ziegfeld finally took in Will's part of the *Frolic* for the first time. Although Will had gotten good reviews—Heywood Broun in the *Tribune* called him "the most emphatic hit in the show"— the humor escaped the producer. Even more damning was the disappointing crowd reaction. The incongruous cowboy, Ziegfeld told Gene Buck, had to be let go. But Buck realized that much of the problem was that the *Frolic* attracted repeat customers, and Will's routine changed little from night to night. He got his boss to agree to a reprieve and went to tell Will that he, Buck, would supply him with some new jokes. But before he could get a word out, Will asked for a fifty-dollar-a-week raise. This stunned Buck sufficiently that Will had time to talk a little more. "My wife says I ought to talk about what I read in the papers," Buck remembered him as saying. "She says I'm always reading the papers, so why not pass it along?"

Buck said he should give it a try.

THE FOLLIES COWBOY WITH DANCER
ANN PENNINGTON

CHAPTER 7

ZIEGFELD

ANY SEARCH for similarities between Florenz Ziegfeld, Jr., and Will Rogers would be futile, except, perhaps, for the fact that Chicago's World's Columbian Exposition of 1893 changed both of their lives. It was there that Will had seen Vincente Oropeza perform with Buffalo Bill, there that he had become aware of how much could be done with a rope. Ziegfeld, twenty-six years old at the time, had a more direct involvement. His father was a German immigrant who in Chicago had become a rather prominent sheet-music publisher, music-school proprietor, and composer. To coincide with the fair, he established a theater called the Trocadero, and he dispatched his son to Europe to engage a roster of performers. This was something of a risk. Up until that point, young Flo had shown little aptitude for anything besides haunting Chicago music halls and bordellos and spending his father's money. His most notable business venture was to put on an exhibition called "The Dancing Ducks of Denmark." When the local SPCA discovered that the ducks (which came not from Denmark but from a local farm) danced because gas flames were directed at their feet, they shut the show down. In a later, no more successful promotion, he set up a large bowlful of water and advertised it as "The Invisible Brazilian Fish."

Florenz senior expected his son to return with the Continent's most distinguished classical artists. Instead, he had engaged what was basically a series of vaudeville dumb acts—acrobats, jugglers, and someone called "The Great Zanzic," who was advertised as producing "startling unaccountable phenomena by invisible agencies." But these acts, performing each night at the Trocadero near the art museum, proved unaccountably popular, especially when Flo added a headliner, a young German who was billed as "Sandow, the Perfect Man." Sandow was capable of remarkable feats of strength—juggling with one hand while balancing a man in the palm of his other, for example—and had a massive sculpted physique of the kind not yet visible in quadruplicate on every newsstand. Ziegfeld, his promotional genius coming into evidence, instructed

Sandow to wear nothing except a pair of tight silk shorts. On opening night, he announced from the footlights that any woman who pledged three hundred dollars to a charitable fund could have the privilege of coming backstage and feeling the strongman's biceps; two of the grandest ladies of Chicago society took up the offer. After a greatly successful run, Ziegfeld took Sandow on a national tour. On the way to California—or so Ziegfeld told Will years later—a wheel broke and fell off their railroad car. Ziegfeld hired a crew of men to carry it to his stateroom. In Oakland, he announced to the assembled members of the press that Sandow had brought it in himself. They swallowed the tale whole, and Ziegfeld was on his way to becoming the greatest showman of the age.

For the next ten years, he was occupied, professionally and personally, with Anna Held, a coquettish French cabaret singer with whom he had a common-law marriage and whom he had groomed, through careful selection of vehicles and careful engineering of publicity stunts, into a major American star. (One of the strangest of the latter was an attempt, with an actor named Julius Steger, to break the record of one thousand kisses in a row. It was sadly unsuccessful. After the 150th kiss, she wrote later, "I was muscularly exhausted, overwhelmed with such nausea that I could not stir.") In 1907, Ziegfeld and the songwriter Harry B. Smith had the idea of re-creating in New York a show with the atmosphere of a Parisian revue. Klaw and Erlanger hired him at two hundred dollars a week to stage it over the summer at the roof garden of the New York Theatre. The production, called *Follies of 1907*, was a huge hit, and the next year Ziegfeld produced a new edition. In due time, it was a national institution. Every year (until 1925) Ziegfeld would present a new *Follies* that opened in Atlantic City, played New York for the summer, then toured the major cities of the East and Midwest.

Ziegfeld—whose narrow face, with thin lips, small intense eyes, large nose, and overbite, gave him a slightly rodentlike aspect—didn't write songs or dialogue for the *Follies* or his other shows. He didn't direct. He found humor hard to understand and his own sensibilities tended toward the coarse. What he had were unmatched theatrical instincts. He instantaneously knew when a number would go over and when it wouldn't, and he was a formidable talent-spotter, especially when the talent was female.

A key to the success of the *Follies* was the creative team he put together—Smith and later Gene Buck and Dave Stamper wrote the book and original songs; Julian Mitchell and later Ned Wayburn did the choreography; and, after a few years, Joseph Urban designed the sets.

But even more important, in the public eye at least, was the chorus, originally billed as the "Anna Held Girls." There was an endless stream of girls whose costumes—despite outsized feathers and wings and other odd accoutrements—covered less and less of them as the years went by. The drama critic Channing Pollock associated the *Follies* with "that indefinable aroma of impropriety, filliping as the smell of sawdust at the circus. With what a thrill one approaches the box-office to ask for two 'down front, for I'm a little hard of hearing!' " Yet the special genius of Ziegfeld, himself a sensualist, was to transmogrify sexuality, retaining its power and allure but turning it into a public spectacle, at once kitschy, witty, and unthreatening. There was nothing lurid or lascivious about the *Follies*, Ziegfeld insisted; it was merely intent, in the words of the subtitle the show acquired in 1922, on "Glorifying the American Girl." A more penetrating critic than Pollock, Edmund Wilson, remarked in *The New Republic* that Ziegfeld chose girls with "the peculiar frigidity and purity, the frank high-school-girlishness which Americans like. . . . He appeals to American idealism, and then, when the male is intent on his chaste and dewy-eyed vision, he gratifies him on this place by discreetly disrobing his goddess."

The apotheosis of the *Follies'* distinctive blend of titillation and refinement came with the *tableaux vivants* designed by Ben Ali Haggin, a New York society painter retained by Ziegfeld in the midteens. Haggin would people the stage with Ziegfeld girls, put some in period costumes and some in no costumes at all, reverently illuminate them as they stood frozen in space, and thereby reproduce famous works of art and historical scenes. Sex and "art"—it was a dazzling combination.

Ziegfeld tried to establish that the *Follies* was not just a girly show, in part by illuminating the proceedings with stars. For the first production he engaged Nora Bayes, famous for her rendition of "Shine On, Harvest Moon" (and later to star in the 1914 London production of *The Merry-Go-Round*, with Will Rogers). Nearly every year thereafter, a new principal performer was added to the cast. In the *Follies'* first eight years, among those featured were Fanny Brice, Leon Errol, Bert Williams, Ann Pennington, Ed Wynn, and W. C. Fields.

Satirical skits were topical and clever—newsmakers such as Teddy Roosevelt, Enrico Caruso, and Anthony Comstock were made sport of, and there were spoofs of other Broadway shows. But where the wit of the *Follies* shone brightest was in the production numbers, spectacles that transformed current pastimes and concerns into elaborate visual conceits that grew more outlandishly rococo with the years. In 1909, the chorus wore baseball outfits and played catch with people in the audience while singing "Come On, Play Ball with Me, Dearie." The same year, Lillian Lorraine, a stunning young actress who had replaced Anna Held in Ziegfeld's affections, "flew" over the audience's head in an airplane while the chorus sang "Up, Up, Up in My Aeroplane."

In 1913, the *Follies* moved to the New Amsterdam, near the corner of Seventh Avenue and Forty-second Street, a magnificent Art Nouveau theater constructed ten years earlier. The New Amsterdam was actually two theaters: a large main stage for the *Follies* and a smaller "Aeriel Garden" on top of it, reached by taking an elevator eight stories up. The roof was dark for a year until Ziegfeld sensed that his *Follies* customers could be prevailed on to stay around after the show and dance. (The great dance craze of 1912–1916 gave the country the fox-trot, the turkey trot, the tango, and Vernon and Irene Castle, and gave New York scores of cabarets.) He had the roof garden's orchestra leveled and its seats removed. Tables were placed along the sides and in the balcony, and the center became a dance floor. The "Danse de Folles" commenced each night at 11:30. For a one-dollar admission charge, patrons could take the elevator up, dance or listen to a live band, and sit either in the theater or among the actual gardens outside.

This enterprise was such a success that Ziegfeld made it a year-round institution, open for business even when the main theater was dark. He had Joseph Urban make further interior alterations so that performers could be accommodated; notable was a runway encircling the dance floor, made of glass so patrons could look up at the parading chorus girls. And he had Gene Buck, a twenty-nine-year-old songwriter from Detroit who was known for having pioneered the convention of illustrated sheet music, recruit the performers and write what material had to be written. The first *Ziegfeld Midnight Frolic* premiered on January 5, 1915, and was an immediate hit.

The *Frolic* had no skits, but there were songs, production numbers, and individual turns by *Follies* stars and lesser-known performers being groomed for a role in the big show. It was more intimate than the *Follies*, smaller in scale. The stage wasn't elevated, and the audience was part of the entertainment—they danced between acts, an activity given its own program listing. They participated in the show itself, as well. In one number, chorus girls had (male) audience members hold their yarn while they knitted; in another, they sat on the runway and dangled fishing lines over the tables. Patrons were provided with wooden hammers—banging them on the tables was a novel way of applauding—and inter-table telephones. A famous bit of audience participation came about fortuitously. For one number, Buck had the idea of attaching gas-filled balloons to the girls' costumes. A tipsy patron accidentally touched and exploded a balloon, and from then on balloon popping was encouraged. (In 1917, when the country was gripped by the thought of oncoming war, miniature Zeppelins replaced the balloons.)

In pre-Prohibition New York, the *Frolic* was the height of sophistication—a good deal more so than the *Follies*, which was known to cater to out-of-towners. It was the place to go. In the fall of 1915, shortly after Will joined the show, his sisters Maud and Sallie and Theda "Dick" Blake (Betty's unmarried sister, who would spend more and more time with Betty and Will over the years, in time becoming the children's second, unofficial mother) visited New York and went to see the *Frolic*. Just as they stepped into the elevator, Sallie wrote home to her children, "a fine looking, broad-shouldered man" greeted Will with a handshake and a smile. It was William Randolph Hearst. On a Wednesday night in January, Mayor Mitchel of New York and his wife were the guests of Cornelius Vanderbilt, while Jay Gould and party were at another table. The rest of the city came to rub elbows with these social titans, and not merely figuratively: On the elevator ride to the roof, it was possible to spend twenty seconds breathing the same rarefied air as Ethel Barrymore or Diamond Jim Brady.

In retrospect, Buck's idea of putting Will in the second edition of the *Frolic*—it was entitled "Just Girls" and, except for Will, a singer, and a wire walker, it was—appears a stroke of genius, first of all because of the flawless fit between his act and the revue's intimate air. Through a gradual and haphazard process, vaudeville had pioneered the kind of insistent informality that would characterize American popular entertainment for the rest of the century; the *Frolic* was one of the first arms of the legitimate theater to pick up on the change. Will, of course, had thrived in vaudeville because his conversational, improvisational style suited the form so well. On the New Amsterdam roof, where performer and spectator were on the same level (in both senses of the word), and where he was illuminated and set apart from the crooners and acrobats by a brighter, sharper spotlight, his approach was not just effective but electric.

Equally significant, but a little more complicated, was the way his amiable homespun played off against the satin sophistication of the show. When Will roped a champagne bottle underneath a table out front, he was animating a piquant mixed metaphor (whose charm he recognized by making the bit one of his trademarks). But it was more than a matter of aesthetic contrast. The "indefinable aroma of impropriety" that marked both the *Follies* and the *Frolic* was not achieved effortlessly. American culture was still watched over by the forces of moral purity in 1915; indeed, their moment of greatest triumph lay just five years ahead, with the enactment of Prohibition. Ziegfeld knew he was stretching the limits of acceptable entertainment, knew it was incumbent on him to demonstrate that his productions were respectable. Heretofore, his favorite way of doing so had been showering them with money in the form of stars and production numbers. Will Rogers was cheaper and (it would turn out) he made the point better.

Once again, the pattern had been set in vaudeville, which if anything was more risqué, lacking as it did the high-gloss trappings of Ziegfeld's shows. Unlike almost everyone else who spoke from the stage, Will had always put forth a spotless line of patter, and his manifest purity (subliminally reinforced by his cowboy garb and his newspaper image as a family man) assuaged customers who might otherwise have been inclined to fret about the other sights and sounds they had partaken of. Best of all, as far as the audience was concerned, Will didn't denounce, or even ignore, the naughtiness that surrounded him. He winked at it. (One of his first jokes had been a complaint that the management wouldn't let him curse when he missed a trick.) At the New Amsterdam, surrounded by a roomful of imbibers and a sea of pulchritude, the line he had to walk became thinner—he needed to retain his wholesomeness, yet paradoxically refrain from reacting in the way a truly wholesome person would. That he carried it off splendidly is clear from the rough transcript of his routines he left among his papers. "The reason Mr. Z keeps me here is the people seem to after seeing my *act* . . . drink more," one of them began. "These girls certainly got on some aggravating *desires*. You know I am going to stick with this fellow. I am off all the shows that go in for art. I am for Ziegfeld and dames. You know this fellow knows just how to drape em so you don't know just whether they have or have not." Will was a wisecracking Virgil to a theater full of wide-eyed Dantes; and his very equanimity amid all that flesh served to let them off the moral hook.

The balancing act, and the ease with which he performed it, prefigured an important element of the unprecedented national popularity he would shortly begin to build. A world traveler and a show-business veteran, he had been around, knew the score, had seen it all. Yet the Americans who responded to him most enthusiastically were people who had not seen it all, who, in fact, were threatened by the very Broadway-Hollywood values Will Rogers could be accused of representing. Not only did no one make any such accusation but Will's familiarity with the forces of sin made it seem they might not be so bad after all.

He was probably unaware of the moral transactions that were going on below the surface. By now, he wasn't a cowboy or a rancher or a farmer anymore. Entertainers didn't go in for premeditation or analysis; they followed a simple creed—use what works and discard the rest.

At the *Frolic,* there was one last component to Will's unexpectedly complex persona—the abundance of topical commentary in his act. This was no hayseed, the knowing jokes announced; rather, a savvy student of the body politic. However startling this may have been to the New Amsterdam audiences, in truth it wasn't out of character at all. Political talk was in his blood. He had grown up in a household animated by Cherokee politics, and he had no trouble transposing a remark his father might have made about Chief Bushyhead into a joke on President Wilson.

It was Will's good fortune that he joined the *Frolic* at a moment in the country's history when the news was particularly full of noteworthy figures and events. Colorful politicians such as Teddy Roosevelt and William Jennings Bryan were still national presences; the not-yet-triumphant temperance movement was always good for a laugh; and since the United States had still not entered the European war, the sundry diplomatic maneuverings of Wilson's White House were fair comic game, too. And then, as always, a steady procession of New York scandals and society doings occupied the newspapers' front pages. In December 1915, Henry Ford dispatched his famous "peace ship" to Europe, an aggregation of pilgrims charged with ending the war by Christmas, and it gave Will the raw material for his first widely repeated topical joke—a not particularly inspired crack to the effect that if Ford had sent some Ziegfeld chorus girls and had them march between the trenches, he would have had more success getting the boys out. As time passed, Will learned that he didn't have to tie his remarks to the immediate circumstances of the show, and they got sharper and funnier.

There were, he found, two keys to a joke's success. The first was to launch his exaggerations and flights of fancy with a fact or an impression that the audience recognized as true. The second was to be current. If he talked about something from that day's newspaper, he'd get comic credit for immediacy; the older the subject was, the funnier the gags had to be. Also critical to his success was the audience's perception and appreciation of his spontaneity. Thus, while he prepared jokes ahead of time, he realized that the lines that seemed to come to him out of nowhere often got bigger laughs, even if they were throwaways. In a magazine article he wrote about his comic strategy, he told of his line on the day it was reported that German submarines could not operate in the warm Gulf Stream: " 'If we can only heat the ocean we will have them licked.' That didn't get much of a laugh and I was kinda stuck—but I happened to add, 'Of course, that is only a rough idea. I haven't worked it out yet.' This last went big and covered up the other."

But since the *Frolic* had so many repeat customers, new material was needed for every performance. Will read every edition of every newspaper and, he told a reporter, "more newspaper extras than any man in the world." Sometimes he may have been too current, as he acknowledged in a "saver" he liked to use when a joke didn't get a laugh: "I guess I'm a couple editions ahead of you folks." But even with all his reading, by January, when he had been in the *Frolic* five consecutive months, he was finding it hard to come up with new lines every night. "I wish a few more nuts would break into the news soon," he said in another interview. "Why, the Ford peace ship has kept me alive for a month, and poor Bryan has been my meal ticket for years."

In any case, he was a great success. Soon after he started with the *Frolic*, the *Times* was calling him the show's "chief source of entertainment." It's unlikely that the mirthless Ziegfeld had come to appreciate Will's humor, but he did appreciate a hit, and when the next edition of the *Frolic* premiered in January 1916, Will was making more money—$275 a week at the start of the run, $350 a week by May—and had a more prominent place in the show. Besides his monologue and rope dance, he sang a song called "The Thousand Squirrels Have Starved to Death Since the Peace Ship Sailed Away." He also figured in a sight gag that got the evening's biggest laugh. The curtain rose on a series of life-sized drawings of women, placed in descending order of clothing, culminating in a nude. One by one, real-life counterparts stepped through the drawings. "By the time the last bit of lingerie is reached and the nude approached," the *Evening Mail* reported, "there is a general shifting of seats to improve the view, when through that particular drawing steps Will Rogers as a masked marvel of the Western range, where they know more of cattle than they do of chickens."

Will's interplay with the audience became a great feature of the *Frolic*. This was nothing new for him—in vaudeville he had customarily introduced and verbally sparred with any celebrities he spied in the crowd. Now, though, there were celebrities at almost every performance. At one show, he brought to the stage eighty-one-year-old Chauncey Depew, a former senator who was considered the grand old man of New York, and at another Charlie Chaplin, who was induced to untie a chorine Will had roped. He once spied the actress Ruth Draper and the famous Broadway priest Father Francis Duffy sitting separately in the crowd. He had them both stand up, asked them whether they knew each other, and, being told they did not, introduced them. Will soon realized that some likely victims might escape his notice, so he instructed the ushers to send back to his dressing room slips of paper with the seating locations of any celebrities they spotted. This strategy wasn't necessary with the capacious Jim Brady, who until he died in 1917 was a *Frolic* regular and a favorite Rogers target. One time, Will recited a poem of Brady's that he had managed to get his hands on, and another time he said, "I always go to all the first nights. I go with Mr. Brady. He sits in the first row and I stand at the back and if anybody cops a diamond I am supposed to rope 'em before they get away with it."

As comedy material, this is a long way from being prime. But imagine sitting at your table on the roof, glass of champagne in hand, maybe twenty feet away from the legendary Brady himself, and seeing him laugh uproariously. Entertainment experiences more memorable than that were not easily had.

Brady surely was laughing uproariously. Far from being unpleasant to be singled out by Will, it was a considerable and sought-after distinction. This would be the case for years to come. As the novelist John O'Hara later wrote, "A big shot, a major industrialist type, was not a confirmed tycoon until he had been kidded by Will Rogers, and there was a great deal of snob value to a Rogers rib, like owning a private Pullman car and having your daughter presented to the court of St. James, and belonging to the Links Club."

Will "kidded," yes, but he was always solicitous and extremely careful not to give offense; he never singled anyone out, he wrote, "unless I know them personally and know that they will take a joke as it was meant." This would be his characteristic stance toward the prominent men who increasingly began to populate his life and his work. He was rarely other than humorous, for he wasn't foolish enough not to realize that humor was his special gift, his way in. But all barbs were generally removed from the jokes in advance, and the potentially hurtful ones were carefully monitored. Before the United States entered the war, Roosevelt and others thought the country should be better prepared militarily. Will told of seeing a soldier walking down the street with a typewriter under his arm and asking him what it was. "Oh," came the reply, "just a Wilson machine gun." But when tensions between the United States and Germany began to heat up and Wilson became the object of more intense criticism, Will promptly dropped the joke from his act. To someone who complained about the omission, Will snapped, "It's a hell of a time to kid the president."

The thrill he got from his association with those he called "big men," especially politicians, the way he courted them with his jokes and his attention, suggests that in Will's mind there were still unresolved issues in connection with the most prominent politician he had known up until then. In the last years of his life, Clem Rogers had finally bestowed a tacit approval on his son and his trade, but was that enough for Will? He may have needed to seek out substitutes and, over and over again, replay a self-made drama of solicitation and acceptance.

Ziegfeld, a titan compared to Zack Mulhall or Texas Jack, was another surrogate. Nearly humorless, demanding, and involved in what was, to say the least, a colorful private life, the producer was the object of some derision among his employees—but not for Will. To others, he was "Ziggy" or worse; to Will, he was "Mr. Zeegfield" or "Boss." In later years, when Ziegfeld was at rock bottom, wiped out by the stock market crash and ailing, Will was one of the few former *Follies* stars to stand by him. After his death in 1932, Will handled his funeral arrangements.

In the spring of 1916, Will had the chance to court the biggest man in the country. He was part of an all-star touring show put together by the Friars Club, a theatrical organization he had belonged to for years. They didn't play Washington because the National Theater was booked, but they did play Baltimore, and President Wilson attended the show. His presence was remarkable, not only because he had to travel fifty miles but because it was a particularly stressful moment in his presidency. He was preparing for an election campaign, meanwhile battling William Jennings Bryan for control of the Democratic party. In foreign affairs, he was involved in a furious exchange of diplomatic notes with Germany over submarine attacks on British ships, and also dealing with the Pancho Villa incident. The revolutionary/bandit had recently raided the town of Columbus, New Mexico, killing sixteen people. An expedition under the command of General John Pershing was organized to pursue him into Mexico, but it had been withdrawn following the objections of the Mexican president.

Eight years later, in a column he wrote on the occasion of Wilson's death, Will recalled that he was deathly nervous before the performance. Today, chiefs of state are expected to be good sports, but not then: "I had never heard, and I don't think any one else had ever heard of a president being joked personally in a public theatre about the policies of his administration."

His first remark to the audience, in fact, was "I am kinder nervous here tonight." "Now that is not an especially bright remark," he wrote,

". . . but it was so apparent to the audience that I was speaking the truth that they laughed heartily at it."

Then I said, "I shouldn't be nervous, for this is really my second presidential appearance. The first time was when Bryan spoke in our little town once, and I was to follow his speech and do my little roping act." Well, I heard them laughing, so I took a sly glance at the President's box and sure enough he was laughing just as big as anyone. So I went on, "As I say, I was to follow him, but he spoke so long that it was so dark when he finished they couldn't see me roping." That went over great, so I said "I wonder what ever become of him?" [This was a line he'd used on Teddy Roosevelt for years.] That was all right, it got over, but still I had made no direct reference to the president.

Now Pershing was in Mexico at the time, and there was a lot in the papers for and against the invasion. I said, "I see where they have captured Villa. Yes, they got him in the morning editions and then the afternoon ones let him get away." Now everybody in the house before they would laugh looked at the president, to see how he was going to take it. Well, he started laughing and they all followed suit.

"Villa raided Columbus, New Mexico. We had a man on guard that night at the post. But to show you how crooked this Villa was, he sneaked up on the opposite side . . . We chased him over the line 5 miles, but run into a lot of government red tape and had to come back. . . . There is some talk of getting a machine gun if we can borrow one. The one we have now they are using to train our army in Plattsburg. If we go to war we will just about have to go to the trouble of getting another gun."

Now mind you, he was being rode on all sides for lack of preparation, yet he sat there and led that entire audience in laughing at the ones on himself. . . .

After various other ones on Mexico I started in on European affairs which at the time was long before we entered the war. "We are facing another crisis tonight, but our president here has had so many of them lately that he can just lay right down and sleep beside one of those things."

Then I pulled the one which I am proud to say he afterwards repeated to various friends as the best one told on him during the war. I said, "President Wilson is getting along fine now to what he was a few months ago. Do you realize, people, that at one time in our negotiations with Germany he was 5 notes behind!"

How he did laugh at that!

Will was not exaggerating Wilson's appreciation. A newspaper account of the performance noted that "the President was pie for Will Rogers, every point or gag Rogers pulled bringing a laugh from the President." After the show, Wilson briefly came backstage and George M. Cohan, the "Abbot" of the Friars at the time, thanked him for coming all the way from Washington. His response, according to Cohan: "I'd travel ten times that distance to listen to as wise a man as Will Rogers." Will missed the backstage appearance but was invited to President and Mrs. Wilson's box for a private interview. He nervously parked his chewing gum inside his straw hat, and chatted for a few minutes. When he left, still agitated, he put the hat back on his head. For the next five minutes, a newspaper reported, the rest of the cast "was engaged in prying the comedian from his headpiece."

Wilson, not known for his sense of humor, honestly seemed to enjoy Will. He saw him perform on four subsequent occasions, and quoted his jokes in a speech and a cabinet meeting. For Will, the presidential connection meant more—the performances for Wilson were "the happiest moments of my entire career on the stage."

THERE ARE two versions of how Will joined the cast of the *Ziegfeld Follies*. According to Betty, Ziegfeld approached Will in the spring of 1916 and asked him to perform in that year's edition of the show, set to open in July. She was against it. Joining the *Follies* would mean a lengthy national tour, and they were "having the best time we had had up to then" in Forest Hills, with their horses and children. Will saw her logic and declined. But when they attended the *Follies'* opening night (with Mr. and Mrs. Tom Harvey as their guests), he regretted his decision: "Will grew nervous and irritable as one top-heavy number followed another, and he was cross with me because he was not in the show. He knew he could have picked it up. He kept whispering and nudging me, all during the evening: 'See, Blake, what did I tell you. This was my one big chance.'" A few days later, Ziegfeld, agreeing with Will's assessment of the absolute need for something to lighten up the show, asked him again. This time the answer was yes.

The alternate version came from Ziegfeld's publicity machinery. (It appeared in almost identical wording in at least six different newspapers.) According to it, Ziegfeld, happening to encounter Will in the New

Amsterdam lobby during a *Follies* performance, jokingly suggested that he mount the stage and make an impromptu appearance. Will took him at his word and "his success in the revue was so pronounced that Mr. Ziegfeld insisted that he continue with the organization."

For the *Follies,* Will would do just what he had been so successful with in the *Frolic:* a twelve-to-fourteen-minute monologue, punctuated by a few rope tricks. He gave Ziegfeld a two-year commitment, for which he would be paid $600 a week the first year, $750 the second. At Will's request, there was no written contract. This fact has traditionally been put forth as evidence of Will's old-fashioned belief that a hand-shake between honest men was worth more than a piece of paper. But he had signed contracts before and would again. The likelihood is that he didn't want to be bound to Ziegfeld, in case something better (and closer to home) came along.

But, at least at first, nothing did. Working both the *Follies* and (when he was in New York) the *Frolic* over the next three years, Will made good, steady money for the first time in his life. He earned $34,000 from Ziegfeld in 1917 and $44,500 in 1918.* But the *Follies,* then nearing the peak of its national success, gave him something rarer than money. It made him a star. Less than a year after his debut, *The New York Times* was declaring that, in the *Follies,* "Mr. Rogers' name leads all the rest."

Will served a similar purpose as he had in the *Frolic,* with one addition. It was Edmund Wilson who discerned that the bigger show had some of the qualities of a very large and soulless machine. He felt the *Follies* dance numbers represented "not the movement and abandon of emotion, but what the American male really regards as beautiful: the efficiency of mechanical movement" and that the show as a whole was "expensive, punctual, stiff," like an express train. In such an environment, Will supplied a much-needed and otherwise lacking spark of spontaneity and human contact.

Now that he had been provided with such a formidable platform and spotlight, a recognition grew among the critics that he was more than a simple comedian. Once he had been compared to the Virginian; now the references were more elevated. While he was still in the *Frolic,* the *Times* likened him to Mark Twain and the well-known humorist George Ade and approvingly quoted one of his quips—"If I were Lloyd George I'd give Ireland Home Rule, and reserve the motion picture rights"—on the editorial page. *Everybody's Magazine,* in a piece called

*That year, he requested a two-hundred-dollar tax deduction for "Newspapers & pereiodicals [*sic*] used daily for material."

"The Philosopher with the Lariat," said his satire brought to mind
W. S. Gilbert. Channing Pollock dubbed him the "poet lariat," and the
popular New York *Tribune* columnist Heywood Broun, an enthusiastic
Rogers fan, praised his "comment on American life." One writer, getting a little carried away in his enthusiasm over Will's apparent improvisation, stated that "he deserves the attention of all serious students of the
modern school of dramaturgy. He is the only actor at large in New York
who is dedicating his time to the revival of an ancient art. He is the
greatest living exponent of the commedia dell' arte, a form of dramatic
entertainment that flourished in Italy during the fifteenth century."

He was no longer merely one of dozens of vaudeville stars, but a celebrity. And so his comings and goings were recorded in the newspapers,
which realized that he made copy of the very highest order. The papers
cooked up "feuds" with Frank Tinney and Willie Collier, another comedian. One day, readers were informed of Will's arrest on a charge of
"boisterous conduct." He had "moved on" after a policeman's request
but refused to do so a second time, and was brought before a judge who
asked him, "Ever had any trouble with the police before?" "Only haul-
ing them home in my car on Long Island and playing at police benefits," Will replied, and the case was dismissed. Another time, soon after
the United States declared war on Germany, he showed up at a recruiting office on Chambers Street and gave an impromptu monologue, the
highlight being the line, "Bryan says that he will go to war if they want
him, but Roosevelt says he will go whether they want him or not."

The incident that got him the most publicity—it was covered by at
least four New York papers—was a bizarre "deer drive" on tiny Shelter
Island, between the two forks of eastern Long Island. Deer had been de-
vouring local farmers' crops, so some seventy state game wardens and
volunteers, in a line, traversed the island, driving the deer onto a beach
where they would be rounded up and shipped upstate to the Adiron-
dacks. Will had volunteered to stand in a motorboat and rope any animal that tried to get away by sea. Sure enough, one buck "headed
straight for the glistening waters of Shelter Island Sound and was in with
a plump, the spray dashing high above him. . . .

"Rogers, dancing in excitement and whirling the loop end of his
rope until it hissed and sang, made ready to lasso the brave swimmer. . . . Rogers cast with pretty precision, and the rope settled snugly
around the swimming deer's neck."

Will Rogers had caught New York's imagination. The infatuation
crystallized at a 1917 benefit held to buy cigarettes for our soldiers in
France. Will had taught Billy, Mary, and Jimmy to ride at the age of

two, and after a baseball game between the *Follies* team and the "Hitchy-Koos" he and his three children all galloped out onto the Polo Grounds. Bill and Mary rode toward him, and he

> roped them gently but firmly, let them go, lassoed them from another angle, nipped the ponies by one foot, two feet, all four feet and finally with a shrill yell of delight in his own work (nobody has more fun out of the grind of making a living than Will Rogers) went careering around the far rim of the Polo Grounds, the whirling lasso beautifully outlined in its perfect circle as he raced by the dark background of the far away stands. Shouts of pleasure went up from the crowd such as are seldom heard in this town. It wasn't altogether the uncanny expertness of Will Rogers that they were applauding. Partly, indeed, it was the buoyant cheerfulness of the man—delight in his merry way of doing things.

Will thrived in the *Follies*. Adapting the act was easy: On arrival in a new city, he would interview the reporters who came to interview *him*, gleaning enough for a few good local jokes. (By now his discomfiture among the press had totally vanished.) Nor were the extended separations from his family (the show was on the road half the year) a grave problem. Except for the tour right after their wedding, Betty had never gone out on the road with him, and by now they had both accepted without a second thought the lengthy absences his career demanded. Indeed, this may have been one of the secrets to their marriage's success. (Even surrounded by beauteous *Follies* girls, dalliances were out of the question; in fact, Will's modest uneasiness in their presence was a backstage joke. Asked by the reporters about the difficulty of being a faithful husband in such surroundings, Will generally took the line that the exotic beauties were just folks. "They're all wool and a yard wide, these girls," he told one interviewer. "They're great pals. And they know how to work.")

One year, Will did have a family member along to keep him company. This was Dopey, a coal-black pony he'd bought from Zack Miller in the summer of 1915, the first horse since Comanche to win a prominent place in his affections. ("I don't know why we called him Dopey," Will wrote years later. "I guess it was because he was always so gentle and just the least bit lazy. Anyway we meant no dissrespect [*sic*] to him.") All three Rogers children learned to ride on Dopey. That had been accomplished by 1918, and Ziegfeld paid to have him and another horse travel from city to city in the *Follies* scenery car. Each day of the tour, Will and Charley Aldridge, an Oklahoma cowboy, went out to a convenient stockyard or field and practiced roping and riding.*

As for his human companions, they were at least entertaining. The *Follies* cast in 1916–1918 included the great singer Fanny Brice; the black performer Bert Williams, who in his early vaudeville days had helped start the coon song and cakewalk crazes, and who Gene Buck thought was the greatest comedian he had ever seen; and Ed Wynn, a scene-stealing buffoon known as "The Perfect Fool." Will's principal cohorts were two other *Follies* comedians, Eddie Cantor and W. C. Fields. Although Cantor later claimed that the trio was so close that Ziegfeld dubbed them "the three musketeers," that they "were ready to lay down their laughs for one another," this is certainly a piece of after-the-fact mythologizing: Cantor was a prodigious sentimentalist.

Which is not to say that he and Will weren't friends. They had first met on the Orpheum circuit in 1912, when Cantor, a banjo-eyed, loose-limbed native of the Lower East Side (real name: Isidore Itzkowitz) was part of Gus Edwards's "Kid Kabaret." (George Jessel was in the troupe, too.) Cantor joined the *Follies* as a featured comic five years later, and on opening night his number "That's the Kind of a Baby for Me" stopped the show. Will came by his dressing room to offer congratulations and found Cantor sobbing on his dressing table: His beloved grandmother, who had raised him, had died a few months before, and he was devastated that she hadn't been there to see his triumph. Will's response, according to Cantor, was to say, "Now Eddie, what makes you think she didn't see you? And from a very good seat?" As far as Cantor was concerned, that clinched it; from then on, he idolized Will.

Their performing styles were diametrically opposed—where Will's shtick was limited to the head scratch and the grin, Cantor would do anything to sell a song or a routine: wear blackface, make effeminate gestures, take pratfalls, roll his eyes, mug, do accents—but in matters of living, he later wrote, "Rogers was my grammar school, high school and college. He taught me that the world doesn't end at the stage door and that politics are every man's business, actors not excluded. He kept on giving me an education as long as he lived." He also introduced Cantor to the pleasures of chili (just as Cantor introduced him to kosher cook-

---

*When Dopey died in 1934, Will wrote a touching obituary that called him "the gentlest and greatest pony for grown ups or children anyone ever saw" and concluded: "He was of the family. He raised our children. He learned 'em to ride. He never hurt no one in his life. He did everything right. That's a reputation that no human can die with. Goodbye, Dopey, from Mama, Dad, Bill, Mary and Jim."

ing), but the main courses of instruction were in the importance of family—Cantor would eventually have five daughters, to whom he was very and publicly devoted—and charity. In his early *Follies* days, Will began what would be a lifetime habit of contributing heavily, in both benefit performances and anonymous donations. In this respect Cantor would, if anything, outstrip the master.

Fields was another story altogether. He and Will shared an uncanny list of similarities—born the same year, with the same first name, they were both vaudeville dumb acts (juggling in Fields's case) who had branched out to verbal comedy and would later achieve great success in movies. Both had even been in South Africa in 1902 (though Fields's claim that they made each other's acquaintance at the time is doubtful). But what they had in common only underscored the elemental difference between the two men. Fields, escaping an abusive father, had run away from his Philadelphia home at the age of eleven. He was a misanthrope, rude, grouchy, alcoholic, miserly, and pessimistic about the human prospect. Onstage, he was howlingly funny, but he held the audience at arm's length; his comedy relied on balletic slapstick and feigned exasperation, helped along by funny hats and props and punctuated by mordant asides. Audiences, sensing his disdain, laughed at him but never took him to their hearts. They did love Will, who came to the *Follies* after Fields but soon became its biggest attraction. The ground-floor star dressing room was given to Fields only because Will, who came as he was, didn't need it or want it. (Instead, he was ensconced in a "little third-floor dressing room, a dingy, uncarpeted place, with one small window that looked out on a back street.")

Fields didn't badmouth Rogers in public, but, like other humorists who lacked his common touch and enormous success (Ring Lardner, Fred Allen), denigrated him privately. Fields' biographer Robert Lewis Taylor describes a Fields-Rogers meeting long after their *Follies* days. After Will had left the room, a young woman who was there said, "Isn't he a wonderful man? I just love that voice." To which Fields replied, "The son of a bitch is a fake. I'll bet a hundred dollars he talks just like everybody else when he gets home."

Once, driving back from a show in Baltimore with Will and some other members of the cast, Fields tried to pass a motorcycle and drove into a ditch, and Will suffered a badly injured leg. (He received a one-thousand-dollar insurance payment.) It would probably be unjust to ascribe the accident to Fields's jealousy, but the special delight that Fields, an energetic practical joker, took in victimizing Will was surely significant. One year, a beautiful singer named Allyn King had a costume change so quick, she didn't have time to close her dressing room door. Fields would stand outside while she was taking off her clothes and shout for Will to come quick, then put an arm around his shoulders and turn him so he was in full view of the bare King. "Rogers bit on that gag a dozen times," Cantor wrote years later, "always turned red and fell over himself escaping." Once, Fields came into Will's dressing room before the show and told him he'd heard a great crack in response to the Germans' "Big Bertha," a huge cannon that shelled Paris from a distance of eighty-five miles: "That's nothin'. Uncle Sam's now got a gun that can shoot everybody in Berlin right from Staten Island, and all those it don't kill, it takes prisoner." Will liked the line so much he said he'd put it into his monologue, whereupon Fields went to Cantor—who came on earlier in the show—and gave him the same joke. After Will finished his act, Fields asked him how the crack had gone over. Not well, came the answer. "It sounded like a funny line to me, but nobody laughed except the musicians."

The most elaborate gag had to do with Will's old Texas roping buddy Clay McGonigle. One night in Pittsburgh, weary of hearing endless stories about what a great fellow and sterling roper Clay was, Fields and Cantor counterfeited a handwritten note, purportedly from McGonigle, telling Will he was on his way to the front in France and would be in the audience that night. Will was overjoyed, and in his act that night he addressed endless remarks to his old friend, despite the fact that he couldn't spot him in the crowd. He didn't take part in the finale, in order to get to the lobby early and catch Clay on his way out. But there was no Clay. He called all the hotels and clubs he could think of, then tried the railroad station. He concluded he had somehow offended his pal and was so miserable when he got back to the hotel that the pranksters didn't have the heart to tell him the truth.

ON NEW YEAR'S DAY 1918, on tour with the *Follies* in Chicago, Will Rogers, thirty-eight years old, was on top of the world. His marriage, now entering its tenth year, was all that he could have hoped it would be. Betty had long since dropped her objection to a life in show business (though they still planned to retire one day to their property in Oklahoma, now ably overseen by Will's nephew Herb McSpadden). Indeed, she essentially managed her husband's career, advising him on gags and job offers, handling his correspondence, and taking charge of the family's financial affairs. Decades later, when Jim Rogers was about to take a wife, his mother confided that on more than one occasion in the early years the frustration and uncertainty of the vaudeville life might have tempted her to walk out of the marriage—if she hadn't controlled the purse strings.

An emotional division of labor had developed within the marriage, as well. Before their marriage, she had been a master practical joker, and he had managed a cattle ranch; but in Betty's presence Will became more high-strung and impulsive with each passing year, and in his she became more responsible, gracious, and calm. A few years later, one of the few reporters who was ever able to secure an interview with her wrote, "She is the eternal type, characterized by gentleness and an exquisite refinement." It was fitting that she called her husband "Billy" (within the family, their older son was Bill), for in a subtle but unmistakable way she was the levelheaded guardian to his headstrong child, a second mother to replace the one he had lost so long ago.

The family's long summers together were a joy. Each year, they would rent a house in Amityville near the Stones, and the days would be filled with swimming, ball playing, and riding. Through Jim Minnick, his first assistant in his vaudeville act, who was now a trainer of and dealer in polo ponies, Will was introduced to the game that was to become his favorite pastime. He formed a team with Minnick, Stone, and Ed Borein, a "cowboy artist" in the manner of Charles Russell who was trying to establish himself in New York and had become a good friend; sometimes Douglas Fairbanks, Vernon Castle, Frank Tinney, or Leo Carrillo played, too. Will was so intent on fun that he frequently missed his train into Manhattan for his *Follies* performance. But Long Island was still undeveloped enough that he could hop into his car and beat the train into the city.

He took great delight in the children, and was so determined not to subject them to the maternal deprivation he had suffered that he saw to it they had a second mother, their Aunt Dick. He used them as playmates and straight men and as a way to relive his cowboy past, dressing them in chaps and spurs and bandannas at every photo opportunity. One of Will Rogers, Jr.'s earliest memories is of being put in such an outfit and reciting "Zebra Dunn," a poem about a dude who went west and was put on a bucking horse. The refrain was still etched in his mind three-quarters of a century later: "Not every educated fellow is a darned greenhorn." The posse was about to grow again. Betty was pregnant with a fourth child, due in July.

Professionally, the three years with Ziegfeld had been nothing short of astonishing, unleashing a flood of creativity of which not even Will could have known he was capable. He had spent ten years in vaudeville with an act that changed only minimally from year to year. But now the jokes poured out. He filled a notebook with them, and sheet after sheet of paper. Nervous energy coursed through him; he couldn't sit still and he always had to be doing something with his hands. In a letter to Ed Borein, Charley Russell—who saw all the world in cowboy terms—remarked on the way Will would "loap [*sic*] up to your camp quirting himself on the hind leg with a paper."

Even after doing a different routine every night (two when he was playing the *Frolic,* and three on matinee days), Will still had more to say. So he turned to the printed word. His first effort was in the summer of 1916, a series of articles for the New York *American* on a "Stampede" (or rodeo), put on in Sheepshead Bay, Brooklyn, by his friend Guy Weadick.* Will was a little self-conscious in print. Contrasting himself to ball players Christy Mathewson and Ty Cobb, who used ghostwriters for the literary efforts credited to them, he proclaimed, "I am not only going to sign my name, but I am going to take a shot at the whole works myself, and I want it to go as she lays, even if the guy that has to set up the type has to get drunk to do it." But he was intrigued enough by the experience to want to do it again. When a magazine writer asked him for some background material the following summer, Will forwarded with it a note, stating "I wish they would let me write them an article just on things that are in the paper or one on a trip I took around the World. You talk to the Editor for me, will you, and see what he thinks of the idea." Nothing came of that overture, but, on tour with the *Follies* that fall and winter, Will wrote two "guest" columns each for the Detroit *Journal* and the Chicago *Examiner,* on topics as diverse as the performance of Connie Mack's Philadelphia Athletics, the troubles of Detroit's streetcar system, crime in Chicago, and the recent Russian Revolution.

Far from being an aberration, his productivity would increase as the years went by. His published output would eventually reach several million words, contained in twenty-one volumes. In the years to come, he would venture into, and achieve great success in, medium after medium—motion pictures (silent and, more dramatically, sound), phonograph records, the lecture circuit, radio. There was so much he wanted—needed—to do, so many places he decided he had to get to, that he would embrace air travel, treating it as a commonplace when it was really in its infancy, a misprision that contributed to his premature

*Weadick was trying to duplicate the success he'd had at the Calgary Stampede, started four years before, and he'd induced Theodore Roosevelt, as well as Lucille Mulhall and nearly every other rodeo star, to attend. Will, if he hadn't met Roosevelt with Zack Mulhall sixteen years before, certainly met him here.

death. Behind all this activity, this explosive fecundity, it is hard not to find, once again, the presence of Clement Vann Rogers. In the Clem Rogers view of things, Will didn't like to work, hadn't accomplished anything, wouldn't amount to much. Clem was gone and his son was the toast of New York; but there would always be room in Will's brief for more evidence against the old perception.

In Chicago that January, Will was in possession of a thrilling piece of news, something that seemed the culmination of all he had worked for up until then. Ziegfeld had told him that he intended to give Will his own show—the first time he had ever accorded this honor to anyone other than Anna Held or his second wife, the actress Billie Burke, whom he had married in 1914.

Will responded with a four-and-a-half-page, single-spaced letter outlining his ideas for the production. It would be a revue: one-third production numbers, one-third "sure-fire vaudeville specialties," and one-third Will Rogers features. For his first scene, he envisioned the curtain opening on a motion picture company at work on a Western. Will is brought out to audition, even though the "big, loud talking director (we could use Wayburn) . . . says, 'You don't look like a moving picture cowboy.' " Will would proceed to unfurl some dazzling rope stunts, which would go over especially well with the audience, he reckoned, because "they do not know that I have kept up on that kind of work." Next, he proposed "a way to do a lot of my newspaper stuff": a country post office setting with three or four codgers sitting around a hot stove. "I am the old Rube that reads all the papers and knows about everything they ask me."

There would be a new rope dance with a girl, a blackface skit, a rendition of a Bert Williams song, and then his regular act, doing rope tricks and telling jokes. For the finale, he had in mind a bit that reveals both his fascination with self-referential plays within a play (as does the first scene) and his doubts about this new venture. On one side of the stage would be a mock dressing room where, even as Will was doing his act, the other male principals would be changing out of their costumes. Will finishes and goes into the dressing room, "with all of them asking me how I did and we talk and discuss things and gags and how they have gone that night and who we saw out front. . . ."

> Now the people, one by one, dress and leave saying "good-night." Some are to meet the girls; some say they are going out to hit you for more money; well I am the last one and I am not satisfied with the way I have done and feel disappointed. Some-

one impersonating you comes in and says, "Oh, cheer up, you
didn't do so bad," or something to that effect. You go out and
I am alone; watchman comes in and says "all out" and I leave
with either some little pathetic touch—"Well I guess that act was
right; this thing is too fast for me; back to The Follies and just
be one of the mob" or some comedy line. . . .

Will had a title in mind, too: "A Mess of Junk."

Ziegfeld may have thought this apt, for he backed down and the
show never came off. Will was back with the *Frolic* that spring and the
Follies in the summer. His disappointment must have been acute, but it
wasn't enough to stop his momentum, or to delay his next big move.
The groundwork for this was laid at the opening night of the *Frolic* on
the New Amsterdam roof just two months after his letter to Ziegfeld. Sitting at a table as night turned to morning, watching Will with intense interest, was a young man with the unlikely name of Samuel Goldfish.

A STILL FROM <u>DOUBLING FOR ROMEO</u>
(JIM ROGERS IS AT RIGHT)

CHAPTER 8

HOLLYWOOD, I

Straight on I didn't look so good, and even sideways I wasn't so terrific, but a cross between back and a three-quarters view, why, Brother I was hot. The way my ear (on the side) stood out from my head was just bordering on perfect. That rear view gave you just the shot needed. In those old silent picture days, that back right ear was a by-word from Coast to Coast.

—WILL ROGERS

THE *Follies of 1917* had ended its forty-eight-week run in Montreal on April 20, 1918. The new *Frolic* opened four days later at the New Amsterdam. At the start of his monologue, Will apologized to the audience that he hadn't had time to read the papers yet; he expected to be considerably funnier by the end of the week. But he and Eddie Cantor amused the sophisticates who had mounted the roof with their in-joke impressions of Gene Buck, Ned Wayburn, theater owner Charles Dillingham, and Ziegfeld himself. And there was, as always, a knockout production number: "Try a Ring, Dear," in which audience members at their tables were handed large rings and told to toss them onto canes held by the chorus girls. The first to score, reported the *Herald,* was "Miss Lynn Fontaine, the bright Australian ingenue."

There is no record of whether Sam Goldfish tried his luck.

Like the rope-spinning cowboy he watched onstage that night, Goldfish—who had a jutting jaw, a pointed nose supporting a pair of pince-nez, and a scalp that was already approaching the state of barrenness—was thirty-nine years old. He had been born Schmuel Gelbfisz, in Warsaw. At the age of fifteen, dreaming of America, he had displayed some of the tenacity for which he would be famous by walking five hundred miles to Hamburg. A few years later, he was working in a glove factory in upstate New York. Starting out as a three-dollar-a-day cutter, he eventually became the Elite Glove Company's top salesman. In 1913, he entered the motion picture business with his brother-in-law Jesse Lasky; they produced—and Cecil B. DeMille directed—*The Squaw Man,* a Western that was one of the first feature-length silent films and one of the first movies to be shot in California.

From the various nineteenth-century contraptions that led to Thomas Edison's development of the kinetoscope in 1891, up until the midteens, the American movie business was catch-as-catch-can, open to anybody—even an erstwhile glove salesman—with enough moxie and ambition to think he could produce the kind of fantasies a lot of people would pay five cents to see. Its maturity can roughly be traced to the astonishing success of D. W. Griffith's *The Birth of a Nation,* which opened in February 1915, grossed at least $50 million in its first run (tickets cost as much as two dollars each), and proved beyond any doubt that film could be a medium of artistry and enormous profit. Convinced that autonomy was the only way he could capitalize on the great opportunities that lay ahead, Goldfish formed a new company in 1916. The playwright Edgar Selwyn contributed capital, copyrights, and the second syllable of his surname to the Goldwyn Pictures Company, but Goldfish ran the show.

One of the axioms of the fledgling business—based on the observation that the public would go to see Charlie Chaplin or Mary Pickford at every opportunity, no matter what the picture—concerned the supreme importance of stars. It so happened that the initial roster of Goldwyn Pictures was predominantly female—Maxine Elliott, Mae Marsh, Madge Kennedy, Mary Garden, Mabel Normand, Geraldine Farrar, Pauline Frederick—prompting the competition to refer derisively to the company as "the old ladies' home." To remedy that situation, Goldfish signed the author Rex Beach, famous for his virtually all-male adventure stories set in the West, to a three-film-a-year contract. Beach's wife was the sister of Mrs. Fred Stone, and it was Mrs. Beach who had the idea that Will would be the perfect star of the film version of Rex's novel *Laughing Bill Hyde,* the story of an escaped convict who shows his heart of gold while on the lam in Alaska.

Presumably, Goldfish took in the *Frolic* premiere to assess Will for himself. He must have liked what he saw, because *Laughing Bill Hyde* commenced filming in August, at the Goldwyn studio in Fort Lee, New Jersey. On the eighteenth of the month, a brief item appeared in *The New York Times,* beginning, "Florenz Ziegfeld, Jr. announced last week that he had exclusive control of the professional services of every member of the *'Follies'* cast." Ziegfeld was clearly talking to Will, but talk was all it was. Without a contract, there was no way he could stop his star from making the movie.

The world of motion pictures was altogether new and somewhat disconcerting for Will, not least because for several weeks he had to do his act in the *Follies of 1918* every night, go home to Long Island, and then (after an auto trip that in those pre–George Washington Bridge days, when the only way to cross the Hudson was by ferry, must have taken at least two hours) appear on the set in Fort Lee, New Jersey, at 8:30 the next morning. The "Alaska" scenes were shot on location in the town of Boonton, about twenty miles west of the studio, and on the nights before those days Will didn't bother going home. One night, he left Manhattan after the *Follies* finale and ran into thunderstorms so heavy that his car stopped running. He arrived in town on foot at 4:00 a.m.; two hours later, he had to wake up to get ready for his first scene.

The actual process of making a movie was trying, too. One day, a reporter visited the set, to find Will carrying an actor "up and down" the Palisades, the sheer cliffs on the Jersey side of the Hudson. The director, Hobart Henley, shouted to him, "Register fatigue!" To which Will yelled back, "I register all-in. I don't have to pretend if I don't want to, do I?"

In an unpublished article called "Breaking in the Movies," he described his bafflement at some of film's technical peculiarities:

> The Director says, "Now, Will, we are going to take the scene where your old pal dies. You have broken out of jail and he gets hurt and you are bringing him into the Doctor's office at night to get him treated and he dies. It's the dramatic scene of the whole opera."
>
> I says, "But I havent got out of Jail yet."
>
> He says, "No, you won't for a couple of weeks yet, besides the jail is not built yet."
>
> That's the first time I learned that they just hop around any old way. We took a scene [with] a fellow and I fighting outdoors and a lot of rainy weather come and a week later he knocked me down in the same fight. . . .
>
> [The director] instructed me as follows: "No thought photographs. If you are thinking a thing the camera will show it." So I told him I would try and keep my thoughts as clean as possible.

Despite all that, *Laughing Bill Hyde,* which opened in New York in late September, was a success. Will got a sheaf of good reviews, including one in *Variety,* which was now covering the movies with the same authority as it had the stage, welcoming "a new star to filmdom." When the favorable box-office tally came in, Goldfish offered Will a contract. The catch was that the Goldwyn operation was moving to Los Angeles, then in the process of becoming the center of film production, and Will would have to move there, too. But he and Betty didn't have to deliberate long before agreeing. The biggest incentive was financial: Goldwyn was offering $2,250 a week, with an option for a second year at $3,000. Even though he had gotten a 33 percent raise that year, Will was still making only one thousand dollars with Ziegfeld. The extra money was irresistible, especially with the arrival on July 15 of Fred Rogers, named in honor of Fred Stone.*

There was a sense, too, that Will had gone as far as he could with the *Follies.* He had never been as prominent as he was in the 1918 edition. He appeared in skits as well as his monologue, and the New York *Evening Post* commented that he "pervaded the piece." But the reaction to his efforts was disheartening—for the first time in his career, he got bad notices. A blackface bit appropriated from the stillborn Will Rogers show went over so poorly that it was dropped shortly after opening night. And even his biggest fans in the press didn't care for his other skit. In her review in *Vanity Fair,* Dorothy Parker wrote, "The life of the evening is Will Rogers, who, to me, is one of the Greatest Living Americans. But they don't do right by him. There is a horrible stretch of time when they make him play the role of Satan in an unbelieveable scene supposed to represent the lower regions on a busy day." (In the sketch, W. C. Fields played Senator La Follette and Allyn King was "The Girl in Hell"; Will twirled his devil's tail like a lariat.) Will's longtime fan Heywood Broun agreed: "Rogers can't seem to do much with other men's lines even when he can remember them."

The notion of California was alluring as well. Will had been based in New York for thirteen years, but he had yet to buy a house there: The city had never really felt like home. He and Betty were Westerners, and so were their children, their place of birth notwithstanding. There were mountains and beaches and open spaces in Los Angeles, and unlimited room for horses. And you couldn't get any farther west.

On November 30, Will and Goldfish met in Cleveland, where the *Follies* were appearing. Will affixed his signature to an agreement affirming, among other points, that Goldwyn would employ him "as an actor

---

*The salary was a step up for Will, but it was a modest one for the movie world. A year earlier, Charlie Chaplin had signed a million-dollar-a-year contract.

in and about its business of producing plays and scenes and taking, making and producing motion pictures thereof" and would "furnish to the Artist first class transportation, parlor and sleeping car expenses from New York to California." The term of employment was not to commence until June 16, 1919; despite his lack of a contract with Ziegfeld, Will felt morally obliged to finish out the *Follies of 1918* tour. The document is of some historical interest, not only because it is Will Rogers's first movie contract but because it bears one of the last signatures of Samuel Goldfish. Two days later, he petitioned to change his name legally to Samuel Goldwyn.

Will was so busy on the *Follies* tour that he didn't have time to worry whether he had made the right decision. The Goldwyn people were sending him novels, plays, and short stories to read as possible film properties. (A nice gesture, but possibly disingenuous: "Everything I don't like they buy," he later complained.) And he applied himself to another project for which he could thank the Beach family. Rex Beach had suggested to his own publisher, Harper and Brothers, that Will might make an author. An agreement was reached, and in Pullman cars and hotel rooms Will worked on a humorous book about the Peace Conference under way in Paris. (The armistice ending World War I had been declared November 11, 1918, and the twelve-month Conference, with President Wilson in attendance for much of it, began January 13, 1919.) *Book* is probably not the correct word, for the manuscript that Will finished in the spring consisted of about two hundred brief paragraphs, each one a more or less discrete gag. But Harper liked it and proposed a series of six volumes in all, each on a different topic. "The more I think about it the more tickled I am about undertaking these books," an editor wrote him. "There is going to be real joy in publishing them, and we want to start the first one off with bells." The book would be published in September, with a title befitting the respect now accorded Will: *Rogers-isms: The Cowboy Philosopher on the Peace Conference.*

But he had still more to say. He found a market in S. L. "Roxy" Rothafel, the celebrated owner of the Strand, Rialto, and Rivoli motion picture palaces in New York. Rothafel was famous for giving the audience something extra with their movies, most notably a full-sized orchestra that played film scores as well as brief concerts between attractions. Now he arranged for Will to write a series of gags that could be projected on the screen. These ran for a time, and then Pell Mitchell, the editor of the Gaumont News and Graphic, one of the first of the newsreels that had begun to be featured in movie theaters, had a better idea: Why not intersperse gag titles with footage of Will actually talking, and send a new batch out to all the subscribing picture houses every week? Mitchell put forth the idea in a letter to Will, guaranteeing, if he agreed to participate, that "I . . . will make you the best known individual in the world within a short time." Will signed on—he had jokes enough for everybody.

In Kansas City in March—where Will's presence was described as "attracting Oklahomans by the trainload" to see the *Follies*—a newspaper reporter produced a verbal snapshot of this thirty-nine-year-old human gag factory: "in his derby hat worn well forward and tilted down over his right eye, his soft collar and small black bow tie, belted overcoat of plain everyday cheviot, he looked like any matter of fact young business man."

Once again, the *Follies* ended its tour in Montreal. The second week of May, Will was back in New York. There was still a month before his Goldwyn contract started, so he agreed to appear in the new *Frolic* for three weeks. On May 31, a Saturday night, Ziegfeld presented him with a gold watch engraved, "To Will Rogers, in appreciation of a real fellow, whose word is his bond." That was his last scheduled performance, but he couldn't resist coming in again the following Monday "to fling a few parting shots," as *The New York Times* put it. Even the chef on the New Amsterdam roof realized the importance of the occasion. He stopped work in the kitchen, stuck his head through the swinging doors, and listened until the final shot had been flung.

Betty and the children repaired to Arkansas for the summer and Will boarded a train for California on June 5. He chatted with movie star Wallace Reid, also bound for Los Angeles, and in his first-class accommodations he worked on his second book for Harper, about Prohibition (the Eighteenth Amendment had entered the Constitution five months back).* He also pecked away at a letter he had agreed to send to the Kansas City *Star*. Datelined "on Board Cal Limited trying to get out of Kansas," it began: "You asked me to drop you a few lines on my way west to Los Angeles, where I hear the call of ART to act a fool for the bucking Pictures, I think they want to use me as the horrible example in some way. . . ." Will touched on some points of local interest, then played on the sense he had that the entire country was going Hollywood: "In fact everybody on this train is going to Cal to go into the

---

*The Rogers books were at least a modest success for Harper, *The Cowboy Philosopher on the Peace Conference* selling six thousand copies and going through two printings. But for some reason, the four additional projected volumes—one of them was to be about the movies—were never published or (presumably) written.

movies. Its the Movie Special. The Porters will tell you they are not black they are made up for a part. . . . There is a Carona [*sic*] Typewriter in every birth writing Scenarios."

When the train arrived in Los Angeles, it was met by someone who had gone Hollywood a few years before. Waiting at the station, "all dolled up in one of his quietest yellow suits and a red tie," was Will's old roommate Tom Mix, now the biggest cowboy star in the movies.

WILL QUICKLY found temporary lodgings on West Adams Street. He had nothing else to do, so on June 9, a week before he had contracted to begin work, he showed up at the Goldwyn studio in Culver City. (This was five miles southwest of Hollywood, where most of the other fledgling picture operations were located. But Sam Goldwyn had gotten a good deal on the sixteen-acre site of the defunct Triangle Films: the whole spread, including stages, buildings, and equipment, for $325,000.) A story *(Almost a Husband),* a supporting cast, and the necessary sets were all ready for him, but the planned director, Victor "Pops" Schertzinger, was still at work on another project. So Goldwyn assigned to the film Clarence Badger, a contract director who had started in the business four years before as a writer for Mack Sennett. The pairing was propitious: Will was so pleased with the experience that he arranged with Goldwyn for Badger to direct all his subsequent films.

With one exception, Will's pictures for Goldwyn were not comedies. One obvious reason is that he was brought on to make features, and the primary receptacle for cinematic humor was still the two-reeler. Moreover, the Goldwyn story department had the sense to realize that he was not cut out to be a silent-film comedian. The great clowns could extract laughter from anything—a derby hat, a broom, a slow burn; Will was equipped to get it only from words. Over and above the balletic grace of a Chaplin, Keaton, or Lloyd, the camera magnified, transformed, and somehow crystallized them. Chaplin as a tramp was larger than life; Will as a tramp was just Will.

But what kind of picture did suit him? Goldwyn answered that question by creating a genre: the rube melodrama. *Almost a Husband,* the story of Sam Lyman, a simple schoolteacher in a small southern town, was typical. As part of a parlor game, Sam has to go through a mock wedding ceremony with Eva, a banker's daughter, whom he secretly loves, to be performed by the next man to enter the house. This gentleman, not surprisingly, turns out to be a minister—the marriage is official. The villainous Zeb Sawyer wants Eva for his own, and in many dastardly ways tries to get Sam to divorce her. But he's ultimately defeated, and Sam works up the courage to ask Eva to honor the marriage.

This set the pattern for the other films Will would make for Goldwyn over the next two years—*Jubilo; Water, Water Everywhere; The Strange Boarder; Jes' Call Me Jim; Cupid the Cowpuncher; Honest Hutch; Guile of Women; Boys Will Be Boys; An Unwilling Hero; Doubling for Romeo;* and *A Poor Relation.* He's a country fellow—not particularly successful, ambitious, or bright—who, following plot developments of greater or lesser improbability, achieves newfound confidence and potency, gets the girl, and usually comes into some money to boot. (The character was varied in *Guile of Women,* where he played a Swedish fisherman given lines such as "Vot good did it do you to make all dis fool out of me, when I love you, Hulda Swenson?" Goldwyn wired him on location that he wanted him to wear a blond wig, to which Will remarked, "If he wanted me to be a blond he should have took it up with my mother forty years ago.") The stories were not sterling, as even the Goldwyn promotion department realized. Publicity materials sent to theater owners showing *The Strange Boarder* began with the sentence, "This is a very fair Rogers picture in which the star gets a great deal out of a story that is not of the best."

The films were not without humor, but the only outlet for it was verbal, the written titles that silent film used for exposition and dialogue. Will often wrote or helped write these, and Goldwyn astutely saw to it that he contributed even when they were credited to somebody else. A reporter visiting the studio one day noticed a man following Will with a clipboard, jotting down his comments: "The Goldwyn people had engaged him to do nothing else than trot around behind Rogers, the walking subtitle factory, to catch . . . gems of repartee." Will walked up to a schoolroom set, where a girl and a boy were rehearsing a fight. The title for the girl's dialogue, he was told, was, "He hit me with a spitball." Will said, "Hell, course he hit you if he threw at you."

"And that retort," wrote the reporter, "went down in the assistant director's pad as a subtitle."

Judging by the surviving films he did for Goldwyn—*Jubilo, Jes' Call Me Jim,* and *Doubling for Romeo*—Will was a surprisingly effective actor. The reservoir of good will he had been building up carried over to the screen, and, though he tended to rely on a limited set of moves—the ocular double-take, the grin, the bowed head, the head scratch—his ingrained restraint and naturalism presented a refreshing contrast to the hypercharged emotionalism and/or acrobaticism silent-film audiences were used to. Tom Mix, William S. Hart, Douglas Fairbanks, Buster Keaton—everything was right angles and jutting jaws. Will was a shambling parenthesis. The innovation did not go unnoticed. "He makes you forget you are witnessing a piece of acting," a reviewer asserted. "Without the aid of facial contortions and wild gesticulations, he draws human and real characters, and by his simple and easy bearing he makes them all the more natural and understandable." In an interview with *The New York Times*, Erich von Stroheim, the Austrian-born director who had succeeded D. W. Griffith as the reigning "genius" of silent film, cited Will's work as one of the few examples of the "realism" the medium desperately needed.

Another distinctive feature of the Rogers pictures was their wholesomeness, moral suitability having already come to the fore as a critical Hollywood issue. One day, the Goldwyn publicity office issued a release declaring that all Will's films had been recommended for exhibition in churches by the Film Committee of the Methodist Episcopal Church, adding, "He is the only star so distinguished."

His most successful film for Goldwyn was the second picture of the contract, *Jubilo*, based on a *Saturday Evening Post* story by Ben Ames Williams. There was nothing distinctive about the plot, which concerned a lazy tramp who is nearly framed for a train robbery but who, supported by the friendship of a rancher and his daughter, finds courage and energy and unmasks the true villain. As Will wrote in the draft of an advertisement he was asked to put together (the experimental approach to promotion was abandoned as soon as the Goldwyn operatives read it), "Story? There's no use telling you wise Birds. Same as usual. Looks bad for the hero right up to the last Close Up. First reel introduces Hero dividing last crum of bread with dog, which they all do in the movies but nobody ever did in real life. Second reel looks bad for hero. Third reel looks even worse for hero. Fourth reel all evidence points to hero being the robber. Villain looks slick and satisfied. End reel five the winners. The tramp wins 100 percent HERO."

But—possibly because of the popularity of the original story, possibly because of the fun the film registered in charting the depths of Jubilo's laziness, and possibly because of the resonance of the song "In the Days of Jubilo," an old Negro spiritual that was played ad infinitum through the film—it struck a chord. Clarence Badger recalled that, on location for subsequent pictures, whenever he and Will would go into the local movie theater, the organist or pianist, immediately on recognizing the star, would play the "Jubilo" melody. "In fact, until the coming of talking pictures, the strains of the old hymn followed Will as a sort of

aura, liable to become manifest whenever he entered a picture theatre."
A dozen years later, when pictures had learned how to talk, he made a
remake of the story called *Too Busy to Work*.

Will seemed to sense that *Jubilo* was something special. After shooting was completed, word came that Sam Goldwyn was considering
changing the title. Will dashed off an outraged telegram:

THOUGHT I WAS SUPPOSED TO BE THE COMEDIAN BUT WHEN YOU
SUGGEST CHANGING THE TITLE OF JUBILO YOU ARE FUNNIER THAN I
EVER WAS. . . . I DONT SEE HOW LORIMER OF THE POST EVER LET IT
BE PUBLISHED UNDER THAT TITLE. THAT SONG IS BETTER KNOWN
THROUGH THE SOUTH THAN GERALDINE FARRAR'S HUSBAND. WE
HAVE USED IT ALL THROUGH BUSINESS IN THIS PICTURE BUT OF
COURSE WE CAN CHANGE IT TO EVERYBODY SHIMMIE NOW. SUPPOSE
IF YOU HAD PRODUCED THE MIRACLE MAN YOU WOULD HAVE
CALLED IT A QUEER OLD GUY. BUT IF YOU REALLY WANT A TITLE
FOR THIS SECOND PICTURE I WOULD SUGGEST JUBILO. ALSO THE FOL-
LOWING:

A POOR BUT HONEST TRAMP
HE LIES BUT HE DONT MEAN IT
A FARMERS VIRTUOUS DAUGHTER
THE GREAT TRAIN ROBBERY MYSTERY
A SPOTTED HORSE BUT HE IS ONLY PAINTED
THE HUNGRY TRAMP'S REVENGE
THE VAGABOND WITH A HEART AS BIG AS HIS APPETITE
HE LOSES IN THE FIRST REEL BUT WINS IN THE LAST
THE OLD MAN LEFT BUT THE TRAMP PROTECTED HER

WHAT WOULD YOU HAVE CALLED THE BIRTH OF A NATION?

WILL ROGERS

The title stayed *Jubilo*.

On a train back from San Francisco, where he had gone to film
some scenes for *Guile of Women*, Will ran into Elmer Rice, a young member of the Goldwyn story department who had been lured out from New
York the year before. Will started complaining about the poor quality of
his material and asked Rice to come up with something a little better.
The writer eventually proposed a variation on *A Connecticut Yankee in King
Arthur's Court*. Rice's superiors liked the idea, but he would let them have
it only if they released him from the last three years of his four-year contract: he had had enough of Hollywood and wanted to go back East. He
made the right decision; he would soon gain fame, and the Pulitzer

Prize, as the author of *Street Scene, The Adding Machine,* and many other plays.

Doubling for Romeo—as the Rice idea was eventually titled—was a real artistic success, the one Goldwyn film that gave Will the opportunity to display his unique kind of satire to full advantage. The opening titles set the tone:

Story by Elmer Rice, Will Rogers and Will Shakespeare
(One of these boys is well known)
Modern Sub-titles written by Will Rogers
Ancient Sub-titles by Shakespeare or Bacon. . . .

We see a shot of a Wild West main street, then the title: "We open our masterpiece with a shot of a western town. Why? Because they all do it."

As this suggests, *Doubling for Romeo*—the first half of it, anyway—is a send-up of the movies. Will plays Sam Cody, a bashful Arizona cowboy ("To prove that he is a cowboy, we show him with cows") whose sweetheart, Lulu, moons over an autographed photo of Douglas Fairbanks and declares, "How wonderfully he makes love. Oh, if only I could be made love to like that." Realizing that "the best way to learn to make love is to go to the movie factory where they manufacture it," Sam heads to Hollywood and gets a job in a picture called *Why Live with Your Own Wife?* (a reference to C. B. DeMille's risqué comedies of the previous couple of years: *Old Wives for New, Male and Female,* and *Why Change Your Wife?*). He's a complete bust as a screen lover; in his big seduction scene, he giggles uncontrollably and can't stop looking at the camera. He doesn't do any better as the villain's stunt double in a fight scene, stopping in midpunch and asking the director, "When do we knock the table over?" The director is too dumbfounded to reply. Sam explains that he's never seen a movie fight where the table stayed on the floor; he just wants to know when he can expect the upheaval.

Back home, still untutored in lovemaking, he borrows a copy of *Romeo and Juliet* from the town parson, reads it, and falls asleep. He dreams a version of the play, with himself as Romeo and the townspeople in the other parts. In the opening scene, he's serenading Juliet/Lulu on the ukulele: "I have the Juliet blues/I have the Juliet blues/But I be-eth too darn mean to cry." There follows a fairly complete condensation of the play, Shakespeare's lines alternating with Rogers's jazzy comebacks. (Example: gesturing at Paris, Romeo/Sam tells Juliet, "Go ahead and marry him—then shoot him. Any jury in the world would acquit you.")

What's impressive about Will's acting is the contrast he's able to draw between the two characters he embodies. Where Sam is sleepy and stooped, Romeo is a gum-snapping, grinning . . . well, Romeo, of the drugstore variety, leaning his elbow against the wall and chatting Juliet up with the slimy self-confidence of a lounge lizard. Rather remarkable, too, is that the last third of the dream sequence is done straight and manages to achieve a real poignancy. (This makes up for the fact that, after Sam wakes up, there's no proper punch line, just a wham-bam happy ending.)

The critics recognized the film's wit and originality. "At last something new in pictures!" began *Variety*'s review. "The picture is a laugh from start to finish, and is the best out-and-out full length feature comedy that has been turned out in a couple of years. . . ." *The New York Times* called *Doubling for Romeo* "about the most hilarious thing Mr. Rogers has ever done," and *Photoplay* and *Reel Journal* put it on their lists of the year's best films.

WILL ALMOST always got good reviews for his Goldwyn pictures. But the films were generally box-office disappointments. Arthur Mayer, a Goldwyn salesman at the time, said he was under explicit instructions never to sell a popular picture "without 'wrapping around the exhibitor's neck' three or four Rogers features. . . . One lady operator in the north woods of Wisconsin turned him down with the criticism, 'He's too much like home folks. He don't seem like an actor.' " Another Goldwyn salesman, however, wrote Will an encouraging letter praising him as a "showman of the old school" (in contrast to the "butchers, barbers, Jews and others" with which the theater business had been "run over") and reassuring him that "your pictures are being sought after by the small towns daily; it is only a question of putting you over in the big centers."

The movies did well enough, in any case, that Goldwyn picked up Will's second-year option. And Will had no hesitations about re-signing; he liked his new career. He found his colleagues amiable and the work itself not taxing, although he continued to have trouble with the subtleties of continuity. (While he was making *Jes' Call Me Jim*, shooting once stopped for the day in the middle of a scene. Will went out and got a haircut. The next day, in order that eventual viewers not be completely baffled, part of a wig was pasted on the back of his head.) Bemusing as well, to someone so obsessively self-effacing, was the level of physical vanity the business seemed to demand. He was an oxymoronically camera-shy movie star, to the point where one fan magazine complained that in its vast files it had only one photograph of Will Rogers. He refused to wear any but the most perfunctory makeup, and he detested close-ups. "Don't you think it distracting," he asked a reporter, "when you see a picture, for the camera to suddenly switch from a whole scene to the hero's beaded eye-lashes, magnified so they look like Zeppelins?"*

But easily outweighing the oddities of the medium was the fact that, for the first time, his work did not take him away from Betty and the children, whose arrival in Los Angeles had followed his by a few weeks. At the end of shooting every day, he could go home to them and the spacious house, complete with swimming pool, they were renting on Van Ness Avenue in the Hancock Park section of Los Angeles. "We are very delighted with California," Betty wrote to Will's sister Maud shortly after her arrival, "have a nice house, very comfortable, such a beautiful yard, and the climate is perfectly wonderful—cool nights are really cold, and the air is glorious. . . . It is quite a treat to us to have our evenings." There was no room for horses, but Goldwyn offered to fix up an old building on the lot as a stable. The land around the studio was deserted and securely fenced, and young Bill and Mary Rogers rode there every afternoon. Jimmy, meanwhile, had substantial parts in three or four of Will's films and even built a following of pint-sized fans.

It wasn't just the regular hours that appealed to Will: He and Southern California were made for each other. The open land and palpable sense of unfettered opportunity were vivifying, stoking his already formidable energy to the point that three-hundred-mile drives across the desert were necessary to release it. And he found the ethos of the place deeply congenial. He had been participating in fictive commemorations of the end of the open range since entering his first roping contest in 1899; now he had discovered a culture that elegiacally honored the cowboy as enthusiastically as he did.

It was from people who shared this sense that Will drew his California friends; although he would occasionally socialize with fellow actors or other movie people, mainly ones who went in for riding or polo, and though he was always comfortable in the movie culture, it was clear from the start that he would never be part of any Hollywood social scene. Arriving in Southern California at roughly the same time he did were Ed Borein and Charley Russell, part of the second generation of

*Will had to use makeup for the Shakespeare scenes in *Doubling for Romeo;* not knowing how to put it on, he asked for help from Lon Chaney, "The man of a thousand faces," then under contract to Goldwyn. "Never again," Chaney commented to a reporter. "Bill kept springing his wisecracks and chewing gum until I grew dizzy trying to make the lipstick meet with his mouth. Half the time I'd jab at the wrong time and Bill would take a bite out of the stick."

"cowboy artists" after Frederick Remington, both of whom Will had known for years. Each had achieved a considerable national reputation for nostalgic depictions of roundups and gunfights that may not have reached the highest level of aesthetic sublimity or emotional profundity but compensated with their historical accuracy and unmistakable sincerity and depth of feeling. (Unlike Remington, both Russell and Borein had worked as cowboys, albeit briefly.) Beginning in 1919, Russell, a native of St. Louis who had long lived in Montana, began spending part of every winter in Southern California, where he found a ready market among such movie people as William S. Hart, Douglas Fairbanks, and Noah Beery. Borein moved from Oakland (where he had been born) to Santa Barbara a couple of years later. Will spent a lot of time with both men—Russell sometimes went along with him on movie locations—and began purchasing their works. In 1919, he saw a painting of Russell's called *Buffalo Hunt No. 39* that was about to be shipped to the Minneapolis Institute of Arts for an exhibition. When Will expressed his admiration, Russell sold it to him; a few days later, *Buffalo Hunt No. 40* was ready to be sent to Minnesota.

Of the two artists, Russell—whose expressionless demeanor belied his great warmth and humor—was the more self-conscious about honoring cowboy traditions, a cast of mind most readily seen in the diction of the wonderful illustrated letters he wrote to his friends. (Once, when Betty and Will invited him to visit, he wrote back, "We wont be able to worke your range this year wev got a six month old boy at our camp and we think hes a little young for trail work so we are going to class herd him a while.") But another California friend of Will's (and of Russell's and Borein's), though less interested in cowboys than Indians, had elevated the West to an entire philosophy of life. Will had met Charles F. Lummis when he played Los Angeles on the Sullivan-Considine circuit in 1907; after Will settled in California, they developed a warm friendship. Lummis was born in Lynn, Massachusetts, in 1859, but had been a resident of Los Angeles since 1885, when he arrived there after walking from Ohio (a journey even longer than Samuel Goldfish's). Lummis was a true American eccentric. He liked to be called "Don Carlos" and always dressed in the same limp green corduroy suit (when one wore out, he had an identical replacement made), Stetson sombrero, Mexican work shirt, and red Pueblo belt, wound several times around the waist, Indian-style. He was short of stature and wiry, and unruly white hair extended generously from the sides of his head; there was nothing on top. At one time city editor of the Los Angeles *Times*, he now edited, published, and wrote a monthly called *Out West*. But he was less a journalist than an indefatigable promoter of the Southwest (he coined the term) in all of its manifestations. He popularized Mexican and Indian lore in his many books, and he was an amateur anthropologist and archaeologist whose personal collection formed the basis of what became the Southwest Museum.

There was a regrettably and characteristically (for the time) racist aspect to Lummis's view of the Southwest, which began in New Mexico and ended at the Pacific Ocean; he saw it as the last frontier, a place where Anglo-Saxons could escape the teeming immigrants then contaminating the East and, in the salutary presence of sunshine and native culture, actually improve its stock. "The ignorant, hopelessly un-American type of foreigner which infests and largely controls Eastern cities is almost unknown here," he had written of Los Angeles in 1895. But Lummis did have an honest, surprisingly unpatronizing respect and admiration for Mexican and Indian culture, and his sense of the West was, in any case, more religious than invidious. What he was really doing was contradicting Frederick Jackson Turner: There still was a frontier, and it had an ocean view. "Well, there is not a dead black line on the map that can define it," he wrote.

> Out West is anywhere that is far enough from the East to be Out from Under. It begins whenever man can find elbow room, and Freedom; wherever he can escape from crowds and the obsession of their strange superstitions; wherever he has space to stand erect and must stand because he will and not because he is so wedged in that he could not fall down if he tried.

Lummis lived in "El Alisal," a structure of extremely eclectic design he had built himself on two and a half acres of wild land along the Arroyo Seco, a mostly dry river six miles west of downtown Los Angeles. It was a combination home, museum, and shrine to his vision of the world. He was a frequent and enthusiastic host, whether for a few close friends or as many as seventy-five, in one of his famous "noises"; whatever the occasion, the menu was almost always *albondiga* and frijol (meat loaf and beans). Lummis's diary description of the dinner where Will met the cowboy writer Eugene Manlove Rhodes for the first time makes it obvious that for the newcomer to California these were extremely congenial surroundings:

> . . . we had the usual official supper of the albondiga and the brown frijol done in Elena's incomparable way and eaten in vast profusion by each of the whole crowd and some of my Satsuma

jam in which Mrs. Rogers claimed partnership as I was putting it up the last time she was here and I gave her a taste of the making. And we had a good homely talk . . . it was a great thing to get these two old-timers [i.e., Will and Rhodes] started and they kept each other in constant action. They are both original and droll as all good cowboys are. . . . it was a long matching of numerous cowmen and old characters, although both of them together haven't a tenth part of Ed Borein's narrative genius. . . . Will was going to take us all to see his new picture "Jubilo," but he got so fascinated with the jabber that he passed it up and said later he just couldn't tear away to take us to any old theatre where he couldn't talk and he had enjoyed the evening more than anything else in years. He had a pretty good dose of it from 5 till 11:30. . . . and Will took them all home in his wonderful $9000 car.

Sometimes Charley Russell would be there, telling stories in sign language while his wife, Nancy, "interpreted" (in the middle of a story, she would occasionally blush and say, "Charley, I'm not going to say that!"), and it took precious little prompting for Will to do some tricks with his "Magic Rope." Lummis had been irascible as a youth, but by the time the Rogerses met him he was in a grand-old-man mode, and he came to have a deep affection for Will and "Bonnie Betty." He wrote her a few years later, when Will was in the hospital after a gallstone operation: "There isn't a man alive that I value more than Will—& I'm free to say so anywhere. And there isn't a more useful American. I'm saying this as a historian. And as myself, I love him Dearly, & love you, & love the children & the Home. It's all a marvelous, wide wholesomeness reaching all over the Country."

The glorification of the West wasn't taking place only in the upper realms of art and ideas; suddenly and improbably, Southern California was becoming the capital of cowboy culture. More responsible for this than the work of any artist or writer was the remarkable popularity of that genre of motion picture known as the Western—which, looked at one way, was not much more than a roping contest writ large. As early as 1909, the annual routine of many cowboys revolved around three seasonal happenings: the spring rodeo circuit, the fall cattle roundups, and a winter stop in Southern California. They would congregate at what became known as "the Waterhole," the corner of Cahuenga Avenue and Hollywood Boulevard in Hollywood, where they would await selection by production crews as stuntmen or extras. There was even the chance of becoming a star—hadn't Tom Mix done it? After World War I, and as large ranches in Arizona and Colorado went under, cowboys streamed into Los Angeles—much like Sam Cody in *Doubling for Romeo*—trying to find a place in the movies. It was from these dinosaurs in chaps that Will selected a less elevated group of California friends. Forty years old in November 1919 and a success by any definition of the word, he had outgrown his need for father figures; now he was drawn to younger men, maybe because only they had the energy to keep up with him. A $7.50-a-day extra on *Almost a Husband* was a six-foot-two-inch, two-hundred-pound nineteen-year-old named Guinn Williams, Jr. As a boy he'd worked on the ranch of his father, a Texas congressman, but after serving in the army during the war had landed in Hollywood. Will took a liking to him, gave him the nickname "Big Boy" (later abbreviated to "Big"), and struck up a warm friendship that would continue through sixteen years of roughhousing and mutual joshing.

On the spur of the moment, Will would gather Big Boy, one or two other movie cowboys such as Buster Brown or Wally Cameron, and sometimes a young Goldwyn production manager named J. J. Cohn, jump into his "$9,000 car," a 1919 Pierce Arrow, and just set out. It was a way to simulate, with a team of simulated cowboys, the treasured cattle drives of his youth. Sometimes their destination would be Victorville, north of San Bernardino, and sometimes they would go all the way to Mexicali, through the Imperial Valley and over the Mexican border.

"Bill would come in and say, 'Joe, let's go somewhere,' " Cohn remembered. "I'd say, 'I don't have any clothes with me.' He'd say, 'We'll buy you a shirt.'

"We'd sleep overnight somewheres. Sometimes I'd end up sleeping in the same bed with Bill. One time, about three in the morning, he kicked me. I said, 'What do you want?' He said, 'How much did *Polly of the Circus* cost?' "—referring, inexplicably, to a Goldwyn film of the year before.

One day in 1920, he told Big Boy to go home and get his suit—they were going on a longer trip than usual. They got on a train and rode it all the way to the Round-Up in Cheyenne, Wyoming, the oldest rodeo in the country. The winner of the riding contest that year was a local boy named Ray Bell, and he took Will and Big Boy out to his family's ranch. The visiting celebrities immediately started in roping, ruining their clothing in the process. Ray Bell took them to the local men's store, where Will bought a new suit.

"The owner said, 'Mr. Rogers, if you can come back in two or three hours, I'll get the pants fixed for you,' " Ray Bell recalled.

"Bill says, 'Have you got a scissors?' Rogers just put the pants on the table and cut them right off. He wore 'em right out of there."

Will convinced Bell to go back to California with him and go into the pictures. When he got to town, he stayed with the Rogers family for a month. By this time, they had bought their own house at 925 Beverly Drive in Beverly Hills, catty-corner from the Beverly Hills Hotel. It was a three-acre property around which Will had constructed a tall brick wall. Besides the obligatory pool, it had a stable, a floodlit tanbark riding ring, a gymnasium and miniature theater in the basement, and two log cabins in a corner of the garden. One was for Mary and the other, concealed by trees and shrubs and containing five bunk beds and open fireplace, was a family gathering place on holidays and special occasions. When Will's sister Maud came to visit, she took one look at the hideout and said, "Will, you're just like an old fullblood. You buy a big house, then build a little cabin at the foot of the hill and live in it."

"We used to saddle up in the morning and ride to Culver City," said Bell, who had found work as a cowboy extra on the Goldwyn lot. It was about a five-mile journey. "We'd ride down Robinson Boulevard. Down on the corner of Robinson and Pico, the Rodeo Land and Water Company had a place there about 50 acres, with a lot of cows and calves. We'd get there about 6 o'clock in the morning, open the gate and rope those calves. One morning we were roping there and a guy comes up in an old Model T car and he says, 'Hey, what are you guys doing roping my cattle?' He looks up and sees Will Rogers. 'Oh, Mr. Rogers, you can come in and rope this cattle any time you want to, day or night.' " The man was Burton Green, the owner of the company.

It was the same Burton Green who was indirectly responsible for Will's new home. Decades before, Green had purchased some land west of Hollywood and edging up into the Santa Monica Mountains; it was covered with lima bean fields at the time, but he hoped to find oil. In 1906, after two unsuccessful strikes, Green hired a landscape architect to plan a community of suburban estates; he named it Beverly Hills, after Beverly Farms, Massachusetts, where he had once lived. The Beverly Hills Hotel was constructed in 1911, as a kind of beacon in the wilderness, and the town was incorporated in 1914, with a population of 550. Beverly Hills was etched into the international consciousness when Mary Pickford and Douglas Fairbanks decided to live there following their marriage in November 1920. Their estate, "Pickfair," was an ersatz English mansion that became to the world at large the very symbol of Hollywood glamour, and their example made Beverly Hills the residence of choice among the Hollywood elite.

The Rogers family actually moved to Beverly Hills a few months before the Pickford-Fairbanks wedding, demonstrating Will's long-standing
acuity in matters of real estate. For a real estate aficionado, of course,
there could be no better place than 1920s Los Angeles. As if he were
playing some real-life version of Monopoly, Will almost immediately
started buying. By 1923, he was making payments on no fewer than five
pieces of property, including three additional lots in Beverly Hills (cost:
$49,500, $18,500, and $15,000) and a lot and some beachfront property
in Santa Monica ($16,000 and $45,000).

Ray Bell described what was probably Will's typical method. "One
.day I was driving on Wilshire Boulevard and noticed a For Sale sign on
the corner of Wilshire and Beverly [Drive]. They were building the Beverly Wilshire Hotel. The Brown Derby restaurant was right on the other
corner, on Rodeo Drive, but it was the only thing around there—the
rest was vacant. The next morning Rogers and I decided we were going
to drive over. He took a look at it and told me to wait in the car. 'I
won't be but a few minutes.' He came back twenty-five minutes later
and said, 'I bought it. I bought that whole block.' "

Will's new working schedule occupied his days, but it still left him
time for other projects. In a venture reminiscent of his newsreels for
Pathé, a San Francisco film company agreed to pay him $750 a week,
for a six-month period starting March 1, 1920, for "at least fifteen original sayings or comments or witticisms." Will himself produced "The Illiterate Digest," another such series distributed by Pathé.*

*The title was a takeoff on *The Literary Digest*, a magazine that at the time was producing
its own newsreel. Its lawyer, William Beverly Winslow, sent Will a letter complaining that
"the prestige of 'The Literary Digest' is being lowered by the subject matter of your films as
well as the title of your film because the public naturally confuse the two subjects" and
threatening to "take such steps as I may deem advisable." Will's reply noted that he had
stopped making the newsreels:

> as the gentlemen who were putting it out were behind in their payments and my hu-
> mor kinder waned. . . .
>   Now you inform your editors at once that their most dangerous rival has with-
> drawn, and they can go ahead and resume publication. But you inform your clients
> that if they ever take up rope throwing, or chewing gum, I will consider it a direct in-
> fringement of my rights and will protect it with one of the best lawyers in Oklahoma.

Expertly punctured, Winslow didn't respond. A year or so later, Will was playing in the
Follies "and who should call on me but the nicest old gentleman I had ever met, especially in
the law profession. He was the one I had written the letter to, and he had had photographic
copies made of my letter and had given them around to all his lawyer friends." Will told the
story in the introduction to his first collection of columns, for which he resuscitated the title
The Illiterate Digest; he dedicated the book to Winslow.

Will was contacted by the Newspaper Enterprise Association (NEA), a syndicated feature service owned by the Scripps-Howard newspaper chain, to provide the gags for a daily cartoon called "What's News Today." The cartoon apparently never reached publication, but another NEA venture did: a series of columns by Will on the Republican and Democratic conventions of 1920. The Republican convention was held in Chicago in the beginning of June, while Will was shooting *Cupid the Cowpuncher*, so he could not cover the proceedings in person. But the NEA promotional sheets promised that the FAMOUS OKLAHOMA COWBOY HUMORIST AND GOLDWYN MOTION PICTURE COMEDIAN would provide at least ten jokes a day. His first few dispatches really were just a series of gags, along the lines of the Prohibition and Peace Conference books. ("Mexico don't know how to get rid of Villa. Loan him to us for Vice-President. That would get both nations rid of him.") But his fourth article introduced a conceit carried through in the remaining six: Will pretended he was in the Philadelphia bedroom of Senator Boies Penrose, a Republican power broker who wasn't able to attend the convention because of illness. Possibly unwittingly, he was following in the comic tradition of Major Jack Downing, Artemus Ward, Petroleum V. Nasby, and Bill Arp, nineteenth-century characters whose creators (Seba Smith, Charles Farrar Browne, David Ross Locke, and Charles Henry Smith) had them report on fanciful interactions with Andrew Jackson, Abraham Lincoln, and other political figures. (Penrose may have been in Will's thoughts because he had been a Harvard classmate, close companion, and frequent anecdotal subject of Charles F. Lummis.)

Will and "Pen" listened in by telephone as the three front-runners— Senator Hiram Johnson, Gen. Leonard Wood, and Governor Frank Lowden of Illinois—fought among themselves and allowed Warren Harding, a first-term senator from Ohio who had been a distant fourth in the first ballot, to slip away with the nomination.

> I said: "What makes the delegates change? Don't they stay with their man?" Pen. said: "The delegates vote the way their people tell them the first ballot. But after that they sell to the highest bidder."
>
> I said: "But that's not honest, is it?"
>
> Pen. said: "No, just politics."

Will probably intended to cover at least part of the Democratic convention in person: It was to start on June 28 in San Francisco, and he would be nearby on location for a movie. But tragedy intervened. Suddenly, Bill, Jimmy, and twenty-three-month-old Freddy Rogers all took ill with diphtheria. Will was informed on June 16 and immediately set out for home, traveling all night by a relay of cars. He was greeted at the door with the news: Fred Rogers had died at 4:00 a.m.

Publicly, Will referred to Freddy on only two subsequent occasions, both times indirectly; within the family, according to his sons, the subject was never broached. Of course, no one knows how many tears Will and Betty shed behind closed doors. But it seems clear that thirty years after the wrenching death of his mother, eleven years after Betty Blake agreed to be his wife and saved him from despair, he was a man who not only controlled his emotions but subjugated them. This psychic economy was indisputably adaptive for Will, but he may have carried it too far. Later on June 17, in an act that went almost frighteningly beyond professionalism, he slipped a piece of paper in the typewriter and began his first Democratic convention piece for the NEA.

GOLDWYN DID NOT sign Will to a new contract when his first one fully expired in May 1921. The decision was less a reflection on Will than on Goldwyn Pictures' financial condition. For the year, the company would report a loss of $686,000, and the very month the Rogers contract came up the decision was made to cut spending by 22 percent. Sam Goldwyn reported to the board of directors that almost all star contracts had either been canceled or not renewed. Within a year, Goldwyn himself would be forced out, becoming an independent producer; in 1924, the studio merged with two other operations to become Metro-Goldwyn-Mayer.

Will had a standing offer from Flo Ziegfeld to go back to the *Follies*. But he had a better idea. Two years before, Charles Chaplin, Mary Pickford, Douglas Fairbanks, and D. W. Griffith had decided they wanted to produce their own films, joining forces to form United Artists. Will thought he could do the same thing, on a substantially smaller scale. He would, for example, employ no stars other than himself and start with two-reel shorts rather than five-reel features. To the "so-called wise guys" who might say that making shorter movies was a comedown, Will with some logic replied that he would rather "tell the same story in two reels. I have made fourteen [*sic*] two-reel pictures, which were released in five reels."

He hired Clarence Badger to direct, put Betty on salary, bought one script and wrote two more, and got to work. For his first effort, *The Ropin' Fool*, he devised a story about "Ropes" Reilly, a man determined to rope anything, including the rat running around his bedroom; he ropes in his dreams and he ropes at the dinner table, and when he wants to propose he throws a tiny rope around his sweetheart's finger. Obviously, a self-portrait. There's a wisp of a plot, but the film, charming even today, mainly exists as a showcase for Will's splendid tricks. The centerpiece is a series of horse-and-rider ropings, presented in slow motion as well as normal speed; the rope was whitened with shoe polish so it would show up well against the coal black Dopey. Will hadn't done them for an audience since changing to a single act ten years before, but he doesn't look a bit rusty.

One Day in 365 (working title: *No Story at All),* his next film, was perfect for an independent producer, at least as far as costs were concerned. Not only did Will star in it and write the script but the cast was his own family and the only set was his own house. The script (no complete print survives) is a delightfully self-referential comic variation on reality, anticipating radio and television serials of a quarter of a century and more later, in which Jack Benny, George Burns, and Jerry Seinfeld played "Jack Benny," "George Burns," and "Jerry Seinfeld." It's a day in the life of the Rogers family. Will desperately tries to find a suitable scenario for a picture due to start shooting that day, but he is constantly interrupted: by the kids fighting across the breakfast table, by one phone call after another, by a series of motorists driving up and wanting to know how to get to Douglas Fairbanks and Mary Pickford's house. Meanwhile, the camera crew loafs and shoots craps and Clarence Badger—playing himself, naturally—stews. In the evening, Will agrees to put on a show for the family; after the first Bryan gag, Jimmy says, "I've heard that one for four years; come on Mama, put me to bed." By 1:30 in the morning, there's still no script; in a final close-up, Will speaks into the camera. "Some of these days I'm going to put on a story from real life—but then no one would believe it."

There is no surviving print or script of the third production, *Fruits of Faith,* but a *New York Times* description of the plot reveals it as a throwback to the Goldwyn features: Will plays a lazy hobo who finds, to his surprise, that he really can get what he wants by praying for it; along the way, he encounters and adopts a mule and a boy (played by Jimmy Rogers). The *Times* reviewer much preferred it to *Drums of Fate,* the feature it followed at the Rialto: "There is more genuine entertainment in any hundred feet of [*Fruits of Faith*] than in all the celluloid miles of agony and adventure that prolongs the heavy hour of the photoplay."

The movie was made in the summer of 1921; the above review was published January 15, 1923. The gap had profound significance for the Rogers family. After the first three two-reelers were completed, Pathé, the distributor, suddenly announced that in order to release them it would need a series of eight films. Having already spent almost fifty thousand dollars of his own money, Will had no desire to spend more without a guaranteed return. So he closed up shop.

The failure of Will Rogers Productions has sometimes been described as having ruinous results for the Rogers family finances. But $45,135.07 (the loss Will declared on his 1921 tax return) was in itself a manageable amount of money, especially when you consider it included the salary paid to Betty, that there was still reason to believe that the three films could one day be marketed, and that it was tax-deductible. What made the loss pressing was all the real-estate buying Will had done: Funds to make the monthly payments had to be found from any conceivable source. The house in Beverly Hills had to be mortgaged; Will Rogers, Jr., ten years old at the time, remembers going to a bank and signing his Liberty Bond over to his parents.

This was Will's first major setback after sixteen years of successes, show-business forms mastered, and new worlds conquered. Determined never to put himself, his wife, and his children in such a position again, he threw himself into his labors with an awe-inspiring fervor. But his efforts resulted in something more than the permanent financial solvency of the Rogers family. By the end of the next half-decade, through an ineffable, ineluctable, and peculiarly American process, Will Rogers would become someone the mere mention of whose name would call up a well-delineated image, complete with homely details, broad brushstrokes of feeling, and a certain singular way of looking at the world. He wouldn't be just a person anymore: He would be a national presence.

SKIPPING ROPE WITH PRIZEFIGHTER
BENNIE LEONARD, 1924

CHAPTER 9

"ALL I KNOW IS JUST WHAT I READ IN THE PAPERS"

We are living in an age of publicity.

— WILL ROGERS

THE ASCENDANCE of Will Rogers in the early 1920s was not just a product of hard work. He was also the right man in the right place at exactly the right time. The mass media as we know them now began in the aftermath of World War I: The ten years after the armistice saw the development of radio, phonograph records, newsreels, and syndicated newspaper features, and great growth in the technological sophistication and influence of motion pictures and advertising. All were predicated on the notion that millions of people, people who hitherto had been separated by geography, outlook, and class, could share the same symbolic experience at roughly the same time. What the new media needed were voices. Will's was ideal for their purposes, being inclusive, accessible, amusing, and marketable. And its down-home twang also immediately defused any intimidation or distaste Americans might have felt at the now-inescapable prospect of being talked to by machines.

The point bears further attention. Technological advance was just one reason many in the country felt a growing sense of anxiety in the postwar period. On a variety of fronts, truths previously held to be unshakable were beginning to tremble. One such was Jeffersonian agrarianism: The 1920 census revealed, for the first time in its history, a country where the majority of the population lived in the city and not the country. Traditional assumptions about money seemed to slip away as the stock market bubble grew and more and more of the accoutrements of life were mortgaged. Meanwhile, signs from all over the culture—jazz, bobbed hair, avant-garde poetry, Chicago gangsters, spiraling divorce rates, Hollywood sex scandals—testified to a shake-up in morals. Even the Russian Revolution of 1917 could be—and was—seen as a threatening signal from abroad that past certainties were certain no more.

The reinvigorated temperance movement, the Red Scare, and the emergence of such xenophobic organizations as the Ku Klux Klan and the American Legion were all reactions to the perception that things had changed in unwelcome ways. What they had in common was a distended national self-consciousness, an obsession with *Americanism,* such as had never really been evident before. An odious phrase of the time referred to the "100 percent American"; anything less, so it was implied, was unacceptable.

Far from pandering to this strain, Will sent some splendid torpedoes its way. "It seems that before the war come along," he once wrote, "we were really kinder lax in our duty toward declaring just what we were."

> The war come along and about all we could do was muster up five or six million men of every breed and color that has ever been invented. Now these poor fellows dident know whether they were "100 percent Americans" or "Better Citizens," or what they were, and we started them drilling so fast they dident have time to go through a clinic and find out.
>
> You see up to then they dident know what all this meant. They thought that as long as they paid their taxes, tended to their own business, went to their own churches, kept kinder within the law, that that was all they was supposed to do. And it was like that in the old days. But you see we was a backwards nation and dident know it.
>
> What we had to learn was to be better Americans. Why here was old men that had raised a big family and had never said "America First." Can you imagine such ignorance?

Yet, in a way that must on some level have been intentional, he was perfectly positioned to benefit from this national unease. More than just espousing the old-time values, he *embodied* them, in his italicized geniality and horse sense. He was there to tell his listeners that maybe things hadn't really changed so much, after all. If you looked at Will Rogers the right way, you could see Ben Franklin. You could see Davy Crockett. You could see Abraham Lincoln. You could *not* see the farmer down the road, for Will was no hick. Indeed, his sophistication, his *Follies* tenure, and his famous friends, made him a more credible prosecution witness. Take one of his favorite jokes of the early 1920s: "I am the only man who came out of the movies with the same wife he started with." One brief sentence simultaneously mocks Hollywood's reputation for loose morals, affirms his own allegiance to monogamy and tradition, and— what is probably most important of all—reassures the listener. *Believe me, I know,* Will is saying—all that talk of fast living is nothing to get worked up about.

A cowboy, an *Indian,* an apostle of decency and common sense. The conclusion was inescapable: The 100 percent American was Will.

None of this concerned him in the summer of 1921, however. What did was the absolute necessity of making some money. His first chance to do so was indirectly related to, of all things, the Hollywood Babylon. C. B. DeMille's leering sex farces, Charlie Chaplin's series of marriages to ever-younger teenagers, the whispers that heartthrob Wallace Reid (with whom Will had ridden to California) was a drug addict, the revelation that even virginal Mary Pickford's marriage to Douglas Fairbanks had been preceded by an adulterous affair—it couldn't all be coincidence. Or so the guardians of official morality believed. These ministers, women's auxiliary groups, and editorial-page oracles, flushed with the triumph of the Eighteenth Amendment, were campaigning to curb the Hollywood debauchery with censorship, a kind of cinematic version of Prohibition. To forestall this eventuality, Hollywood executives began a well-publicized attempt at "self-censorship." They cracked down on their stars' colorful behavior, to the point of inserting morals clauses into their contracts; publicity departments were bolstered and instructed to accentuate the positive. Baseball, its image gravely tarnished by the 1919 "Black Sox" scandals, had tried to redeem itself by appointing an unimpeachable figurehead, Judge Kenesaw Mountain Landis, and in 1921 the major studios asked Will Hays, Warren G. Harding's squeaky-clean postmaster general, whether he would become their industry's "czar."

Even as Hays was considering the offer, the worst scandal of all struck. Over Labor Day weekend, Roscoe "Fatty" Arbuckle—after Charlie Chaplin, the era's most succcessful comedian in the movies— threw a three-day party, fueled by hot jazz and bootleg liquor, in three adjoining rooms on the twelfth floor of the St. Francis Hotel in San Francisco. A guest at the party, an actress named Virginia Rappe, became very ill; the following Friday, she died of what was diagnosed as a ruptured bladder. Witnesses came forward to say that Rappe had been injured during an attempted rape by Arbuckle, and the day after her death the comedian was arrested for murder.

During one of Arbuckle's three trials (the first two ended in hung juries), Will gave a speech to an industry gathering that took a caustic look at the way anti-Arbuckle hysteria had turned into an indictment of Hollywood. "In case this is not a respectable party, I left an assumed name as I came in in case I was called on to testify," his notes opened.

> Adam and Eve made the rib famous, Corbett made the solar plexus stand out but it remained for Roscoe to bring the bladder into a prominence that was never enjoyed by any other organ. Now at all the fashionable teas and gatherings sooner or later the conversation drifts to it. . . .
>
> The toughest charge he has against him now is being from Los Angeles. The Grand Jury is out now and are going to turn in a verdict favoring cremating everybody south of Bakersfield. The District Attorney has been promised if he can hang Arbuckle he will be Mayor. And if he can hang ten other Picture people with him he will be made Governor.*

He also mentioned that he was "working over at Lasky's now." What he didn't say was that his job at the Famous Players–Lasky studio—his first since the Will Rogers Productions debacle—was courtesy of Roscoe Arbuckle. Shortly before his arrest, Arbuckle had begun preproduction on a picture called *The Melancholy Spirit*. Will was hired to take over his part, at a salary of $7,500. (He was happy to take the money, but in truth the studio took *him:* Arbuckle's salary at the time he got into trouble was a million dollars a year.) The film, directed by James Cruze and retitled *One Glorious Day* when Will came on, was about Professor Ezra Botts, a meek expert on spiritualism, whose body becomes inhabited by a rash spirit named Ek. Thus, as in *Doubling for Romeo*, Will played a dual role. Again he got excellent reviews; *Variety* said that casting him in the part was "an inspiration" and *The New York Times* called him "a revelation." The film itself—whose double-exposure special effects were at the cutting edge of technical sophistication—won higher praise than anything he'd done for Goldwyn, making many newspapers' ten-best lists and being chosen the top film of the year by the National Board of Review.

---

*Arbuckle was acquitted in his third trial, but the case ruined his career. Shunned by an industry desperate to dissociate itself from any suggestion of loose morals, and broken in spirit, he was not able to return to the screen until 1932. He died the next year.

But Will's entrepreneurial fiasco had soured him on Hollywood, for the time being at least. While he couldn't take up with Ziegfeld right where he had left off—the *Follies of 1921*, with W. C. Fields, Fanny Brice, and Ray Dooley, was on the road—vaudeville hadn't gone anywhere. A price war between the rival Shubert and Keith organizations had momentarily inflated salaries, and Will's Hollywood tenure had, if nothing else, made him a more valuable commodity on the boards. On October 18, Will's old agent Max Hart sent him a telegram at Famous Players–Lasky: OKAY THREE WEEKS THREE THOUSAND DOLLARS EXCLUSIVE ENGAGEMENT OPENING WINTER GARDEN OCT THIRTY FIRST CONFIRM. He actually appeared only two weeks at the Shuberts' showcase theater, the Winter Garden; during the second, he also played their Crescent Theatre in Brooklyn.* The total fee of $8,600 was, according to a Shubert press release, the highest salary ever paid in vaudeville. After the engagement ended, Will went up to the New Amsterdam roof to headline a new edition of the *Midnight Frolic,* which ran through the year. Will had gotten used to early retiring and rising in California; maybe because he knew he had gotten the star cheap, at one thousand dollars a week, Ziegfeld let him go on before intermission. In December, there was a Christmas bonus: Every night from the twelfth through the seventeenth, he made personal appearances at four or five of Marcus Loew's movie theaters. Another fifteen hundred dollars.

Shortly after New Year's, Ziegfeld sent an edition of the *Frolic* out on the road, something he had never done before. The production was built around Will, whose name was billed in type as big as the show's; for the first time, instead of being given a straight salary, he was paid a share of the gross receipts each week. His 10 percent share ranged from $1,520.60 to $2,519.30.

He came out right after the opening production number. Playing on his reputation for spotting celebrities in the audience, he introduced and brought up onstage "David Belasco" (really actor Brandon Tynan, made up to look like the playwright/producer who was the grand old man of the American theater). After a few pleasantries, Will asked "Belasco" for acting lessons, possibly a reference to his own less-than-sterling success in Hollywood. In fact, he did a lot of acting in the *Frolic,* appearing in three skits as well as his monologue. There was a mock melodrama called "The Curse of Gold," where he took the role of Nellie Beaumont

*According to Eddie Dowling, another performer on the bill, Will did not do well at the Crescent: "Well, I never saw a man die such a horrible death. Brooklyn was no place to put Will Rogers, with his sly talk and all that."

(appearing in drag for the first and only time in his career), a movie
spoof along the lines of *Doubling for Romeo,* and "The Disagreement Conference," a takeoff on the naval disarmament conference then under way
in Washington. Will played Secretary of State Charles Evans Hughes
and had such lines as "Now, we made a mistake in the last war by fighting it on credit. The next war has got to be C.O.D." When he called
on the delegate from Italy, played by John Shannon, Will would substitute the name of a prominent Italian citizen of whatever city they were
in, then hit Shannon on the head with a rubber mallet. According to
notes penciled in a copy of the script, this piece of business got the "biggest laugh in the scene."

The show opened in Philadelphia in early January, then played
Pittsburgh, Washington, Baltimore, Rochester, Cleveland, Toronto, and
Detroit before closing in Chicago in May. Betty, sometimes accompa-
nied by one or more of the children, came along. "In the afternoon,
Rogers would go to the theater to practice his rope tricks on the empty
stage, while his children roller-skated around," recalled Betsy Rees
Bevan, a featured dancer. "I would go to do ballet exercises. One day
Rogers turned and said to me, 'You and I are the only ones in this show
who really work.' "

Lucille Zinman, a chorus girl, remembered the star as a benignly
paternal figure. "Roy Rosenbaum was the show manager," she said.
"His wife was a serious poker player. After our last show in Toronto, we
got on an overnight train for Detroit, and Ma Rosenbaum picked six or
seven dopes to play poker. She took our salary. When we got off the
train the next morning, Will Rogers was leaning against a column in the
station, his hands in his pockets, his hat brim over his eyes. Somehow,
he knew exactly who was in the game. He said, 'How much you have
left?' 'She took it all.' He took my hand and put in a wad of bills." Will
was protective of the girls. In a later edition of the *Follies,* Ziegfeld had
inserted a production number that approached—if it didn't actually
achieve—full nudity. Will saw it in dress rehearsal and told Ziegfeld he
was quitting the show if it wasn't modified. It was.

One notable milestone on the tour occurred in Pittsburgh, the first
week of February. Over KDKA—which, at fifteen months, was the nation's oldest commercial radio station—Will made his first broadcast.

From Pittsburgh, the *Frolic* traveled to Washington for a heady week.
Seventeen years before, on his way to Madison Square Garden, Will
had palled around with Theodore Roosevelt, Jr. Now he and Betty were
the luncheon guests of young Roosevelt, his half-sister Alice and her husband, Congressman Nicholas Longworth, a powerful Ohio Republican.

What joy the invitation must have held for Will. He would never hold any politician in higher esteem than Theodore Roosevelt. In Texas, many years before, he had tried to enlist in the Rough Riders; Roosevelt had provided the name for his vaudeville horse and the subject for his first political joke. There was even reason to believe that the former President admired *him*. Shortly before he died in 1919, he told an aide that Will had such a keen insight into the American mind that he was bound to be a "great factor" in the political life of the nation. Through young Theodore—whom the newly elected Harding had appointed assistant secretary of the navy, just as his father had been—and Mrs. Longworth—who had already developed a reputation as an unsurpassed Washington wit—Will could vicariously commune with the great man.

Later in the week, through Will Hays—who had accepted the "movie czar" job but would not begin it until March 14—Will met Warren Harding at the White House. In his Washington hotel room, he scribbled an account of the encounter:

> Well Hays the minute he spied me said Have you met the President yet. I said no. So he dragged me through three rooms filled with Ohio office seekers. Didn't even knock, just busted right on in. Well I felt shamed. I felt we would both get thrown out on our ear. But he didn't even get to start to introduce me before the president said, "Hello, where's your chewing gum?" So instead of me telling him anything funny, he starts in repeating things I had said in the Midnight Follies for years. . . .
>
> So the fellow who tells you he's right from a farm to the White House is cuckoo. I told him I wanted to tell him the latest political jokes. He said, "I know em. I appointed most of em." So I saw I couldn't match humor with this man so I called it a day. I felt just like I was shaking hands with some old cow man from Oklahoma.

The ambrosial taste of presidential fellowship and approval quickly turned bitter. In the "Disagreement Conference" sketch, there were a number of cracks directed at Harding, whose readiness to delegate responsibility and taste for golf were both well known. At one point, Will, as Secretary Hughes, picked up a ringing telephone and said, "Hello, Mr. Harding. You lost by two holes? Well, you can't win every day." Everywhere in Washington, people were repeating this and other gibes, and one day a White House secretary came to Will's dressing room and asked him to drop them. According to Gene Buck, Will began to cry on learning that the President had taken offense, and immediately agreed to take the jokes out. He thought that was the end of it, but though he sent tickets to the President and expected him to attend the Friday performance, word came that Harding was going to *another* show that night: According to Betty, still peeved two decades later, this was "a road company on tour for the second season."

The next night, Will struck back. He praised the speech on foreign affairs Harding had given to the Senate the day before: "In fact, it sounded like one of the best speeches Hughes ever wrote." Referring to a fire that had recently damaged the Treasury building, he said, "The fire started on the roof and burned down and down until it got to the place where the money ought to be and there it stopped. The Harding administration had beat the fire to it. A fire in the Treasury building is nothing to get excited about during a Republican administration." (The Teapot Dome and other financial scandals for which the Harding White House would be known had not yet been exposed, so Will can be credited with striking prescience.)

When he was brought out for a curtain call, he made an indirect but nonetheless pointed reference to his tiff with the President, which had become grist for the Washington gossip mill. "I have cracked quite a few jokes on public men here, both Republicans and Democrats," he said. "I hope I have not given offense. In fact, I don't believe any *big man* will take offense." He went on to detail what good sports Roosevelt and Wilson had been and concluded, "After all, it is the test of a *big man* whether he can stand the gaff."

The display of pique was uncharacteristic of Will, and, given the opportunity, he reverted to solicitous form. Harding died some eighteen months later, and in his syndicated column Will determinedly tried to make posthumous peace with the President. The highest praise he could come up with was, "HE WAS A REAL HONEST-TO-GOODNESS MAN"; the capital letters indicate Will knew the compliment was less than overwhelming and the volume had to be pumped up. Referring to the press reports of the hard feelings between him and Harding, he wrote, disingenuously, "Now, I want to say nothing was further from the truth. That was simply newspaper stuff."

He also took the occasion to reiterate his comic credo. It was an odd one for a satirist, but it was Will's through and through: "No, I don't think I ever hurt any man's feelings by my little gags. I know I never willfully did it. When I have to do that to make a living I will quit."

THE TOURING *Frolic* got Will back on his financial feet; the *Follies of 1922* gave him a platform from which he could soar. The sixteenth edition of the show was the most elaborate yet, costing $300,000, or more than ten times the budget of the first *Follies*. Because of the expense, the customary Atlantic City tryout was forgone, and it opened cold in New York on June 5. Unironed kinks stretched the show to about twice its normal length. Right before the finale came some free-form patter among Will, Andrew Tombes, Ed Gallagher, and Al Shean. On opening night, this didn't transpire until 12:45 a.m., and Tombes asked Will why he was carrying an umbrella. "Because it was raining when they began this show yesterday," he replied. But the reviews were glowing (the *Herald* said the show "was like a composite picture of the best bits from all the best musical shows you've ever seen or ever hoped to see") and by the second night people were standing five deep at the rear of the theater. The demand for tickets had not abated by September, when the *Follies* traditionally went on the road, so Ziegfeld kept it at the New Amsterdam. It ran for another year.

Will had agreed (orally, of course) to remain with the production only while it was still in New York, so this decision can be seen as a ploy by Ziegfeld to hold on to his star. But a letter he wrote when Will finally left, in June, averring that "we are all surprised that we are still at the old stand where we started," seems sincere. "I want you to know that I appreciate the fact that your word is good for anything on this earth," the showman declared, "and to have you say you will do a thing is the same as if it was done."

But staying in New York with the *Follies* (with the rest of the family back in California, he lived at the Hotel Astor in Times Square) suited Will's purposes, anyway. The two-thousand-dollar-a-week salary gradually served to bring his finances to health. (It was helpful, too, that Pathé finally began to release *The Ropin' Fool* and *Fruits of Faith* late in the year, from which Will eventually recouped more than $32,000 of the $45,000-plus he had put in.) The celebrities who streamed into the New Amsterdam to see him perform solidified his national standing; among those he asked to take a bow were former Secretary of the Treasury (and future Democratic presidential candidate) William McAdoo, Governor Henry Allen of Kansas, financier Bernard Baruch, Will Hays, Ambassador to Great Britain George Harvey, artist Howard Chandler Christy, Gen. John Pershing, and the Russian actor/director Constantin Stanislavsky. During one memorable week in the fall, Douglas Fairbanks, Mary Pickford, John McCormack, Sir Thomas Lipton, Al Smith, Rudolph Valentino, Pola Negri, and Adolph Zukor all showed up.

While in Chicago with the *Frolic*, Will had been approached by a film producer named Carl Clancy and offered the part of Ichabod

Crane in a film adaptation of Washington Irving's "The Legend of Sleepy Hollow," set to be filmed in July and August. In search of historical accuracy, Clancy had persuaded John D. Rockefeller to let him rebuild the Hollow's schoolhouse on its original site, which was then part of Rockefeller's Tarrytown, New York, estate. The nearby location meant that Will could appear with the *Follies* and still work on the film every day except Wednesday and Saturday (when there were matinees).

Though he had to stretch his budget to pay Will's fee (it totaled $19,583.20), Clancy was extremely impressed by the enthusiasm and vigor the star brought to the set. On the occasion when the reckless night ride of Bram Bones and his gang was to be filmed, one of the stunt riders didn't show up. Will, Clancy recalled, "volunteered to double for the missing 'extra,' quickly changed his make-up, leaped into the saddle, and led all the other riders in repeated thundering dashes up and down the rock-strewn road until the scene had been taken." In the final editing, the footage of the ride was intercut with a scene of Will as Ichabod Crane hearing the hoofbeats and pulling the covers over his head in fear. When Will saw the sequence, Clancy reported, "he was greatly amused to see himself in two places at the same time."

That fall Will seemed to be in a dozen places at once. He put out yet another series of gags to be projected in movie theaters, of interest because it was the inspiration of David Selznick (he had not yet added the *O.*), then twenty, whose father, the early movie mogul Lewis J. Selznick, had put him in charge of a fledgling newsreel operation called the Selznick News. Possibly unaware of the earlier ventures, Selznick presented this to Will as a new idea, so high in publicity value that a salary wouldn't be necessary. Will, atypically, agreed. Later, he asked for one hundred dollars a week; "since this was still cheaper than any other footage I could get," recalled Selznick, "I gave it to him."

A request from Theodore Roosevelt, Jr., got Will started on a new venture. A friend of the family, Ogden Mills, was the Republican candidate for Congress in the "silk stocking" district of Manhattan, and Roosevelt asked Will to give a talk at a Mills fund-raiser. He agreed even though, fanatical about his impartiality, he had never endorsed candidates, much less passed a hat for one—but, as he noted in his speech, "Nobody can refuse a Roosevelt."* Actually, nothing he said that night compromised him. "Now I don't know or have never met my candidate," he started out, "and for that reason I am more apt to

---

*He made only one other speech at a political rally. The year was 1932 and the candidate was Franklin D. Roosevelt.

say something good of him than anyone else." He spent most of the rest of the speech telling jokes about how much money Mills had: "Most people take up politics through necessity, or as a last resort. But I find this guy was wealthy before he went on. Not as wealthy as now, but rich."

It so happened that *The New York Times* had sent a reporter to cover the Mills affair, and Will's speech was prominently featured in the article that resulted. The following day, the *Times* ran an editorial, "Humorists as Campaigners," musing on the oddity of the Mills campaign engaging "the alert and incalculable Mr. Will Rogers. . . . Mr. Rogers was characteristically amusing in his speech on behalf of Mr. Mills, but laughs are not votes, and whether the candidate whom Mr. Rogers was ostensibly supporting gained more by the performance than did his opponents it would be hard to say."

Will did not, in any case, harm the campaign enough to prevent Mills from winning the election. But his address, and the attention it attracted, did have one definite result: It made him the most widely sought-after public speaker in New York. Suddenly, he was the performer every actors' benefit wanted, the after-dinner speaker every trade group demanded. He did his best to comply. In the seven months following the Mills speech, he spoke no fewer than sixty-one times—to the National Association of Waste Material and the Salvation Army, to the Newspaper Owners and Editors and the New York Building Superintendents, and to anyone else who asked him. The speeches helped him break into yet another medium: Several of them were recorded by the Victor Company in 1923 and included on phonograph records put out under Will's name.

One week in February was packed to the bursting point. On Sunday the eighteenth there was an appearance at a Lambs Club benefit, and on the nineteenth a speech for the Retail Milliners, a trade association. The next night's schedule was breathtaking. Will addressed the United Corsets Manufacturing Association before the *Follies*, something he referred to in his diary as the "Show Men's Assn" between the acts, and the Allied Leather Association after the curtain went down. And the following night, there was a dinner at Delmonico's for an upstate New York police commissioner.

This wasn't easy money for Will. Painfully nervous when he had to address a large group, he could not rely on himself to wing it, so he prepared his remarks in advance, tailoring them to each audience. For his speech to the corset manufacturers, for example, he typed out extensive comic musings on the existential status of the industry, plus discussions of various recent trends and mentions of prominent figures in the field. "You gentlemen shape the world," he wrote.

> Just think if flesh were allowed to wander around there is no tell-
> ing where it would wind up. What you have to do is gather it
> in at some given point and see if you cant arrange something
> like an equal distribution. In other words you gentlemen have a
> Herculanian task, you have to really improve on nature. . . .
>
> Now one of the greatest fears has always been right in the
> midst of a party the fleshy woman's string broke. I sat next to
> one when that happened once at a Table, and the spread come
> so gradually that we dident notice it till my friend on the other
> side of her and myself were being gradually shoved off of our re-
> spective chairs. To show you what a wonderful thing the corset
> art did for her she came to the party in a Small Roadster and
> had to go home in a Bus. Now one of you smart men worked
> out what you call an emergency string or what might be called
> a second line of control. Then all the modern Corsets have now
> a place on the back where you carry or park your extra strings.
> You can change a string now while you wait.

Early on in this regimen, Will realized that it would be a grave mis-take to eat the food at all the banquets he was compelled to attend. He found a chili joint at Broadway and Forty-seventh Street, with just a counter and a few stools, and ordered chili and enchiladas there before every dinner he was required to attend. After that kind of meal, he wrote, "I was fortified, not only to refuse anything that might be offered to me at the dinner, but I would sit through almost any kind of speeches."

The location of the publishing industry in New York gave him a chance to resume his career as a writer. He seems to have arranged with the New York *Evening Herald* to undertake a regular column; at least one installment (seemingly ghostwritten or at the least clumsily edited) ap-peared in October under the headline WILL ROGERS'S SAYINGS THIS WEEK. The next month, he began sending jokes to the humor magazine *Life* (no relation to the picture weekly started up years later by Henry Luce), which printed them under the heading "All I Know Is What I Read in the Papers." (Whether the slogan was Will's invention or an anonymous *Life* editor's will, sadly, never be known.) The fit between writer and publication was not perfect—*Life*, an urbane precursor to *The New Yorker*, published the literate musings of Robert Sherwood, Robert Benchley, and Dorothy Parker, plus a great deal of light verse—and Will was displeased with the percentage of gags that were printed. "I read the ones you used last week (both of them)," he wrote to an editor in a note that accompanied a batch of gags. "You have *some* man on your Paper whose Geinus [*sic*] I dont believe you fully appreciate. The way he can take 48 Jokes and pick out the absolute poorest is positively uncanny."

Soon afterward, the cartoonist and humorist Rube Goldberg called on Will in his dressing room at the New Amsterdam. Goldberg, a friendly acquaintance of long standing, told Will that his own work was being sold to newspapers around the country by the McNaught Syndicate, a recently formed company in the forefront of the burgeoning field of newspaper syndication. Goldberg said that McNaught's owners, two young ex-newspapermen named Charles McAdam and V. V. McNitt, would pay Will five hundred dollars to write a weekly column. That was good money, but what sold Will on the idea, McNitt later told Homer Croy, was the willingness of Carr Van Anda, managing editor of the grand and hitherto humorless *New York Times*, which Clem Rogers had subscribed to when Will was a boy, to use the feature. The *Times* paid the syndicate $150 a week for exclusive rights to the column in the territory bounded by Baltimore, Pittsburgh, Buffalo, and Springfield, Massachusetts, and twenty other papers signed on, paying weekly fees that ranged from three dollars (Galveston *Tribune)* to fifty dollars (Chicago *News*, Boston *Globe)*. The first column ran Sunday, December 24, 1922; from then until Will's death, a new one appeared every week.

Will was a little slow getting out of the box. His first effort, headlined BATTING FOR LLOYD GEORGE, opened with a self-conscious and rather clumsy fiction about the recently resigned British prime minister: "It seems THE TIMES had Lloyd George signed up for a pack of his memoirs. Well, after the late election Lloyd couldn't seem to remember anything, so they sent for me to fill in the space where he would have had his junk." Following was a series of political gags along the lines of what he had been doing for years.

But in the weeks and months that followed, there were fewer and fewer gags. Will emerged—remarkably for someone who had never thought of himself as a writer and had only rarely set anything down on paper that sustained a thought for more than one line—as an estimable comic essayist and political commentator, comfortable with the form (the column ran as long as fifteen hundred words), with an impressively broad rhetorical and thematic range and an unmistakable and unique voice. It was that voice, unquestionably, that made him into the most widely read columnist in the country. (More than one hundred newspapers were subscribing within two years and some four hundred by the early 1930s.) There was nothing out there like it. It was the sound of a letter from a good, wise, and funny friend, rambling on in a syncopated stream of consciousness. In a style that approximated transcribed speech (without the redundancies, non sequiturs, and logical ellipses), Will let his readers know what he had been doing and what he had been thinking, and talked about the celebrities of the day—and there had never been as many celebrities as there were in the 1920s—as if they were his *own* friends. Somehow, he had taken the secret of his stage success—the way he included his audience, let them in on things—and translated it into prose.

Will never aspired to Literature, and his columns were anything but well-tempered Grecian urns. The beginnings were usually just throat-clearings, the endings throwaway exit lines. After he had typed a piece out, he would give it a once-over and pencil in a few revisions; the idea of a second draft would never have occurred to him. Years later, when the Hannibal *Courier* asked him to contribute to a special Mark Twain edition, he declined on the ground of presumptuousness: ME IN YOUR MARK TWAIN EDITION WOULD BE LIKE SISTER AIMEE [Aimee Semple McPherson, discredited evangelist] BEING ASKED TO THE LORDS SUPPER, he wired. . . . THERE IS ONE THING THAT OUGHT TO BE ELIMINATED IN THIS COUNTRY AND THAT IS EVERY TIME SOMEBODY GETS A LAUGH OF SOME SMALL DIMENSIONS, WHY HE IS CALLED THE MODERN MARK TWAIN. But if he wasn't a literary artist, he was—once he had gotten up a head of steam—a formidable craftsman of words, humor, and ideas.

And, to his readers, he was fresh air. In 1922, the country's literary standards were still set by the remnants of the genteel tradition, the sort of elegant circumlocutions and bodiless babble that novelists such as Sherwood Anderson and Ernest Hemingway would soon explode for good. In the newspaper realm, Will's untutored directness and absolute absence of hokum made an equally welcome contrast to the well-made gentility and "good" writing of such now forgotten figures as O. O. McIntyre, Arthur Brisbane, and Christopher Morley. Indeed, the most noticeable thing about Will's prose was that it was bad. Whenever he used a word of more than three syllables, he fell all over himself insisting that he was on unfamiliar ground.* He was partial to outlaw contractions like *aint* and, for the third person singular, *dont,* and in all contractions left out the apostrophe. He tended to use the improper past tense

---

*Talking of Henry Ford's business genius, he wrote, "When Henry gets his hands on anything, it is, what do you call that word, Superfluous (that's hitting close to it) well it's (what I said it was just now), to say that he had made a success out of it."

for irregular verbs—*come* instead of *came, run* instead of *ran*. He liked to flag the reader's attention by starting a thought with *Well, Now,* or *Say*. He used a few regionalisms—*kinder* and *sorter* were treasured modifiers—but also a good deal of urban Jazz Age slang—*bird* (for person), *junk, cuckoo, gumshoe* (as a verb). His spelling was terrible, his syntax shaky, his punctuation unfathomable, and his capitalization a crap shoot.

To his great credit, McNitt realized that these idiosyncrasies were what gave Will's writing its flavor, and the syndicate's editing was minimal. In asking that the *Times* follow suit, he wrote to Van Anda, "I believe that the stuff will look more genuine if the copy is left as nearly as possible like the original manuscript. We are accordingly leaving in the copy some of the unnecessary capital letters, which tend to emphasize the points that Rogers makes."

Will's fractured style led some to surmise that he was a direct descendant of nineteenth-century "Phunny Phellows" such as Charles Farrar Browne (creator of Artemus Ward), Henry Wheeler Shaw (Josh Billings), and David Ross Locke (Petroleum Nasby), and their follower Finley Peter Dunne (Mr. Dooley). Yet those humorists were all ventriloquists, fashioning untutored characters through whose broken grammar, thick dialect, and shot-in-the-dark orthography the comic truth could be spoken. (Mark Twain bowed to the tradition in *Adventures of Huckleberry Finn.)* Will was speaking as himself—more or less. As the people who imitated and (sometimes) mocked him didn't seem to understand, he *didn't* affect ignorance; his mistakes were his by right.

Which is not to say that he had no link to the earlier humorists. The Phunny Phellows' illiteracy was really just another way of playing dumb—a pose of mock simplicity being possibly the most dominant strain in the American comic tradition. Will had been intimately familiar with the pose since his first days at Keith's Union Square, and now he found literary equivalents for the sly winks and grinning head scratches with which he signified onstage that he was aware of more than he let on. One was the opening phrase that he first used in September 1923 and within a few years was, in some variation, the way every column started—"Well, all I know is just what I read in the papers." But what's striking about the column is, in fact, how rarely Will resorted to an aw-shucks pose. He revealed himself, in fact, as a sophisticated rhetorician, capable of expressing himself in every stop on the line between flat-out sincerity and Swiftian irony.

A passage from a column he wrote in March, just three months after he started, shows a number of things: how quickly Will had transcended one-liners and become capable of sustained exposition, using a range of

rhetorical strategies; the rough-hewn but cogent populism that, in the forum of the column, emerged as the principal component of his personal
political credo; and his tendency, as pronounced now as it always had
been, to back away genially from hard truths, especially if they reflected
negatively on prominent men. Talking about a pending farm loan bill
got Will thinking about banking (incidentally, Clem's final profession):

> Borrowing money on what's called "easy terms," is a one-way
> ticket to the Poor House. Show me ten men that mortgage this
> land to get money and I will have to get a search warrant to find
> one that gets the land back again. If you think it ain't a Sucker
> Game, why is your Banker the richest man in your Town? Why
> is your Bank the biggest and finest building in your Town? In-
> stead of passing Bills to make borrowing easy, if Congress had
> passed a Bill that no Person could borrow a cent of Money from
> any other person, they would have gone down in History as
> committing the greatest bit of Legislation in the World.
>
> I was raised on a Cattle Ranch and I never saw or heard of
> a Ranchman going broke. Only the ones who had borrowed
> money. You can't break a man that don't borrow; he may not
> have anything, but Boy! he can look the World in the face and
> say, "I don't owe you Birds a nickel."

These two paragraphs are straight from the heart, the up-to-date
lingo ("search warrant," "Sucker Game") contrasting piquantly with the
old-fashioned hearth values. Now Will begins to add comic highlights.
Characteristically, he is self-deprecating, and, even more characteristically, he is personal, calling J. P. Morgan and the other financiers he dis-
cusses not only by their first names but by their nicknames, as if he, they,
and all his readers were sitting around the stove in a country store.

> You will say, what will all the Bankers do? I don't care what
> they do. Let 'em go to work, if there is a job any of them could
> earn a living at. Banking and After Dinner Speaking are two of
> the most Non-essential industries we have in this country. I am
> ready to reform if they are.
>
> Now, of course, I am not going to put these bankers out of
> business right away. This article will kinder act as a warning or
> a 6 months dispossession clause, in other words. Of course, the
> Ali Baba of this gang is J.P. Now, I give John credit. It's no small
> job, when you have to handle the finances of the world, in ad-

dition to your own country, to suddenly have me deprive him of his livelihood.

Then there is Otto Kahn. I talked to him at a dinner the other night and he is one of the most pleasant men I ever met. And Charlie Schwab, who without a doubt has the greatest personality of any man in America. Of course Charlie don't hardly come under the heading of Banker. He only owns just the ones in Pennsylvania. He was so darn nice and congenial. I didn't have any money with me at the time, but I really felt like borrowing some and handing it to him. And he may have been disappointed that I didn't.

Thus the sly wink (and note the eloquent redundancy in "He only owns just the ones in Pennsylvania").

Then the other night Barney Baruch was in the theatre with all the War Industries Board. They are just sitting around waiting till another war shows up. You remember Barney. He was the Tutankhamen treasure of the Wilson Administration. Well, he is another great fellow. So you see it's not from a personal view that I am abolishing Banks. It's just that I don't think these Boys realize really what a menace they are. As far as being good fellows, personally, I have heard old timers talk down home in the Indian Territory and they say the James and Dalton Boys were the most congenial men of their day, too.

Will's principal subject, predictably, was politics. His great ability to get at the comic heart of people and issues had been on display in his Peace Conference and Prohibition books, and at the *Follies*, but was easy to overlook, given that he was both a cowboy *and* a comedian. The forum of the column gave him confidence to shed the protective coloration of one-liners, and with its dissemination more people recognized his keen perception and good sense. A powerful piece he wrote late in 1923 in support of giving a bonus payment to World War I veterans—he proposed paying for it by putting a tax on then tax-exempt securities—was quoted approvingly on the floor of the House of Representatives.

It's easy to pick out comments that in retrospect appear positively Nostradamesque. In 1924, writing of the inflated stock market, he declared, "You mean to tell me that in a Country that was really run on the level, 200 of their National commodities would jump their value millions of dollars in two days?" The next year he wrote, "As soon as Germany gets strong enough so she thinks she can lick both of them [England and France] there will be another war." Some of the strong stands he took assume in the light of history a glow of great wisdom. He was against military intervention in Latin America ("What the Devil business is it of ours how some other country runs their business?"), in favor of increasing U.S. air power ("Why a battleship will be as obsolete in the next war as a sword was in the last one"). He took William Jennings Bryan to task for trying to legislate religion in the Scopes trial, and he considered Prohibition a hypocritical joke. In taking off on U.S. Steel chairman Elbert H. Gary's resistance to the eight-hour workday, he was scathing (and, for once, personal):

> Now Mr. Gary says it will take time. You see, a man who has been working for years for 12 to 14 hours a day, and you cut him down to 8, and you have a physical wreck on your hands. You take a person who is used to the cool air of the steel furnace for half the 24 hours of each day and bring him to the stuffy atmosphere of outdoors, or a home, and he can't stand it.

But there were limits to his vision. His attitude toward blacks was as patronizing and unenlightened as you would expect from the son of a slaveholder and Confederate veteran. There was no overt contempt or cruelty on his part; indeed, he expressed warm feelings toward people like Dan and Babe Walker and his *Follies* co-star Bert Williams. But he might not have been so friendly if the blacks he encountered had not known their place, or if it had been suggested to him that there was something offensive about darky stories. The essential point here is that he showed no awareness that blacks in America might possibly have a grievance.

Such an awareness, of course, would have required his transcending a commonsense, cracker-barrel worldview, and this Will, for all his perspicacity and even wisdom, was not equipped to do. The cracker-barrel view has a hard time with tragedy (though it does fine with sentiment), with ambiguity, and with evil, and so it was with Will. Whenever any of these phenomena appeared on the horizon of his discourse, he would reflexively retreat into the safe port of comedy. For the Ku Klux Klan, for Hitler (even in the early to mid-thirties, when the dictator was consolidating his power and leaving no doubt as to his racial theories), he had only mild gibes. As for Mussolini, Will, through the twenties at least, thought he was a great man.

The millions who were beginning to open their Sunday newspapers to Will Rogers's column—saving the rotogravure section, the box scores, and the serialized novels for later—wouldn't have had it any other way. If Will had been just a national version of the wise-cracking codger in the general store, others would have been able to duplicate his success. He was more than that. Nevertheless, part of his appeal lay in his implicit refusal to challenge the core beliefs of his audience, to address moral or political complexities or human suffering, to upset the applecart. Americans, maybe more than most other peoples, like to take refuge in what they have always known to be true. Will, as he was now defining himself, was a kind of apostle of common sense, with all the virtues and all the limitations that perspective implies.

As such, it wasn't surprising that he was most comfortable commenting on politics, which, being a self-contained world, didn't open itself up to larger questions. Will quickly became known for his analyses of particular politicians, which were put forward in a humorous vein but were nonetheless pithy, pointed, and usually right on target.

Starting in February 1924, he devoted a series of columns to the Senate probe of the Teapot Dome and the other scandals that proved to be the Harding administration's chief legacy, and his coverage of that bumbling exercise was hilarious and superb. Posturing and hypocrisy were always Will's two favorite targets, and there was plenty of both on display in Washington, as Republicans stonewalled and Democrats sought to extract every ounce of political gain from the proceedings. Meanwhile, investigation begat investigation, and the parade of witnesses continued. Eventually, Will wrote, "The only one you never hear mentioned anymore is ex-Secretary Fall"—Harding's secretary of the interior, whose questionable oil leases to wealthy friends had started the whole affair. "He and the oil leases passed out of the picture so long ago that people have about forgotten them."

Will concluded his coverage with a modest proposal:

I have a scheme that I think would be very beneficial and add to the efficiency of this investigation. That is, have certain days for certain things. Now, say for instance, Mondays. That is for confessions. Everybody that wants to confess come and confess Monday. Tuesday is for accusations. If you want to accuse anybody come Tuesday, and accuse from 9 A.M. to 6 P.M.

Then that leaves Wednesdays, Thursdays, Fridays and Saturdays for denials. You see it takes you longer to deny than anything else. That would make it a lot easier on the spectators. They would know then just when to go.

They could sell the house out on Tuesdays. Everybody

wants to hear accusations, and nobody wants to hear denials. So you are just taking up spectators' time by having them there on days when all they hear is, "It's absolutely false. I didn't receive the money, and if those 18 witnesses have testified that I did they must have been mistaken." Or here is another favorite line: "I don't remember."

I tell you folks, if American men are as dumb as some of them have appeared on the witness stand this year, civilization is tottering.

Will was frequently serious but rarely solemn. He never indulged in sanctimony, stridency, alarmism, or cant, and he saw right through those who did. His sense of perspective, in fact, was the area in which he transcended the realm of common sense and approached wisdom. "That's why I can never take a Politician seriously," he wrote. "They are always shouting that 'such and such a thing will ruin us, and that this is the eventful year in our Country's life.'

"Say, all the years are the same. Each one has its little temporary setbacks, but they don't mean a thing in the general result."

Bunk touched everything in the 1920s, not just politics. Every day, the same media apparatus that had allowed Will Rogers to flourish was filling a new balloon with the helium of publicity and sending it up in the cultural sky. The process fascinated Will, and he wrote about champion prizefights and marathon dances, Rudolph Valentino and Babe Ruth, "Yes, We Have No Bananas" and bathtub gin. A favorite device was merely to present an incongruous list of celebrities; like the famous names in a Cole Porter song, these ballyhoo catalogs were perfect expressions of the Zeitgeist. Yet Will never lost sight of the fact that these were all temporary manifestations, never lost his down-home values and horse sense—and that may have been what made him most valuable to readers fearful that their world was changing beyond recognition.

In a gem of a column, he wrote, "Everything nowadays is a Saying, or Slogan."

You can't go to bed, you can't get up, you can't brush your Teeth without doing it to some Advertising Slogan. We are even born nowadays by a Slogan: "Better Parents have Better Babies." Our Children are raised by a Slogan: "Feed your baby Cowlicks Malted Milk and he will be another Dempsey." Everything is a Slogan and of all the Bunk things in America the Slogan is the Champ.

Even if you want to get married a sign will stare you in the face: "You get the girl, we will furnish the Ring." That has led more Saps astray than any misinformation ever published, outside the Prize one of all, which is: "Two can live as cheap as one." . . . Yes, two can live as cheap as one if you don't want to eat or wear anything during its lifetime. Two can't even live as cheap as two, much less one. . . .

We even got into War on a Slogan that was supposed to keep us out. After we got in we were going to "Make the world safe for Democracy." And maybe we did—you can't tell, because there is no Nation ever tried Democracy since. . . .

The next President was elected on the slogan: "Back to Normalcy." Back to Normalcy consisted of the most Cuckoo years of spending and carousing and graft we ever had. Another Slogan knocked crosswise. . . .

Coolidge ran on "Economy" which is always good for the Boobs. It's like getting up a Dinner and saying "I am proud to be here." It's an old Gag but it always goes. Economy beat Honesty by 8 million, and as soon as he got in he raised Congress' and the Senate's Salary and redecorated the White House. So away goes another Slogan! . . .

You see a fool Slogan can get you into anything. But you never heard of a Slogan getting you out of anything. It takes either Bullets, Hard Work or Money to get you out of anything. Nobody has ever invented a Slogan to use instead of paying your Taxes.

Will had only been doing the column for two months when he wrote his first obituary, of his old railroad companion Wallace Reid, dead of complications from his drug addiction. ("He was just a big overgrown Kid," Will concluded, "who never knowingly harmed a living soul.") He developed an affinity for the form, and took to paying tribute whenever a friend or a prominent American passed away. These pieces were Will's only indulgences in any form of sentimentality, but they were often eloquent and touching, and they gave him an outlet for feelings he did not otherwise allow himself to express. When his sister Maud Lane died in 1925, he traveled to her funeral and wrote a column that exuded overwhelming emotion:

Today, as I write this, I am not in the Follies, the carefree Comedian who jokes about everything. I am out in Oklahoma, among my People, my Cherokee people, who don't expect a laugh for everything I say. . . . I have just today witnessed a Funeral that for real sorrow and affection I don't think will ever be surpassed anywhere. . . .

Some uninformed Newspaper printed: "Mrs. C. L. Lane sister of the famous Comedian, Will Rogers." They were greatly misinformed. It's the other way around. I am the brother of Mrs. C. L. Lane, "The friend of Humanity." And I want to tell you that as I saw all these people who were there to pay tribute to her memory, it was the proudest moment of my life that I was her brother.

His greatest death notice came not in the column but the introduction to a posthumous book by Charley Russell, who died in 1926. Using the cowboy talk that was Russell's own trademark, he addressed the artist in heaven, a corny conceit that in Will's hands became exquisitely moving (and permitted him to express, for the only time in his writing life, some of what he must have felt over young Freddy's death):

I bet you hadent been up there three days till you had out your old pencil and was a drawing something funny about some of the old Punchers. . . . I bet you Mark Twain and Old Bill Nye, and Whitcomb Riley, and a whole bunch of those old joshers was just a waiting for you to pop in with all the latest ones. What kind of a Bird is Washington and Jefferson? I bet they are regular fellows when you meet em aint they? Most big men are. I would like to see the bunch that is gathered around you the first time you tell the one about putting the Limberger Cheese in the old Nestors Whiskers. Dont tell that Charley till you get Lincoln around you, he would love that. I bet you and him kinder throw in together when you get well acquainted. Darn it when I get to thinking about all them Top Hands up there, if I could just hold a Horse wrangling job with em, I wouldent mind following that wagon myself. . . .

You will run onto my old Dad up there Charley. For he was a real Cowhand and I bet he is running a wagon, and you will pop into some well kept ranch house over under some cool shady trees and you will be asked to have dinner, and it will be the best one you ever had in your life. Well when you are a thanking the women folks, You just tell the sweet looking little old lady that you knew her boy, back on an outfit you used to rep for, and tell the daughters that you knew their brother, and if you see a cute little rascal running around there kiss him for

me. Well cant write you any more Charley dam papers all wet.
It must be raining in this old bunk house.

Course we are all just a hanging in here as long as we can.
I dont know why we hate to go, we know its better there. Maby
its because we havent been like you. We havent done anything
that will live after we are gone.

from your old friend.
Will.

HAL ROACH was a twenty-nine-year-old native of Elmira, New York,
who had been a prospector in Alaska, a mule skinner, and a cowboy extra in the movies. In the late teens, he began to produce them himself,
making a great success with the comedies of Harold Lloyd; he would go
on to present Laurel and Hardy and the "Our Gang" series of kid comedies. But now, in 1921, Roach found himself in need of talent: Lloyd
would soon begin to produce his pictures on his own, Laurel hadn't yet
hooked up with Hardy, and "Our Gang" was just about to get under
way. One night, visiting New York, Roach went to the *Midnight Frolic*
with Lloyd and Victor Shapiro, the exploitation manager for Pathé,
which distributed Roach's pictures. Shapiro was there to effectuate some
publicity for Lloyd: Before the show, it had been arranged that Will
would rope the comedian and bring him onstage. (The stunt might have
been a complete dud had not Shapiro, noticing at the last minute that
Lloyd was not wearing his trademark eyeglasses, without which he was
unrecognizable, lent him a pair of his own.) Roach met Will after the
show and offered to put him to work in two-reel comedies.

But Will's Hollywood scars had not yet healed; it was not until January 1923 that he signed with Roach. And he didn't start work for another five months after that: The contract stated that it wouldn't go into
effect until "after the Follies closes." The agreement gave Will a 25 percent share of his pictures' profits—but also a guaranteed salary of two
thousand dollars a week. It was the biggest salary Roach had ever paid.
The Hardy-less Stan Laurel was earning $400 at the time, the about-to-
depart Lloyd $1,000 (plus 80 percent of his extremely successful pictures'
profits), and Roach himself $1,750.

Years later, Roach recalled that his "Irish Dad," the treasurer of the
company, hated to give a paycheck to anyone making over five dollars
a day and was outraged about the salary of this high-priced newcomer.
On Will's first payday, Roach senior was prepared to give him a piece
of his mind along with his check. But Will didn't stop in to pick it up.
The same thing happened the second week, and the third.

"Now the old man was about to have a nervous breakdown," Roach said. "I happened to be on the porch, near my Dad's office, as Will was walking by, and dad walked over to him and said very humbly, 'Please, Mr. Rogers, would you mind picking up these checks?' "

Will earned his keep. The Roach pictures—each budgeted at about thirty thousand dollars—were shot in two or three six-day weeks; the morning after one was finished, the next would begin. So busy that he had no need for his dressing room once his makeup and costume were on, Will offered the use of it to a young staff writer he found sitting on a lumber pile with a piece of paper and a pencil, scribbling out gag ideas for an "Our Gang" comedy. Frank Capra would always remember the star's thoughtfulness.

The work was physically demanding, too. Roach's experience had been in knockabout comedy, and Will's first few pictures—*Hustlin' Hank, Jus' Passin' Through, Uncensored Movies* (where he impersonated and spoofed Tom Mix, William S. Hart, and Rudolph Valentino), and *Gee Whiz Genevieve*—were loaded with pratfalls and leaps into lakes. "All I ever do on the Roach lot is run around barns and lose my pants," he complained to Rob Wagner, a director he met at actress Irene Rich's house. On Will's recommendation, Roach hired Wagner to take over the direction of *Gee Whiz Genevieve* and work up some other projects for Will. In the evenings, they traded ideas on how to tone down the slapstick, and what to replace it with. Following through on his long-held notion that the fresher the event a joke referred to the better, Will wanted to make a parody of *The Covered Wagon,* James Cruze's epic Western that was the box-office hit of the moment. He and Wagner put together a complete script—the first one the Roach lot had ever had, according to the director—and set out for Lake Elsinore, sixty miles east of Los Angeles, to shoot it. "If we stick around here," Will told Wagner, "they'll be building barns for me to lose my pants behind."

The completed picture was a mild amusement. The wagon train traverses the country in an arduous journey—yet each piece of landscape it passes looks suspiciously similar. The pioneers arrive in Los Angeles, only to be besieged by "Escrow Indians," real estate men who pull each one of them aside and talk up properties that are "between the mountains and the sea—swept by ocean breezes." But the film struck a chord with the public and the critics, who didn't always review short subjects; *The New York Times* said, "It is as funny as anything we have ever seen on films." In Los Angeles, it ran for seven weeks at the Miller Theater as the featured attraction. Will himself was pleased with it: "I like the snaps," he told Victor Shapiro, using his personal slang for subtitles. "Makes the people overlook my face."

There were scattered funny ideas and bits of business in Will's other pictures for Roach. In *The Cowboy Sheik* he played a dim cowpuncher who can't make a move without drawing straws; *Don't Park There* stretched to comic absurdity the struggle to find a parking place. In *Going to Congress*, Will created the character of Alfalfa Doolittle, a small-town dimbulb who becomes a member of the House, and he continued Doolittle's adventures in two more shorts. The conceit prefigured a number of Will's talking pictures, and it gave him the chance to use some political gags. But the series as a whole was neither an artistic nor a financial triumph—it posted a total loss of more than eighty thousand dollars, meaning that Will's share of the profits was 25 percent of nothing. And though Roach wanted to pick up his option for another year when the contract expired, Will declined. He knew that this was not his medium.

Even so, the Roach pictures gave extra momentum to the now-irreversible process by which Will was becoming a national figure. With that process came some inevitable inconveniences. On November 5, 1923, someone on Betty Rogers's staff wrote her a note: "I took the matter up with the telephone company relative to the discontinuance of Mr. Rogers' name from the next issue of the telephone directory, and am informed that this will be done."

THE CALIFORNIA AIR had a peculiar effect on Will: It made him want to buy land. The work for Ziegfeld, McNaught, and Roach had, as Will's son Jim later described it, put the family "back on the gold standard," and with some capital in the bank he acted as though the financial disaster of two years earlier had been only a bad dream. In January 1924, he made his biggest move yet. Alphonzo Bell, the developer who created Bel Air (his decision to drop the second *l* in his surname shows his marketing genius), had recently bought 22,000 acres of undeveloped land in the Santa Monica Mountains. Will signed an agreement to buy 159.721 acres, at a price of two thousand an acre; the down payment was to be thirty thousand dollars, and the interest rate 6 percent.

It was a beautiful spot—between the mountains and the sea and cooled by ocean breezes, as it happened. About six miles southwest of Beverly Hills and barely a mile and half from the Pacific Ocean north of Santa Monica, the property rested at the southern toe of a ridge between two canyons, Temescal and Rustic. It was extremely steep, rising rapidly from an elevation of 225 feet to 751 feet; from the heights, one could make out downtown Los Angeles, Santa Monica Bay, and Catalina Island. Thanks to the elevation and the breezes, it was delightfully temperate, with high temperatures in the low seventies in the summer and the low sixties in the winter. Despite the site's proximity to population centers, it was wild—uninhabited except for some Japanese tenant farmers cultivating a mesa—and covered with rocks and chaparral.* There were no paved roads anywhere near it.

But Will had plans for the property. His old Wyoming cowboy friend Ray Bell, fed up with the hokeyness of cowboy movies, had left California to ride on the rodeo circuit. He came back in 1923, and Will took him to see his new treasure. They drove on Beverly Boulevard (later to be renamed Sunset) until Sepulveda Boulevard, where it stopped. "From then on it was all dirt roads," Bell said. "We went out this old country road and took it all the way to the top. He said, 'This is my Shangri-La.'"

At first, Will saw the place as a kind of wilderness retreat, unexpectedly close to the city, where he could construct stables and comfortably keep many more horses than in a Beverly Hills backyard. That first year, the family would ride out on a Saturday or Sunday with a picnic lunch; the children, even eight-year-old Jimmy, would sometimes continue on down to the Pacific and go for a swim. Will probably thought that one day he might build a larger version of his Beverly Hills cabin on the property, so he could escape from "so called civilization" for longer than an afternoon at a time.

The passage by Los Angeles voters, in September 1924, of a bond issue that would extend Beverly Boulevard all the way to the ocean put his imagination into high gear. The route, no doubt devised with Alphonzo Bell's significant input, took the road right past the front of Will's property; it meant that he would be able to drive to Hollywood or downtown Los Angeles in well under an hour. Within six months, he had decided he wanted one day to put a proper house on the land and was making elaborate plans for where the house would be set and how the steep hills could possibly be graded to make for a navigable entrance

*The first year, Will collected $961.50 in rent from the farmers, but in 1925 his foreman informed him that, because of a California law prohibiting the leasing of farmland to Japanese, they had to be kicked out: "There is no way we can keep them on the place except to hire them straight out and give them no share in the crop whatsoever. . . . if any trouble should come, you will suffer most by loosing [sic] your land and the Japs and your humble servant would have to go to San Quentin for a spell."

THE MOST FAMOUS PUBLICITY PHOTO FROM THE <u>FOLLIES</u> YEARS.

Above: THE DAY WILL ARRIVED IN
LOS ANGELES TO MAKE MOVIES FOR
THE GOLDWYN STUDIO IN 1919,
STAFF PHOTOGRAPHER CLARENCE
BULL (LATER RENOWNED AS
HOLLYWOOD'S PREMIER
PORTRAITIST OF GLAMOUR)
SNAPPED HIM AT THE TRAIN
STATION. TYPICALLY, WILL IS
CHATTING UP SOME REPORTERS.
BULL ALSO SHOT THE PHOTO AT
RIGHT, OF WILL AND WESTERN
ARTIST CHARLES M. RUSSELL
RELAXING ON THE GOLDWYN LOT.
Below: IN A 1922 <u>FROLIC</u> SKETCH,
WILL ROGERS APPEARED IN DRAG
FOR THE FIRST—AND ONLY—TIME
IN HIS CAREER.

BILLY ROSE THEATRE COLLECTION, NEW YORK
PUBLIC LIBRARY FOR THE PERFORMING ARTS

WILL GENERALLY PLAYED A BUMPKIN OR DRIFTER IN THE
GOLDWYN FILMS, WHICH IS PROBABLY ONE REASON WHY THEY
DIDN'T DO VERY WELL. HE EYES FOOD IN A POOR RELATION
(ABOVE) AND ACCEPTS SOME FROM JOSIE SEDGWICK IN JUBILO.

Above: "THE WALKING SUBTITLE FACTORY" POLISHES A SCRIPT. *Below:* ON THE SET OF <u>AN UNWILLING HERO</u>, CHARLIE CHAPLIN TRIES HIS HAND AT THE LARIAT WHILE WILL IMITATES THE FAMOUS CHAPLIN STANCE.

Above: SNUB POLLARD, STAN LAUREL (SOON TO TEAM UP WITH OLIVER HARDY), AND WILL (IMPERSONATING THE STONE-FACED WILLIAM S. HART) IN HAL ROACH'S 1923 SATIRE UNCENSORED MOVIES. *Below:* THE ROGERS HOUSE IN BEVERLY HILLS HAD A SWIMMING POOL AND A RIDING RING.

WITH MARY.

LIBRARY OF CONGRESS

Right: JUST BEFORE GOING UP
WITH BILLY MITCHELL, 1925.
Below: WILL BEING TRANS-
PORTED PIGGYBACK FROM HIS
FIRST PLANE RIDE, ATLANTIC
CITY, 1915.   *Bottom:* IN
DECEMBER 1927, WILL WAS
NAMED HONORARY MAYOR OF
BEVERLY HILLS—A CURIOUS
STUNT FOR A CITY THAT DIDN'T
NEED THE PUBLICITY AND A
MAN WHO NEEDED IT EVEN
LESS.

Al Signor Roger cordialmente 28 maggio 1926

Villa Torlonia Roma Mussolini

Above: A MEMENTO—
INSCRIBED "AL SIGNOR
ROGERS"—FROM WILL'S
INTERVIEW WITH
MUSSOLINI. *Left:* GIVING
89-YEAR-OLD JOHN D.
ROCKEFELLER A DIME.
Below: WILL WITH H. L.
MENCKEN, LOOKING
UNCOMFORTABLE IN A
COWBOY HAT. AT RIGHT
IS THE FORT WORTH
NEWSPAPER PUBLISHER
AMON CARTER, A GOOD
FRIEND OF WILL'S.

Above: WHEN FRED STONE WAS INJURED IN A PLANE CRASH, WILL
TOOK HIS PLACE IN THE MUSICAL <u>THREE CHEERS</u>. HERE—WITH
STONE'S DAUGHTER DOROTHY AND ANDY TOMBES—HE GIVES
STONE AND HIS WIFE, ALLENE, A PRIVATE RENDITION OF THE
BAREFOOT DANCE NUMBER FROM THE SHOW. *Below:* ON WILL'S
1931 RELIEF TOUR OF THE DROUGHT-STRICKEN SOUTHWEST,
"BLUE YODELLER" JIMMY RODGERS WAS PART OF THE BILL.

Above: THE LIVING ROOM OF THE PACIFIC PALISADES RANCH WAS PACKED WITH THE ARTIFACTS OF THE WEST. THE PICTURE WINDOW AT REAR WAS CONTRIBUTED BY FLO ZIEGFELD.
Right: THE FAMILY ON THE PORCH OF THE RANCH. BILL IS IN FORE-GROUND. *Below:* IN CONSTRUCTING THE RANCH, WILL DEVOTED MOST OF HIS ATTENTION TO THE RIDING RING (FOREGROUND) AND THE BARN.

MUSEUM OF MODERN ART

FOX PROVIDED WILL WITH A
BUNGALOW IN A SOUTHWESTERN
MOTIF, BUT HE PREFERRED TO
POUND OUT HIS COLUMN IN THE
FRONT SEAT OF HIS LASALLE.

Right: BY 1934—THE YEAR OF <u>THE COUNTY CHAIRMAN</u>, WITH A YOUNG AND VERY FRECKLED MICKEY ROONEY—WILL WAS THE NUMBER-ONE BOX OFFICE ATTRACTION IN THE COUNTRY. *Below:* WILL'S BEST FILM WAS PROBABLY <u>JUDGE PRIEST</u>. IN A KEY SCENE, HE COMMUNES WITH HIS LATE WIFE'S SPIRIT. *Bottom:* WILL HUMS ALONG WHILE A GROUP OF ACTORS (STEPIN FETCHIT IS AT CENTER, WITH HATTIE MCDANIEL TO HIS LEFT) REHEARSE A SPIRITUAL. DIRECTOR JOHN FORD LOOKS ON.

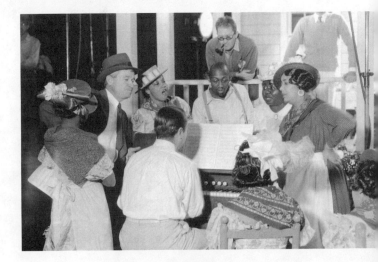

Above: WILL'S CLOSE FRIENDS WERE FEW. TWO OF THEM WERE FRED STONE (CENTER) AND WESTERN ARTIST ED BOREIN. *Below:* WITH VICE PRESIDENT JOHN NANCE GARNER, A POLITICAL CRONY.

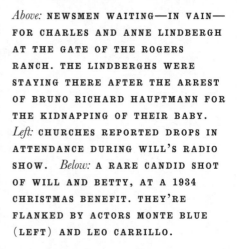

Above: NEWSMEN WAITING—IN VAIN—
FOR CHARLES AND ANNE LINDBERGH
AT THE GATE OF THE ROGERS
RANCH. THE LINDBERGHS WERE
STAYING THERE AFTER THE ARREST
OF BRUNO RICHARD HAUPTMANN FOR
THE KIDNAPPING OF THEIR BABY.
Left: CHURCHES REPORTED DROPS IN
ATTENDANCE DURING WILL'S RADIO
SHOW. *Below:* A RARE CANDID SHOT
OF WILL AND BETTY, AT A 1934
CHRISTMAS BENEFIT. THEY'RE
FLANKED BY ACTORS MONTE BLUE
(LEFT) AND LEO CARRILLO.

Above: FROM SEATTLE, WILL SENT HIS FAMILY THIS PHOTO OF WILEY POST'S PLANE AND SCRAWLED ON IT THE MESSAGE, "SHE IS A <u>BEAUT</u> AINT IT. THIS WAS WHEN WE WAS TRYING IT OUT FIRST WITH THE <u>PONTOONS</u>." *Below:* CHARLES BROWER (ON CRUTCHES) AND SEVERAL ESKIMOS STANDING OVER THE BODIES OF ROGERS AND POST. THE PHOTO WAS TAKEN BY AN ESKIMO AND NOT DEVELOPED UNTIL 1956.

road. This was not an easy proposition; Will wrote to his brother-in-law Lee Adamson, an engineer who was supervising the project, that he needed his and his colleagues' thoughts on "how to get up the West Hill without an Aeroplane."

These deliberations were carried on by mail because Will wasn't in California. When his contract with Roach ended (his last day of work was May 10), he had numerous offers to appear on stage in the East, for three thousand dollars a week—or so he wrote to Ziegfeld, who wanted him, too. Will said that if he did go back to the *Follies,* he would need one hundred dollars more than that: "This Hundred Dollars is in the Nature of a Fine for not engageing me in advance . . . for 3 thousand. Also Transportation for Myself, One Wife, Three Kids, 2 Cars, and not over 12 Horses, and a retinue of Dogs and cats." Will got the $3,100, a salary that made him, by far, the highest-paid performer in the *Follies.* Second, at $1,750 a week, was W. C. Fields.

The *Follies of 1924* were to open on June 24, following a week of try-out performances in Atlantic City. The timing was perfect for Will. He had contracted with McNaught to cover both parties' presidential conventions; the Republicans' was to begin in Cleveland June 10, and the Democrats' in New York on the same day that the *Follies* started (a co-incidence naturally made much of by Will in his coverage). In the month he had free, he visited the home folk in Chelsea and Claremore (he made a point of going out to see Dan Walker, the black man who had taught him to rope nearly four decades before), spent some time making the rounds in New York (where he made a proposal to Pathé, apparently stillborn, for a self-produced weekly satirical film), and traveled to Washington, where his reception and the heady company he kept befitted his new status as a political presence. Sitting in the gallery of the House of Representatives, he was spotted by Congressman Thomas Blanton of Texas, who took the floor and declared, "Mr. Speaker, I want to call attention to the fact that the House of Representatives is honored by having one of the big men of the United States sitting in the gallery. I refer to Mr. Will Rogers, who is up there looking on." *The New York Times* noted that Will "turned a fiery red and bowed his acknowledgment as the members applauded." He had lunch with the Oklahoma congressional delegation, then went over to the Senate and met William Borah of Idaho and Oscar Underwood of Alabama, and renewed his acquaintance with the Senator from Missouri. "My old fighting friend Jim Reed asked me out for dinner," Will wrote, "but I had just made a previous engagement." This was to sup at the home of Nicholas and Alice Roosevelt Longworth, "where you get the smartest and most authentic political dope in Washington." The next day he had lunch with Ned McLean, the inordinately wealthy owner of the Washington *Post* (and the Hope diamond).

"All in all," Will concluded, "I had a very pleasant visit in Washington, found that with all my kidding and knocking our public men, they all seemed to be my friends."

The Republican National Convention of 1924 had all the suspense of a telephone directory. In the first ten months of his presidency, Calvin Coolidge had maintained a striking popularity—despite the continuing Teapot Dome revelations. His nomination was a foregone conclusion, and the delegates in Cleveland were sadly unable to manufacture any intensity. "All my life I have been longing to attend a convention and see the excitement and hear the shouts," Will told his readers. "Now, when I do get a chance I draw this one. . . . The city is opening up the churches now and having services so the delegates and visitors can go and hear some singing or excitement of some kind."

But the convention nonetheless gave Will "the thrill of my entire life"—the chance to rub shoulders with William Jennings Bryan, a towering figure in national politics for nearly thirty years, who was also covering it for McNaught. He and Will got acquainted in the press stand, had lunch together, and traded observations on the proceedings— including this exchange:

"Mr. Bryan turned to me and said: 'You write a humorous article, don't you?' "

"I looked around to see if anybody was listening and then I said: 'Yes, sir.' "

"He said: 'Well, I write a serious article, and if I think of anything of a comical or funny nature, I will give it to you.' " (The best Bryan did was a comment on Theodore Burton's keynote address, which had a "finishing gag" in the middle. Quipped the Great Commoner, "The speaker suffered from a premature climax.")

A remarkable alchemy had transpired, one that Seba Smith or Charles Farrar Browne could never have foreseen. The device Will had used in reporting the 1920 conventions from home, imaginary conversations with political eminences, had become real.

Where Cleveland was uneventful and brief, New York was chaotic and endless. It took the Democrats three weeks and 103 ballots at Madison Square Garden to decide that the dry William Gibbs McAdoo, former Secretary of the Treasury under Wilson (and the husband of Wilson's daughter Eleanor), and the wet Al Smith, governor of New York, were hopelessly deadlocked. Almost as an afterthought they nominated former Ambassador to Britain John W. Davis of West Virginia for President and William Jennings Bryan's brother, Charles, for Vice President. This was also the convention where Franklin Delano Roosevelt made himself a national figure with his galvanizing speech nominating Smith as "the Happy Warrior," and where the Democratic party almost destroyed itself in its internal debate over whether to condemn the Ku Klux Klan by name or merely take a stand "against violence" (the latter won by a fraction of a vote, some delegates having partial votes).

To Will, facing a *Follies* performance every night and a deadline every day (and getting no extra money from McNaught for his daily dispatches), the long-winded nominating and seconding speeches were bemusing, to say the least. "We heard nothing from 10 o'clock in the morning until 6 at night but 'The man I am going to name,' " he wrote after the first day of windy platitudes. "Then they talk for another thirty minutes and then, 'The man I am going to name.' There have been guys going to name men all day, and all we ever got named was about six out of a possible 200."

By the next day, he was frankly disgusted:

> Well, I saw something yesterday that for stupidity, lack of judgment, nonsensicality, unexcitement, uselessness and childishness has anything I've ever seen beaten. It was the Democratic National Convention. . . .
>
> It does seem that out of all this barrage of everlasting talk, that maybe just accidentally some one would have made an original remark, or perhaps coined some epigram that could be remembered. But no. . . .
>
> Now, I never propose a thing unless I have a solution to it. Make every speaker, as soon as he tells all he knows, sit down. That will shorten your speeches so much you will be out by lunch time every day.
>
> Or make them be censored and not allow one man to repeat what some other man has said. That would cut it down to just one speech at each convention.

There was still no movement five days later, and Will wired a nine-word demand to William Jennings Bryan: WE WANT AL SMITH AND NO MORE HOT AIR.

Of course, after all the candidates were nominated, that only meant the balloting could begin. A week and a half later, Will's dispatch carried the byline "Will Rogers Jr." and began: "Papa called us all last night and made his last will and testament, he called it. He said he had carried his work on just as long as he could and he realized that he was unable, on account of his old age, to go further with it. He put in the will that I being the oldest was to take up his life's work, that of reporting the Democratic National Convention."

But for all the wearisome and interminable inanity of the gathering, it was an important milestone for Will. The fact that two delegates from Arizona, each representing half a vote, had put the name of Will Rogers in nomination for President and cast their ballots for him could be interpreted as a facetious protest against their party's long-winded meandering. More significant was that for seventeen days he huddled in close quarters with Democratic powers. New York mayor John Hyland called him over to his box for a chat; he talked about children, politics, and show business with the wives of Smith and McAdoo; he conferred on the speakers' stand with power brokers Joe Tumulty and Pat Harrison. One day early in the balloting, John Davis—then still the darkest of dark horses—invited Will to visit him in the apartment where he was staying. As they sat and talked, the radio was broadcasting reports from the convention floor. Mississippi, the announcer stated, was voting for Davis. On the next ballot, Missouri switched to Davis from McAdoo. Will's description of what happened next shows that he wasn't really a reporter at heart:

> A big political leader dashed into the house and remarked: "John, it's going just like we figured." I offered to withdraw, as I knew they had important business, but "No," he said. "You stay right here." And I sat there and heard the inner workings of a national convention.
>
> Some day, with both men's permission, I might tell you what was said. I will start my little newspaper career by taking a tip from our President, Mr. Coolidge, by keeping my mouth shut. I feel mighty proud that these men trusted me enough to discuss things before me without even pledging me to secrecy. So I just listened, but have plum forgot what they said.

But if Will lacked the instincts of an investigative journalist, he was (at least in this case) an impeccable prognosticator. His dispatch began: "Well, folks, I have just come from a private visit with the Presidential nominee of this convention." Seven days later, he was proved right.

Will was probably the only reporter at the convention who, when it was all over, felt obliged to send telegrams to Davis, Charles Bryan, and the two losing candidates. To McAdoo, he wired, CONDOLENCES TO A FELLOW DEFEATED CANDIDATE, I TOO KNOW WHAT IT IS TO SUFFER; he re-

minded Smith, 1928 IS ANOTHER YEAR. The message to Davis was, UN-
DERSTAND YOU ARE TO BE ASSOCIATED WITH ONE OF THE BRYAN BOYS.
FOR THE LORDS SAKE PICK THE RIGHT ONE.

He was certainly the only reporter the candidates sent telegrams *to*.
The best was probably McAdoo's: DONT FEEL BADLY ABOUT YOUR DE-
FEAT. I CAME HERE WITH 530 DELEGATES AND COULDNT GET A SHOW.
HOW COULD YOU EXPECT TO HOLD YOUR ONE.

THE *Follies of 1924* differed from its predecessors in one respect: It had
a plot. Given a coauthor credit for the first time, Will followed through
on his Hal Roach character and wrote some scenes for himself as Alfalfa
Doolittle, an Oklahoma rancher who—between production numbers—is
elected to the Senate, has a powwow with Henry Cabot Lodge, and sits
on a committee "Investigating Investigations." The show ran much too
long the first night in Atlantic City, and a lot of the Doolittle material
had to be deleted. "I have heard of plays that run just one night," Will
told the second-night crowd, "but this plot of ours only run half of one
night. They cut it out between the first and the second act."

It didn't really matter, he acknowledged: "No use to read the papers
in the morning as I can tell you what they will say and have for years:
'Mr. Ziegfeld's Glorification of the American Girl was unfolded last
night. It's a beautiful show, as he alone knows how to do one. It is sadly
lacking in humor. Why can't we have humor in our American revues?'

"As if a Follies audience ever paid any attention to what some comedian was doing in the show. It's just a question of when will the girls
be back."

As he had two years before, Will stayed in New York with the *Follies*
for a lengthy stint—a total of fifteen months, spanning four editions.*
This time he could afford to bring his family east; they stayed at a farm
in East Williston, Long Island, rented at seven thousand dollars for the
year. And this time, he didn't need to make quite so many speeches. But
there was no shortage of outside ventures, pursued with a diligence that

---

*A featured dancer in the final one was eighteen-year-old Louise Brooks, soon to gain
fame as the temptress Lulu in the silent film classic *Pandora's Box*. "My moment of delight
came at the end of the *Follies*, when the whole company was onstage for the finale," Brooks
wrote years later. "Will Rogers and I climbed a ladder to the top of a fifteen-foot tower set in
the middle of the stage. Starting with a tiny noose on his lasso, Rogers would twirl it faster
and faster, bigger and bigger, until the rope hissed in a circle around us like an intoxicated
snake as the curtains opened and the dazzling spotlight shone upon us."

One night Will had the inspiration to remove his chewing gum and park it on Brooks's
turned-up nose. She hissed at him, "You sonofabitch, I'll kill you." He never did it again.

made it clear he wanted every communications medium covered. Radio had become a fact of American life since the establishment of KDKA in 1920, and Will made numerous appearances, including a speech to the Radio Industries banquet that went out over a twelve-station hookup. With the American Tobacco Company, he contracted to write twenty-six humorous ads for Bull Durham tobacco, at five hundred dollars each. He had had great sport at the expense of advertising bunk, and he escaped from this promotional stint with his honor intact—barely. He made it a point not to mention Bull Durham until the very end of his 150 to 200 words of copy, and then only in passing. Once, he asked his readers whether they had ever read a truthful "add."

> No you never did. You read where some Guy endorses an Over-coat, and to prove it he has one on (or one they loaned him for the Picture). Now even if he did like it, what has that got to do with You? Peoples tastes are not alike. . . . You ain't no kindergarden, you know what you wore last year and if it pleased you try it again. Now I don't smoke "Bull" Durham. But if *you* did and you liked it, why dont let some Guys Picture and indorsement tout you off on something else.

He also ventured again into the world of books. Soon after he came back to New York, the firm of Albert and Charles Boni published *The Illiterate Digest,* a collection of the best of his weekly articles, plus the transcripts of a few speeches. Will opened the book with the conceit that since William Allen White, Arthur Brisbane, Ring Lardner, Vicente Blasco-Ibanez, and Elinor Glyn had all refused to contribute the introduction, he would have to supply his own. "I have known Mr. Rogers for years," he began. ". . . I spent my late youth in these shaded oak lands where so many of his scenes are so pictorially laid, and he has made me live over again the scenes of my freshman manhood. . . . His jugglery of correct words and perfect English sentences is magical, and his spelling is almost uncanny. . . . He always remembers that it is dangerous to jest with laughter. This man in writing it has done a service to all thinking mankind. Belinsky, the great Russian Critic to whom Mr. Rogers had read the manuscript, said, 'It looked like another Ben Hur to him.' "

This is exquisite nonsense, expertly pricking literary-critical pretensions. But tucked into the foolery was a kernel of truth. The book showed evidence of the influence of both Cervantes and Dickens, Will wrote, "the first in the matter of structure, the other in background, humor, and detail of characterization." But "the predominating and distinguishing quality of this Author's work is undeniably foreign to both and quite peculiar to itself. Something that for want of a better term might be called the quality of American Soul."

The critics agreed, and their recognition of the unique character of his persona and work raised him to a new standing. Most eloquent and perceptive was David McCord in *The Saturday Review of Literature:*

> Like Mark Twain (but a little differently) he walks with kings and princes and presidents and Henry Ford and Fred Stone. He is at home with the world and its denizens. Someone once gave him a license of free speech (or perhaps he took it without asking); but, at any rate, in the past few years he has probably turned over more heavy stones and thrown sunlight on the poor human grubs underneath than any man in the United States. Will Rogers is a philosopher and crusader in the tradition of Walt Whitman. He passes generally for a humorist, but that is not the whole of him.

The book was a popular success, too. Six weeks after its publication, a newspaper reported that Boni had gone through five ever-larger printings, totalling 64,000 copies; a Chicago bookstore reported that *The Illiterate Digest* was its second-best-selling title.

Early in 1925, Will asked McNaught whether they would be interested in a daily column. The Kentucky humorist Irvin S. Cobb was then syndicating a comical story every day; Will's notion, assented to by the firm, was to present (in the words of the column's title) "The Worst Story I Heard Today." He began his first offering by complaining that people were always telling him stories and saying, " 'You can switch that around and use it in your Act.' Now I never in my life on the Stage told a Story. . . . I hate a Story and I hate the Guys that are always telling them." But since he had to suffer through these "good ones," his readers might as well, too.

With as convoluted a premise as that, it wasn't surprising that the column failed to make much of an impression on the public. For the most part, the jokes really *were* bad, and Will took up more space apologizing for them than telling them. Although they were all attributed (to celebrities, pals of Will's, or people he ran into on his travels), Betty Rogers reported that she herself supplied a lot of the howlers by prowling from one used bookstore to the next, hunting up old joke books. "People were amused to find their names attached to some ancient story or to a joke of which they had never heard." The best—or at any rate the least numbing—of the worst was probably the story credited to Ring Lardner, who, Will wrote, "claims that an Englishman can't understand it and has never been able to get it." It seems a man has been invited to dinner "at a very swell home." When the salad is served, he picks some of it up in his fingers and rubs it in his hair. The lady sitting next to him says, "Why that is Watercress. You are rubbing it in your hair!" To which the man replies, "Is that so? I thought it was lettuce."

The column died a merciful death after a run of about a year. But it got Will another three hundred dollars a week from McNaught, bringing his paycheck up to thirteen hundred dollars. And, while it lasted, it got him into the newspapers every day.

Another literary venture never even got off the ground. *The Saturday Evening Post,* then the most popular magazine in America with a circulation of some 2.5 million copies every week, had recently found success in printing the memoirs of celebrities. Soon after Will's return to New York, the *Post's* venerable editor, George Horace Lorimer, commissioned him to write the story of his life. Will dutifully scratched out some opening lines. Yet his flow of words, unstoppable on any other subject, somehow could not coalesce into more than a trickle on this one. Two years later, he apologetically wired to Lorimer that the article still wasn't ready, noting that there was a bright side: HOWEVER THE LONGER I LIVE THE MORE LIFE YOU GET ALL AT ORIGINAL PRICE.

Newspaper columns, books, motion pictures, radio appearances, recordings, Bull Durham advertisements—in what seemed every way imaginable, the image, voice, and words of Will Rogers were being disseminated all over the country. But there was another, easily overlooked, medium, one that came into its own in the American 1920s. The medium was publicity. By the middle of the decade, a capacious and efficient mechanism was in place and humming, its component parts being press agents, wire services, newsreels, radios, a public hungry for ideas and images and gossip, and celebrities, none of whom could have been more willing to participate in the process than Will. In earlier years, if he made a choice remark or chatted with a prominent person at the *Follies,* it might have been picked up by one or two New York papers, or it might have remained the sole property of the people in attendance that night. But in July 1925, when he introduced Thomas Edison and said, "Next time you invent a talking machine see that there is no screech to it," the Associated Press sent the story to dozens of newspapers all over the country. (The clipping service Will had retained sent them back to him.)

That same July, a former Oklahoma congressman came to the conclusion that Will should be the next governor of the state. The AP picked up the story, and it appeared in newspapers around the country on July 10. That day, the editors of the Bartlesville (Oklahoma) *Enterprise* and the Oklahoma *News* of Oklahoma City both had the same idea. Within three hours of each other, they wired Will at the McNaught Syndicate, asking for a comment. He duly sent out two facetious telegrams (the one to the Oklahoma *News* read: I MUST HAVE ELECTION GUARANTEED BEFORE I WILL GIVE UP MY PRESENT JOB. WIRE BEST OFFER AT ONCE). The AP sent out a story featuring one of the wires, the United Press sent out a story featuring the other, and the country was blanketed. Even the Rogers, Arkansas, Kiwanis Club wanted to get into the publicity act. On July 24, it telegraphically asked Will whether he had any interest in the governorship of Arkansas. Another facetious reply. Another sheaf of clippings.

As a communicator, Will was throwing his rope wider and wider. A similar process was taking place in the social sphere. In the summer of 1924, the Prince of Wales, later to be Edward VIII, still later to be the Duke of Windsor, had visited America. The Prince had come in for a good deal of kidding, rather like Gerald Ford, over the frequent tumbles he had taken in steeplechase races; Will—who had been playing more and more polo and fallen several times himself—had spoken out on the royal visitor's behalf in his column and onstage at the *Follies*. He pointed out that his and the prince's *horses* had lost their footing: "Are the Prince and I supposed to fall with the horse, or are we supposed to stay up there in the air until he gets up, and come back under us?" Word of this defense got to the prince, and Will was invited to speak at a dinner given for him at the exclusive Piping Rock Country Club in Long Island. He was a hit—primarily, he wrote in his column, because of his target's willingness to laugh at jokes at his own expense. The prince "even worked it up to such an extent that he grabbed me by the coat tails and whispered suggestions in my ear, of ones he had heard of me telling on him but which I had not told there yet. I never do over 15 or 20 minutes and out there I did 50." He told a reporter: "Why say, I couldn't have hired a straight man to do straight for me what he did." The next day, Will played polo and had lunch with the prince.

Needless to say, Will was in ecstasy. He wrote to Lorimer at the *Post*, offering to send along a copy of the speech for publication. Before he got the negative reply (the magazine's policy precluded the publication of material previously used in any form), Will typed out a third-person introduction, titled "The Prince and the Cowboy," that glowed with the pride he felt:

The Prince of Wales has traveled all over the World and has been the Guest of Honor at hundreds of Banquets. But never has he been made to enjoy himself as he did the night of the Polo Dinner given in his honor at the Piping Rock Club on Long Island, given by the Polo Association. It was the most exclusive gathering of the representatives of both England and America. There was only 150 chosen Guests, all men. It was the only formal affair arranged for even before he left England. There was no music or entertainment of any kind, just formal speeches, and exchanges of good will and sportsmanship between the two Countries. The Prince himself expressed a desire to see and hear Will Rogers, The Cowboy Comedian, and he was invited as a Guest and Speaker, to follow the Prince's Speech. It was the first time in the History of English Royalty that they had ever been kidded in Public, and the hearty laughter, and good wholesome manner in which he received it, made him live up to the good fellow reputation, that has made him so universally popular. Will's speech went over so big with him that he was asked to play Polo with the Prince, and also appeared for him again before he left for Canada. There was no reporters allowed there and the speech has never been printed before. It was considered by everyone who heard it as being the best of Will's career.

Presidents weren't royalty, but they were the best America had to offer. In November, Calvin Coolidge won in a landslide, and Will got a chance to make his acquaintance the following May. (Still angry about the Madison Square Garden circus, Will wrote after the election: "There is something wrong with a Party that sits in a Hall for 6 months trying to nominate a Presidential Candidate, when it will only take from 7 o'clock in the morning on election day, to 7:30 A.M. on the same morning to beat him.") In town to share the podium with Coolidge at the annual Gridiron Dinner of the Washington press corps, Will and Nick Longworth, newly elected as Speaker of the House, had a private meeting with the President beforehand. Will reported to his readers that he was hoping Coolidge would be as taciturn as advertised; he needed material for his Gridiron routine. But the President, of all things, was warm and funny: "as agreeable as an Insurance Agent." Talking of the dinner, Coolidge remarked that it was " 'hard on the President.' I thought of course he meant the jokes and Sketches they put on about him, but he said no, it is the time it 'keeps me there till after 12.' "

"Now there is a joke right there. You see the subtle thing about a joke is to make it look like it was not a joke. I told him I was very anxious to see one of these Dinners as I had heard they put on great stuff. He said, 'Yes, the singing is good.' Now there is another kind of a Subtle one."

So much for stone-face material. "He outsmarted me," Will concluded. "He says to himself, 'Here is a smart Aleck Guy coming in here just to get a lot of Jokes on me and speechlessness, so I will just fool him. I will talk for 15 Minutes IF IT KILLS ME.' Nick said going out that he had never heard him so gabby in his life."

WITH LINDBERGH

CHAPTER 10

SELF-MADE DIPLOMAT

A truck ran over me, oh, 'twas a shame,
I think it had two tons of wet sand in it.
Stars flashed, bells rang and ambulances came
Life changed for me all in a tragic minute.

I waked and saw a nurse who held my head
The plasters and the bandages adorning,
And then she grinned a broad grin as she said:
"Did you see what Will Rogers said this morning?"

—ANONYMOUS

BY NOW, Will Rogers had been disseminated to the country at large by every currently available mechanical means. It remained for Charles L. Wagner to think of sending him in the flesh. Wagner was a concert promoter who had recently had great success in presenting the tours of singers such as John McCormack and Mary Garden. He had been involved in the American lyceums of the turn of the century, in which such figures as Jack London, James Whitcomb Riley, and William Jennings Bryan had lectured from town to town, and he had long wanted to try to revive the tradition, on a grander scale. He decided Will was his man and offered extraordinary terms: for seventy-five performances between October 1 and December 16, 1925, he would pay $82,500, plus all expenses. Will was hesitant, less because of the grueling pace than because, after all those years of fifteen-minute Follies routines, he didn't know whether he could hold an audience for the fifty minutes

Wagner's contract specified. (Filling out the bill was to be the the de Reszke Singers, a male quartet named after their teacher, the great French tenor Jean de Reszke.) But for that kind of money—more than twice what he was making from Ziegfeld—he could live with the doubt. He signed up in June.

As opening night approached, he warmed to the idea. For ten years, except for occasional Ziegfeld tours, he had been tethered to New York or Los Angeles; he had forgotten the scent of the Middle American air, the sound of lunch-counter conversation, the look of Main Street on a Saturday afternoon. The tour—hitting seven times as many towns a week as the most grueling vaudeville circuit—would be a chance to re-acquaint himself with it all. "All I used to know was just what I read in the papers," began his first weekly article after he hit the road. "But that was when I was 'Shanghaid' in New York, because all anybody knows is just what they read in the papers. But NOW all I know is just what I see myself. . . . I am out to see how America is living. . . . I am meeting the regular Bird."

The tour opened in Elmira, New York, once the home of Mark Twain. This was no accident: Wagner was not subject to Will's humility, and it was his intention to market his star as Twain's successor. The two were explicitly compared in the pages of the twenty-five-cent program; on its cover, Will was pictured in a bow tie, business suit, and crew cut (no cowlick!) and billed as "America's Greatest Humorist." But audiences did not immediately accept this proposition. Will was still far less widely known in the hinterlands than in Manhattan, and for the first two weeks of the tour, Wagner lost from two to eight hundred dollars a night. The problem, remembered Bruce Quisenberry—Will's nineteen-year-old nephew, who served as his rope cleaner and all-purpose aide-de-camp—was that "we were getting into towns, or cities, and hardly anybody knew we were coming. Local impresarios . . . thought all they had to do was put their tickets on sale and wait for the people to show up." Soon Quisenberry began to act as advance man, local sponsors were induced to pay more attention, and Wagner's "problem," he wrote in his memoirs, "changed to one of finding halls large enough to hold the throngs he attracted."

Any doubts Will himself may still have had were dispelled by his five appearances in Oklahoma, two weeks into the tour. In Tulsa, just thirty-five miles west of the home place, he was so tense that he paced around Convention Hall three times while the de Reszke Singers performed. The collective reason for his agitation was gathered just inside the hall: He had accumulated "twenty years of doubt and expectations just to what they would think of you," and he was about to find out. "They" were his boyhood and youth's entire cast of characters, who had driven in from Nowata, from Talala, from Oologah, from Vinita, from Claremore, and from Chelsea to finally see for themselves, after all these years, exactly what it was that Willie Rogers did. When he came out on-stage, he saw a bigger audience than he had ever played for—three thousand people filling every seat, standing at the rear, and sitting in the aisles and in chairs on the stage. Someone handed him a jug of flowers, a gift from the town of Claremore. "That did stick me," he wrote in his weekly article.

> Well, after what seemed like ages, I got started, and they laughed, and they would laugh so long it gave me time to think of another one. . . .
> Well, they kept on seeming to want more till I did two Hours and fifteen minutes. That's I think a Minor League Record for Monologists. That made all the opening nights in New York I have worried with, seem like rehearsals. Just think, back home and they liked you! That was a Kick. It's not the highest type of work, this acting a fool, and a Comedian may not excite much envy. But it's the best I will ever get, and I felt good enough that night to last me the rest of my life.

"Gee, I am lucky," he concluded. "I fooled 'em at home."

The concert tour was the final turn of the screw to the mechanism that transformed Will Rogers from a vaudeville rope thrower to a national presence. It cemented his connection to America. With some interruptions, it lasted for two and a half years, and it hit big towns and small, high school gymnasiums and civic arenas, New England churches and Carnegie Hall. By the time he was through, there was no one in the country who had not had the opportunity, in most cases more than once, to plunk three dollars down and see Will Rogers in the flesh.

What was most gratifying for Will, that first season, was the chance to make a nostalgic grand tour of his past—on Charles Wagner's dime. In Bartlesville, Oklahoma, he met with Dick Parris, his old South American traveling companion; in Denver, a week later (the farthest west he would get that season), a classmate from Scarritt College. He saw Fred Tejan and Tom Harvey and Gene Buck and Rex Beach and Ring Lardner and Annie Oakley (he'd met the sharpshooter years ago through her good friend Fred Stone) and even Roy "Pop" Rosenbaum, husband of the *Ziegfeld Follies* poker shark. In the course of one week in Texas, he met with Jim Minnick, his first vaudeville assistant; Billy

Johnston, the Kemper boy who had sent him to the Ewing ranch; Frank Ewing himself; Billy Connell, who had been overcome by gas with him in a San Francisco hotel room a quarter of a century before; and the widow of Clay McGonigle. Outside of Amarillo, he journeyed out to the spot where he and Ewing had had such a time crossing the Canadian River with their herd, twenty-eight years before.

He made new acquaintances, too. In Kansas, he called on the legendary newspaper editor William Allen White and the mother of his favorite baseball player, Washington Senators pitcher Walter Johnson. In Florida, where Betty joined him for a two-week working vacation in January, he got together with two fellow humorists, George Ade and Kin Hubbard. (Will thought Hubbard, a cracker-barrel wit from Indiana and the creator of the character Abe Martin, was the funniest man in America.) He met Amon Carter and L. E. Phillips, a publisher and an oilman, respectively, who would become good friends. There were also encounters with several governors, dozens of mayors, and untold legions of newspaper reporters.

The reporters were key. When Will arrived in a town with Bruce Quisenberry, one or more of them would invariably be at the train station, notebooks in hand. Before an interview could proceed, Will, who had learned that local references were essential to his show's success, turned the tables: "Instead of allowing the reporter to ask him questions," wrote a frustrated newspaperman in Birmingham, Alabama, "he shot them forth himself.

"What's happened in your town lately? What's going on."
He was told that we had a recent election.
"What's your form of government? Commission? Did they have a close race? Is Senator Underwood still here? Nick Longworth told me once that he was one of the greatest Americans and Nick's Republican, you know.
"Where does Roy Cohen live? I'd like to see that clever bohunk. We were on the same movie lot once. How's 'Twenty-four Votes for Underwood' Brandon?"

Will genuinely enjoyed the reporters—he was now one of them, after all—and they got a huge thrill out of him. Nearly three decades after the fact, in a letter to Will Rogers, Jr., a newspaperman named Robert Ranord recalled having breakfast with Will one morning in Sioux City, Iowa. "I think I enjoyed that meal more than any I ever had eaten," he wrote. "I ate the usual reporters breakfast, which, if you know newsmen, is light, but he ate the whole corn country breakfast, ham and eggs, straight through." As they were leaving the dining room, they ran into William J. Bulow, the governor of South Dakota. "Will asked if he had had breakfast and Bulow said no," Ranord recalled. "Your father just turned around and took us all back to the table. He urged me to have another breakfast but I could not do it. He, himself, ate another breakfast just like the one he ate before and got along fine with everyone. I just sat in awe and watched."

There was a postscript: "I have spent my life dealing with people but I never met anyone that I liked more than your father."

The pace was grueling. "We jumped back and forth," Quisenberry complained years later, "zig-zagging here and there; in my opinion making jumps too long for the average engagement. The policy of Mr. Wagner and his booker seemed to be to take any date that was offered, and then later on get a time table and see whether we could make it or not."

After a show, Will would usually get right into a train or a hired car (or in later years an airplane) and head for the next city. The down time was anything but restful: Will would pull out his portable typewriter and work on "The Worst Story I Heard Today," his weekly article, engineering plans for the California ranch or a magazine piece. As far as Quisenberry could tell, his uncle never felt the strain.

> I never saw such amazing energy. He never seemed to be tired. Sometimes, when I was utterly exhausted, he would say, "Boy, what are you so draggy about? You slept till six this mornin'." Always, after a lecture, he wanted to eat. He dearly loved chili con carne, but this wasn't so bad—he also loved onion sandwiches. On the train we slept in the same compartment. Of a morning, when we were in a hotel, he would be the first person up; he would grab the newspapers and go in to breakfast. We didn't dare talk to him, then.

A week in late November had a typical itinerary. On successive nights, he played Utica, Ann Arbor, Buffalo, Rochester, and Washington. The next day, there was a matinee in Waterbury, Connecticut, and an evening performance at the New Amsterdam in New York, and then it was on to Richmond. He was in Ann Arbor the day before Thanksgiving, when he and Betty always celebrated their anniversary, and he sent her this night letter:

> YOU KNOW WHAT DAY I AM SENDING THIS LETTER AND YOU KNOW WHAT DAY YOU WILL RECEIVE IT THIS IS ONE BARGAIN WE MADE WHERE WE DIDN'T SELL OUT TO QUICK THE LONGER WE HOLD

IT THE MORE VALUABLE IT SEEMS TO BECOME HOPE YOU HAD A
GOOD TRIP WE HAD A GREAT LAST NIGHT IN UTICA AND IT LOOKS
GOOD TONIGHT I DO WISH I WAS THERE TOMORROW I WOULD
BREAK REDUCING FOR ONE DAY LOTS OF LOVE TO YOU ESPECIALLY
ON THIS WONDERFUL DAY AND A MIGHTY LOT OF THOSE WONDER-
FUL LITTLE NESTERS GOOD NIGHT DADDY

After the initial uncertainty, the shows themselves were not only relatively effortless but, in the extended and unmediated communion they
offered with an adoring crowd, thrilling. Will would say later that they
gave him the most personal satisfaction of anything he ever did professionally. Far from finding it difficult to hold the stage for fifty minutes,
he'd generally stay on for at least two hours, and sometimes as long as
three. There were two segments to the show, his appearance in each
preceded by the de Reszke Singers, who had a repertoire of semi-
classical pieces, folk songs, and spirituals. In the wings during their first
set, Will would study scraps of paper he pulled out of the pockets of "the
Old Blue Serge with the mirror effect in the seat and knees"—the notes
he had made from his conversations throughout the day. Then he came
out to a bare stage.

His openings were usually self-conscious deflections of grandeur designed to put himself and the audience at ease. "I can't think of a way
to start my act," he'd say. "Guess there's no reason why it should be
started." Or: "I don't know what to call the fool thing. If a smart man
was doing this it would be a lecture; if a politician was doing it it would
be a message." Then came the local references, some custom-crafted,
some boilerplate. A favorite was: "The children of [name of town where
concert was held] are taught two things. To fear the Lord and hate
[name of town's biggest rival]." He had a whole speech prepared to follow the glowing introduction of a member of the town's upper crust:
"That ought to set me in pretty nice in case I want to come back here
and settle down and borrow some money. Can I get it? I can? I would
like to have you put that down in writing if you don't mind. You can
never trust these men, and the more prominent they are the less you can
trust them.

"He got by on his pluck and perseverance. The trouble is we can't
find somebody to pluck like he did."

Young Bruce Quisenberry was always good for a few laughs. Will
would say, "Hey, bub, c'mere," and motion for him to start moving the
piano off the stage. Will would follow with the stool, saying "I'll help
you." That, Quisenberry recalled, always broke the audience up. One

time, quite by accident, the piano collapsed and broke into pieces as it was being pushed off. This was comic gold for Will. "You know how scared old Bruce can look well you should have seen his eyes," he wrote to his son Bill. "He thought he had ruined the whole show, Theatre, act, and everything, Well I wish it would happen every night, I got a dozen laughs out of it."

The heart of the talk, as the tour continued, was material Will found to be surefire. There was stuff on the Klan, Prohibition, the Florida land boom, aviation, evolution, and his own meetings with Coolidge and the Prince of Wales. For Will the lectern was vestigial: As he spoke (without a microphone, except in the very largest halls), he walked across the stage, leaned on the piano, sat on the stool. His speaking style, polished to a high gloss of efficiency in the two decades he had been talking from a stage, appeared just the opposite. He would look at the floor or over at the wings, as if he were too shy to regard the audience directly. He was just thrilled to be there, his body language announced; every now and then, the excitement, or the sheer humor of it all, would overcome him and he would erupt in a girlish giggle. His own enjoyment was infectious. Each of his extended comic sallies would be leisurely, drawlingly offered, and interrupted by asides and digressions, by his frequent "you know's," by his studied stammer. By the time he got to the climax, everyone would be right there with him, and he'd be looking into a sea of rapt, delighted faces.

For the second act, he would come out in cowboy regalia, ropes in hand, and do a few tricks. By the end of the show, if it had gone well, he would be sitting on the end of the stage, dangling his legs, and just "gassing and gossiping," as Quisenberry put it. When he could finally think of no more to say, he would tell the crowd, only half in jest, "Go home, I'm sick of looking at you."

The tour was a triumph beyond Will's or even Wagner's dreams. The financial success was most dramatic. The eventual arrangement was that Will would receive 75 percent of each show's gross, payable to Quisenberry by each manager as soon as the house was counted. (Wagner got 5 percent, proving once again that Will was a nonpareil businessman.) Assuming an average crowd of fifteen hundred, an average ticket price of $2.50, and an average of six performances a week, this works out to a $22,500 paycheck.

But it also meant a great deal in terms of esteem. No one had ever done quite what he was doing. Certainly no comedian had ever played Carnegie Hall—which is what Wagner arranged for Will to do in April 1926, near the end of the first season. The prospect made the performer extremely nervous—so much so, according to Wagner, that Will offered him one thousand dollars to call the engagement off. He needn't have worried. "It was a Rogers house," *The New York Times* reported the next day, "and roared uproariously at his every sally."

FOUR DAYS LATER, Will had lunch with George Horace Lorimer of *The Saturday Evening Post*. The story of his life remained unfinished (it "still is on," he had assured the editor—"I am living some of the best part of it so it wouldent do not to get it in"), but while on tour he had put together two other long pieces for the *Post*, a humorous meditation on the Democrats' desperation for a viable campaign issue and a mock debate between Florida and California. Delighted with them, Lorimer had proposed that in the summer Will go to Italy, where Mussolini's reign was attracting worldwide curiosity, and write about it for the magazine. It was probably at the Philadelphia lunch that the idea expanded into a series of articles on the European scene, in the guise of diplomatic reports to President Coolidge; he would be paid two thousand dollars per article.*

Will hadn't been to England for twelve years, hadn't been to the Continent for twenty. The children had never visited either, and Will arranged to use the *Post* assignment as an excuse for a family excursion. He and Bill, now fourteen years old, would sail for England from New York on May 1, to be joined later in the summer by the rest of the family. The lecture tour ended on April 20, and Will used the free time to lay groundwork for the trip. He accumulated about thirty letters of introduction, including one to American diplomatic and consular officers from Secretary of State Frank Kellogg, one from William Borah of Idaho, possibly the most distinguished member of the U.S. Senate, two from Father Francis Duffy (Will hoped for an audience with the Pope), and six from Vice President Charles Dawes, who wrote, "Mr. Rogers is a friend of mine." He also asked Charles Dana Gibson, the illustrator who had created the Gibson Girl, for an introduction to his sister-in-law, Lady Nancy Astor, a native of Virginia who in 1919 had become Britain's first female member of Parliament. "This is our friend Will Rogers," Gibson wrote on *Life* magazine stationery. "He has heard of you.

---

*The running title of the series, "Letters of a Self-Made Diplomat to His President," was an indication of the editor's enthusiasm for the project. It echoed Lorimer's own novel, *Letters from a Self-Made Merchant to His Son*, serialized in the *Post* in 1901–1902. It was one of the most successful series the magazine ever ran and, in book form, an international best-seller.

And in time you will hear of him. I will be famous for having brought you together."

Will also paid a visit to Adolph Ochs, the publisher of *The New York Times*. The *Times* had stopped carrying the weekly article in 1924 (the New York *World* had picked it up), but Ochs and Will remained on good terms. At lunch together in New York, the publisher made the offhand remark that in the course of his travels Will should be on the lookout for potential news items. If he sent them on, the newspaper would pay cable costs.

Will ended up being overseas for five months. It was an amazing trip. Most of the first couple of months was devoted to reporting and writing his pieces for the *Post*. He had the journalistic good fortune to arrive in England in the middle of a general strike, and his coverage set the tone for his subsequent pieces: funny without being clownish, looking for absurdities but even more for a germ of truth. His main impression of the strike was how incongruously civilized it was.

> The strike was carried on something like this: Some government man would approach a man and ask, "Could I get you to drive a Tram for us? We are really in great distress at not being able to perambulate."
>
> "No, sir, I can't drive it for you; I am on strike. I am a Tram driver by profession. However, I should be very glad to assist you if it's not presuming too on your short acquaintance. I will see who I can find that's not on strike and send them around to you."

Lorimer was very pleased with Will's first piece, and used it as the lead article in the July 10 issue of the *Post*. "The start is a running one," he wrote Will, "and we are going to have a big series, I am sure." All told, Will would write eleven pieces, and they continued to get a favorable reception in Philadelphia. "There is only one fault to find with these articles," Lorimer wrote later, "and that is that they don't come often enough." They were eventually collected in two books—*Letters of a Self-Made Diplomat to His President* (1926) and *There's Not a Bathing Suit in Russia & Other Bare Facts* (1927).

Four days after his arrival, Will visited Parliament, where he got more good stuff. From the gallery of the House of Commons, he watched David Lloyd George—formerly the prime minister, now a Liberal MP—criticize the government's strike newspaper for not publishing a settlement plan put forth by the Archbishop of Canterbury. Winston Churchill, who as chancellor of the exchequer was responsible for editing the paper, rose to defend himself. "He explained to Lloyd George that it was very hard, as some connected with the paper had never been in a Newspaper office before; and some Laborite hollered out, 'Including the Editor.' That was what I would call a real Nifty, and, say, it went over with a bang."

Spying Lady Astor on the floor, Will sent along the letter from Charles Dana Gibson. She sought him out and, as soon as she heard him talk, said, "Boy, where did you get that Nigger dialect? It sho sounds like home to me." Lady Astor (born Nancy Langhorne) was an unmistakable figure in between-the-wars England, as much for her Virginia accent as for her good looks (still striking at the age of forty-seven). She was a Conservative but was in the process of beginning a close friendship with the venerable Fabian socialist George Bernard Shaw, who in appreciation of her effervescence called her "a cocktail of a woman . . . a whirling atom." She and her husband, Lord Waldorf Astor, assiduously collected the wealthy, the prominent, and the accomplished, entertaining them in London and at Cliveden, an Italianate mansion in Berkshire overlooking the Thames. Immediately recognizing Will's star qualities, she saw to it that he was a frequent guest at her home, where he was introduced to such social luminaries as Sir Thomas Lipton and Lord Thomas Dewar. At one dinner party, he was seated next to Sir James Barrie, the author most famous for *Peter Pan*. (He had also written *What Every Woman Knows*, which Will and Betty had seen in St. Louis on their wedding night.) While Lady Astor was driving the two of them home, Barrie asked Will whether he wanted to continue their conversation in his apartment. "Well Lady Astor whispered to me, 'You go. He don't invite many up there, and don't you miss this.' " He didn't. For once he was silent, as Barrie regaled him with stories of his life in the theater and the world of letters.

A few days later, he received a note from the Prince of Wales, who had heard he was in London and invited him to come to York House for a visit. It was not an interview, the Prince stressed—" 'just renewing old acquaintanceship.' " But in the course of an hour's conversation Will caught something essential about the prince, who was then thirty-two years old but still somehow unformed. The room where they talked, Will wrote, "just gave you the feeling of some boy's room off to school, or some boy that was fortunate enough to have his own room at home and fixed it the way he wanted." There was also this prescient comment near the end of the piece: "Just between you and I, Cal, he don't care any more about being King than you would going back to Vice President again."

On May 16, Will and Bill left their rooms at the Savoy, flew to Paris, and commenced to tour the Continent. Will's comments in his *Post* articles on the lighter side of European touring recall Twain's *Innocents Abroad,* with an important difference. Twain mocked the American philistine who narrated; Will, for whom the art of painting began with Ed Borein and ended with Charley Russell, *was* that philistine, and proud of it. It was a reminder that Will Rogers was a package deal; along with the insight and the largesse and the great good humor, an admirer had to accept a certain provincialism that had not proved subject to adjustment. About his stay in Rome, he wrote:

> I am, I bet you, the only one that ever visited that city that dident run myself ragged dragging from one old Church to another, and from one old Oil Painting to the next. In the first place, I don't care anything about Oil Paintings. Ever since I struck a dry hole near the old home ranch in Rogers County, Oklahoma I have hated oil, in the raw, and all its subsidiaries. You can even color it up, and it don't mean anything to me. I don't want to see a lot of old Pictures. If I wanted to see old Pictures I would get D. W. Griffith to revive the Birth of a Nation. That's the best old Picture there is. . . .
>
> Say Charles Dana Gibson and Herbert Johnson can assemble 'em good enough for me. They may never hang in the Louvre. But they sho do dangle from the front page of many an old News stand.

A graphic example of his limitations was his encounter with Mussolini. This time, it was Will who made it clear that their meeting was not to be considered an interview; instead, as he said when they met, he had "come to see is Mussolini a Regular Guy." (The dictator's response, according to Will's account, was, "Hurray. Bravo. No Interview.") This was a happy decision, since the literary persona Will had fashioned to rake pompous senators over the coals was not (as he probably on some level realized) equipped to do justice to all the implications of the dictator's rise to power and his rule. Mussolini had taken control of the country in 1922, and while his initial achievements in centralization, efficiency, and morale had won considerable international admiration, there had since been clear indications that his thirst for power was unquenchable and had potentially brutal consequences. Indeed, just three days after Will saw him, Mussolini put through a law that gave him the right to exercise judicial and legislative prerogatives—thus ending the division of governmental powers in Italy. The implications of such acts were lost on Will, who in his *Post* account made admiring comedy of the Fascist habit of force-feeding castor oil to their opponents and who gushingly called Mussolini "the man that has done more for one race of people in three years than one man ever did; a Napoleon, but with peace."

The non-interview was one of the oddest encounters in the history of journalism. Will entered Il Duce's chambers with a broad and deliberate grin on his face—"I thought he has got to be a pretty tough Guy if he don't grin with you." Sure enough, the man who was famous all over the world for his stone face gave his visitor a smile along with the Fascist salute. As translator, Will had brought along Warren Robbins, counselor of the American embassy in Rome, but Mussolini gave most of his answers in a broken English that, in Will's rendition, made him sound like a fruit peddler in a bad vaudeville sketch.

The first question concerned the number of cabinet posts Mussolini held. He started counting on his fingers: "Me—one, two, three, four, five, six—Me, Six Ministers."

What kind of salary did he draw for all that work? "He understood without an interpreter, and said, 'Oh, not so much,' and did his fingers together, as one does when they insinuate money."

Will then asked whether he had thought up the castor-oil treatment himself.

> He laughed and winked and said, "Very good, eh?" He dident say outright that it was his idea, but he winked as he said, "Very good, eh?". . .
>
> He then said, through Mr. Warren [*sic*], "No castor oil in two years. When we were fighting and trying to save the country against the Bolsheviks, we used to find them and"—he then dropped back into English—"one fellow, he not so bad, we give him half leiter [*sic*], next fellow, he bad boy, we give him ONE leiter," and he laughed and sure got a kick out of telling this. . . .
>
> I said I was going to Russia, and he interrupted me. "Oh Russia, See, See! You take recipe to Russia, very good for Russia, castor oil. I give you free."

As the hour drew to a close, Mussolini brought out a photograph of himself on horseback and signed it "Al Signor Rogers." For his last question, Will asked whether he had any message for Italian-Americans.

"Well, he laughed and put his hands on both my shoulders and said in English, 'You can tell 'em Mussolini, R-e-g-u-l-a-r G-u-y. Is that right Englais?' He said, 'Mussolini no Napoleon, want fight, always look mad;

Mussolini, laugh, gay, like good time same as everybody else, mayby more so'—and he winked."

From Rome, it was on to Venice, Nice, and then Spain, where Will interviewed dictator Miguel Primo de Rivera and chatted with King Alfonso XIII before the latter played polo. He also went to see a bull-fight, where the *suerte de picar,* the part of the spectacle in which the bull charges and kills blindfolded horses, not surprisingly unnerved him. He would watch until the moment of truth, then duck his head down behind the wall in front of his seat. "A very nice Spanish Chap who I had met in New York was my host, and he would tell me when to look up again," Will wrote. "I am a pretty tough egg, but I couldent go that Horse business."

The climax of his European reporting was his visit to Russia at the beginning of July. He flew from London to Moscow in thirty-three hours. There were three changes of planes, the last in Königsberg, where Will was the only passenger to board a single-engine plane. "It was piloted by the funniest looking old chuckleheaded, shave-haired Russian boy that dident look like he was over twenty. But say, Bub, that clown could sure rein that thing over and make it say Uncle and play dead and roll over. He was an Aviator." All summer, Will had been impressed by the ease with which he could fly all over Europe; the swift flight into Moscow was probably the final push in his becoming an apostle of aviation.

Will had with him a letter from Edwin James, managing editor of *The New York Times,* to Walter Duranty, the *Times'* Moscow correspondent. It said, in full: "This will introduce you to Will Rogers. Please help him out if he gets in too bad." Not exactly a sterling recommendation, but it was all he had, and he set off to find Duranty, eventually being taken to him by the correspondent's friend Armand Hammer, a young American in Moscow who was prospering greatly with a pencil factory and some other business ventures. Influential as he was, Duranty was unable to get Will a meeting with the man he really wanted to interview: Leon Trotsky, who had lost influence in the Party since the death of Lenin two years before—at the time of Will's visit he was head of the Central Committee for Concessions—but was still the Russian leader best known to Americans. As sharp on Soviet politics as American, Will discerned the reason why Trotsky was being kept under wraps: he was "not in so good with the present government."

The real fellow that is running the whole thing in there is a Bird named Stalin, a great big two-fisted fighting egg from away

down in the Caucasian Mountains. He is the Borah of the Black
Seas. He is kinder the Mellon and Butler combined of the Russian administration. He is the stage manager of Bolshevism right
now. He don't hold any great high position himself, but he tells
the others what ones they will hold. He has served his term in
Siberia under the Czar. Well, Trotzky is kinder not sitting at his
round table for lunch.

Will thought the Soviets made a mistake in not letting him see
Trotsky: "I bet you if I had met him and had a chat with him, I would
have found him a very interesting and human fellow, for I have never
yet met a man that I dident like. When you meet people, no matter
what opinion you might have formed about them beforehand, why, after
you meet them and see their angle and their personality, why, you can
see a lot of good in all of them."*
But he got along all right without the interview. He had the good
fortune to visit the country in a period of relative freedom, and in the
week he was there he was able to visit Moscow, Leningrad, and a
number of villages without any interference or even supervision. His
three *Post* pieces—published the next year as *There's Not a Bathing Suit in
Russia*—showed an impressive, sober grasp of current realities and anticipation of future developments (especially in his sense that the Commu-
nists had underestimated the continuing strength of both the peasants
and the church). Among his observations:

> You see, the Communism that they started out with, the
> idea that everybody would get the same and have the same—

---

*The last clause of the first sentence of this quotation was Will's first statement of the
claim that would become his most famous line. He restated it at least seven subsequent times,
in speeches and writing. Speaking at a Boston church in 1930, he said, "When I die, my epi-
taph or whatever you call those signs on gravestones is going to read: 'I joked about every
prominent man of my time, but I never met a man I dident like.' I am so proud of that that I
can hardly wait to die so it can be carved."

A surprising number of people have taken the statement literally, leading them to see
Will as a liar, a saint, or a fool, but it's clearly better viewed as both a piece of hyperbole and
an inverted expression of Will's need to *be* liked. Will himself gave an interestingly Talmudic
interpretation to Pinky Tomlin, an Oklahoma songwriter who once challenged him on the
impossibility of liking *everyone*.

"Well, young man," Tomlin reported him saying. "You and me are from the same part
of the country. We both know everyone that pulls on britches ain't no man."

Trotsky, incidentally, was expelled from the Communist party in 1927 and expelled
from the country two years later.

Lord, that dident work at all. . . . That talked well to a crowd, but they got no more of it now than we have. . . .

If Socialists worked as much as they talked, they would be the most prosperous style of Government in the World. But the thing is they don't know anything about it themselves. There is not two of them in the world with the same idea of what it is. . . .

It seems the whole idea of Communism, or whatever they want to call it, is based on propaganda and blood. Their whole life and thought is to convince somebody else. It looks to me like if a thing is so good and working so fine for you, you would kind of want to keep it to yourself. I would be afraid to let anybody in on it, and that generally seems to be about the usual brand of human nature everywhere. But the Communist has so many good things he just wants you to join in and help him use some of them. . . .

There is as much class distinction in Russia today as there is in Charleston, South Carolina. . . .

Russia hasent changed one bit. It's just Russia as it has been for hundreds of years and will be for the next hundreds of years. A hundred million people are out in the Country and small Villages, and are living just the same lives they lived under the Czar, and their existence wouldent be changed even if the Prohibition, the Populist, the Farmer-Labor or even the Democrats run Russia.

Will was back in London by the middle of July. He did not rest on his laurels. Two days after his return, he signed a contract to act with Dorothy Gish in a feature film called *Tiptoes,* a comedy about a vaudeville team down on its luck in London. That same week, he agreed to appear nightly in a revue put on by the English showman Charles B. Cochran. The show was a great success, but Will's monologue, which took some potshots at English coffee and Britain's debt to America, among other targets, drew several scathing notices, the press currently being in a nationalistic mood. Most offended was *Everybody's Weekly,* which headlined its review "GO HOME WILL ROGERS—A Comedian Propagandist Who Is Not Wanted." Its critic wrote that when Will's presence in the show was announced,

> naturally, we of the audience assumed that we would see this quaint American comedian in some of his inimitable drolleries. Nothing of the sort! To the amazement, and I may truthfully say

consternation, of the bulk of the audience, we were compelled to listen to a long diatribe which mainly consisted of gratuitous insults aimed at Great Britain, France and Belgium.

In other words, this comic man from New York, dressed in an ordinary lounge suit, walked up and down the stage chewing gum, at the same time keeping up a running fire of caustic criticism of the present European crisis. His remarks throughout were insulting, insolent, provocative and in the worst of bad taste.

According to press reports, Cochran had agreed to give Will a blank check at the end of the engagement, amount to be filled in by the star. Supposedly, Cochran handed him a check after the four-week run and Will tore it up, saying he had enjoyed the show so much he couldn't accept payment.

When the Cochran show ended, Will played three weeks in a cabaret. He gave a radio speech for what was reported to be "the largest fee ever paid to a radio talker in this country"; he turned the check over to a hospital charity. When a movie theater fire in Ireland killed forty-eight people, Will flew to Dublin to give a benefit for the victims' families. Carl Clancy, the producer of *The Headless Horseman*, hired him to make a series of comic travelogues, and through August and September he traveled around the Continent with Betty—she had arrived with Mary and Jim on August 7—posing in front of landmarks and mugging next to natives. Back in America, the footage would be edited into twelve one-reelers, humorous titles supplied by Will.

His social life was not neglected. He went grouse-hunting with Bernard Baruch at the financier's estate in Scotland and dined with Irving Berlin in London. Among the guests at a stag dinner given for him at the Savoy were James Barrie, G. K. Chesterton, the Scottish music hall comedian Sir Harry Lauder, the novelist Michael Arlen (a newspaper reported that he "came over especially from Paris"), and his old friends Lord Dewar and Sir Thomas Lipton. Through a misunderstanding, both of the last two expected Will to be their guest on the same day. Dewar resolved it, reporting to Will that he had "arranged matters with Lipton and he quite understands that you are coming to see me on Sunday. He says he will be delighted to see you and your wife out at his place any time you may choose to select."

Easy to overlook in the daze of activity were fifty-eight words Will banged out on his portable typewriter on July 29:

Nancy Astor, which is the nom de plume of Lady Astor, is arriving on your side about now. She is the best friend America has here. Please ask my friend, Jimmy Walker, to have America take good care of her. She is the only one over here that don't throw rocks at American tourists.

Yours respectfully,
Will Rogers

He was taking Adolph Ochs up on his offer. He wired the *Times,* asking whether it would indeed pay the cable tolls on a dispatch. The answer came back in the affirmative, and Lady Astor's letter of introduction came over the wire. It was addressed as a letter to the editor, but Joseph Tebeau, the night managing editor, decided to put it on the first page of the second section rather than on the editorial page. Will would continue to send the *Times* a pithy message every day for the rest of his time in Europe, excepting a few days when he was in the Alps and couldn't get to a telegraph office. When he returned to America, the McNaught Syndicate arranged to syndicate the daily telegram in the *Times* and a roster of newspapers that would grow to more than four hundred. It ran six days a week until August 16, 1935, when the 2,317th, and final, one appeared.

Will's conquests continued. Sailing home on the *Leviathan,* he organized a series of shipboard benefits for the victims of a hurricane in Florida, raising more than forty thousand dollars, and even persuaded the notoriously solemn former Secretary of State Charles Evans Hughes, whom he had impersonated in the "Disagreement Conference" sketch, to give a humorous talk. When reporters met the ship in New York, they found Will and Hughes walking arm in arm on the deck. "Hughes was reluctant to have his photograph taken," said the *Telegram,* "but Rogers' coaxing words of, 'Come on Sec, give the boys a shot at you!' brought the desired result."

The flock of reporters was just one piece of evidence that Will's European dispatches in the *Post* and the *Times*—respectively, the most popular and most prestigious publications in the country—had elevated him to a new level of fame. Another was that, while he was gone, his photograph occupied the cover of Henry Luce's three-year-old weekly, *Time,* with a one-word caption: "Funny." A third was the wire he received two days after his arrival in New York. It was from President Coolidge's secretary, Everett Sanders, and it invited him to be an overnight guest at the White House. It did not state that the President wished to be briefed on European affairs, but it might as well have, so striking was the sense that Will's comic fancy of self-made diplomacy was coming true. He immediately typed out a draft of a reply:

> If that gentleman is not kidding me that is the greatest honor that ever fell my way and I not only appreciate it but I am going to take you up on it. . . . Just think the only non office seeker that ever slept in the White House. I have an awful lot to report. I will be there one night if I have to put a cot in the Blue Room. . . . Just think it will be the first meal I ever had on the Government, and its just my luck to be on a diet now. Its Mrs Coolidge I want to meet. Regards till somebody wakes me up.

Will's stay at the White House was, if anything, odder than his Mussolini visit. His train from Philadelphia was delayed by an accident, so he walked into the dining room just as the Coolidges were sitting down to dinner. "This is what I call true democracy," he announced, "the President and his wife waiting dinner on me, such as I am." (Irwin "Ike" Hoover, chief White House usher for six Presidents, included a snippy account of Will's visit in his memoirs, noting, "Of course they had not waited at all, but the remark went over well, drew a smile from the President and something a little more than a smile from Mrs. Coolidge.")

Will's account, published a couple of months later in the *Saturday Evening Post*, stressed the homeyness of the visit, making much of details like the Coolidges' predilection for feeding their two dogs with dinner-table scraps. As for his depiction of the President, if Mussolini was a stock Italian in Will's hands, Coolidge was a Central Casting Maine farmer, a Zen master of gnomic utterance. Over a fish dinner—Will was the only guest—the conversation touched on a new passenger airline from Washington to Philadelphia. Mrs. Coolidge asked, "Does anybody ride on it?" "I don't know," replied the President. "I don't."

After the meal, Will and the President retired to a study for cigars and conversation. Sure enough, Will offered his impressions on foreign affairs, including the observation that people in Britain resented having to pay off their debts to the United States. The President's comment was, "Well, England's got a right to holler. They are paying."

Presently, they rejoined Mrs. Coolidge, who was knitting in the "main living room." Ike Hoover adds a detail: Jigsaw puzzles were brought out and worked on. At 10:25, the President said, "Grace, where is Will going to sleep?" He was assigned to the State Room, which was "big enough you could have roped a steer in it" and contained "the biggest bed I ever saw, a regular Brigham Young affair. I knew that evidently a great many famous people had slept in there at various times, and I knew I had no business even in the house, much less in that bed—I wouldent have felt right." He slept instead in a single brass bed in a small adjoining dressing room.

The next morning, he was served breakfast in his room, then talked for a while to various White House staff members. (Ike Hoover: "Time rather dragged on his hands. He seemed to have no plans, except that he appeared anxious to get away as soon as possible. He really seemed uncomfortable.") Finally, a White House car took him for visits to Secretary of Labor James Davis and Evelyn Walsh McLean. He returned in time for lunch, which was fish hash. The President eyed the dish, then remarked, "Same old fish?"

Will reported the following lunch-table conversation (at Lorimer's request, he attributed all Coolidge's quotes to a "White House Spokesman"):

I said to Mr. Coolidge, "I see you had a lot of Visitors today." And to get in a little bit of my bum comedy I asked him, "What Notables and horse thieves did you have call today?"

As quick as a flash, and without the least semblance of a smile, the White House Spokesman replied, "The Cabinet."

Well, that one got such a laugh with us that he followed it up with: "And Senator Butler."

Mrs. Coolidge then asked, "Who else was over, Papa?" She calls Mr. Coolidge that. You see, they were just in the usual family conversation now. I had been there so long I was one of the family.

The White House Spokesman said, "Burton, from Ohio."

Mrs. Coolidge said, "What did he want?"

He replied, "Wanted me to go to Cleveland and make a speech."

She asked, "Are you going?"

"No, I ain't. Made two speeches there already and they don't know it yet."*

---

*In Ike Hoover's view, Will's visit was no more notable than hundreds of others to the Coolidge White House. "That he afterwards made so much of it, in amusing his audiences, is to his credit, for in reality his field was very limited. He seemed to interest Mrs. Coolidge just a little, and the President a great deal less. In fact, when someone remarked later to the President that it was hoped he got a good 'kick' out of Mr. Rogers's visit, he replied casually, and without a smile, 'Oh, Will! He is all right.' " In a December 1927 nationwide radio broadcast, Will announced that Coolidge was with him, and proceeded to do an imitation so

Will's account of his White House visit was the high point of his presentation on his fall lecture tour, which began in Bronxville, New York, three days after he got back from Washington, and continued until December 20. The tour was highlighted by one symbolic event and concluded by another. The former was the premiere broadcast of the National Broadcasting Company, a four-and-a-half-hour program sent out on November 15 over telephone wire to twenty-four stations and heard by 5 million listeners. It was an historic happening, if for no other reason than the spectacle of all of this entertainment being offered to so many listeners free of charge. An NBC official confided to the Associated Press that "it is expected to make advertising ultimately pay the entire expense for the elaborate programs to come." But it was also the first time the country realized how powerfully unifying a medium radio could be, that it could, in ways unavailable to movies, recordings, or the printed word, simultaneously involve masses in the same event. Should it have surprised anyone that Will was a participant, speaking from Independence, Kansas, on a remote hookup? Such a communion was what he had been working toward, one way or another, for five years.

The second event was a kind of *ne plus ultra* publicity stunt. While Will was on tour, a group of Beverly Hills elders—Douglas Fairbanks, Sr., and Stanley Anderson, proprietor of the Beverly Hills hotel, were the ringleaders—cooked up the idea of making Will honorary mayor of the city, whose actual presiding officer was the president of the board of trustees. Telegrams were exchanged, and, when the Rogers family arrived in the Los Angeles train station on December 22, a Rolls-Royce motorcade was there to take them back to Beverly Hills. Hundreds of people stood in a driving rainstorm outside the Beverly Hills Hotel and held up elaborate banners (WE LOVE OUR DOUG, BUT OH, YOU WILL, read one) as a mock ceremony was conducted. The Associated Press covered the "inauguration" and it got good play in papers all over the country—the Christmas season being a notoriously slow one for news. Calvin Coolidge, Vice President Dawes, Al Smith, W. G. McAdoo, and New York Mayor Jimmy Walker all sent congratulatory telegrams.

It was a curious enterprise. Will didn't need publicity anymore and

accurate that many listeners thought the President was speaking. Will immediately sent an apologetic telegram to the White House, and the President reassured him: "I thought the matter of rather small consequence. . . . I hope you will not give the affair another troubled thought." However, according to Hoover, Will "never got back into the President's good graces. Coolidge especially disliked the nasal tone Will adopted imitating him. He remarked that Rogers had been a guest in the house once, but, if he was to be again, some other President would have to do the inviting."

neither did Beverly Hills. Yet publicity had helped create both, such as they were, and it was too late to arrest the heliotropism that still sought it out.

WILL HAD NEVER been thrilled with his opening act on tour. His poor opinion of the De Reszke Singers was confirmed when John McCormack came to see the show one night in the fall. The great tenor sent for one member of the group and bawled him out for an excessively esoteric repertoire, saying (Will reported to his son Bill) that if he, McCormack, "could afford to go out and sing Popular songs with what he thought was a better voice than they had why he dident see why they should object. I hope it does them some good, they can pick out the poorest songs there is, it looks like."

When he went back on the road in January 1927, just two weeks after his "inauguration," he was alone. Less singing meant more Will Rogers, and audiences responded with enthusiasm. "We have seated them on the stage in every town," Will wrote Bill in March. But now he performed at least two hours a night, and the pace was punishing: "I am traveling so fast I dont know where we go the next day." The strain was surely not unrelated to the fact that on three separate occasions that winter and spring, he suffered severe stomach pains. On June 1, he closed the spring tour with a performance in New Orleans to benefit the victims of a cataclysmic Mississippi River flood that had killed 214 people and caused $300 million in property damage. A week later, he was back home in California and finally went to see his doctor; the diagnosis was gallstones, the prescription surgery. Will's condition was amply documented in the press, and he received 178 get-well telegrams, from such diverse personages as Max Hart, W. C. Fields, Alice Longworth, Ty Cobb, Ring Lardner, Calvin Coolidge (again), and Flo Ziegfeld. (Ziegfeld, who had been pestering Will to come back to the *Follies* since he had left them in 1925, took the opportunity to get in another shot: I ALWAYS WAS WORRIED ABOUT THE TERRIBLE LIFE YOU ARE LEADING IN DUMPS AND ON RAILROAD TRAINS NO HUMAN BEING CAN STAND THIS LIFE. . . . GO IN THE FOLLIES AUGUST FIRST AND GET YOURSELF A NICE COUNTRY PLACE WITH A POLO FIELD AND REST FOR AT LEAST THREE OR FOUR MONTHS.*) Although there were serious complications to the

---

*Will declined, but Ziegfeld kept trying to get him back. One year, he tried a different tack and sent the Rogers children extravagant Christmas presents—Bill got a car, Jim a fifteen-foot boat, and Mary a gold-inlaid mah-jongg set. That didn't work, either—Will never returned to the *Follies*.

surgery—the poison in his system did not drain properly, and he ran an extremely high fever—Will permitted himself to miss only one daily column. The next day, he dictated this brief piece: " 'Relax—lay perfectly still, just relax.' " Those last two words were the subtitle to *Ether and Me*, the slim volume he wrote about his hospital experience. It was his last book and it was a great success (thanks in no small part to brisk sales in hospital gift shops), his publisher putting out a total of eighteen printings, the last one in 1943.

Five years of pushing himself to his limits had caught up with him. And the stress was not only physical. Three years before, in a letter to Maud Lane, Betty had commented, "It is wonderful to be a big man before the public, but oh, what a price Billy pays for it." Will had hired Jim Hopkins to take care of the horses at the Pacific Palisades property, and, about this time, Hopkins thought that his boss and old friend was going through something like a nervous breakdown. "He talked to himself all the time," Hopkins remembered in 1955. "I was worried." One day, Ray Bell and another cowboy drove up and Will started to speak to them, his foot on the running board. "The first thing I knew," Hopkins said, "his eyes were kind of asleep and he was talking to something way off. When they left, I said, 'Will, if you don't lay off, you'll go to the bughouse.' He said, 'I don't know what I was doing.' He was terribly embarrassed. After that, he was very different."

But still nothing like idle: His schedule for the rest of 1927 and early 1928 was breathtaking. His scars from the gallstones operation had barely healed when he was in Washington, D.C., shooting location scenes for *A Texas Steer*, which would be his last silent film. Producer Sam Rork paid him $100,000 to play the familiar part of Maverick Brander, a Texas rancher who is elected to Congress.* While he was there, the National Press Club, reacting to the fact that the California legislature had recently amended the Municipal Corporations Act so that the trustees were known as councilmen and the president as mayor, thus ending Will's administration, named him congressman-at-large. His mandate—which sounded suspiciously similar to what he was already doing—was to "roam over the country, pry into the state of the Union, check up on Prohibition enforcement, and report at regular intervals."

Back in California to shoot studio scenes for *A Texas Steer*, Will was invited to speak at a San Diego banquet honoring Charles Lindbergh,

---

*The star's salary apparently put a big crimp in Rork's budget. Douglas Fairbanks, Jr., who played the juvenile lead, remembers that no one would give him an advance on his own pay, so he had to spend the night before shooting started on a park bench.

whose New York–Paris solo, nonstop flight had electrified the world four months before. He immediately said yes. "He is the one man in this world that I would stand on a soap box on the corner and try to get a peek at," Will wrote in his daily telegram.

His enthusiasm was a product of his latest—and greatest—passion: aviation. According to Betty, Will first flew in Atlantic City in 1915, in a five-dollars-a-ride "flying boat" that took off from the ocean. But he had given serious thought to it only since 1925, when, at a Gridiron Dinner in Washington, he met Brig. Gen. William "Billy" Mitchell, the army officer who had caused great controversy by scathingly criticizing the preparedness of the aviation divisions of the Departments of War and the Navy. The next day, Mitchell invited him for an aerial tour of the capital. Will was petrified, but he agreed to be Mitchell's passenger. Unfortunately, he told his readers, he didn't get a chance to see any sights: "I have always heard when you are up on anything high, don't look down; look up. So all I saw was the sky. The trip from a sightseeing point of view was a total loss to me, outside of seeing the sky at short range." After they had landed and gotten out of the plane, Mitchell told Will that had been his last flight as a brigadier general; he was about to be demoted to colonel for his outspokenness.

In fact, Mitchell was court-martialed, and in December Will attended the proceedings. He tried to slip undetected into the room, but the presiding officer spotted him, announced his presence, and called a recess so he could be properly greeted. After a ringing speech against Mitchell by the army attorney, Will came up to him and offered some words of encouragement; Mitchell later said it was the one moment of the entire "nightmare" he would remember with pleasure. He was sentenced to a five-year suspension from duty, and he resigned from the army the next year.

Mitchell convinced Will of the importance of a well-armed and technologically up-to-date air force; Will's travels in Europe the next summer rid him of his fear of flying and showed him how remarkably convenient it could be. He was continually impressed by the abundant passenger routes, the ease with which he could hop from city to city. The swift flight from London to Moscow was probably what converted him into (as he was dubbed in a *Scientific American* article three years hence) "the Patron Saint of Aviation." "Here I am," he wrote:

for no apparent reason, able to fly from London, England, to Moscow, Russia, in two days, part of it over a country that we laugh at and look on as backward and primitive; and here we have hundreds of business men in Seattle, San Francisco, Los Angeles, Chicago, New Orleans, Talala [Oklahoma], and hundreds of cities like those that want to gets somewhere, mebbe on account of illness, or thousands of other reasons, and the best they can get there is just like their forefathers got two generations before. We do more talking progress than we do progressing.

Back in the United States that fall, he didn't let the paucity of passenger lines keep him out of the air. Whenever he could, he would just hire a pilot and hop to the next town on his lecture tour. Prone to airsickness at first, he gradually acclimated himself; aviator Nathan Browne said that when he flew a bunch of newsmen to the Republican convention in 1932, the stormy weather got to all of them but Will. And on every possible occasion, he promoted aviation in his lecture and columns. Each time an airplane crash made headlines, Will downplayed the danger of flying, usually pointing out that getting in a car and braving the roads posed a greater risk. He tirelessly reiterated the theme that the air was the way of the future, and, probably more than any other individual besides Lindbergh, he contributed to its acceptance among the American people.*

The efficiency of flying had an obvious appeal to someone as restlessly peripatetic as Will. But the ability to cover more ground in less time wasn't the only reason why he promoted it with more fervor than any other cause, why he flew to Managua and over the Andes and, of course, to Alaska, why he was first on the passenger list for the first transatlantic passenger flight (he didn't live to make it), why by the time of his death he had logged some 300,000 miles—more, it was estimated, than any non-pilot in America. (Will never expressed any interest in learning how to fly himself.) Flying struck a deep chord in Will. Early pilots—gruff, hard-drinking, loyal to the fraternity, courageous—were like no group so much as the cowboys he had grown up with. Both sets of men had to harness an entity far more powerful than themselves; significantly, both traveled mile after mile over unspoiled country. It may have been the sight of the world in miniature that had such a calming effect on Will. Or maybe it was how being in a plane mercifully elim-

---

*Among other aviation-related causes, Will pleaded that towns have their names painted on top of local buildings as an aid to help pilots and navigators who in the early days of flight often found themselves lost. At first, he said he would supply the paint himself, then modified the offer: "Paint has been put down to towns of three letters. Ada, Oklahoma, for instance. Mooselokmeguntic, Me., sent me a bill for $79. They had to put a letter on each house and borrowed three houses from Connecticut."

inated all other options for action besides staying in the plane. Whatever
the reason, he found to his delight that he could relax in the sky to a degree that wholly eluded him on the ground. It was no accident that
when he wrote about flying he attempted a lyricism that rarely appears
elsewhere in his work, even venturing into simile. "They had just had
their first snow," he wrote about a flight over northern California, "and
the Mountain tops were covered, and the Railroad and Highway was
winding along down there like a couple of black snakes." People were always comparing Will with Mark Twain, but he really had more in common with Twain's greatest creation. Thus his near-reverence for flight
calls to mind Huck Finn's musings about life on the Mississippi: "Other
places do seem so cramped up and smothery, but a raft don't. You feel
mighty free and easy and comfortable on a raft."

It wasn't surprising, then, that the announcement of Lindbergh's
transatlantic flight early in 1927 had captured Will's imagination. He was
taken as much with the "slim, tall, smiling, bashful American boy" as
the feat, and he continually boosted Lindbergh in his column and lec-
tures. Will Rogers, Jr., says his father "picked him up like a guy that had
bet on a horse." There was no question about accepting the invitation
to a San Diego banquet. The following day brought an even bigger
thrill: The aviator invited Will and Betty to fly with him to Los Angeles.
During the flight, the plane became tail-heavy and he had to make a sta-
bilizer adjustment. The problem persisted, to the point where he could
adjust no more. Lindbergh was probably not capable of panic, but he
had never encountered anything like this before and, he later said, he
"passed some pretty uneasy moments." At that point, he looked into
the cabin and found the source of the trouble: Ten of the eleven passengers were jammed into the back of the cabin with Will and Betty, while
the eleventh was focusing a camera at them.

Later in the flight, Will rode in the cockpit with Lindbergh. To escape the crowds waiting for him at Los Angeles Airport, he planned to
land at small Mines Field, which lacked equipment that could show him
the force and direction of the wind. Lindbergh had already remarked on
the importance of this information, and Will asked how he would be
able to discern it. The answer: "Didn't you see the way those clothes
were blowing on that line back there a while ago?" Thus establishing the
aviator's powers of observation, Will decided to see whether he had a
sense of humor. "What would you do," he asked, "if it wasn't Monday?"
"I wouldn't fly over such a dirty place," was the aviator's response,
which, while not sidesplitting, at least proved he was willing to attempt
levity.

Even so, Will realized that the twenty-five-year-old Lindbergh had directed his energies and intellect so forcefully into one area that he remained somewhat unformed as a person. "He eats, sleeps and drinks aviation," he wrote after their flight together. "He is not particularly interested in anything else. This is an era of specialization. He picked out aviation, and he certainly has majored in it. His whole expression and attitude changes when he is in the air with no banquet table in front of him, and nothing under him but the clouds."

It may have been the excitement of riding with Lindbergh that inspired Will to set up a cross-country, round-trip flight for himself less than a month later. There was no transcontinental passenger service as yet, but, for the intrepid, the government permitted passengers to ride in regularly scheduled mail routes, for a fare that roughly translated to first-class postage for the weight of a human being. Will paid $814 and completed the trip—including a morning in New York taking care of business matters—in three and a half days. It was hardly luxurious transportation. He wore goggles and a leather flight suit and had to share his seat with packs of mail; several legs of the trip were made in open planes. And on the way from Cleveland to New York, his pilot got off course and made a forced landing on a muddy farm near Beaver Falls, Pennsylvania. The mishap did nothing to temper Will's aviation enthusiasm. "I was kinder disappointed it came down so nice," he wrote in his account of the trip in *The Saturday Evening Post*. "I was just sitting there looking at all that mail around me. If it had tipped over on its nose, I was just thinking what a lot of fun they would have picking air-mail stamps out of me."

Indeed, after he had conquered his initial fear, Will appeared blithely unconcerned about any danger posed by his frequent flying. This sometimes resulted in recklessness, as when he insisted that the aviatrix Blanche Noyes fly him to Cleveland through an ice storm because his column had already been filed with a Cleveland dateline. He got through all right, but he had several minor accidents over the years, the worst coming in 1929 when his pilot ran out of gas and had to come down in a vacant lot near Chicago. Miraculously, he was able to land without hitting anything. But the plane did turn over, and Will was thrown against the cabin, in the process fracturing all of his ribs. Fearing that news of the incident would damage the cause of aviation, he was able to keep it out of the newspapers.

Two weeks after the cross-country flight, Will and Betty were off on a whirlwind cross-country train tour. The reason? "For the first time in my life had nothing to do and nowhere to go." Over the next ten days, his datelines read Adamana, Arizona; Laguna and Santa Fe, New Mexico; Topeka, Kansas; Culver, Indiana (they visited Bill, a student that year at the Culver Military Academy); Detroit (Will spent the day with Henry Ford and got an advance look at the much-anticipated Model A); Chicago; Dodge City, Kansas; and Winslow, Arizona.

After a week at home, Will set out for Mexico. In October, just two months before, Coolidge had named as ambassador to the country the Wall Street banker Dwight Morrow, an old friend and Amherst classmate. The president had turned to the universally respected Morrow because relations with Mexico—whose revolutionary government was a decade old—were at an extremely low ebb. U.S. Secretary of State Frank Kellogg had recently discerned a "Bolshevist threat" in the country and warned that "the government of Mexico is now on trial before the world." Mexicans were naturally displeased with such posturing, and easing tensions was Morrow's main mission. That one of his first acts was to invite Will to visit the country shows how shrewd Coolidge was to appoint him. Directly on his arrival, Will joined Morrow and Mexico's President, Plutarco Elías Calles, on a six-day railroad tour of dam sites and points of interest in northern Mexico. Thanks to the presence of a gifted interpreter named James Smithers, Will's humor was a hit with Calles and the Mexican party. "He was all over the place making jokes, very impertinent, making fun of everybody and getting away with it," said George Rublee, the legal adviser to the American embassy. "The Mexicans roared with laughter and there was much good feeling and excitement." On their return, Morrow gave a dinner for Will, who was his guest at the embassy, and invited Calles; it was the first time the president of Mexico had ever set foot in the U.S. embassy.

Morrow's other brainstorm was to invite Lindbergh to fly to Mexico. (Meeting with Morrow in his New York apartment to discuss the idea, Lindbergh met the ambassador's daughter Anne, whom he would later marry.) The notion appealed to the aviator: He wanted to make one more long flight with *The Spirit of St. Louis* before it was retired to the Smithsonian, and the Washington–Mexico City route presented intriguingly different conditions from the New York–Paris one. He left shortly past noon on December 13, 1927, flew over Tampico, on the east coast of Mexico, at 8:50 a.m., Mexican standard time, and proceeded to get extravagantly lost. He climbed more than twelve thousand feet in an attempt to get his bearings and searched for a landmark for three hours. "Any other aviator in the world would have come down to see where he was," Will wrote, "but that determination made him stay up there till he found the name of a hotel [written on its roof] . . . and found it on the map, and laid a compass route from there." Meanwhile, at the airfield in Mexico City, some 150,000 people, including the president, waited for him, Morrow and Will having gotten there at 7:15 a.m. The scheduled arrival time of noon came and went, and nobody budged. "There wasn't even as much as a sandwich served on this stand even to the President or any of the folks up there," Will told a lecture audience a few months later. "There wasn't even a pitcher of water, there wasn't a thing in the world. The idea of eating never entered their minds in their anxiety about this boy coming in there."

Lindbergh finally landed at 2:40 p.m., to a tumultuous welcome. He had covered 2,100 miles, had been in the air twenty-seven hours and fifteen minutes. "The throng on the field shouting and screaming with joy was indescribable," wrote Morrow's wife, Elizabeth, in her diary. Will, too, was struck with the Mexicans' spontaneous demonstration of love for the aviator: "In France and America they like to tore up the plane to tear off souvenirs. Here hundreds took it up on their own shoulders and carried it to the hangar." Later, Will, Lindbergh, and the Morrows stood on a balcony at the embassy and received the cheering throngs. At one point, Will nudged the flier in the side and said, "Smile, Lindy, smile."

The next day, over breakfast at the embassy, somebody told Lindbergh he should see some of Mexico. His response showed that his sense of humor had made some strides: "I saw all Mexico yesterday but the Gulf of Lower California."

In January, Will was in Washington, where he spoke at the annual Jackson Day dinner, and went on to Havana, for the Conference of American States.* A month later, he started a new lecture tour; he continued it through late July (with time off to cover the Republican convention in Kansas City that nominated Herbert Hoover and the Democratic convention in Houston that nominated Al Smith).

All the while, he was writing his daily telegram. At the beginning, in the fall of 1926, McNaught sold the column to the *Times* and ninety-one other newspapers, a response sufficiently positive for the syndicate to allow the "Worst Story" feature to die a merciful death. (For a while, it was written by a McNaught editor under Will's name, with the humorist and the syndicate splitting the proceeds.) Within three and a half years, the number had increased to about four hundred papers, making Will—who by then was receiving a guarantee of $2,500 a week, against 70 per-

---

*H. L. Mencken, covering the meeting for the Baltimore *Evening Sun*, wrote to his future wife that he "got an overdose of stimulants last night with Will Rogers."

cent of the gross proceeds—the best-paid columnist in the country, according to McNitt, and probably the most widely read. (His rivals were O. O. McIntyre, also syndicated by McNaught, and Arthur Brisbane, whose "Today" column ran in the Hearst papers.)

The column, headlined WILL ROGERS SAYS in most papers, was strikingly different from his meandering weekly piece. Ranging from fifty to two hundred words in length, it was pithy and almost terse, with a no-nonsense lead, insistent internal rhythm, and, invariably, a chuckle-inducing kicker at the end—a prairie haiku. Rampant *ain't*'s aside, there were few mistakes of grammar, punctuation, or spelling. This was not because of editing by the *Times*, to which Will sent his copy before distribution by the other subscribing newspapers. The copyeditors there made only minimal changes (although they occasionally succumbed to the temptation to standardize Will's prose, once prompting a memo to the proofroom from managing editor F. T. Birchall: "Please do not correct Will Rogers's English or spelling. His little pieces are unique because he makes his own English. When you 'improve' it you are taking away part of the personality he is selling to readers.") Rather, Will labored on the daily pieces as he did not on the weekly ones; friends reported seeing him fiddle with a line over and over again, sometimes reading it out loud, until he was satisfied that it was exactly right. Which is not to say that he wasn't capable of turning out a piece quickly. A visitor to Will's house once noted the time when he excused himself to write his column. He emerged with the finished product precisely twelve minutes later.

Most of the time, the column was a comment on the previous day's events. (Will had until 3:00 p.m., Pacific time, to deliver it to the telegraph office, so he was able to be fairly current.) It was generally comically framed, but rarely without a pointed message. Here, for example, is what he had to say on August 3, 1927, the day after Calvin Coolidge announced that he did not "choose to run" for the presidency.

> I think Mr. Coolidge's statement is the best-worded acceptance of a nomination ever uttered by a candidate. He spent a long time in the dictionary looking for that word "choose," instead of "I will not."
>
> It don't take much political knowledge to know that a man can get more votes running on the people's request than he can running on his own request.
>
> Mr. Coolidge is the shrewdest politician that ever drew government salary.

More than anything else that he did, the daily telegrams forged an intimacy between Will and a national audience. In a way, they were a diary of his life. Readers could track his frequent travels by the datelines, participate in his bull sessions with Henry Ford and John D. Rockefeller, Speaker of the House John Nance Garner and Al Capone, Thomas Edison and Huey Long. Inclusive as ever, Will wrote in a breezy shorthand that assumed the reader shared his own political sophistication, his own large-mindedness, his own easy familiarity with the famous and great, whom he usually referred to by their first names. (Indeed, he assumed so much knowledge that many of the pieces are unintelligible today to a reader without an annotated edition.) It was the daily column that allowed him to become a kind of national oracle. His readers found his sensibility an irresistible way of filtering the news; many of them literally did not know what they thought about an issue or an event until they found out what Will Rogers had to say. This was especially the case with the most momentous stories, when he tended not to be humorous at all. While Lindbergh was still somewhere over the Atlantic Ocean, Will wrote this:

> No attempt at jokes today. A slim, tall, bashful, smiling American boy is somewhere out over the middle of the Atlantic Ocean, where no lone human being has ever ventured before. He is being prayed for to every kind of Supreme Being that has a following. If he is lost it will be the most universally regretted single loss we ever had. But that kid ain't going to fail. . . .

Five years later, Charles and Anne Morrow Lindbergh's infant son was kidnapped in a crime that shocked the nation. It was a wrenching piece of news that, somehow, was a little more bearable when it was presented by Will. The day the news was announced, he wrote about his visit to the Lindberghs' house in New Jersey two weeks before. The baby, he told his readers, "had his father's blonde curly hair, even more so than his dad's. It's almost golden and all in little curls. His face is more of his mother's. He has her eyes exactly.

"His mother sat on the floor in the sun parlor among all of us and played blocks with him for an hour. His dad was pitching a soft sofa pillow at him as he was toddling around. The weight of it would knock him over. I asked Lindy if he was rehearsing him for forced landings."

The next day, when the news had sunk in, Will wrote:

> Did you ever see such a day. Nobody don't feel like doing anything, taking any interest in anything.

The attention of the world is on a little curly haired baby. Till he is found we can't get back to normal.

Never since the two days and a night that this same kid's father was out over the Atlantic has the attention of everybody been centered so completely on one thing.

The greatest single "kick" that a whole nation got, outside of the signing of the armistice, was when the news had flashed that Lindbergh had landed in Paris.

The next one we hope and pray will be when this baby is delivered home.

By this time, the column was such a fixture in the nation's newspapers and on its breakfast tables that its tag line—probably originally devised by an anonymous *Times* copyeditor—took on a literal truth. Every day, the last three words were "Yours, Will Rogers."

IT WAS the daily column, without question, that made it possible, on January 9, 1928, for a Congressman from Oklahoma to stand up in the House of Representatives and say, "Col. [*sic*] Will Rogers, the humorist, the philosopher, and statesman, is a man able, capable, and filled to administer the great office of President of the United States." This was not the first time the idea had been mentioned; at the 1924 Democratic convention Will had received a vote for the presidential nomination. But his stature had grown since then. Early in the year, a Rogers for President movement sprang up in Oklahoma, numbering among its supporters former governor Charles Haskell. (The interest it attracted doubtless had something to do with the fact that the likely Democratic nominee was the wet, Catholic New Yorker Al Smith, who had never been popular in rural areas.) The idea of people taking him seriously as a candidate shocked Will, and he knocked it down in his daily telegram with an uncustomary lack of humor. "When that was done as a joke it was all right," he wrote, "but when it's done seriously it's just pathetic. . . . There is no inducement that would make me foolish enough to ever run for political office. I want to be on the outside where I can be friends and joke about all of them, even the president."

Yet the idea had an appeal that would not permit it to die. In April, Robert Sherwood, the future playwright who was then editing *Life* magazine, had the idea of promoting a mock candidacy for Will in the magazine's pages, in the interests of humor, publicity, and a recognition that, as an editorial put it, "the Republican elephant and the Democratic donkey have come to resemble each other so closely that it is practically impossible to tell them apart; both of them make the same braying noise, and neither of them ever says anything." In a meeting at the Hotel Astor in New York, Will agreed to let his name be used and, for a weekly fee of five hundred dollars, to provide a few hundred words of copy for every issue until Election Day.* He also came up with a name for his political party: Anti-Bunk.

Life was a humor magazine, and the Will Rogers candidacy was presented purely facetiously, along the lines of comedian Pat Paulsen's runs in the 1960s, 1970s, and 1980s. Campaign buttons were printed up proclaiming, HE CHEWS TO RUN; in the magazine, *Life's* drama critic, Robert Benchley, sometimes followed Will's contributions (themselves less engaged with real issues than his daily or weekly columns) with accounts of his own goofy straw poll. (Explaining his methodology, Benchley wrote, "The author of this article . . . goes up to the voters on the street or in bed or wherever they happen to be and asks them certain questions, all beginning with 'W.' Most of this was explained in last week's issue and if you didn't read it you missed a very funny piece and it serves you right.") But where some people saw comedy in his candidacy, others discerned good sense. Still others saw both, their statements slipping back and forth between facetiousness and sobriety. The famous Colorado judge Ben Lindsey contributed an endorsement for the magazine, and none other than Henry Ford (who had mounted a maverick campaign for the senate himself in 1918) wrote in to say, "The joke of Will Rogers' candidacy for President is that it is no joke. It is a serious attempt to restore American common sense to American politics." *The Saturday Evening Post* said, "We're not sure the idea is only a joke," *The Nation* that Will's campaign was "as invigorating as a bright fall day."

In the election, Hoover, riding a wave of prosperity, trounced Smith. Robert Sherwood had the impression that the write-in vote for the bunkless candidate was sizable, but, he wrote to Homer Croy, "It was impossible to check the figures, or at least it was too difficult for us to go into it after the election story was cold, and so was I."

---

*According to Sherwood, "We had one hell of a time getting copy out of him. When he did get it in it was very sketchy and never nearly enough of it to fill the necessary space. So I filled it out, imitating Will's style as best I could. This had the unfortunate effect of convincing Bill that he need write practically nothing and I think there were one or two weeks when he did supply nothing and I had to write the whole piece. He never complained about my work. The only allusion he ever made to it was that now and then he would say to me, with a slight grin, 'That was a pretty good piece I wrote for you folks last week. If this quality keeps up I'll have to be asking you for a raise.' "

• • •

FRED STONE had caught the aviation bug from Will, but typically he wasn't content to ride in planes; he had to pilot them. In the summer of 1928, he flew from the east to California for a visit to the Rogerses. A few months later, he was to open in a new musical comedy called *Three Cheers,* costarring his daughter Dorothy, and he decided that with so many people's livelihoods depending on the show he would give up flying during its run. For his last flight, near Groton, Connecticut, he decided to try something new—a forced landing. Just as he was ready to land, a gust of wind hit the wing and flew him into a flat spin. He was unable to fly out of it, and he crash-landed in a farmer's beet patch. Stone had broken his ankle, shin, thigh, and five ribs, dislocated his shoulder and bitten his tongue almost in two. He was put in a full-body cast and told he was lucky to be alive, that he might possibly walk again but would never dance.* In order to save Dorothy's opportunity to star—and Stone's longtime producer Charles Dillingham's investment—Will impulsively decided to "pinch-hit" for his friend. He was in New York on September 11, ready to start rehearsals and able to see Babe Ruth help the Yankees beat the Philadelphia Athletics.

Will's generosity in taking his stricken friend's place won him exorbitant praise in the press. Charles Wagner didn't see it that way. Although *The New York Times* reported that Will told Wagner he would pay him $250,000 to cover the lost business, the manager wrote in his autobiography that "If he ever made that offer it was in a whisper too faint for my ears to catch. Rogers did send a check for $3,000 to pay actual booking expenses, but nothing at all for my work and possible profits that season." Two years later, when Will again canceled an already-booked tour (to go on a relief tour of the drought-stricken Midwest), Wagner considered taking legal action but was dissuaded by his lawyer,

---

*Stone's recuperative powers were remarkable. "When they brought him in to the hospital," Dorothy Stone Collins told interviewer Bryan Sterling in the 1970s, "the doctor said that had this been anyone but Fred Stone, that he would have amputated both legs immediately. . . . But the doctor said that he had seen those legs in action, that he could not bring himself to take them off. As time went by the doctor refused to make any predictions. 'I don't know what this man can do,' he said. 'Everything that I predict, he upsets.' First the doctor had said that Daddy would have to be in a wheelchair for the rest of his life. Then he said that Daddy would never walk again; then that he would walk, but never dance again." That was wrong, too. Stone's acrobatic days were over, but, a year and a half later, having convalesced at the Rogers ranch in California, he was on Broadway in another show. At that point, he was nearly 60 years old, however, and he wisely made a transition to dramatic roles.

who sensibly pointed out, "If you sue and Rogers testifies, what chance would anyone else have with a jury?"

The plot of *Three Cheers* was typical nonsense about the royal family of a mythical European kingdom who go to Hollywood; musical-comedy books had not appreciably progressed since the days of *The Wall Street Girl*. All through rehearsals, Will read the part of King Pampanola from an opened script. He still hadn't memorized it the day before the out-of-town opening, in Springfield, Massachusetts, and Dorothy Stone told Charles Dillingham she thought the New York opening, set for October 15, should be postponed; the star clearly wasn't ready. Dillingham told her, she remembered, "Dorothy, I have news for you. Will is never going to know that part." In an interview with Bryan Sterling, she described what Will did the next night:

> He walked down to the audience, took the script out of his pocket, and said, "Now here it says that Fred is to do a flip-flop, a back somersault, a stiff all, and an eccentric dance to open the show. Now I'm not going to do that! I'm going to talk about Hoover!" And he threw the script into the orchestra pit. . . . Well, Will proceeded to do a marvelous monologue about Hoover. . . . Just as I was wondering whether I should change clothes, or go on, or stay there, or what, Will turned and saw me in the wings. He said, "Dorothy, honey, come here! Come on stage and meet your Daddy's friends." I came on, and he put his arm around me, and he talked to me for a while; I know we didn't do our scene at all. . . . He finally said, "Now you run and change your clothes for that number you're going to do with your leading man." The audience didn't even know there was a leading man, because I hadn't met him yet on stage. "You know," Will went on, "that nice young man back there that I seen; he's all dressed up; he's very handsome. Now you just go and do that song with the leading man, because after that, I want to talk about Congress."

The next day, the director called a cast meeting and announced that, except for musical numbers and Will Rogers's pieces of business, the entire show was cut.

Opening night in New York was so emotional for Dorothy Stone, who had never before appeared without her father, that she feared she wouldn't be able to perform. What saved her was Will. As the orchestra struck up the overture, he burst into her dressing room in tears. "Nobody can take your father's part, nobody can do it," he said, sobbing. "That's his music, his audience. What am I doing here?" Being the comforter rather than the comfortee allowed Dorothy Stone to function, and Will got hold of himself too. The highlight of his monologue was a straw poll on the presidential election then in full swing. "We won't pay for your votes," he announced, "which puts you on a level with the Democrats, who have been voting for nothing for years." (Al Smith won by a hair, proving either the invalidity of straw polls or the unrepresentativeness of first-night audiences.)

The critics were charmed by Will's blatant disrespect for the script, most concurring with Percy Hammond of the *Tribune* that "Mr. Rogers made havoc of 'Three Cheers' as a drama last night, while adding considerably to its assets as an entertainment." And the consensus was that while he was no Fred Stone, he acquitted himself honorably in his two song-and-dance numbers. New York audiences, perhaps sensing in some way that this would be their last chance to see Will Rogers on Broadway, made *Three Cheers* the hottest ticket in town. The playwright Noel Coward saw an early performance and sent Will a telegram: YOU GAVE ME SUCH A GRAND EVENING IN THE TEATRE [*SIC*] LAST WEEK I FEEL I MUST WIRE AND TELL YOU. Even the publicity-shy Lindbergh made a rare public appearance to see Will (who thoughtfully didn't introduce him to the audience).

Three Cheers closed in New York in April 1929, then went on the road until June 1. It could have played indefinitely, but Will had another commitment, something that would prove to be the most significant professional move of the rest of his life. Attempts had long been made to link sound to film, but since 1925, when some engineers at Bell Labs made a technical breakthrough and sold the patent rights to Warner Brothers, it was clear that one day pictures would talk. In 1926, Warners produced *Don Juan*, with John Barrymore and a musical sound track in their so-called Vitaphone process. The next year saw the release of *The Jazz Singer*, the first film to have portions of synchronized dialogue, and in 1928 came *Lights of New York*, the first all-talking picture.

Along with the excitement over the new possibilities came anxiety, especially among actors, over surviving the transition to what really amounted to a new medium. "The whole business out here is just scared cuckoo," Will had remarked in his column. "The girl that left a ribbon counter and won a beauty contest and then was made a 'star' overnight just because somebody told her every move to make and when to smile, she can just see her finish." And so the stars desperately tried to learn how to speak. "You meet an actor or girl and in the old days where they would have just nodded and passed by, now they stop and start chattering like a parrot," he wrote in another column. "Weather, politics, Babe Ruth, anything just to practice talking, and they are so busy ennunciating [sic] that they pay no attention to what they are saying. Everything is 'Annunciation' [sic]. I was on the stage 23 years and never heard the word or knew what it was."

Will could afford to make sport of the turmoil over sound because he had nothing at stake. As the poor performance of *A Texas Steer* had made clear once again, he wasn't much as a silent-film star. But to be able to talk in a motion picture—that was something else again.

The man who gave him a celluloid voice was William Fox. Like Samuel Goldwyn and so many of the other early movie moguls, Fox was an Eastern European immigrant who had started out in the garment trade. In 1904, he sold a business called the Knickerbocker Cloth Examining and Shrinking Company and with the profits proceeded to buy a string of nickelodeons. Not long afterward, he went into production, and an antitrust lawsuit he filed in 1912 effectively ended the monopoly Thomas Edison's Motion Picture Patents Company had on the field. The Fox Film Corporation grew through the teens and twenties, both in theater acquisition (by 1927, it owned one thousand of them) and film production. But although he had developed stars such as Theda Bara, Tom Mix, and Janet Gaynor, and such directors as John Ford, Frank Borzage, and Howard Hawks, William Fox felt in the mid–1920s that the company was stagnating, stuck in the second tier of the industry. Seizing on sound as the way to advance, he was second only to Warner Brothers in exploiting the new technology. In 1925, he began to develop a synchronizing process called Movietone, which, in fact, was more sophisticated than the Warners' Vitaphone, being able to record sound directly on film. Fox's Movietone News pioneered the sound newsreel, its most dramatic instance coming on May 20, 1927. At 7:52 a.m., Charles Lindbergh took off for Paris; that evening, at the Roxy Theater in New York, audiences watched—and listened to—Fox Movietone News' report on the event.

Fox used Movietone in portions of the 1927 film *What Price Glory?* and a number of 1928 features. On March 24, 1929, William Fox announced that henceforth the company would produce all-talking pictures exclusively. Production chief Winfield Sheehan told *The New York Times* that the company had spent $15 million on new studios and machinery, and that he had placed some two hundred "show folk" under contract—directors, singers, songwriters, and playwrights. At the head of the list was Will Rogers. Ten days earlier, Will had signed a contract with the company, agreeing to make four "talking motion pictures" over a period of sixteen months, for which he would be paid $600,000. Next to his signature, Will wrote these words in ink: "If Winnie Sheehan and William Fox say this is O.K. it goes for me."

JIM, BILL, MARY, WILL, AND BETTY ROGERS,
ON THE PORCH IN PACIFIC PALISADES

CHAPTER 11

HOLLYWOOD, II

Up betimes and at my stint. My first stint is a lot of sliced fresh peaches, then some ham and then some eggs washed down with about a dozen saucers of coffee. I lay late, almost till 6:30. The papers came, but having nothing but politics, I cared not one whit for 'em. It does seem that our country could be run much better by someone if we could only think who. Mrs. Rogers came down and we had the usual argument as to how late the boys stayed out. They have to drive over a cattle guard coming in and it's as good as an alarm clock as it rattles under car wheels.

— WILL ROGERS, 1932

Will Rogers is the man talkies were invented for.

— NEWSPAPER REVIEW OF
"THEY HAD TO SEE PARIS" (1929)

ON A FEBRUARY DAY in 1933, Will Rogers had three guests for dinner at his ranch—Charlie Chaplin; Chaplin's paramour, Paulette Goddard; and Will Durant, a philosophy professor at UCLA whose book of a few years earlier, *The Story of Philosophy,* had been a great popular success. (He and his wife, Ariel, had not yet begun to record the story of civilization.) "Will Rogers sent a nifty Cadillac Roadster for me," Durant wrote in a letter to Ariel, who was at their home in New York, "and after a 50-minute ride I found myself in his immense ranch—an expanse of farmland, grazing pasture, polo field, golf links, bridle paths, barns, garages and a rustic home. He was in his stables when I arrived, and greeted me, out of overalls, boots, leather jacket, bronze wrinkled face, and tousled gray hair, with the broadest, wholesomest grin in the world."

"He looks like a cowboy," Durant added, "but has the nerves and mental activity of an artist."

It would be just four for dinner. Bill was away at Stanford, Mary at Sarah Lawrence, and Jim at boarding school, and Betty was upstairs recuperating from an appendectomy. As Lilly, the cook, served the meal on the patio overlooking the polo field, Will described the story of *Down to Earth,* his next picture for the Fox studio. Chaplin immediately jumped up, full of suggestions for the film; as he demonstrated bits of business and acted out possible scenes, the awestruck Durant could see the movie take on a "subtler and ampler" form before his eyes.

After the meal, the four drove to an auditorium in Santa Monica where Durant was to lecture. Asked to introduce him, Will delivered a speech that Durant thought was one of the most amazing pieces of extemporization he had ever heard—"every line a witticism, until the house was convulsed." Afterward, everybody went back to the ranch and talked about economics, politics, and philosophy until 1:30 a.m. At that point, Chaplin and Goddard went home and, as Durant wrote in his letter to Ariel, "I fell asleep in Will Rogers' gigantic pajamas."

The only unusual thing about Will Durant's impression of Will Rogers is that he formed it in person. By the time of the magical dinner Durant described with such star-struck delight, the majority of Americans thought of Will in just these terms—as the effortless host to philosophers and kings, the brilliant but down-to-earth lord of a graceful manor.

What gave him, in the last phase of his life, a new level of fame and financial security was his second career in the movies. He made a total of twenty feature films for Fox. The neglect into which they fell (and remained) soon after his death should not obscure their prominence at the time. He quickly supplanted Janet Gaynor as the studio's biggest star and, in fact, was its only dependable moneymaker until a pint-sized trouper named Shirley Temple came along. The company signed him to a new contract, paying $187,500 a picture, as soon as his first one expired, and although subsequent deals were more modest (a result of the depression and Fox's internal problems) they still permitted him to earn a minimum of $300,000 a year from film work. (He also made more than $125,000 from his column.) Within two years of his debut, he had cracked the motion-picture exhibitors' ranking of the top-ten box-office attractions; in 1932–1933, he was number two; and the next year, he headed the list, beating out Joan Crawford, Mae West, and Clark Gable.

Fox had made a substantial investment in Will (his first contract was three times higher than Gaynor's) and for his debut talking feature it made sure that all the elements for success were in place. To direct, Winfield Sheehan selected Frank Borzage, a silent-film veteran who, surely not coincidentally, was a Westerner and a polo devotee. Will's co-star would be Irene Rich, an old friend who had played his wife in several Goldwyn features. And the story, based on the novel *They Had to See Paris* by his old Forest Hills neighbor Homer Croy, fitted Will like a pair of twenty-five-year-old overalls. He was to play Pike Peeters, an Oklahoma garage owner (the film gave him Claremore as a hometown) whose oil well suddenly gushes, making him hugely wealthy. His social-climbing wife (Rich) insists that the family relocate to Paris; Pike grumblingly goes along. In France, the pretensions get out of control, and through some canny maneuvers Pike brings the clan back to reality.

The sound technology was new for everybody, but Will's special style made the filming particularly challenging. The sound man complained to Borzage that he would set up his microphones based on where Will had placed himself in rehearsal, only to find that, when the cameras rolled, the star was on the other side of the room. "I'm not going to change Will Rogers' naturalness," Borzage replied. "Wherever he is, that's where the scene's going to be played. . . . You put microphones in his beard if he has one. . . . Put 'em behind pictures. Put 'em under the sofa. Put 'em any place you want. And just watch him and then you play like you're playing an organ. You just tune him in." It wasn't only where Will talked that was unpredictable; it was what he said. A *New York Times* reporter visited the set and commented, "Mr. Rogers has an original way of speaking lines. He varies them according to the inspiration, keeping, of course, to the sense of the idea." In 1929, *improvisation* was not yet a part of the actor's lexicon.

The film had its world premiere on September 18 at the Fox Cathay Circle Theatre in Los Angeles; Jack Benny was the master of ceremonies. Will wasn't there. "I figured I better kinder take to the woods till the effects kinder blew over," he later wrote in his column. "I wanted 'em to kinder fumigate around before I appeared in person." And so he had embarked on a ten-day jaunt to visit relatives in Oklahoma and his old friend Jim Minnick's horse ranch in Texas. When he returned, he wrote, "My picture had opened amid no casualties and I had been practically forgiven for it: wasent bad enough to shoot or good enough to cheer."

He was being modest. The picture was a great success. The *Times* said it gave Will his "best screen role" and included it as one of the top ten films of the year; another reviewer declared, "Will Rogers is the fellow talkies were invented for." "I don't remember the time when I enjoyed an evening so much," Will's old boss Sam Goldwyn wrote him. "I have never seen an audience enjoy a performance so much as it did yours." Best of all, *They Had to See Paris* made a profit of $700,000. Will Rogers was back in the movies to stay.

It's not too surprising that his films have aged poorly. They constitute, for one thing, the only portion of the Will Rogers oeuvre that was not written by Will Rogers. Moreover, comedy generally doesn't travel well over the years; the Marx Brothers and W. C. Fields, also vaudeville alumni who made movies in the same era, may have been able to retain some freshness because they had a certain demotic edge, an edge sharp enough to cut through history. (Interestingly, they were much less popular than Will at the time.) Most of Will's first films, by contrast, played out a theme that had immediate resonance for contemporary audiences, very little for later ones. As in *They Had to See Paris*, he played a country fellow, unsophisticated but blessed with common sense, whose family lose their heads and forget their station, until he brings them down to earth. An emblematic image: in *They Had to See Paris*, Idy Peeters forces Pike to taste caviar, and he makes a face of profound disgust. A substantial part of Will's whole persona, of course, and a large reason why he struck such a comforting chord in the 1920s, was the spectacle of a plain man keeping his feet on the ground in the midst of rampant pretension—a man who didn't like caviar and wouldn't pretend that he did. These films gave the metaphor sight and sound, and perhaps that is why they are often obvious, scolding and tiresome in a way that his writing never was.

The rest of Will's early films had him as the same unpretentious fellow placed in unfamiliar surroundings, but they lacked the disapproving subtext; the incongruity was played strictly for laughs. One such was *A Connecticut Yankee*, an extremely loose adaptation of Twain that was Will's only costume picture. (Myrna Loy played the seductive Morgan le Fay.) In *Ambassador Bill*, he plays an Oklahoma businessman appointed ambassador to a mythical Eastern European country; in *Business and Pleasure*—probably his funniest film because of a few broad-comedy bits—he's a razor-blade mogul from Oklahoma (again) who goes to Syria to obtain the secret of Damascus steel and gets involved with a fortune-teller and various sheiks.

None of these roles, obviously, was a major stretch for Will. An advantage of playing different versions of himself was that it mitigated any tension he may have felt over starting what was really a new career. In fact (possibly because he already earned a comfortable income from his writing and had lecturing to fall back on), he was completely relaxed about his new venture in movies. This attitude manifested itself in a number of ways, one being his near-total disregard for scripts. John Ford, who directed three of Will's later films, told Bryan Sterling, "I don't think he ever read a script at home." On the set, he would take a look at the speech to be shot and ask Ford, "What does that mean?" "And I'd say, 'Well, that's rather a tough question,' " Ford recalled. " 'I don't know what it means exactly.' Then we would finally figure out what it meant, and I'd say to him, 'Say it in your own words!' And he'd go away, muttering to himself, getting his lines read, and when he came back, he'd make the speech in typical Rogers fashion, which was better than any writer could write for him."

His lines may have been better, but the other actors were still working from the ones that had been written. This clearly presented difficulties. One of his costars commented that "listening for cues that never came had me ad libbing to myself in my sleep long before my first picture with Bill was finished." Another solved the problem by not looking at the script herself until an hour before the cameras rolled: "I just wait and hear what Will says and then try to fit the script's dialogue to it." Will made things easy for Joel McCrea, an improbably handsome young man who had grown up in Hollywood, of all places, and who starred with him in *Lightnin'* and *Business and Pleasure,* becoming a protégé of sorts. He told McCrea that he would surreptitiously poke him in the stomach whenever he, Will, was finished with a speech. Helping ease any resentment other supporting players might have felt was Will's great generosity as an actor. As spooked by close-ups as ever, he always pushed others into the middle of the frame and edged away himself.

They had to admit, as well, that Will's off-the-cuff approach really did work. Sometimes he would come up with a genuinely funny impromptu quip. In *They Had to See Paris,* he forgot his line and said, "I'll answer that just as soon as I think of something to say." The ad-lib stayed in the picture. More often, he would improve on the script in subtler ways. Screenplays in the early sound era, still under the influence of silent-movie titles, tended to stilted, melodramatic language with little relation to actual speech; Will's changes almost always made his lines fresher, funnier, better.

The point is clear if you compare final-draft scripts with what Will actually said on the screen. The script for *In Old Kentucky,* has his character, a horse trainer named Steve Tapley, put forth this bit of circumlocution: "If Emperor wins, I'll see to it that you get that strip of land without any further trouble—in any event, we'll call off the feud. What do you say?" In the actual film, Will says: "Well then if Emperor wins you get the land and the old man drops the feud." In Tapley's response to the cue, "Grandpa's harmless. He really hasn't shot anybody," the screenwriter clearly tried to inject a Will Rogers flavor: "I know—but there's always a first time—and when Grandpa's chasing you you're bound to wonder a little if you ain't going to be on the receiving end of the first time." Will's changes made the line sound more like himself, improved the joke and even included a current-events reference (John Dillinger had recently been shot):

> No, he ain't shot nobody but—but he's aimed at enough people and at his age, you know, them fingers—is—they're kind of nervous, you know—say, he's jagged that gun in my face so much that even I wouldn't call him public benefit number one.

Will may have been playing himself, but this was a more difficult proposition than it sounds, involving a deliberate resistance to effects and affectation. Indeed, in his use of improvisation, his preference for natural behavior instead of unnatural declamation, he was at least twenty years ahead of his time. When they worked together in *State Fair*, Lew Ayres regarded him as a kind of amiable amateur; when Ayres talked to Bryan Sterling in 1970, he was amazed by Will's anticipation of future trends: "His relaxed attitude when you watch him in those old films is like the most modern New York laboratory theater performance. There is nothing stilted, static about Will Rogers. He was alive and real." Will knew what he was doing, too. Joel McCrea—whom Will for some reason always called "Joe"—described to Sterling the time when David Butler, the director of *Business and Pleasure*, rather histrionically demonstrated the way a scene should be played. "Will nudged me and said, 'Joe, watch Dave. He's *acting*.' And I'd ask him, 'Are you going to do it that way?' And Will said, 'I can't. I can't remember what he done.' "

Like his acting style, his view of the entire moviemaking enterprise was casual. Thus even though his contracts gave him script approval, he dutifully accepted whatever Fox chose for him. Only once did he resolve to get more involved, demanding that Sheehan allow him to select his own stories. The executive couldn't refuse outright this request from his main meal ticket, but he wasn't happy about it. McCrea described his solution: "He got a five-ton truck with every script, every property, every synopsis that Fox ever had, and he sent it to Will's ranch, with an inter-office communication, saying, 'Dear Mr. Rogers, these are a few of Fox's properties. Will you read these and tell us which ones you want to do?' Will turned the memo over, and wrote on the back, 'You win, Winnie!' and sent the whole truck back."

Casual also described Will's working demeanor. Often the entire production would have to wait while he finished pounding out his daily telegram, seated either on the front seat of his car or in the adobe bungalow, complete with front-yard sand and cactus, that Fox had constructed for him on the lot. (In the days before the Depression hit Hollywood hard, studios could afford to carry out such fanciful conceits. When John McCormack went to Fox to make a movie, the studio built him a thatched-roof cottage next to Will.) When the piece was finished to his satisfaction, there were always guests to receive; for Will, a movie set was a little like a salon. According to a Fox press release, on just one day he "was visited by a South American Ambassador, a U.S. Senator, Cleveland builder and poloist K. A. Wigmore, [Fort Worth newspaper publisher] Amon G. Carter, Fred Stone and reporters from London and Paris."

Eventually, the cameras did roll, but between takes Will would supply rope tricks and a steady stream of patter. He also made it clear that he wanted to wrap it up every afternoon at 4:30. When that time came, according to one of his costars, he would say, "'O.K. Now comes the window shot.' Which meant that he quit."

HE WAS SO eager to leave the set because of what was waiting for him at the other end of his car ride. Over the years, as he had gotten used to the idea of the Pacific Palisades land he had bought in 1924, he had come to look on it less as a weekend retreat and more as an eventual full-time residence. (It was never seen as a place where horses or cattle could be raised for profit, but that didn't inhibit Will's nomenclature. The property was "not really a ranch, but we call it that," he admitted. "It sounds big and don't really do any harm.") Following Will's (usually) long-distance instructions, his brother-in-law Lee Adamson supervised the construction of a road that wound two hundred feet up from Beverly Boulevard, with four switchbacks to ease the grade; to prevent flooding, stone culverts were put in. Hundreds of eucalyptus trees would one day provide both stability and shade; Jim Rogers remembers bringing them in in five-gallon cans and planting them by hand. In January 1926, Will bought an adjoining eighty-four acres for $120,000, and later that year he added a U-shaped barn and, remarkably (considering the steepness of the site), a polo field, the laborious grading done by 150 mules dragging fresnos.

The following spring, while he was on his lecture tour, he sent a letter to Adamson that seemed to jump out of the envelope: "Now look out we got a big Idea, We want a house over on the ranch that we can have this summer whether we sell the home place or not."

Will was very specific about what he had in mind:

> Dont get it too high up the hill. We just want it high enough so it gives us a good view of everything Ocean and all, and still low enough that we can do some grading and get a bit of level ground around the edge of the porch. . . . We want a pretty good size house, in fact a big living room, dimensions about 48 by 24. Then a kitchen and a couple of bed rooms. Betty is enclosing an idea of her plans. Just want a plain what we used to call a box house, Not weatherboarded, just 12 inch boards up on edge and the batting nailed across the cracks, want it white with the green roof, and a big wide porch. . . . Now get this its to be very plain and ordinary, all on one floor. It will look more like a Club House. . . . I want it there so we can ride our horses and hitch em right in front of the house, and all our Roping and riding and everything we will do in that space down in front of the place where we build the house.

It hadn't been long before, in his farewell to Charley Russell, that Will had written fondly of a place that sounded very similar: "Some well kept ranch house over under some cool shady trees." The Pacific was a long way from the Verdigris, and eucalyptuses were no oaks, but, in some indefinable way, he knew he was coming home.

The house was built that spring, at a cost of about five thousand dollars. Except for the fact that the width was closer to thirty-four feet than twenty-four, it met Will's specifications exactly. The long living/dining room, running the length of the house, had a fireplace made of stones found on the ranch. Aligned behind it were three small bedrooms, a kitchen, and a bathroom, and in front was a southeast-facing porch. The next year, flying home from his lecture tour in July, he had the pilot circle the ranch: "as though," the Pacific Palisades newspaper wrote, "a bird's-eye view of polo field, corral and paddock was needed as a tonic for weary and homesick eyes."

Over the next couple of years, as the family began to come out most weekends and stay in the summers for weeks at a time, Will added amenities, most having to do with horses and/or polo. The showpiece was a new stable, always called "the barn" by the family. It was composed of two rows of horse stalls Will had found in, and had transported from, the San Fernando Valley, connected by a large, almost majestic

rotunda encircled by two rows of windows and one of open wooden lou-
vers; he wanted it high so he could practice roping in bad weather.
(When people inevitably teased him about his barn looking so much
nicer than his house, he had one row of windows taken out and the roof
lowered by about ten feet.) The barn housed as many as thirty horses at
a time, many more than the family needed for polo and recreational riding. "They stayed till they died," Jim Rogers said. "We didn't get rid of
very many."

Between the barn and the house was a long, narrow corral that the
children used for trick riding—Jim became expert—and below that was
a kidney-shaped roping ring, complete with chute. Will designed it—
taking special pride in the way the walls went outward, instead of
straight up and down, so you could ride very close to them without hitting them with your stirrups—and it became his favorite retreat. He
would spend hour after hour in the ring, rediscovering, as he approached and passed fifty, the great pastime of his youth. (There were
some differences in the way he pursued it now. He roped calves instead
of steers, and, since he had no great desire to jump off his horse and tie
them, he used a breakaway honda that let his prey escape as soon as it
was caught.) Roping helped calmed him down. He spent so much time
at it that he wore out a set of calves every few weeks. "They wouldn't
run," Bill Rogers said. "You couldn't even kick 'em away. And so, he
would trade that bunch of calves and get another wild bunch." One
time, William G. McAdoo, who had stayed friendly with Will since their
meeting at the 1924 Democratic convention and who was elected U.S.
senator from California in 1932, paid a call at the ranch with a few other
people. Will made the visitors wait while he got in enough roping to satisfy him. They drove off before he was done.

Polo, though more closely linked with Will in the public mind, was
less of a passion. Indeed, in a draft of a 1928 letter to the Internal Revenue Service, which had balked at his attempt to deduct his polo expenses, he claimed, "I am no polo player, I am not even fond of the
game. I could ride a bit and I took it up solely for what there was in it
from a publicity angle."* But the fact was he did enjoy playing, notwith-

*The letter belies the image of Will as an unworldly soul who gained and retained his
fame despite himself, and offers substantial insight into his view of public relations. "Us Birds
that try to keep before and interest the public have various ways of doing it," he wrote. "The
more you do anything that dont look like advertising the better advertising it is. I never take
out adds in Theatrical papers, and in no one of my income tax blanks will you find one cent
charged off to a Press Agents salary. . . . I have never paid one cent to any man in my life for
publicity, and I get paid for being fairly well known. Well I had to do it some way, and the

standing this tax-relief hyperbole. His field was the first in the Rustic Canyon area (it was swiftly followed by layouts at the Uplifters Club and the Riviera Country Club), and the weekly contests at the Rogers ranch were a principal reason why polo became a Hollywood fad. There would be a game every Sunday when Will was in town, followed by a buffet brunch, and the players included executives such as Hal Roach, Darryl Zanuck, and Walt Disney and such stars as Spencer Tracy, Leslie Howard, and James Gleason—not to mention Big Boy Williams, who had become a successful character actor over the years. (One day Disney was involved in a polo accident in which another player lost his life. He never played again.)

Another player was a local youngster named Robert Stack, whose father was a regular known for his untamed style. "Will Rogers was the only polo player as wild as dad," Stack remembered years later. "He used to tear down the field twirling the polo mallet around his head like a cowboy about to rope a steer." Habitually wearing blue jeans and an old white sweatshirt instead of the customary britches, Will was an effective player, his horsemanship and ardor—he was the only player on the field who never stopped talking—making up for his lack of polish. A Los Angeles columnist who covered the sport called him "the puzzle figure of polo. He misses the easy shots and returns all the impossible ones. He rides so well that he gets away with murder." Also helping out was his one-goal handicap, the same rating received by novices. After a few years of frequent polo activity, Will began to cut back on his playing; Jim Rogers thought it was no coincidence that this happened just after his elevation to three goals.

Significantly, the ranch never had a swimming pool, but there was an asphalt tennis court (used exclusively by the children) and an odd golf layout. To afford Fred Stone some exercise when he came to stay in 1929 for a lengthy recuperation, Will had two greens put in, at either end of a broad lawn next to the house. In time, there were two more, and, by approaching them in different ways, a nine-hole course could be approximated. Will would ride along with Stone, sometimes mischievously whacking his friend's ball with a polo mallet. He caddied on horseback for Bobby Jones when the golf champion visited, and he would sometimes tee up a ball and whack it 250 yards into the hills, but

reason I figure I have made myself maby better known than the majority is because I have done the publicity end of it differently.

"If I dident have to make my living out of my name before the public," he concluded, "you would see me hitch those polo ponies to a plow and turn that polo field into a corn patch, thats how much the game means to me."

he never formally played the game. Betty, on the other hand, liked golf, more or less as a vehicle for a brisk walk. Jim Rogers described her style: "She took one golf club, one golf ball, and a sweater with a pocket and she would tee off in front of the house, hit the ball, walk over, pick up the ball, put it in the pocket of the sweater, walk down to the green, drop the ball, putt it, pick it up, and walk."

If nothing else, all the outdoor activity kept Will in excellent physical shape. He never appeared tired, showed no signs of aging as he passed fifty (other than a little farsightedness and a little gray in his hair), and would constantly surprise people with his strength. Once, he picked up Big Boy Williams and literally threw him over a fence. When he was traveling in Shanghai, a weight-guessing specialist put him at 175 pounds. This was twenty-three pounds too low.

Will and Betty finally put the Beverly Hills house up for sale in 1929. The final impetus was the discovery, in attempting to put a new bathroom in for Mary, that the place was termite-infested. But a move had been inevitable for some time. One reason was an itch for a new challenge. Two years earlier, in a letter to Bill, Will had remarked that he was anxious to get to work on new ranch projects: "There is no more fun now at home, everything is finished." There was also the fact that, over the years, Beverly Hills had become nearly urban; another thing Will had in common with Huck Finn was an overwhelming urge to light out for the territory.

The small house at the ranch was obviously insufficient for a full-time residence. The newspapers reported that Will would build "a beautiful home of Italian-Spanish architecture to cost approximately $100,000." Plans for this villa, complete with a marble fireplace, were drawn up by a Pasadena architect; predictably, Will threw them out. He engaged another architect, a young man named Ken Reese who had helped lower the stable's rotunda and designed his bungalow at the Fox studio, and told him that what he wanted was to replicate the main house of a Montana sheep ranch he had visited recently. Reese eventually presented Will and Betty with plans for a two-story, thirteen-room companion ranch house, separated from the original cottage by an outdoor patio. A building permit was taken out in April 1930; the estimated cost was eleven thousand dollars.

By the end of that year, the Beverly Hills place was sold for $150,000 and the family was living at the ranch. The north wing, furnished and laid out under Betty's direction, had all the necessary gentility and creature comforts (there were eventually eleven bathrooms), but it was the big room in the original house that was the heart and soul of the place.

It was still the living room and (when it was too cold or wet to eat on the patio) dining room, and over the years it filled to the breaking point with emotionally laden objects and furnishings: a double-tree lighting arranagement from the Clem Rogers ranch, pictures and sculptures by Charley Russell and Ed Borein, Navaho rugs, a light fixture made of an ancient wagon wheel found on the property, a swing from the porch of the Beverly Hills place, a picture window courtesy of Flo Ziegfeld (rocked by the stock market crash, he went to California in 1930 to try his hand at the movies), a quirt from the Prince of Wales, any number of saddles and branding irons, and a stuffed calf on runners, given by Ed Borein so Will could rope on rainy days.

Will very quickly settled into a routine. He would wake up at 6:00 a.m. or so, have coffee and look over the papers in the kitchen, and then go for a ride in the hills and canyons in the back of the property. Or he might repair to his second-floor study to work on a daily telegram. The study, furnished (like the living room) in heavy Monterey-style pieces, was in a back corner on the second floor of the north wing, and a large window next to Will's desk looked out on the barn and hills where horses grazed. If the view got too tempting, he could climb down a special "sneak stairway" that got him outdoors without encountering any guests who might have stopped in. He would peck away at his pieces on a specially made all-uppercase typewriter that had resolved his capitalization confusion once and for all. (When he was done with a column he would leave it in the machine and Emil Sandmeier, a young Swiss man who with his wife had been hired to run the house, would remove it and take it to the telegraph office in either Santa Monica or Beverly Hills in time for the 3:00 p.m. deadline.) If it was a weekday, Will would drive off to the Fox studios in his LaSalle coupe; with the completion of Beverly Boulevard, the trip took less than half an hour.

He always tried to get home in time to do some roping. Or maybe he would ride out to a place where a fence needed mending. Then he would join Betty and whichever children were home for an informal supper on the patio. (His favorite meal was still beans; if he had been on the road and needed to reduce, he would go on a regimen of lamb chops and spinach.) The radio would rarely be turned on unless it was time for "Amos 'n' Andy," of which Will was a fanatical devotee. He claimed in his column that he wasn't much for book reading—"it takes 'em so long to describe the color of the eyes of all the Characters. Then I like my sunsets from eyesight and not from adjectives." But he was protesting too much. Jim remembers frequently seeing him in bed with a book at one, two, or even three in the morning. A particular favorite, according to Bill, was Twain's *Life on the Mississippi*.

Most of his social ventures outside the ranch were related to the movie industry. He was regularly called on to preside over openings. (At *Grand Hotel*'s, he announced he would produce the even-then reclusive Greta Garbo after the screening; "Garbo" turned out to be Wallace Beery in drag.) He was the master of ceremonies for the 1933 Academy Awards. There would be occasional dinner parties at the homes of Hal Roach or Oscar Lawler, the Rogerses' personal attorney, who had been their next-door neighbor on Van Ness Avenue and in Beverly Hills. Each August, Will tried to spend a few days with Ed Borein, who had settled in Santa Barbara, taking in the Old Spanish Days Fiesta.

Of course, Will would leap at any opportunity to spend time on a real ranch. He took special pleasure in his stints at the Kleberg family's million-acre King Ranch in Texas, not least because of the bill of fare: "That's what makes a good Cow outfit, is good beans. Just give me some beans and I will follow you off. I sure wish I was on a ranch. I would like to stay a year on that outfit." He developed a warm friendship with Sarah Kleberg, daughter of the ranch's owner, and as a present she shipped the Rogerses a purebred Brahma calf that the family dubbed Sarah and took to their hearts as their only real pet. She "followed the children around like a big dog," Betty wrote. "Sitting out on the lawn, the first thing we'd know Sarah would come and curl herself up comfortably at our feet."

But his feelings about more elevated social gatherings can be discerned from what happened when he was invited to be a guest of William Randolph Hearst's at San Simeon. He was late. Hour after hour passed, and finally Hearst dispatched a rider to look for him on the sprawling grounds. He found Will on horseback, deeply engrossed in conversation with a group of Hearst's cowboys. Maybe he was telling them about how he couldn't ask for a job there thirty years before because be couldn't speak Spanish.

What he liked to do on a free day was to hop into the car with Betty and drive. "He would call to me, 'Come on, Blake, let's get going,' and away we'd go," Betty wrote. "I think I had my happiest times with him on these expeditions. We were alone; I had him all to myself. There was no reading, no calf roping, no hundred and one other things that he always seemed to be doing." Sometimes they would have no particular destination, but frequently they headed for a (real) ranch, with possible purchase in mind. ("He loved the ranches," Jim Rogers said. "He wanted a ranch in the worst possible way, except he didn't want one bad enough to get one. Every one—there was something wrong with it.") Not surprisingly, given his ingrained impatience, Will had little regard for the speed limit, and he was frequently stopped by the police. He didn't mind paying tickets; what he didn't like were the wisecracks attributed to him on these occasions by the newspapers. "I am going to get a regular slip written and hand it to em, when they pinch me and ask them to give it to the papers," he wrote to Bill, "so they will at least have some decent jokes to print."

By an uncanny, surely unintended process, each of the Rogers children had inherited one set of their father's inclinations. Bill was interested in journalism, literature, humor, and politics; Mary in the theater; and freckle-faced Jim in horses and nothing but horses. From an early age, he had determined that he wanted to go into the cattle business, and living at the ranch was "seventh heaven" for him, especially on the frequent occasions when his like-minded cousin Jimmy Blake was there to keep him company. (Betty's brother Sandy had moved to Beverly Hills to run Will's office.) "I lived in the barn," he remembered, exaggerating only slightly. But both of the others had reached their automotive majority by the time of the move, and it wasn't tragic for either of them. Bill was an enthusiastic, skilled polo player, and he was able to retain his enrollment in Beverly Hills High School, where he was a standout swimmer and debater and editor of the school paper. Being in the comparative wilderness was a little tougher for Mary, who had developed into a beautiful young woman, with blond hair and features that suggested a softened version of her father's. "She was in the romantic stage, and it was a little far out," Jim said. "All the guys aren't going to drive that far." But there was no shortage of "Mary's blokes" (as Jim called them) around the ranch. One suitor was Howard Hughes. He sent bowls and bowls of gardenias, but when he showed up, to Mary's dismay, he spent the whole time talking aviation with Will.

For as long as they could remember, their father had been absent more than present, and the children were raised more by Betty and their Aunt Dick than by Will. Once, Jim was in a school speaking contest and saw his father's figure sneaking into the back of the room. He was so unnerved by this unfamiliar presence that he forgot the rest of his talk. When Will was in residence during the California years, he was devoted, if a little distant. He tried to coach the children in riding and roping but found he didn't have the patience. "What are you trying to do," he'd shout after a rope trick went down to defeat, "kill snakes?" So the instructional duties were delegated to others. He wasn't particularly comical; Jim was always struck when they were out in public to see his father "step into his act" and mug and tell jokes. He seemed unconcerned about their performance in school ("I would rather have you give up that Latin and some of that than the riding. You know Son it is your health and the Athaletic [*sic*] end of it that I want you to get right into as much as anything else or more," he wrote to the bookish, still somewhat frail Bill when he was at Culver Military Academy). But he supported their vocational fancies, making no attempt to substitute his own; Jim thought this was because he himself had been pushed so hard by Clem. He got Jim and Jimmy Blake summer jobs as cowboys in Texas, and, after Bill graduated from Beverly Hills High in January 1931, arranged for a position on the Fort Worth *Star-Telegram* until he started at Stanford in the fall. He encouraged Mary in her theatrical aspirations, too, suggesting that she try summer stock and consenting to Winnie Sheehan's suggestion, after Mary's year at Sarah Lawrence, that she take a small part in a Fox film called *My Weakness*. (Neither she nor Will wanted it to seem as though she were trading on her name—they were never photographed together after she started her career—and so she was listed in the credits as Mary Howard.) But there were a few guidelines whose flouting was greeted with a high-volume eruption. Animals were not to be mistreated. And, most important, any attempt to take advantage of being a celebrity's child was unthinkable. The only time Jim Rogers remembers his father screaming at him was when a traffic ticket he'd been issued was inadvertently fixed.

Will never referred to Freddy, who would have been ten on July 15, 1928, and was not inclined to reminisce. He never talked about his mother and when he mentioned his father the subject was invariably equitation. "You'd be sitting on a horse and throw your leg up over it," Jim recalled, "and he'd say, 'Sit up on that horse straight. Papa fired cowboys for doing that.' "

The marriage of Will and Betty, which completed its twenty-fifth year in November 1933, continued to thrive, a happy product of mutual respect and what had turned out to be a remarkable compatibility. Important, too, was the joint realization that Will's frequent forays away from home—which continued even when his association with Fox would have allowed him to stay put in his cowboy Shangri-la—gave them both some salubrious breathing room. His delight in her, his need for her calm presence, was evident in the genuine affection with which he framed every reference to her. And one need only have seen some newsreel footage of them together—she standing by his side as they met the press after getting off a ship, wearing the obligatory hat, chuckling over a quip—to comprehend that one of the first things she had noticed, and liked, about the "Injun Cowboy" still held true: She thought he was funny. As they grew older, the filial quality of his feelings toward her, always a basis of their relationship, grew even more pronounced. Shortly after Will's death, Allene Stone gave a canny description of how the dynamic between them sometimes worked.

"He not only adored Betty, he came to depend upon her as a child upon his mother," she told a reporter. "He would be heartbroken if she scolded him.

"Bill loved to tease Betty. I remember one night Betty had some friends at the ranch for dinner. Bill wouldn't come in when she called him—and called him, just stayed out on the polo field with his roping. Finally we all sat down to dinner without him—Betty quietly stern. In due time Bill came up on the long porch in front. He knew he was late but didn't come in. Just stood out on the porch—roping all the chairs.

"At last he came in and sat down at the table. Betty didn't look at him. Suddenly he inquired solemnly, 'Well, what's the matter with you, Blake?'

"We all howled and laughed."

There was no shortage of visitors to the ranch. Will duly noted the prominent ones in his column, in much the same way that, from the *Follies* stage, he used to announce celebrities in the audience. But his circle of close friends was still small. There was Fred Stone, of course, and such longtime cronies as Ed Borein, Tom Mix, Hal Roach, Big Boy Williams, and Leo Carillo. W. C. Fields came out once and showed young Bill how to juggle with balled-up pieces of bread. Among the movie folk, Irene Rich, Will Hays, and Pauline Frederick were occasional guests. Will renewed his friendship with his boyhood schoolmate Ewing Halsell, son of the mighty W.E., who was now running the family enterprises from Texas; when Betty wasn't available, he liked to get in the car and prowl with a California cattleman named Eddie Vail.

Billie Burke was now based in California, pursuing a successful film career, and she and her daughter, Patricia, were regular visitors, as was Flo Ziegfeld whenever he went west for a film project. Will's star now outshone his former boss's, who had never recovered from his losses in the 1929 Crash, but he still deferentially called him "Mr. Zeegfield." During the summer of 1932 Ziegfeld developed pleurisy and journeyed to Los Angeles to recuperate near his wife and daughter. Shortly after his arrival he suffered a relapse, and he died on July 22. Will (who paid funeral expenses) wrote in his daily column that Ziegfeld "left something on earth that hundreds of us will treasure till our curtain falls, and that was a 'badge,' a badge of which we were proud, and never ashamed of, and wanted the world to read the lettering on it, 'I worked for Ziegfeld.' "

One afternoon, there was an eclectic gathering: Mr. and Mrs. Will Hays, Will's McNaught stablemate O. O. McIntyre, McIntyre's wife and his eighty-two-year-old aunt, Billie Burke, Irvin Cobb, and Cobb's daughter Elisabeth. For the occasion, Will brought out a new buckboard carriage drawn by two mules and announced that he was going to drive the company high up in the hills on a newly cut road. On the way down, the brake broke and the mules began galloping out of control. "A mighty narrow road, a real deep drop down one side into a deep canyon, down hill, mules picking up momentum here and there," Will wrote in his column a few weeks later. "Sounds kinder komical now, but not so hot at the time." Fortunately, he had asked his ranch foreman, Buddy Sterling, to ride along with the party, and now Sterling sprang into action. "I swear that blessed cowboy galloped off the path into thin air," recalled Elisabeth Cobb, "somehow swung his horse back onto the path, was alongside the flying mule team, had leaped from his horse onto the back of the nearest one and was sawing so savagely at its mouth that the mule began to see reason, and reflect himself and slow up." When the ride resumed, it was short three passengers who had elected to walk the rest of the way: Betty, Billie Burke, and Irvin Cobb, who "said he dident mind staying in, but he dident like to see the ladies walk down the hill alone as no telling what leading man might attack 'em."

Will felt a special, paternal bond with Joel McCrea, making sure he got good roles at Fox, advising him to invest in real estate (a strategy that made McCrea one of the wealthiest men in Southern California at the time of his death in 1990), and acting out for him the kind of moral object lessons he rarely offered to his own children. One day, he drove the young actor home from the *Lightnin'* location and asked whether he wanted to stop at a bar. McCrea said his mother had impressed on him the evils of drinking, and he had never tasted liquor. Will responded that this showed no strength of character. "You're just going on your mother's say-so. You haven't built any character yourself, because you're just doing what you're told to do. But if you try it and say you don't care for it, then there's no argument, you're not a drinker. Then you got character!" So they went into the bar, and Will ordered a sugary concoction called a Sherry Flip for both of them. He had a second— McCrea didn't—and they left. "Never, from that day on," McCrea said, "did he ever mention drinking again, or did I ever see him take a drink." Once McCrea took Mary out to a party. "You know, we resent you a little bit," she told him during the course of the evening. "You take so much of our father's time."

Probably the best friend Will made in his later years was Amon Carter, the flamboyant, ten-gallon-hat-wearing publisher of the Fort Worth *Star-Telegram*. They had met in 1922 at the New York apartment of New York Giants manager John McGraw (Carter was a more ardent sports fan even than Will), and their friendship was cemented at the 1928 Democratic convention in Houston, where they shared a steaming hotel suite with H. L. Mencken and Baltimore *Sun* publisher Paul Patterson. They'd see each other at the Capitol, heavyweight prizefights, and other masculine venues, and Will would stop as often as he could at Carter's always-jumping suite at the Fort Worth Club, where the specialty of the house was "soup salad": "Open all the cans of tomatoes you have, all the cans of cove oysters, lots of sliced onions, raw, mix 'em in a big bowl."

The one thing everyone who met Will remarked on was his restlessness. Not content with jiggling coins in his pockets, he would take them out and rattle them in his cupped hands, like a gourd. O. O. McIntyre sat next to him at the 1928 Democratic convention and described his antics: "His jaws snap 100 times a minute and when he is not wriggling his feet he is shifting from one hip to another or rolling a lead pencil between his palms." Finally McIntyre told him, "If you can't sit still, go on home." When he started to need reading glasses, Betty always had to keep a large supply on hand; Will kept chewing through the temples. One night at the ranch, he got so agitated over a column he was trying to finish that he kept rubbing the lenses of his glasses between his thumb and finger. Each time, Betty would take them away and wipe them off with a cloth. After the fourth repetition, a friend who was there said, "Betty, why don't you just wash his thumb?"

Will's fervent peripateticism, as evident at the end of his life as at the beginning, sprang from something deep within him. Now, when there were no *Follies* tours or lecture dates, he sent himself out. He traveled to gather material for his column, to raise money for the humanitarian causes that increasingly commanded his concern, to aerate his marriage, but mostly because he was still "fiddle-footed," as Jim put it: "he just had to see what was on the other side of every mountain in the world." After he completed *They Had To See Paris*, Will met Winfield Sheehan in New York to discuss his second picture for Fox. The company wanted him to do a story based loosely on his life; Will vetoed the idea. Since it would take several weeks to prepare another property, he decided on

the spur of the moment to sail that night to England, where a disarmament conference was under way. The only problem was that he had no
passport and no change of clothing. Sheehan handled the first problem
through his Washington connections; Will took care of the second.
"That evening he came to my hotel, wearing a new, hand-me-down
blue serge suit he had bought," Sheehan recalled. "Under his arms he
carrried several paper parcels containing some changes of underclothes,
a half-dozen shirts, six red bandana handkerchiefs, a five cent comb and
a nickel cake of soap. He refused a bag I offered him and that evening
boarded the Bremen with his wardrobe under his arm."

In time, Will refined his packing technique. "I got one little old soft
flat red grip, or bag," he wrote

> that if I just tell it when I am leaving it will pack itself. A few
> old white shirts with the collars attached, and a little batch of
> underwear, and sox, now all these you can replenish at any store
> anywhere, (I know for I have done it) then throw the old ones
> away. . . . So me and my little red bag and typewriter, one extra
> suit in it. It's always packed the same, no matter if it's to New
> York or Singapore.

While in London, Will met George Bernard Shaw for the first time.
The encounter between England's and America's greatest wits was a little disappointing. According to journalist Charles Graves (the poet Robert Graves's brother), who arranged the session, Shaw pretended that he
had never heard of Will Rogers. "When I finally brought the two men
together, Will did not have a chance of getting a word in edgeways,"
Graves wrote later. "At last he put up his hand like a small boy asking
permission to leave the room and, in fact, stemmed the torrent of words
for a few moments."

Will began 1931, his most-traveled year, with a marathon benefit
tour of drought-ravaged Oklahoma, Arkansas, and Texas that covered
fifty towns and cities in eighteen days. Piloted from city to city by the
aviator Frank Hawks, who had set most of the extant speed records, and
accompanied by the pioneer country singer Jimmie Rodgers, rope spin-
ner Chester Byers, and the Revelers singing group, he raised a total of
$221,191. Before his appearance in Stillwater, Will had Walter Harrison,
editor of the *Daily Oklahoman*, arrange for a meeting with Zack Mulhall,
who was quite ill. "The old cowman, in red shirt, bandanna and broad-
brimmed Stetson met us at the flying field," Harrison wrote. "He was
crying like a baby as he put his arms around Will, and the tears in Rogers' eyes were not caused by the biting wind that was blowing. . . . I saw

Will hug the old boy like a mother hugs her baby. Then he whispered in his ear, and stuck a roll of bills that would choke a horse into the old man's hand." Mulhall died seven months later.

In April, he toured Latin America by air, landing in Managua just eight days after an earthquake had ravaged the country; in his daily telegram, he made an impassioned appeal for charitable donations, and he gave five thousand dollars out of his pocket. Before returning home, he stopped in Costa Rica, Panama, Trinidad, Venezuela, Puerto Rico, and the Virgin Islands.

In the following months, he made two trips to Mexico and in the fall set off for a part of the world he had never seen before, the Far East. Early in November, Japan invaded Manchuria, precipitating a war with China. Will sailed, as he put it in a telegram to *The New York Times*, TO SEE WHAT THIS WARS ALL ABOUT. His dispatches were published by *The Saturday Evening Post* under the running title "Letters of a Self-Made Diplomat to Senator Borah." (Will had not warmed to Herbert Hoover as he had to Coolidge, or vice versa, hence his apostrophizing the chairman of the Foreign Relations Committee.) Will didn't see any fighting, but—traveling much of the time with the foreign correspondent and radio commentator Floyd Gibbons, famous as "Your Headline Hunter"—he visited Korea, Japan, and three Manchurian cities, ate dinner with the emperor of Manchuria, had tea with Japan's minister of war, and formulated a much-quoted analysis: "China owns the lot, Japan owns the house that's on it, now who is going to furnish the policeman?" "America could hunt all over the world," he concluded, "and not find a better fight to keep out of." On his way back, he stopped in Peking, Shanghai, Singapore, and the island of Penang. He flew across India, and filed his telegram from Cairo, Baghdad, Athens, Rome, and Paris before arriving in London. He met Betty there and they toured the Continent for two weeks before sailing for New York.

He made shorter jaunts, too. Whenever there were four or five free days strung together, he would drop everything and make for New York or Washington. If he was crossing the country by train, he would never miss an opportunity to stop in Oklahoma, where his visits were relished by an always-growing group of relatives.* The stops were good for his

---

*On one of these trips, he walked into the Chelsea telegraph office to file his daily column and found the operator strumming a guitar and singing a tune. The young man started to put the instrument down, but Will motioned for him to continue. When he finished, Will told him he had talent—he should think about going to New York and getting a job on the radio. Gene Autry went west instead of east and into movies instead of radio—but he has always considered Will Rogers responsible for his show-business career.

soul, if not his waistline. "About all I do when I go home to Oklahoma is just shake hands and eat," he told his readers.

We always have such good things to eat at my sister's in Chelsea. Beans, and what beans, kinder soupy navy beans cooked with plenty of real fat meat. Well when I can't knock off a whole bowl of those myself, why I am sick before I start. And then the ham, fried ham; they cure their own ham. Tom McSpadden my Brother in Law, he is the prize ham curer of any I ever saw. Smoked 'em with the old hickory log fire, then salts 'em away for all this time. . . .

Then the cream gravy. You know there is an awful lot of folks that don't know much about eating gravy. Why not to be raised on gravy would be like never going swimming in the creek. They got their own cows and real cream. Ham gravy is just about the last word in gravys. Course good beefsteak gravy is good. . . . Well, you can get some awful good gravy by putting the old milk in the skillet after you fried a lot of good beefsteak. There's an awful lot of good gravy! A good old home cook can mix up a tasty batch of gravy just about out of anything. No sir the old city eaters missed some mighty fine grub when they don't take advantage of making gravy one of their regular dishes at every meal.

Now then comes the corn bread. Not the corn bread like you mean. I mean corn pone, made with nothing but meal, and hot water and salt. My old daddy always had that at every meal, said it was only the high toned folks that eat biscuits, and light-bread or loaves like you all eat now. He called that "wasp nest," and thought that was just for the heathen. Well this corn pone is mighty hard to go hungry after. . . .

Beans, cornbread, country ham, and gravy, and then just raw onions, either the young ones if they are in, or the sliced ones. Sallie had some dandy Bermudas that Tom had raised. He has the best garden in that part of the country. . . .

Then for desert? Don't have room for any desert. Had any more room would eat some more beans.

These paragraphs could only have been written by a happy man. Will had everything he could ever have hoped for; he was fulfilled, he was loved, he had the capacity for joy, and he was grateful. Yet there was another side to the man, and his nearly obsessive jumpiness and wanderlust were an intimation of it. So was his shyness, which was merely camouflaged, not erased, by his public expansiveness. Asked to describe him years after his death, his longtime banker, neighbor, and friend Oscar Lawler said, "He was rather diffident—quite so in fact." Mrs. Fred Stone said, "He was the most sensitive . . . sentimental man I ever met." Homer Croy, who came to know him fairly well and wrote a canny biography, observed, "Beyond this hail-fellow-well-met personality he was vastly reserved; there was a wall that no one went beyond; and there were dark chambers and hidden recesses that he opened to no one." In his later years, he sometimes permitted himself to open the door a crack.

He became, for one thing, extremely sensitive to criticism—an odd stance for someone so habitually modest. When a columnist such as Ed Sullivan or Heywood Broun took a shot at him, however offhand, he would immediately dash off a lengthy letter of protest. He bristled at suggestions that he shouldn't meddle in politics, that he should stick to jokes, taking the trouble to write to the editor of a small newspaper in the state of Washington that had reported a lecturer's slighting of his knowledge of international affairs: "I'll come out there and debate him on anything foreign he can think of, whether its an affair or not. He says he gets all his news out of a Magazine called 'Foreign Affairs.' When a magazine can learn him foreign affairs, I want to tangle with a guy like that." When a writer named Corey Ford referred to him in *Vanity Fair* as "an uneducated lariat thrower," Will typed out (and, it is to be hoped, never mailed) a response that, coming from him, was almost shockingly spiteful and small. "Your name is Corey Ford," Will wrote. "Why be so masculine and change the Cora to Corey? . . . There is a bunch of you fellows back there that have your little so called Literary Clique. Among you you have killed off more deserving talent than Editors have. Every laugh you or anyone of you have ever gotten has been at some one elses expense. You sit in New York and write for some magazine . . . and you are the last word. Well listen Brother you hopped on the wrong Guy, I will get your name in more papers than you ever thought existed."

Now, he was sometimes willing to be something other than amiable in public. To a woman reporter who started an interview by asking about his favorite foods, he snapped, "Now who cares what I eat? I eat what I want and when it suits me to eat," then stomped off. As a young reporter, the humorist H. Allen Smith approached him at the Frontier Days rodeo in Cheyenne and asked him to visit the press box. Will told him to get lost. The rebuff so shocked Smith that, forty-six years later, he used it as the sole basis of a magazine article called "Will Rogers Was No Damned Good."

One memorable eruption came during an appearance before a large group of Cherokee Indians. The beginning of his performance was like any other. "Then, suddenly, he became furious," reported a newspaperman who was there. "His transformation was terrifying, and for three minutes his astonished audience was treated to a demonstration of what primitive, instinctive hatred could be." The object of his hatred was Andrew Jackson, who in the distant past had started the chain of events that sent the Cherokees on the Trail of Tears. "The Indians listened, and then the quiet was ripped by the screaming war cry of the tribe, while Rogers stood, white, trembling and actually aghast at himself."

The fact that Will did not permit himself such outbursts until late in life had something to do with his elephantine need for approval. (So, for that matter, did the fact that he was loved more than any American has been loved before or since.) On rare occasions, he displayed it more directly. During one political convention Will shared a hotel room with Rube Goldberg. One night, Goldberg was shocked to find his friend in a state of "abject misery," so depressed that he refused to speak and spent the whole night lying on his back and staring at the ceiling. In the morning he got up and dressed, still without saying a word. V. V. McNitt later told Goldberg that Will was in this state because a few days earlier some sentences had been cut out of his copy.

There was one more factor that contributed to his occasional black spirits. His commonsense cosmology was a wonderful humor-producing engine, as it punctured all pretension, cut through all the verbiage that cluttered the cultural ether. It also tended to disassemble the structures of language and belief that gave comfort to others. Will was too respectful to publicly doubt the existence or beneficence of God. But he didn't belong to any church. He was inaccurately dubbed "The Philosopher with a Lariat" by an uninspired headline writer—philosophy had nothing to do with his special abilities—but to the extent that he had a general view of the world it was nihilistic, stark, and rather cold. His clearest expression of it came in response to a letter from Will Durant, two years before his dinner at the ranch with Charlie Chaplin. Durant had asked prominent people to summarize their "philosophy of life" (eventually collecting the responses in a book called *On the Meaning of Life*). In his column, Will obliged:

> What all of us know put together don't mean anything. Nothing don't mean anything. We are just here for a spell and pass on.

Any man that thinks that Civilization had advanced is an ego-
tist. Fords and bathtubs have moved you and cleaned you, but
you was just as ignorant when you got there. We know lots of
things we used to dident know but we dont know any way to
prevent 'em happening. . . .

We have got more tooth paste on the market, and more
misery in our Courts than at any time in our existence. There
ain't nothing to life but satisfaction. If you want to ship off fat
beef cattle at the end of their existence, you got to have 'em satisfied on the range. Indians and primitive races were the highest
civilized, because they were more satisfied, and they depended
less on each other, and took less from each other. . . .

The whole thing is a "Racket," so get a few laughs, do the
best you can, take nothing serious, for nothing is certainly depending on this generation. Each one lives in spite of the previous one and not because of it. And don't start "seeking"
knowledge for the more you seek the nearer the "Booby Hatch"
you get.

And don't have an ideal to work for. That's like riding toward the Mirage of a lake. When you get there it ain't there. Believe in something for another World, but don't be too set on
what it is, and then you won't start out that life with a disappointment. Live your life so that whenever you lose, you are
ahead.

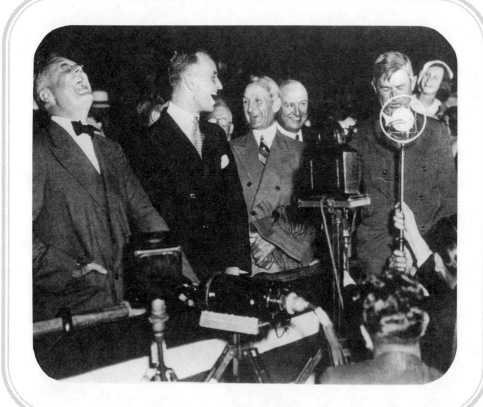

AT A 1932 RALLY, WILL BREAKS UP (FROM LEFT) FDR, JAMES
ROOSEVELT, WILLIAM G. MCADOO, AND JAMES FARLEY

CHAPTER 12

REVERSIBLE FIGURE: WILL ROGERS AND POLITICS

No nation in the history of the world was ever sitting as pretty. If we want anything, all we have to do is go and buy it on credit.

So that leaves us without any economic problems whatever, except some day to have to pay for them. But we are certainly not thinking about that this early.

— WILL ROGERS, SEPTEMBER 6, 1928

Why not name Will Rogers president of the U.S. by acclamation? His so-called "applesauce" seems to be just what the world needs right now.

— COLUMBUS DISPATCH, JUNE 23, 1931

POLITICALLY, Will was a little hard to pin down. What was one to make of a columnist who, as occasion demanded, would praise Calvin Coolidge and Al Smith, Dwight Morrow and Robert La Follette Jr., William Borah and Franklin D. Roosevelt? The inconsistency, however, was more apparent than real; certainly Will was not unaware of the sizable differences among these men of affairs. It was just that as he developed as a commentator through the 1920s and into the 1930s, he was able to pick and choose his issues, never blindly casting his lot with any camp. One explanation for this catholic perspective is his childhood and youth in the Indian Territory, whose political parameters corresponded in no way with those of the twentieth-century United States, and which therefore spared him partisan baggage. Another is his own resistance to doctrinaire ideology in any form.

His main impulse was a broad neo-Jeffersonian populism tempered by an across-the-board skepticism. He had a general and instinctive distrust of bankers, big business, and Wall Street. (Talking to a banquet a few months after Herbert Hoover took office, he offered a scathing, difficult-to-dispute two-sentence assessment of Hoover's laissez-faire predecessor: "Coolidge went in and just turned his head. And say, brother, if you didn't get yours then you was just dumb.") Pro–income tax and antitariff, he doggedly stuck up for the farmers, whom he (correctly) saw as getting the blunt end of Republican economic policies of the 1920s. He felt that consumer buying on credit and stock-market speculation, both of which reached unprecedented proportions by the end of the decade, were something close to an evil and he (correctly) felt they would end in disaster. But unlike many populists, Will was no proselytizer. He saw Prohibition—a divisive litmus test in the Democratic party for more than a decade—strictly as a political issue, with negligible relevance to morality or the public good; the position got him into trouble with many of his rural admirers, including his pious sister Sallie. "Talking about Prohibition is like whittling used to be," he said in a radio broadcast in 1930. "It passes away the time but don't settle anything." And he found stridently racist Bible-thumpers like Alabama Senator Tom Heflin distasteful. He simply didn't trust crusaders, which was why he never warmed to William Jennings Bryan, Huey Long, or, for that matter, Woodrow Wilson.

Another area of contention with Wilson and Wilsonians was in the realm of foreign policy. His skepticism about the efficacy of the League of Nations, the World Court, and the succession of international conferences held in the twenties and thirties qualified him as an isolationist, although unlike many people traditionally designated as such he was consistent, opposing U.S. military intervention in such places as Nicaragua, Mexico, and the Philippines, as well as Europe. At the same time, he favored a strong military—especially, of course, in the air—and had little doubt that there would eventually be another world war. In the matter of World War I debts owed to the United States by its European Allies, he was a strict collectionist, a stance that left him open to the wrath of internationalist voices such as Walter Lippmann and *The New York Times*. But Will's position had less to do with ideology than with the commonsense feeling that money borrowed ought to be paid back. He approvingly quoted Coolidge's five-word assessment: "They hired it, didn't they?" ("They" being the Allies, "it" being the money.)

Will was famous for making fun of Congress—a good half of his most famous quips were directed at that body's collective denseness, crookedness, and/or inefficiency. There was a venerable tradition for this sort of thing, participated in among others by Twain, who once observed, "It could probably be shown by facts and figures that there is no distinctly native criminal class except Congress." Like Polish jokes or mother-in-law jokes, swipes at Congress had entered a rhetorical realm in which the message imparted was subordinate to the convention itself, and its relative truth was of little consequence. But the way Will returned to the theme, again and again and again, bespoke a genuine disdain on his part for legislators (in general—typically, he had nothing but praise for most of them as individuals); he saw their posturing, blatant pork-barreling, and sheer windiness as a permanent, only slightly less egregious version of the endless 1924 Democratic convention that had so infuriated him. Drawing any conclusions from the fact that the country's most celebrated Congress-basher was the son of a three-term Cherokee senator and master legislative politician would require aggressive speculation. But the irony is no less striking for that.

Will genuinely admired Mussolini for taking the reins of power as completely as he did, thus bypassing the messy legislative process, and as late as 1933 remarked, "Say, Mussolini could run this country with his eyes shut, in fact that is the way our Congress has been running it." When a San Diego newspaper criticized this comment and pointed out some of the drawbacks to life in Italy, Will responded to the "long winded editorial" with a personal letter that averred, "Dictatorship is the best government in the world provided you have the right dictator."

Statements like that lent credence to the proposition that Will was a mere comedian and not to be taken seriously as a political commentator. As such, they were welcomed by more conventional pundits, who were habitually bemused by the political and popular influence he wielded. Arthur Brisbane, the dully oracular author of the "Today" column in the Hearst papers, frequently made patronizing remarks about the very "useful" (faint praise indeed) Will Rogers. (In 1931, Brisbane wrote that Will's "early training at Eton and Oxford" made it hard for him to maintain the "cowboy style"—a weak joke that revealed more about Brisbane than Will.) In the pressroom of the 1928 Republican convention, with Will (and a reporter from the St. Louis *Post-Dispatch*) present, H. L. Mencken, the sage of Baltimore, fumed at Will's influence in the body politic.

> "Look at the man," he shouted. "He alters foreign policies. He makes and unmakes candidates. He destroys public figures. By deriding Congress and undermining its prestige he has virtually re-

duced us to a monarchy. Millions of Americans read his words daily, and those who are unable to read listen to him over the radio. . . . I consider him the most dangerous writer alive today."

"Come on, now, Henry, you know that nobody with any sense ever took any of my gags seriously," remonstrated Rogers.

"Certainly not," was the retort. "They are taken seriously by nobody except half-wits, in other words by approximately 85 percent of the voting population."

Mencken's outrage was in some measure mock (the *Post-Dispatch* reporter is no help in trying to determine the exact proportion). But there was an undercurrent of seriousness in his tirade as well.

The good gray *New York Times*, which by the time Will started writing for it had assumed its identity as the voice of what would later be called the Eastern Establishment, never knew quite what to make of its cowboy columnist. From the beginning of his association with the *Times*, in 1922, it was an odd fit, a fact the paper recognized two years later when it dropped his weekly column. (The McNaught syndicate had also been angling for a hefty rate hike at the time.) In January 1927, just months after his daily telegram had begun, Arthur Hays Sulzberger, who had married Adolph Ochs's daughter and would become publisher of the *Times* on Ochs's death in 1935, sent his father-in-law a memo asking, "Don't you think Will Rogers is getting pretty bad—and if so that we have been paying him long enough to feel that we have wiped out any obligation that we may have incurred last summer [when Will filed from Europe for free]?

"My suggestion would be that we give him due notice of desiring to stop at the earliest possible time."

Ochs didn't follow the advice. But he—and the editors who worked for him—consistently treated Will with condescension. A reader once wrote in to complain that Will was "going into fields that are outside of his jurisdiction" and wanted the *Times* to "swap" him for Walter Lippmann, then with the New York *World*. "It has been our idea," replied managing editor Edwin "Jimmie" James (who doubtless wished he could make the trade), "that our readers understood that he wasn't presented as a serious oracle, but as a jokesmith." This was not Will's self-assessment. Since his 1926 European trip, he had considered himself a bona fide reporter. The *Times* did not. In 1930, in London to cover the disarmament conference, Will received this cable from Ochs:

AM SURE YOU SHARE OUR HOPE FOR SUCCESS OF DISARMAMENT
CONFERENCE. IN THAT BELIEF SUGGEST YOU DO NOT UNWITTINGLY

EMBARRASS THIS COUNTRY'S NOBLE PURPOSE IN ENDEAVORING TO
PRODUCE GOOD LASTING RESULTS. LETS TRY TO BE HELPFUL

He got the same treatment the following year. Before his trip to
Manchuria, he asked Ochs for credentials indicating that he was a *Times*
correspondent. The publisher's return telegram answered in the negative
and included, by way of explanation, a memo written to Ochs by F. T.
Birchall, James's predecessor as managing editor:

> It should be remembered that neither the Japanese nor the
> Chinese know Mr. Rogers, nor will they be able to understand
> his keen wit. These two are perhaps the most sensitive nations
> on earth. They have no sense of humor, and if he is going to be
> humorous, he will be misinterpreted and misunderstood. . . . On
> the other hand, if Mr. Rogers proposes to be a serious corre-
> spondent, it should be borne in mind that it would take a long
> time to convince the public that he had become one. . . . Also a
> good Far Eastern correspondent requires years of training and
> absorption of history and customs. . . .
>
> Whether the situation be drawn out or short lived, Mr. Rog-
> ers will be better able to comment from Beverly Hills, basing his
> material on what he reads in the Times.

On at least two occasions, the *Times* killed Will's column, the first
time explaining the censorship by sending him this supercilious anonymous wire: "WE DID NOT USE YOUR PIECE TONIGHT. WE DO NOT CARRY
ATTACKS ON CHARACTER OR CREDIT.*

Usually, Will grinned and bore this sort of thing. Once, he didn't.
Late in 1932, England and France asked for postponement of their next
war-debts payment. Will would have none of it. "One message of three

---

*The "attack" in question came in a 1933 column criticizing what would later come to
be known as the "trickle-down" theory. "The Reconstruction Finance Corporation is made
up of fine men, honest, and mean well and if it was water they were distributing it would help
the people the plan was meant to help," Will had written. "For water goes down hill and
moistens everything on its way, but gold or money goes uphill. The Reconstruction loaned
the railroads money, medium and small banks money, and all they did with it was pay off
what they owed to New York banks. So the money went uphill instead of down. You can
drop a bag of gold in Death Valley, which is below sea level, and before Saturday it will be
home to papa J.P. [Morgan]."

In the second column, Will wrote, "Frank Phillips, of oil fame was out the other day,
said he was going to Washington. The oil men were going to draw up a code of ethics. Everybody present had to laugh. If he had said the gangsters of America were drawing up a code of
ethics, it wouldn't have sounded near as impossible."

words," he wrote, "will make every nation in Europe dig it up and send it over by plane, they would be in such a hurry to get it here—'Pay or default.' " He hammered home the theme in several other columns. The stance went counter to the prevailing view (editorially endorsed by the *Times* and Lippmann) that debts should be canceled, or at least their terms adjusted, and the newspaper received a spate of irate letters, including one from a recent Harvard graduate named Charlton Ogburn, who accused Will of "destructive obscurantism," called him "the most vociferous expositor of the 'hick' or 'dirty foreigner' viewpoint in the country," and accused the *Times* of "augmenting his already appalling influence." An editor wired Ogburn's letter to Will for reply and noted in a memo to James, the managing editor, "No answer to this tonight. Will probably is looking up the big words, or having someone interpret it for him." But Will did puncture Ogburn's pretensions masterfully in a wire that was addressed to James and published in the Letters to the Editor section. ("... HE MADE ME MAD JIMMIE, HE CALLED ME A 'BUCOLIC WIT,' " wrote Will. "JIMMIE I AIN'T HAD THAT SINCE I WAS A CHILD. . . .") It was followed by eleven letters from readers: five pro-Will, six con.

The next day, the newspaper itself half-apologized for Will's views, in an editorial that swelled with condescension. "Let the raw, untutored voices be heard," it stated, and concluded: "Mr. Rogers will doubtless recall the advice of Matthew Arnold not to be disturbed by 'the fever of a differing soul.' The Times tries not to be." But Will got the last word in his daily telegram the following week:

> I would like to state to the readers of THE NEW YORK TIMES that I am in no way responsible for the editorial or political policy of this paper.
>
> I allow them free reign as to their opinion, so long as it is within the bounds of good subscription gathering.
>
> But I want it distinctly understood that their policy may be in direct contrast to mine.
>
> Their editorials may be put in purely for humor, or just to fill space.
>
> Every paper must have its various entertaining features, and their editorials are not always to be taken seriously, and never to be construed as my policy.

It's worth noting that, except for the (not uncommon) use of *reign* for *rein* in the second sentence, the entire column contains not a single error of punctuation, grammar, or spelling.

In his next weekly article, Will put forth a lengthy defense of his political seriousness. He remarked that he'd noticed a lot of people writing to the papers, saying, "I read Will Rogers, but why does he have to dabble in politics. Let him stay on funny stuff where he belongs."

> Well if they would just stop to think I have written on nothing but politics for years, you never heard me on a mother in law joke. It was always about national or international affairs. . . .

> Where do these other fellows get all of their vast stores of knowledge. I never hear of 'em going any place. If I write about Mexico, I have been down there a half a dozen times. Nicaragua, I been there twice and found out things that I couldent ever have by reading about it. Crossed India at the height of their troubles, been in Europe and talked debts till I had everybody's angle over there. There is not a state in this country that I am not in ever once in awhile. Talk to everyone, get the ranchers' and farmers' angle.

> Those New York writers should be compelled to get out once in their lifetime and get the "folks" angle. I know and have known all the time that the real backbone people of America wasent going to cancell any debts. They would never have given the moratorium if it had come to a vote of them. All your Lippmans and all your cancellationists in New York can write their economic theories that want to, but they dident know a thing about our people.

Will's point was well taken. But he was also protesting too much. He wanted to be taken seriously, yes, but at the same time he wanted to retain the comedian's privileges of hyperbole, selectivity, and deflection. He would still frequently back away from the logical conclusion of his comments, still undercut his criticisms of politicians and big business with a public courting of Calvin Coolidge and John D. Rockefeller, still avoid topics or positions that couldn't be explored without running the risk of dullness, still never allow himself to go for more than a few sentences at a time without saying something funny. He still refused to recognize evil. As a result, he became the political equivalent of a reversible figure—the psychological test in which a wavy line on a blank page can be seen to be either a table lamp or a human profile, depending on which side of the line one concentrates on. If you looked one way at Will, he was a jokesmith; if you slightly modified your angle of perception, he was a sage. Far from bothering Will, the ambiguity suited his purposes perfectly.

And, of course, it helped bolster his remarkable popularity. If he had rigorously followed his positions to their logical conclusions, he would have lost the allegiance of millions. As it was, he was adored by Prohibitionists, Wall Street bankers, senators, tariff supporters, internationalists, even Cancellationists with more of a sense of humor than Charlton Ogburn had. Whenever a Rogers opinion was unpalatable, they could with minimal effort shrug it off and turn it into a mere joke.

By the late 1920s, in any case, Will had become a figure of real influence in American politics. He was read every day by millions, many of whom uncritically adopted his views as their own; most of the others at least looked on them sympathetically. This was not lost on politicians, who, over and above the honest affection they generally felt for Will, knew better than to overlook what he had to say on the issues. In 1930, a "Washington statesman" was quoted in *American Magazine* as saying, "You can never have another war in this country unless Will Rogers is for it." Also significant was a subtle but unmistakable sea change in the public climate (a change Will had much to do with bringing about): Suddenly, appearing to be a good sport, a regular guy, had become an important political consideration. In 1933, when Will announced over the radio that he planned to step down as congressman-at-large, Vice President Garner and no fewer than fifty-eight senators (nearly a two-thirds majority!) beseeched him to reconsider. Indeed, in the years since Will's gibes had ruffled Warren G. Harding's feathers, only one politician, Chicago's Mayor William "Big Bill" Thompson, had been foolhardy enough to take him on publicly.*

No doubt many seethed at him in private. One such was Harold Ickes, secretary of the interior under Franklin Roosevelt. Will had criticized him for wanting to change the name of Hoover Dam and had commented, during a radio broadcast, that at least there were no plans to call it "Ikey's Dam." Few things made Ickes angrier than to hear his name subjected to that particular mispronunciation, and the morning af-

---

*In 1930, in the depths of the Depression, Thompson had put forth a plan to solve the city's economic woes with a lottery, and Will had taken a shot at it in his column.

"All I have to say," stated Thompson, "is that if Will Rogers has made so much money that his head is so swelled that he thinks it is funny to crack jokes about people who are starving, I hope to God he goes broke and gets hungry himself and he won't crack any more jokes about those who have to accept charity.

"He has pulled some pretty brutal and unfair stuff about me in years gone by, which means nothing to me, because I consider the source from which it comes. When this nation is suffering and people are hungry, a wisecracker that belittles the condition and efforts of anyone to correct it is to me the cheapest skate on earth."

The next year Thompson was out of office.

ter the broadcast he was livid with rage. "He never again had anything to do with Will Rogers," said an Ickes aide.

Will testified before Congress on the question of flood relief in 1928. Beyond that, he was a frequent, savvy, and welcome presence in the hallways of the Capitol and in informal summits of the powerful. Senators came to his ranch, hat in hand, to talk politics. At the 1928 Democratic convention, he drew Al Smith aside and pleaded with him to withdraw his candidacy. "Wait four years," a Smith associate remembered Will saying. "Nobody ever killed Santa Claus. Times are too good, you can't win in so prosperous a year." If Smith had followed the advice, he would have had a much better chance in 1932, and American history could have been very different. Will was also an unofficial adviser to Frederick Davison, Clarence Young, and David Ingalls, who as (respectively) assistant secretary of war, assistant secretary of aeronautics, and assistant secretary of the navy in the Hoover years were collectively responsible for the nation's aviation policy.*

The friendships Will had cultivated over the years were bearing fruit as his cronies advanced up the ladder of power. His friend Joe Robinson of Arkansas, the Democratic leader in the Senate since 1923, was picked by Smith to run for Vice President in 1928. Nick Longworth died in 1931, but he was succeeded as Speaker of the House by John Nance "Cactus Jack" Garner, a hard-drinking, plain-talking, white-haired Texan Will had known and liked for years (and who will always be remembered for the immortal remark, "The vice-presidency isn't worth a bucket of warm piss"). On the two or three trips he made to the capital each year, Will would use Garner's office as home base, dumping his gear there before prowling the corridors. He also had long been friendly with Franklin Roosevelt, a fifth cousin of Theodore who had been the Democrats' vice-presidential nominee in 1920 and who was elected governor of New York in 1928. Their admiration was sincere and mutual. In 1930, Roosevelt was reelected by a plurality of more than 700,000 votes, and Will wrote in his daily telegram, "The Democrats nominated their President yesterday, Franklin D. Roosevelt." The following year, in

---

*Years later, Davison recalled a day when he, Young, Ingalls, Amon Carter, and Will met at his house for cocktails. Knute Rockne had recently died in a plane crash, and the topic under discussion was whether the airlines should provide parachutes. Ingalls, Davison, and Will said yes; Young thought it would be too impractical.

"I remember Young saying, 'Take that accident. You probably wouldn't have saved more than one out of the whole bunch.'

"Will Rogers with that funny little smile of his looked at the ceiling and said, 'Well, wouldn't he have been tickled.' "

a letter to Will, Roosevelt implored him to come to Albany sometime "and talk to me of cabbages and kings! I want to see you, Oh, most excellent of philosophers."

BY THE TIME Roosevelt wrote these words, the country was two years into the worst depression in its history. It was a moral and political crisis as well as an economic one, and it provoked Will, as nothing had before, to transcend reversibility, to take a firm, serious, and provocative stand.

Like virtually everyone else in the country, he had no idea that the stock market crash of October 1929 would be followed by a severe slump. Given his frequently expressed distaste for financial speculation, his initial reaction was not surprising. "Oh it was a great game while it lasted," he wrote in November. "All you had to do was buy and wait till the next morning and just pick up the paper and see how much you made, in print. But all that has changed, and I think it will be good for everything else. For after all everybody just can't live on gambling. Somebody has to do some work."

In the following months, as the economy continued to turn downward, Will continued to be attracted to the view that hard times might be a good thing in the long run. Americans had been living beyond their means, and financing it all on credit; the slump had brought us down to earth. "It's really not depression, it's just a return to normalcy," he wrote. "It's just getting back to two bit meals and cotton underwear, and off those $1.50 steaks and silk Rompers. America has been just muscle bound from holding a steering wheel. The only callus place we got on our body is the bottom of the driving toe." The temptation, for Will, was to see the Depression as a kind of all-purpose moral cleanser, wiping away the excesses of the 1920s and allowing old-time values to shine once more. "You know this darn thing has made the whole country better off in a lot of ways," he wrote on another occasion. "It's done away with four-flushing. If a man hasent got it, he don't mind telling you right out that he hasent. . . . It's brought out some mighty good qualities in lots of people. There is a spirit of better fellowship among everyone I think."

But as it became clear that there would be no quick upturn, he was forced to come to terms with the fact that any bracing effects the Depression might have had were as nothing compared to the suffering it had wrought. Seven million people had neither a job nor the hope of finding one; untold thousands were without sufficient food or shelter. Will's Red Cross relief tour in the winter of 1931 showed him how bad things really were among farmers, who had to face the consequences not only of drought but of price drops of up to 90 percent over the previous twelve years. Something was not right. Hoover's State of the Union address in December 1930 was a rather pedantic attempt to explain the causes of the Depression, which to Will was beside the point: "Our rich is getting richer, and our poor is getting poorer. That's the thing that these great minds ought to work on."

A month later, he returned to the theme. In England, Arkansas, an armed force of some five hundred people had demanded food from Red Cross officials, graphically illustrating how desperate things were. Yet Congress and the Hoover administration refused to provide any direct relief. Will didn't blame Hoover for the slump ("Mr. Coolidge and Wall Street and big business all had their big party, and it was just running out of liquor when they turned it over to Hoover," he would write), but the government's inaction left him incredulous. "If you live under a Government and it don't provide some means of getting work when you want it and will do it, why then there is something wrong," he wrote. "You can't just let the people starve, so if you don't give 'em work, and you don't give 'em food, or money to buy it, why what are they to do? What is the matter with our Country anyhow?" He proposed that the government hire the unemployed for massive public-works projects, to be paid for by "a higher surtax on large incomes." "It may not be a great plan," Will concluded, "but it will DAM sure beat the one we got now."

Franklin D. Roosevelt would adopt Will's plan almost to the letter, but his inauguration was still more than two years away. In the meantime, the masses were becoming less willing to accept their lot. A general conviction was emerging that some kind of revolution was a distinct possibility. In the fall of 1931, editor William Allen White warned that unless the government provided effective relief, the winter would see "barricades in the street." His prediction appeared to be borne out the following March, when the police opened fire on a group of three thousand protestors at a Ford plant in Dearborn, Michigan, killing four of them. In the spring, World War I veterans from around the country, demanding immediate payment of a bonus they were scheduled to receive thirteen years later, marched on Washington. Twenty thousand strong, they peacefully camped out in shantytowns on the Anacostia Flats until July, when soldiers under the command of General Douglas MacArthur, bayonets flashing, drove them from the city.

It would take a very long stretch to call Will Rogers a radical. His resistance to doctrinaire ideology of all kinds ruled out any attraction to

communism or its variants; indeed, all his views were informed by a vis-
ceral (not political) conservatism, and he was in fact a frequent target of
leftist voices. "Will Rogers likes to pose as 'home folks,' " complained a
socialist newspaper, "but the truth is he's a millionaire. He has never
written a word in support of a worker on strike. He has never spoken a
sentence that doubted the divine justice of the capitalist system. Many of
his wisecracks reveal a hidden sympathy for the Fascist type of Demagogue." (The second and fourth sentences were accurate, and, if we set
aside the question of whether Will was posing, the first was as well. The
third was not.) But, reversible as always, Will was subject to divergent in-
terpretations. Woody Guthrie, a Dust Bowl Oklahoman whose left-wing
credentials are beyond dispute, was once asked who his heroes were. He
gave two names: Jesus Christ and Will Rogers.

One observer bemused by the paradox was his son Bill. A self-
described "intellectual snob" who was cultivating a fashionable radical-
ism in the early 1930s, Bill once collared his father and said, "Dad,
you've been jumping on the bankers day after day. Don't you see the
implications of what you've been saying?" Will brushed him off: "He
didn't feel he had to be consistent," Bill Rogers says now.

But in 1931 and 1932, the spectacle of a government seemingly un-
interested in addressing its people's suffering elicited a palpable anger in
Will. On Washington's Birthday 1931, he wrote bitterly that Washington "would have seen our great political system of 'equal rights to all
and privileges to none' working so smoothly that 7,000,000 are without a chance to earn their living." He was unimpressed when Congress convened early to discuss the unemployment question: "Well, I
believe if I was unemployed and hungry I would want a little more substantial help than just the thought of 'our boys' being gathered in
Washington."

Hoover recognized Will's unique position in the country and tried to
use him to help build support for his program to fight the Depression,
such as it was. But the President understood neither the Depression nor
public relations. Once, he met with Will and merely requested a few
antihoarding jokes. Another time, he tried to explain his opposition to
direct relief. "Had a long talk with the president this morning," Will reported to his readers. "He sincerely feels (with almost emotion) that it
would set a bad precedent for the government to appropriate money to
the Red Cross." The parenthesis was damning.

On October 18, 1931, Hoover was scheduled to make a radio speech
on the issue of unemployment, for which he had devised a two-pronged
strategy—convincing the country that the problem was not as bad as it

seemed and convincing local groups to raise money for relief.* He asked Will to speak on the broadcast, and he did. This was another miscalculation on the President's part. Will said all the right things, asking towns and cities to do their part and even venturing the opinion that Hoover "would rather see the problem of unemployment solved than he would all the other problems he has before him combined." But he also confronted the issue with a solemn and eloquent fervor that put the administration's inaction to shame:

> Now we read the papers every day, and they get us all excited over one or a dozen different problems that's supposed to be before the country. There's not really but one problem before the whole country at this time. It's not the balancing of Mr. Mellon's budget. That's his worry. That ain't ours. And it's not the League of Nations that we read so much about. It's not the silver question. The only problem that confronts this country today is at least 7,000,000 people are out of work. That's our only problem. There is no other one before us at all. It's to see that every man that wants to is able to work, is allowed to find a place to go to work, and also to arrange some way of getting more equal distribution of wealth in the country.

If the notion of Will Rogers as a presidential candidate had caught Americans' imagination in booming 1928, how much more attractive must it have been in 1932, when the country seemed on the verge of collapse. In the intervening four years, moreover, Will's stock had risen even higher. His credentials as a political sage were now established beyond question, and as a result of his humanitarian efforts he had become a nearly universally admired, and in some circles venerated, figure. In an extraordinary editorial written after Will's drought-relief tour and his goodwill mission to Latin America in 1931, *The New York Times* itself compared him to St. Francis of Assissi and praised him for "flying over great stretches of GOD's earth to make it as much of heaven as possible while still a very human mortal." His efforts on behalf of the suffering, in the *Times'* opinion, were "suggestions of a kind of angelic service, though the angel be of a very masculine type and very different from the conventional one."

*The chairman of the President's Organization for Unemployment Relief (POUR), formed in August 1931, was Walter S. Gifford, the president of AT&T. In January 1932, he told a Senate Subcommittee, "My sober and considered judgment is that at this stage . . . Federal aid would be a disservice to the unemployed." An exasperated senator complained, "You are always hopeful!" "I find it pleasant, Senator, to be hopeful," was Gifford's reply.

Newspapers started promoting a Rogers candidacy in 1931, jokingly at first but more seriously by the month. In July, a Kentucky paper reported that "it is beginning to look as if the possibility exists of Rogers being taken seriously as a possible candidate." He was endorsed by the Oklahoma League of Young Democrats; Governor James Ferguson of Texas said he would be no more out of place in the White House than was Lincoln or Andrew Jackson. The *Home Friend* magazine got on the bandwagon early in 1932. "Little did we realize when we published the article about Will Rogers being the man we need in the White House," it reported in a subsequent issue, "that it would arouse so much favorable comment, and strike such a sympathetic chord in the hearts of our readers." *The Home Friend's* editor copied out some of the responses and sent them on to Will. Mrs. C. W. Webb of Oklahoma wrote in to say, "If he could be prevailed upon to accept, I believe he would simply be the saviour or redeemer of our beloved U.S.A." A. C. King of Pennsylvania said, "In my intimate group of friends with whom I chat and play I find manufacturers, clerks, professional men, farmers and laborers, and I have heard your suggestion spoken of hundreds of times within the last few months, and the unanimous opinion that he could handle the job, and give us the faith and confidence we need at this time."

As a publicity stunt, a movie magazine sent a young man around the country in a car bearing a WILL ROGERS FOR PRESIDENT banner. He was surprised to find genuine interest in the idea, and repeatedly had to hurry out of town to escape people's demands to know the particulars of Will's platform.

Even Roosevelt, favored to bear out Will's prediction and win the Democratic nomination, appeared concerned about the possibility of a Rogers candidacy. "Don't forget you are a Democrat by birth, training and tough experience," he wrote Will in June, four weeks before the convention, "and I know you won't get mixed up in any fool movement to make the good old Donkey chase his own tail and give the Elephant a chance to win the race."

As Roosevelt knew very well, conditions in the country were such that, more than at any other time in its history, a candidate outside the political mainstream had an opportunity to attract a sizable following. Sinclair Lewis recognized this in his 1935 novel *It Can't Happen Here,* in which a plainspoken Vermonter is elected to the White House (and proceeds to install a fascist regime). That same year, Louisiana's Huey Long—blasting big business and promoting a redistribution of wealth—attracted enough support that he was considered a serious presidential contender until his assassination in September. Probably even more than

Long, Will would have been able to tap the longings and resentments of the large portion of the country that had been abandoned by conventional politics. But unlike Long, Will had no interest in power. Furthermore, becoming President would have meant a cut in pay of more than 75 percent. There is, in any case, no evidence that he gave any serious consideration to running. When a *Collier's* magazine writer boosted his candidacy, he responded in his daily telegram: "Will you do me one favor? If you see or hear of anybody proposing my name either humorously or semiseriously for any political office, will you maim said party and send me the bill?"

To a friend he wrote, "I couldn't be a politician in a million years. I like to go my own way, and I don't believe I could take dictation. It sure would be an honor, and worth all the monetary sacrifice, but I am going through my life making up my own mind. . . ."

The 1932 Democratic convention began in Chicago on June 27 (the Republicans having already renominated Hoover). On the opening day, during a recess, Will made an impromptu speech that was greeted with gales of laughter. "If some fellow got up and nominated Rogers right then," wrote a Chicago newspaper, "he'd have got two-thirds of the vote as quick as a secretary could have called the roll." Heywood Broun, an admirer since the *Follies* days, wrote, "I think it is a little ironical that the same convention which thinks Will Rogers is a clown accepts Huey Long as a statesman."

But Roosevelt was the man of the hour. Two years younger than Will, he had risen rapidly in the Democratic party, serving in the New York State legislature and as assistant secretary of the navy before receiving the vice-presidential nomination at the age of thirty-eight. The loss in the 1920 campaign was followed by personal calamity the next year, as he was stricken with polio and paralyzed from the waist down. Through sheer perseverance, he recovered the partial use of his legs, and, where previously he had struck many as a callow child of privilege, he emerged from the ordeal with a new and unmistakable authority and presence. While he held no office until 1928, he maintained and solidified his standing in the party, chiefly through his rousing nominating speeches for Al Smith at the 1924 and 1928 conventions. As Will had recognized, his overwhelming reelection as New York governor in 1930 had pegged him as the Democrats' strongest candidate in an election that, because of the Depression, appeared unlosable.

But when the first ballot was taken in Chicago on June 30, 1932, Roosevelt was still short of the necessary two-thirds of the vote; both Smith (now his bitter rival) and Garner (running with the support of

William Randolph Hearst) received significant support. Oklahoma's twenty-two votes had been pledged to its eccentric governor, William "Alfalfa Bill" Murray, who had served with Clem Rogers at the constitutional convention of 1907. During the second ballot, Murray stood up and announced he was throwing the votes to "that sterling citizen, that wise philosopher, that great heart, that favorite son of Oklahoma, Will Rogers." At that very moment, Will was in the press box, fast asleep. "He came out of the trance dazed but smiling," reported *Editor and Publisher,* "and let out a long, loud laugh when he learned what had happened." Oklahoma switched its votes from Rogers to Roosevelt on the third ballot, and the New York governor won on the fourth. On hearing the news, Roosevelt took an airplane from New York to Chicago—the first presidential candidate to fly. He chose Garner for his running mate.

Will made no official endorsement, but there wasn't a soul in the country who thought he preferred Hoover. When Roosevelt went to Los Angeles in September, it was Will who introduced him to the cheering crowd of more than eighty-thousand at Olympic Stadium. "This is the biggest audience in the world that ever paid to see a politician," Will said as Roosevelt lifted back his head and roared with laughter. "Franklin—I can call you Franklin, for I knew you before you were Governor or even Assistant Secretary of the Navy. I knew you when you first started in your career of nominating Al Smith for office. As a young man, you used to come to the Follies, and I would call on you from the stage to say a few words, and you would get up and nominate Al Smith for something."

After the expected landslide, Will typed out the draft of a night letter to the President-elect in Warm Springs, Georgia, where he regularly repaired for the healing waters. It is an extraordinary document, displaying not only Will's affection and concern for Roosevelt but also his own unique position in the country. If anyone could presume to sit a President-elect down and give him some fatherly advice, it was Will Rogers. "I dident wire you on your election because I knew you wasent reading any of em anyhow," he began.

> Now that all the folks that want something are about through congratulating you I thought maby a wire just wishing you could do something for the country when you get in, and not wishing anything for me, well I thought the novelty of a wire like that, when it was backed up by the facts, might not be unwelcome.
>
> Your health is the main thing. Dont worry too much. A

smile in the White House again (by the way when was the last one?) why it will look like a meal too us. Its the biggest job in the world, but you got the most help in the world to assist you. Pick you some good men, and make em responsible for their end. If Europe dont pay up, fire your sectry of the treasurer and get one that will make em pay. If people are starving and your granaries are full, thats your secretary of agricultures business is too feed em. If Nicaragua wants to hold an election, send em your best wishes but no Marines. Dissarm with the rest of the world, but not without it. And kid Congress and the Senate, dont scold em. They are just children thats never grown up, they dont like to be corrected in company. Dont send messages to em, send candy. Let your secretary of state burn up the notes that come from Europe, dont you have to attend to a little thing like that. Europes not going to do what they "threaten to do," all those things are just something to give diplomats an excuse for existing. Dont let these state governors like Pinchot, and all those get in your hair. A state is too the federal government, what an "honery" relation is too any of us. The more you do for em the more they expect. Keep off the radio till you got something to say, if its a year. Be good to the press boys in Washington, for they are getting those "Merry Go Rounds" out every few weeks now. Stay off of that back lawn with those photographers unless you got a Helen Wills. Or your fifth couzin, Alice Longworth. Nothing will kill off interest in a president quicker than "weeklys" with chamber of commerces, and womens political organizations. Now if some guy comes running into your office telling you "what Wall Street was doing" that day, tell him "Wall Street? Why there is 115 million of my subjects that dont know if Wall Street is a thoroghfare, or a new mouth wash, its happenings dont interest me." Why Govenor you can go in there and have a good time. We want our president to have some fun, too many of our presidents mistake the appointment as being to the Vatican and not to just another American home.

And about people wanting jobs, just pass them on down to the next in line, and there is so many working for the government, that by the time they reach the lowest government employee, why the applicant will be beyond the government age limit. Why you handled more different kinds of people as govenor of New York than you will have in the U.S. and if Tammany comes around telling you "what they did," you just tell em, "Yeah?, I know what you did, and thats why you better keep quiet." So go in there and handle this thing just like it was another job. Work it so when we see you in person or pictures, we will smile with you, and be glad with you. We dont want to kill our presidents, but it just seems our presidents want to die for us. If we are going to blow up as a country lets be good sports and blow up with a smile.

Now if you dont like these rules I can send you some more, but you will get the next bunch collect. Just dont get panicky. All you have to do is manage 120 million "hoodlums," and the higher educated they are the bigger hoodlums they are, and the harder to manage. The illiterate ones will all work, and you will have no trouble with them, but watch the ones that are smart, for they have been taught in school they are too live off these others. In fact this last paragraph is about all that is the matter with our country.

Yours with all good wishes,
Will Rogers.

ROOSEVELT was inaugurated on March 4. The following day, invoking emergency powers, he declared a national bank holiday. Will was impressed. "America hasn't been as happy in three years as they are today," he wrote in his daily telegram.

> No money, no banks, no work, no nothing, but they know they got a man in there who is wise to Congress, wise to our big bankers and wise to our so-called big men.
>
> The whole country is with him. Even if what he does is wrong they are with him. Just so he does something. If he burned down the Capitol we would cheer and say, "Well, we at least got a fire started anyhow." We have had years of "Don't rock the boat," go on and sink it if you want to, we just as well be swimming as what we are.

Not surprisingly, FDR's usurpation of legislative authority struck a responsive chord with Will. In the middle of March, Roosevelt more or less unilaterally effected a modification of the Volstead Act, permitting the sale of beer, and Will could only shake his editorial head: "It just shows you what a country can do when you take their affairs out of the hands of Congress." Will liked everything about Roosevelt. On April 30, he began a Sunday-evening network radio program and devoted his talk to the President, concluding, "That bird has done more for us in seven weeks than we've done for ourselves in seven years." A few weeks later, he compared the President to Moses and said, "He swallowed our depression. He has inhaled fear and exhaled confidence."

One of the things Roosevelt's Hundred Days made clear was that he was a new kind of President, a President who was not formal or distant or unapproachable in any way, yet who retained an unmistakable dignity, compassion, and sense of purpose. He conducted himself, as Will had advised, in a manner that made people happy when they saw him. Roosevelt's greatest innovation in the area of communications actually went against Will's counsel to stay off the radio for a year. He had his first Fireside Chat on March 12, and the way his voice came into the nation's living rooms bolstered the sense people had that he was trying to reach out to them personally. In truth, he had not a little in common with Will Rogers, his fellow radio communicator. FDR's second Fireside Chat was scheduled to air Sunday, May 7, after Will's own program. When the Rogers show was over, the White House phoned NBC and said the President wanted to know what Will had said; could a transcript of his remarks be read over the phone? The parallels between President and humorist were so striking that a guest on his show once remarked to Will, "Some people are wondering if the President is writing your speeches or you're writing the President's speeches."

Roosevelt boosted the nation's morale. His decisive moves did give it a much-needed display of direction and action in the White House. But the fact remained that they did not immediately (or even gradually) end the Depression. Nineteen thirty-three, 1934, and 1935 were hard years, better only marginally, if it all, than their predecessors. A reader of Will's columns of that period would have no way of knowing this. Over the previous two and a half years, he had repeatedly decried the plight of the poor, the hungry, and the unemployed; now, it was as if they suddenly had money, food, and jobs.

Will had made such a turnabout once before—in 1908, when an acceptance of his marriage proposal by Betty Blake was followed by the permanent disappearance of the despair and emotional frenzy of the preceding months. His foray into advocacy had been provoked by extraordinary circumstance, and was as anomalous and uncomfortable as his soul-baring had been. He gratefully seized on Roosevelt as a savior, and he turned his attention to other things.

WITH WILEY POST AT FAIRBANKS, ALASKA,
JUST BEFORE TAKEOFF

CHAPTER 13

CEILING
ZERO

I an glad to see that you are riding the airlines. I hope you either take
up parachute jumping or stay out of single motored planes at night.

—CHARLES LINDBERGH TO WILL ROGERS,

MAY 17, 1933

That Post is just full of determination. I would hate to tell him he
couldent do anything.

—WILL ROGERS, JULY 19, 1931

A fellow can't afford to die now with all this excitement going on.

—WILL ROGERS, JUNE 30, 1935

THAT THE Depression was not personally disastrous for Will was due
largely to Bernard Baruch. Even as they were making plans to settle on
the Pacific Palisades property, Will and Betty continued buying land
elsewhere. By the middle of 1928, they owned twelve separate pieces of
California real estate, including nearly half a mile of Pacific beachfront
property north of the mouth of Santa Monica Canyon; its total value,
according to Will and Betty's (presumably optimistic) estimate, was $4.15
million. *Owned* might not be quite the right word, for the land was highly
mortgaged. They owed more than $1.4 million on it, which worked out
to interest payments totaling nearly $66,000 for the year.

In the spring of 1929, Will approached Baruch for some free advice.
The Fox contract, added to his McNaught fees, would guarantee him a

sizable amount of money over the course of the next year and a half, some $900,000. Will owned not a single stock (his net worth, other than his real estate, amounted to less than $200,000 in a bank account), but now he thought it might be time to venture into the market like everybody else. "I looked at him and said, 'What you want to do is gamble,'" recalled Baruch. "'But I want to tell you that you're sitting on a volcano. That's all right for professional volcano sitters, like myself, but an amateur like you ought to take to the tall timber and get as far away as you can. There may come a time when the man who holds your mortgage will want his money and you may not have it, and your friends won't have it, either.'" Will, no doubt relieved to have his own innate distrust of financial speculation confirmed, took the advice.

The Depression did depress Will's movie earnings, his per-picture fee dropping from a high of $187,500 to $100,000 and then, in the contract he signed early in 1934, to $88,000.* But he still made $324,314 from Fox in 1934; only one American, Thomas Watson of IBM, had higher corporate earnings.

By that time, moreover, Will had found a new source of income: the radio. In 1930, for a series of twelve fifteen-minute talks, the Squibb company paid him $77,000—almost as much, as *The New York Times* noted, as Babe Ruth's annual salary. Two years later, he agreed to be a regular on "Ziegfeld's Follies of the Air," one of the ailing impresario's last ventures. Unfortunately, the tight format of the show—Will's segment, done from a Los Angeles studio (the rest of the performances emanated from New York), was allotted just four minutes—did not suit him. Each of the first two weeks he ran over, and the sponsor, Chrysler, sent a man named Al Weeks out to California to rein him in. As the four-minute mark neared on that week's program, Weeks gestured to Will to wrap it up; Will waved him away. So, when his time expired, Weeks went into the control room and cut him off, right in the middle of a sentence. Will kept right on talking, not finding out what had happened until he got home after the show. Professional pride bested personal loyalty, and he promptly sent Weeks a three-word telegram: GET ANOTHER BOY.

He found his platform in the spring of 1933, when the Gulf Oil

---

*Also relevant were Fox's internal difficulties. In 1930, William Fox, unable to refinance his sizable loans because of the stock market crash, was forced to sell the company to his creditors. It lost $19.9 million in 1932. The company never recovered its financial footing, and in May 1935 merged with thirty-three-year-old Darryl F. Zanuck's fledgling Twentieth Century Pictures, Zanuck (a polo crony of Will's) becoming vice president and head of production of the new Twentieth Century–Fox. Winfield Sheehan left two months after the merger, with a cash settlement of $360,000 in hand.

Company signed him for a weekly half-hour live Sunday evening series called "The Good Gulf Show." Gulf paid him fifty thousand dollars for the first seven weeks; in a gesture that was probably born as much from superstition as goodwill, he gave half to the Red Cross and half to the Salvation Army. The show was a rousing hit and continued for the rest of Will's life.

The program would normally originate from Los Angeles, but radio technology had progressed sufficiently that on a given week Will's contribution could be transmitted from wherever he might happen to be. When the commercials, the introductions, and the musical contributions of an orchestra and quartet were taken into account, he was left with twelve to fifteen minutes to fill, a comfortable allotment. Even so, he had a tough time bringing himself to a halt. He solved the problem on his second program by taking an alarm clock into the studio and setting it to ring at the end of his segment. "When that alarm goes off, I am going to stop, that is all there is to it," he told his listeners. "I don't care whether I am in the middle of reciting 'Gunga Din' or the Declaration of Independence, I am going to stop when that rings." Will's "famous alarm clock" (as his announcer soon started to call it) became his trademark for a new generation of fans, just as his lasso and chewing gum had been for their parents. It was more functional than either of them: Only rarely did he exhaust his material before the sound of the bell. And it was also an objective correlative of his own modesty. Let people like Huey Long and the reactionary demagogue Father Coughlin—even like Franklin D. Roosevelt—be carried away with their own words and importance, the clock seemed to say. Here was a radio talker so humble that he would gladly let himself be interrupted in the middle of a sentence by a mechanical device.

The radio was a challenge for another reason: It didn't permit the performer access to his listeners' reactions. This didn't matter much for a singer; for a comedian—especially one like Will, who depended on audience interplay—it was like trying to walk a tightrope with a blindfold on. "On the stage when you tell anything and it gets a laugh why naturally you kinder wait till the laugh is over, and then go on," Will wrote after an early broadcast. "Well that little microphone that you are talking into, it's not going to laugh, so you don't know when you tell anything whether to wait for the laugh, or just go right on." For "Good Gulf," he eventually dealt with the issue by bringing an audience into the studio. (He found the remedy imperfect, complaining on the air that the audience members "laugh at the serious parts for fear they won't be invited again.")

In general, though, the radio was a piece of cake for Will. He had been talking to audiences for nearly thirty years, and the fact that he now had millions of listeners and was being paid more than seven thousand dollars per broadcast wasn't about to make him nervous. One Sunday afternoon, he lost track of time while he was in the roping corral, then suddenly realized he needed to leave for the studio. Fifty-five years later, Emil Sandmeier, the major domo at the ranch, recalled the day. "Mr. Rogers said, 'Since you're here, why don't you drop in and drive? I haven't had a free moment to think of what I'm going to say tonight.' We got stuck behind a streetcar and Mr. Rogers said, 'I have a good notion to ask you to phone. On second thought, keep on going.' When we arrived at the studio, he got out of the car, walked up on the stage and started talking." Will was actually five minutes late. To fill time, J. Frank Drake, the president of Gulf, who happened to be in the audience that day, had been telling a humorous story.

There was no one like Will on the radio. All of the other early comedy programs—Jack Benny's, Ed Wynn's and Fred Allen's shows, "Amos 'n' Andy"—were tightly scripted. During the week, Will would jot down ideas and practice making his points in front of family and friends, but in front of the microphone he would throw away his notes and launch into a more or less free-form stream of consciousness. As a result, his broadcasts were full of *you know's* and *well's*, rampaging non sequiturs, infectious giggles, and mid-sentence changes of subject. Being live, they were obviously unedited as well, and they offered a less mediated, rawer version of Will than his writing did. On the radio, he didn't seem to censor himself as much. He certainly never went on record with a more biting assessment of America's treatment of the Indians than this:

> Our record with the Indians is going to go down in history. It is going to make us mighty proud of it in the future when our children of ten more generations read of what we did to them. Every man in our history that killed the most Indians has got a statue built for him. . . .
>
> The Government, by statistics, shows they have got 456 treaties that they have broken with the Indians. That is why the Indians get a kick out of reading the Government's usual remark when some big affair comes up, "Our honor is at stake."
>
> Every time the Indians move the Government will give them a treaty. They say, "You can have this ground as long as grass grows and water flows." On account of its being a grammatical error, the Government didn't have to live up to it. It

didn't say "flown" or "flew" or something. Now they have moved the Indians and they settled the whole thing by putting them on land where the grass won't grow and the water won't flow, so now they have it all set.

On at least one occasion, he *should* have been censored. Talking about a popular song called "The Last Round-up," he said that the tune was "really a nigger spiritual." He repeated the offensive word three more times. NBC's New York headquarters was deluged with telephone and telegraph protests, which took Will aback. "I wasn't only raised among darkies down in Indian Territory," he said on his next show by way of defense, "I was raised *by* them. And Lord, I was five years out on the ranch before I ever knew there was a white child."*

There were no such things as ratings in the early days of radio, so it's impossible to know precisely how many people heard Will's broadcasts, which continued until June 1935. But in all probability they exposed him to a larger audience than any other medium. Radio had been embraced by the country, and NBC and the Columbia Broadcasting System were the only two networks. Will didn't have the immense popularity of "Amos 'n' Andy," for whose antics he and everybody else in America stopped what they were doing, but the anecdotal evidence suggests that he wasn't far behind. The first week he went on the air, a minister reported a drop of 50 percent in Sunday-evening church attendance. To counter such defections, another church placed a radio in the chapel and tuned it to Will's broadcast.

*He undertook a lengthier defense of his race-relations record in a telegram to a black man who had written him a letter about the issue. In his enthusiasm about the song, he explained, he "reverted to the word that I had used since childhood down home, with never a thought of disrespect. I want to say this Mr Tobias, I think you folks are wrong in jumping too hastily onto someone or anyone who might use the word with no more thought or belittlement than I did. There is millions in the south use that word, and if the race has more real friends among millions of people down there I dont know where it is. I am offering no excuse for using it myself, I was wrong, but its the intention and not the wording that you must look for. What in the world, what particle of action had ever lead a single Negro to believe that I hadent the best wishes toward their race? . . .

"A colored cowpuncher taught me how to rope, and I contributed to him and his wife, and went out of my way to drive by and see them every time I went to my home in Okla. Up to the time of their death, he never worked for a soul during his whole lifetime but us. All these things make this criticism the more unfair and hard on me. If there is a colored performer (I might have known in the old vaudeville days and I knew many) if there is a Negro porter, waiter, or any one of your race, that I have come in contact with in all my years, if you or anyone else can find a onc that will say that I ever by action, or word ever did one thing to humiliate, or show in any way that I was antagonistic to them, I will, ah well I would do anything, for you cant find em, for I never did."

• • •

NINETEEN THIRTY-THREE marked a new stage in Will's film career. *State Fair,* based on a novel by Phil Stong (and twice remade into
a Rodgers and Hammerstein musical), was about an Iowa family's gently
momentous week at the fair. Will, as the father, was part of a strong ensemble cast that included Janet Gaynor, Lew Ayres, and Louise Dresser,
and for long stretches of time he was offscreen. (He was paid only fifty
thousand dollars, about half his regular rate.) While his character was
not without humor, most of it stemming from his undue affection for his
nine-hundred-pound hog, Blue Boy, the film—exquisitely photographed
by Hal Mohr, who would shoot two subsequent Rogers pictures—was
an atmospheric, idyllic piece of Americana. Fox's first production to
open at Radio City Music Hall, *State Fair* brought 1.5 million much-
needed dollars into the studio. And it helped Will's standing among the
critics, who appreciated that for the first time he was playing a real character, not just a slightly camouflaged version of himself. Richard Watts,
writing in the New York *Herald Tribune,* was relieved that Will had been
"divorced from the necessity of being the Homespun Philosopher and,
therefore, no longer forced to carry the destiny of America on his
back."

State Fair set the pattern followed by all but a few of the later Rogers
films. The setting is an idealized America—sometimes an edenic
nineteenth-century land of county picnics and soda fountains and comical darkies, sometimes a contemporary small town so picturesque as to
induce anachronistic nostalgia. The jokes are subservient to the setting.
Will himself is usually a bachelor or widower, free from the tiresome
wives of the earlier films, and free to act as a front-porch Prospero, genially stage-managing the melodramatic intrigues and romantic shenan-
igans that swirl around him. The public liked what it saw: It was with
this new model of film that Will jumped to the top of the motion-picture
exhibitors' poll of top box-office attractions. His pictures of this period
consistently brought in rentals of over a million dollars to Fox.

The Will Rogers persona of these films constituted the second movement of his response to the Depression. The hard times will pass, the
movies implicitly but firmly insisted; behold the real and enduring
America. And behold the real American—trustworthy, wry, incapable of
panic—in the person of Will Rogers. "They give a comfortable feeling,
these Rogers comedies," wrote an unusually perceptive reviewer, "about
the solidity and innate common sense of this country. . . . Will Rogers,
although very much himself in each scene in each film, has a curious na-

tional quality. He gives the impression somehow that this country is filled with such sages, wise in years, young in humor and love of life, shrewd yet gentle. He is what Americans think other Americans are like."

In most of the films, the contrast with the country's present straits is implied. In Fox's adaptation of the enormously popular novel *David Harum,* released early in 1934 and set in upstate New York during the panic of 1893, the point is directly made. Unable to find work in the city, the youthful hero repairs to the country town of Homeville, where one of the town elders says, "I tell you these panics come in cycles every twenty-one years." No great mathematical expertise is needed to ascertain that this takes us up to the present. So the Depression could have been predicted back in the nineteenth century, and therefore is not cause for alarm. And kindly Will Rogers, as horse trader David Harum, has a further message for us: "A panic is just like a war. You can talk your way in, but you've got to fight your way out. . . . The government has to spend some money. . . . I bet you this fellow [ostensibly Grover Cleveland, implicitly Franklin Roosevelt] will pull us through and we'll live to see the day when we'll have 100 million people in this country, and we'll have trouble remembering just when this panic was."

Not surprisingly, the palliative message drew fire from critics on the Left. "At a time when the American farmer is faced with ruin, when the whole Middle West is seething with bitterness and economic discontent, a movie like 'State Fair' is an insulting 'let 'em eat cake' gesture," wrote young Dwight Macdonald. "The vaudeville rusticity of millionaire Will Rogers, the 'cute' doll face of Janet Gaynor—thus Hollywood embodies the farmer." More recently, David Thomson—one of the few contemporary critics to pay attention to Will Rogers films—has written, "Rogers' philosophy was reactionary, dispiriting and provincial, despite every affectation of bonhomie and tolerance. It scorned ideas and people who held them, it relied on vague evolution rather than direct action, its fixed smile concealed rigidity of opinion that middle America need not be disturbed from its own prejudices and limitations."

These attacks, though intemperate, are to some extent justified by the late Rogers films, with three exceptions—his collaborations with John Ford. Born Sean Aloysius O'Feeney in Cape Elizabeth, Maine, Ford had been a contract director at Fox for a decade when he was assigned to work on Will's follow-up to *State Fair, Dr. Bull,* a story of a small-town New England physician. Ford, at thirty-eight, was about to enter the first great phase of his career—in the next decade he would direct *The Informer, How Green Was My Valley, Young Mr. Lincoln, The Grapes of Wrath,* and *Stagecoach*—and he and Will were poised to bring out the best in each other. The director's ability to play the cards of skepticism and sentimentality simultaneously and his complicated, deeply held feelings about the nature of male valor led him away from the easy reassurances that Will's directors and writers usually found so tempting. The New Winton, Connecticut, of *Dr. Bull* is peopled by pinched-faced gossips and scowling businessmen, a gallery of grotesques that Ford, like Bosch or Fellini, employed to express his view of some aspects of society. They make the crotchety Bull's life a trial. Sipping cider and singing old ballads with widow Cardmaker—this is the only Will Rogers film where he is permitted a girlfriend—the doctor says, "I kind of relax when I get up on these windswept hills with thee. . . . Some old settler had it right. Life is like a storm. You need a harbor."

Bull is no saint, grumbling when he gets calls from patients, sometimes dismissing them with a prescription of castor oil. Exasperated with the jerky soda jerk played by Andy Devine, he tells him to shut up; when he is falsely accused by the townspeople of allowing a typhoid epidemic, he gets up in a town meeting and calls them "grinning baboons." But, in Will's finely delineated performance, he is also a genuinely good man, concerned about the welfare of his patients and in touch with the rhythms of the universe. "I've seen a hundred people die," he says, "and none of them seem to mind it."

The next year's Ford-Rogers collaboration was sunnier. Based on a series of *Saturday Evening Post* stories by Will's friend Irvin S. Cobb, "the Sage of Paducah," and set in 1890 Kentucky, *Judge Priest* is a misty-eyed depiction of life in the Old South. Thus mint juleps are ubiquitous and the only blacks in evidence are shuffling Stepin Fetchit and the bandanna-wearing, spiritual-singing Hattie McDaniel. Yet it is part of the movie's charm that the extremely loose-constructionist jurist played by Will relates to these characters with an affectionate, not unrespectful give-and-take. (Asked about his and Will's apparent improvisation, Fetchit, who was also featured in *David Harum* and *Steamboat Round the Bend,* told a reporter, "Paht of the time he suhprises me. Paht of the time I suhprise him. But mos' of the time we suhprises each other." "If you put anyting I say in the papah," he rather astonishingly added, "it might be wise to kind of transpose it into my dialeck.") The plot concerns the unjust prosecution and near-conviction of Gillis, a mysterious stranger in town; as in *Dr. Bull,* society is seen as potentially malevolent. But here, Billy Priest is able to overcome the forces of intolerance, Gillis is acquitted, and everyone joins to march in the Confederate Memorial Day parade.

Will did his most impressive acting to date in *Judge Priest,* his presence establishing the elegiac tone and mood of the entire film. In two separate scenes, he was asked to make a lengthy speech to his dead wife's portrait and grave, a formidable assignment he carried off convincingly. *Judge Priest*—which Ford late in his life said was his personal favorite among his works—also stands as one of the few Rogers films whose humor approaches the wry sublety of Will's own. At one point, a superannuated veteran, caught in an enervating web of nostalgia like nearly everybody else in the town, recites the story of his War of the Rebellion heroism for what must be the thousandth time. Judge Priest takes it all in, pauses in appreciation, then remarks, "Puttin' them gunboats in there was a new touch."

There was a good reason why Will's work was so accomplished in *Judge Priest.* He had been practicing. In the spring of 1934, a California theatrical producer named Henry Duffy asked him to appear on the stage in a West Coast production of *Ah, Wilderness!*—a Eugene O'Neill comedy (the only one he ever wrote) that had been running in New York since the fall. As Duffy realized, the role of Nat Miller, a small-town newspaper owner that was being played on Broadway by George M. Cohan, could not have fit Will better if it had been written expressly for him. After a good deal of deliberation—this would, after all, be his first straight play, an undertaking not to be taken lightly at the age of fifty-four—Will agreed.

Set on the Fourth of July, 1906, *Ah, Wilderness!* mainly concerns itself with sixteen-year-old Richard Miller, a devotee of Shaw, Ibsen, and, the *Rubáiyát* of Omar Khayyam (which provides the title) who in the course of a long day's journey into night comes to some new understandings about sex, love, his family, and life. But Nat Miller—described in O'Neill's stage directions as having "fine, shrewd, humorous gray eyes"—appears in all but two scenes and, though nowhere near perfect, grounds the play with his decency and wisdom. While the part was clearly of a piece with Will's recent movie roles, the additional challenge was to submerge his character in the bittersweet mood masterfully created by O'Neill, all the while projecting to the last row. Fortunately, he had a sympathetic and vastly experienced coach: Fred Stone, who was visiting at the time and helped him rehearse as they went for endless drives in the California countryside, searching for the perfect ranch. The production opened in San Francisco on April 30, and two of the many telegrams that came to the theater had special meaning: one from the playwright, who wanted Will to know Nat Miller was his favorite part of all the ones he had written, and one from his daughter Mary, who had just started a season of summer stock in Maine. THERE IS ROOM IN THE LEGIT, she wired, FOR TWO ROGERS.*

Will and the play each made a great success. The opening was an event of such magnitude that *The New York Times* ran a review, describing Will as playing "with a simple sincerity that brought out handkerchiefs and made tears and smiles mingle." Will's reputation as an improviser was now well known, and the critics were especially impressed with the fact that he gamely stuck to the text. After three weeks in San Francisco, the production moved on to Los Angeles, where the reception was equally enthusiastic. Will agreed to continue with the play even after filming began on *Judge Priest,* and the planned three-week run was extended to six. *Variety* reported that the play grossed a total of $190,000—the most lucrative production ever staged on the West Coast—and "could have continued indefinitely."

Film rights to *Ah, Wilderness!* were purchased by MGM, with production slated for 1935. It would have been logical to assume that Will would re-create his role—Fox would doubtless have been willing to lend him to another studio—yet "for some reason," a newspaper reported in December, he was "reluctant" to participate. "Once he went to Winfield Sheehan . . . and asked his help in getting out of the picture." His efforts were successful; when the film came out in late 1935, Lionel Barrymore was in the part of Miller. (Mickey Rooney was young Richard.) The only explanation for Will's absence comes from Eddie Cantor, who wrote that his friend decided not to do the film after receiving a letter from a clergyman who had taken his fourteen-year-old daughter to see the play and was shocked at the scene just before the curtain in which Nat attempts to explain certain facts of life to Richard. Cantor did not say where he got his information. Yet Will's participation in the scene *was* a little shocking. After a lot of hemming and hawing, Nat tells his son that when the "desires of the flesh" build up to the point where they must be attended to, "a certain class of women" exists to satisfy them.

---

*Mary went directly from a Canadian tour in Robert Sherwood's play *Reunion in Vienna* to a summer with the Lakewood Players, which specialized in employing the sons and daughters of theatrical notables. (Others in the company included the offspring of Ed Wynn, Owen Davis, and Arthur Byron.) But Mary, it was becoming clear, had no need to rely on the family name. Alexander Dean of Yale's Department of Drama (unsuccessfully) tried to lure her down to New Haven during the summer for two repertory parts, and the following February she made her Broadway debut in a comedy called *On to Fortune*. In the *Herald*, Percy Hammond wrote, "It is, perhaps, news to announce that Miss Mary Rogers, daughter of Will Rogers, makes a successful debut as a tactful and decorative ingenue, and that she doesn't in the least look like her father."

"You just have what you want and pay 'em and forget it." It is plausible that even though Will was willing to say those words to thousands, he would have resisted saying them to millions. (He certainly was sensitive to the issue of decency, crossing out the phrase, "Why, you old damned fool" in his copy of the script and replacing it with, "Don't be silly, Dave.") If he had agreed to be in the film, he would have been on location in Massachusetts in the first week of August 1935. Instead, he was in Alaska, on his way to Siberia with Wiley Post.

BUT THAT WAS more than a year away. Will had once written: "Well, after I finish a long siege I sorter begin to look up in the sky and see what is flying over," and the completion of *Judge Priest*, in early July, was the end of a particularly long siege. He took to the air. First stop was Ewing Halsell's ranch in Texas for some calf branding, then Claremore, then Washington, D.C., and finally Waterville, Maine, where he saw Mary perform for the first time. But that was only a warm-up for a two-month, around-the-world trip he, Betty, Bill, and Jim embarked on a week after arriving back home. From Hawaii (where Will and Betty had dinner with President and Mrs. Roosevelt), they proceeded to Tokyo. A representative of a local English-language newspaper met them and reported the following: "With that proverbial outburst of laughter, after rubbing his chin as you often see on the screen, he made a statement, 'We are going to stay several days in Tokyo and see places whence as we extend our trip to Soviet Russia. Don't worry, boys, I won't ever be "Red." Ha! Ha! Ha!'

"Though Mr. Rogers looked older with more gray hairs on the head, he seemed to be the incarnation of youth with his peps [sic]."

This same reporter may have been one of two shown with Will in a Hearst newsreel. "Mr. Roosevelt told me, 'Will, don't you jump on Japan,' " Will is seen telling the unamused pair. " 'You just keep them from jumping on *us.*' "

By way of Korea, the party toured Will's old haunt of Manchuria, then boarded the Trans-Siberian Express in Manzhouli. Boredom loomed menacingly, and nineteen-year-old Jim Rogers had armed himself with a copy of *Mutiny on the Bounty*, settling into it as the train approached the Russian border. When his father saw the title of the book, he grabbed it and threw it out the window, saying, "We don't take that kind of book into Russia."

"But this is *Mutiny on the Bounty*—Captain Bly, Mr. Christian, the British Navy," protested Jim.

"I don't care," Will said. "We don't take it."

From Novosibirsk, in central Siberia, they were supposed to fly to Moscow, but when they arrived there was no plane. "So for six days," recalled Betty, "we were cooped up in a tiny compartment with a big basket of oranges, a purchased stock of canned goods and a little canned-heat outfit for brewing tea." Will, putting a bright face on the ordeal, told his readers, "it's a great trip, only way to go around the world; fine train, great diner, food enough for Primo Carnera."

Jim was enrolled at the Webb School in Claremont, California, for the fall and Bill was to start his senior year at Stanford, so, while their parents toured Russia and Europe (seeing Scandinavia for the first time), the boys traveled back to the United States in early September. When they arrived at the ranch, they were surprised to find two house guests: Charles and Anne Lindbergh. Bruno Richard Hauptmann had just been arrested for the kidnapping and murder of their son, and Will had trans-atlantically offered them the use of the ranch as an escape from the reporters who were hounding their every move. Word of their presence got out in the course of their two-week stay, and, while no reporters penetrated the ranch, a group of them was always camped out at the gate on Beverly Boulevard, waiting for the inevitable day when the Lindberghs would leave. But they were foiled. Emil Sandmeier hatched a plan to put the couple in the Model A and drive them on horse paths through the canyon to a neighboring property, from which they could exit undetected. On their return to the East, where Hauptmann's trial was about to begin, Anne Lindbergh wrote Betty, "Perhaps Charles and I appreciated the place especially because it was so quiet and far away and protected that we felt completely private and free."

Will couldn't have purposely timed it that way, but he and Betty disembarked in New York just in time for two of the most exciting weeks in the history of baseball. September 30 was the last day of the season, and the National League pennant race between St. Louis and New York still had not been decided. If the Giants could beat the Brooklyn Dodgers, they still had a chance to tie the Cardinals. But the Dodgers would not yield easily. They remembered that even before the season started, Giants manager Bill Terry, asked whether he feared Brooklyn, had uttered the immortal question: "Is Brooklyn still in the league?" Will was in the Polo Grounds stands that day as the Dodgers, under manager Casey Stengel, got their revenge, 8 to 5.

He was pleased that it was the Cardinals who would face the Detroit Tigers in the World Series, because the team was led by his favorite ballplayer—Jay Hanna "Dizzy" Dean. Born in Arkansas, raised in Oklahoma, malaprop-spouting, fun-loving, braggadocious, and tremendously skilled, Dizzy was widely hailed as Babe Ruth's successor as the country's most popular ballplayer. He and Will had never met but (unsurprisingly) were enthusiastic mutual admirers. "He is sho chockful of personality and he is boastful," Will wrote of the twenty-four-year-old pitcher, "but it's not in a fresh way. It's in a kidding way, and he is what they call a natural ball player."

"There ain't been nobody like Will since them old times," Dizzy said by way of returning the compliment.

On October 3, the morning of the first game of the World Series, they shared a breakfast table in the Book-Cadillac Hotel in Detoit with Hearst columnist Damon Runyon and Dizzy's brother Paul, also a Cardinals pitcher. Dizzy ordered three eggs, bacon, biscuits, gravy, milk, orange juice, and coffee. Will, taking only grapefruit juice because he was trying to reduce, said just two kinds of people could eat that much and get away with it: cotton pickers and opera singers.

Caught up in the excitement of the Series, which was the first to be broadcast nationally and was attended by such notables as actors Joe E. Brown and George Raft and Father Coughlin, Will was present for five of its seven games. In Detroit, he sat with Henry and Edsel Ford in their box. And before and after every game he visited in the Cardinals' dressing room. The back-and-forth Series concluded with an anticlimactically lopsided St. Louis victory behind Dizzy in game seven, the only excitement coming from a fight in the seventh inning between the Cardinals' Ducky Medwick and the Tigers' Marvin Owen that was followed by a near-riot by the frustrated Detroit fans. To prevent catastrophe, Commissioner Kenesaw Mountain Landis removed Medwick from the game. Will immediately went to the Cardinals' locker room to get Medwick's side of the story. When the game was over, he went to see Owen. "I believe I am the only fellow," he wrote, "who talked with both boys in their dressing rooms directly after the game."

Dean's sudden prominence was an example of what was proving to be a signal quality of the new mass culture: a great alacrity in the manufacture of celebrities. This suited Will wonderfully, of course. He got great mileage out of Mae West, she of the capacious bosom and unlimited double entendres, out of the fugitive John Dillinger, and out of the renowned aviatrix Amelia Earhart (she was his guest one Sunday at the ranch). Upton Sinclair, the novelist who ran for governor in 1934 on the socialistic End Poverty in California ticket, also made good copy. Although business interests, including the motion-picture studios, aggressively opposed Sinclair, and likely denied him the victory, Will was evenhanded. Sinclair was "a darn nice fellow," he wrote just before the election, "and just plum smart, and if he could deliver some of the things he promises, should not only be governor of one state, but president of all of 'em."

The anti-Sinclair forces posited a direct pipeline between the white-haired author and the Kremlin. Earl Warren, for example, a young attorney who had just been named state Republican chairman, declared that "The battle is between two conflicting philosophies of government—one that is proud of our flag, our governmental institutions, the other that glorifies the Red Flag of Russia and hopes to establish on American soil a despotism based upon class hatred and tyranny." Will, of course, would have none of this red-baiting nonsense. "There's some pretty smart birds over there in Russia," he told his radio audience, "and they're not sending any dough to some soapbox orator over here—they know that this country is hopeless as far as Communism is concerned."

Best of all was Huey Long, the "Kingfish" of Louisiana, who entered the U.S. Senate in 1932 and quickly became notorious for his radical Every Man a King platform and his endless filibusters. Will immediately saw that Huey (as he always called him) was bigger than life, full of bluster and hokum, yet not without conviction—a perfect target, in person as well as in print. Once Long was in the middle of a filibuster when Will entered the Senate gallery and began to cough and clear his throat. The senator looked up and saw Will open his jacket to reveal a vest covered with EVERY MAN A KING buttons. At that, Long lost his train of thought and had to yield the floor.

Huey liked Will, perhaps recognizing an authentic example of what he could only pretend to be. Knowing of his friendship with Jack Garner, Long asked Will to see whether he could fix it with the Vice President to recognize him on the Senate floor for a bitter speech against his archenemy Joe Robinson. (Garner agreed. When Long got up to talk, both he and Robinson picked up newspapers and buried their heads in them throughout the address.) In June 1935, without warning, President Roosevelt announced a plan to use taxation to secure a "wider distribution of wealth"—exactly what Long had been advocating for years. Three days later, Long got up on the Senate floor, pulled a clipping of Will's column out of his wallet, and recited it with delight: "I would sure liked to have seen Huey's face when he was woke in the middle of the night by the President, who said, 'Lay over, Huey, I want to get in with you.' "

As the earthiness of that conceit indicates, by now Roosevelt was no longer a sacred cow in Will's eyes. It was inevitable, of course, that New

Deal interventionism would one day become unpalatable to Will's Jeffersonian individualism. As the administration entered its third year, there were hints that this day was about to dawn. "Well the old year will be passing out in a few hours," he wrote on December 31, 1934, "and I don't know personally a thing I can do about it. I guess there will be a lot of people will take it up with the government, as they look to them to do everything else."

But they were only hints. Likewise, the other changes in Will's life as the New Year approached were not earthshaking. On the last day of January 1935, Will shook hands on a ten-picture, $1.1 million contract with Fox. So his fee was starting to climb back; better yet, he had a measure of security. With it, he embarked on a new flurry of improvements on the ranch. (The previous year, he and Betty had bought 95 adjoining acres, making a total of 339.) Added were a new sun room off the master bedroom, where Betty liked to sew and read, and a new three-bedroom second story for the old wing. In the process, the roof to the living room was raised—now Will could rope indoors. And on March 14, they took out a building permit for a three-room cabin to be built deep in Rustic Canyon, at a site reachable only by horseback. By now, Will had found that his hideout needed a hideout of its own.

His search for a ranch had not abated, either. In late February, an Arizona cattleman who had gotten wind of it wrote to tell him about his 135,000-acre spread—"one of the oldest cattle ranches in the state, and the only well watered ranches [sic] in northern part of the state, running creeks and living spring." Will was interested enough to write him back, but the $125,000 asking price may have been a little steep.

Contributing to his desire for getaway places, no doubt, was a discovery he was making about fame: It was cumulative. Previously, he had been able to mingle with people on his travels, drawing crowds, to be sure, but never unable to come and go as he pleased. Now he was assaulted by admirers, many of them wanting him to sign his name on a slip of paper. ("There ain't any unemployed in this country," he wrote of the new fad. "That's what the so called idle are doing, is getting autographs, and say they are working 24 hours a day.") Arriving in Baton Rouge at the end of January, he was besieged by fans, the local newspaper reporting that "three times during the night he was forced to change rooms to get a little rest." The next day, as he paid a call on a local newspaper publisher, "everybody began to gather in the lobby, and everybody's friends. The place soon filled with eager spectators, little babies and businessmen, women out shopping and university students." He needed a police escort to get out of town.

Given this climate, it's not surprising that no fewer than three people should have begun work on biographies of Will Rogers. Two were young men from Oklahoma, David Milsten and Cal Tinney. The third was his cousin Spi Trent, who had moved to California, borrowed considerable money from Will, and discerned that a way to pay it back would be to accept a five-thousand-dollar advance from a publisher who wanted the inside story of the great man's youth. But Spi was not granted an audience when he went out to the ranch, possibly because the idea of someone capturing his life between covers gave Will the willies. "I am a young man (get that) yet, and I haven't even started living," he wrote in a column complaining about the "amateur Carl Sandburgs" who were hounding him for interviews. "I am going to cut loose here someday and try to get some life into my life and even then it won't be fit to tell about. Most of my life has been lived alone. I never run with a pack. In my later years Mrs. Rogers could perhaps give you a few details, but no one of my various authors have ever seen her, or asked her."

Another change was evident in Will's writing. It may not have seemed possible, but his weekly article was becoming even more lax than before. He would spend whole columns describing his mail of the week, the books on his bedside table, or merely the contents of his consciousness. But if anyone could carry off free-form writing, it was Will, as demonstrated by this inexplicably appealing paragraph from one of his February columns, talking about a man he met on a passenger airplane:

> John D. Rockefeller's son-in-law, a Mr. Milton (I am sure it was Milton, maybe it was Minoton, but I still think it was Milton), well he is the nicest fellow you ever saw. I mean he is the son-in-law of young John D. If I remember right back during the wedding I think he was a young lawyer, and his wife got in some little minor traffic jam and he defended her. (What in the world was her name? Was it Aggie?) I hollered at my wife just now to ask her if she remembered it, but she was about half asleep and I might just as well hollered at the bell hop.

His editorial flaccidity had a simple explanation. He was tired. He made five pictures in the eight months following his return from the round-the-world trip, that in addition to his radio show, columns, and trips to Washington (where he was the featured speaker at Vice President Garner's dinner for the President), Louisiana, New York (where he saw Mary's Broadway debut), Chicago, New York again (stopping in

Oklahoma on the way back), and Fort Worth. Late in March 1935, he made what turned out to be his last trip to the nation's capital. At his customary lunch with Garner, there was a new face: the freshman senator from Missouri, whom the Vice President had taken under his wing. Harry Truman felt honored by the invitation and would always cherish his memory of the day.

Will was now fifty-five years old and was starting to feel his age. One day he was roping at the ranch, with Fred Stone looking on, when his pony stumbled to its knees. In getting back up, it cracked Will on the chin with its head, causing no major injury, just some bleeding and a sense that longtime assumptions about his body's capabilities were in need of adjustment. He would take the newspapers to bed with him and wake up a few hours later, his reading barely begun, the light burning and his glasses on. A couple of years before, he'd met a young comedian and cello player named Morey Amsterdam, and occasionally he'd let Amsterdam supply the gags for his daily dispatches.

Readers and listeners who paid close attention that spring saw a good deal of Will's sentimental side. On a Mother's Day broadcast, he got so flustered that he dropped the coins he was jiggling in his hands and stooped to pick them up, resulting in a few seconds of dead air. He wrote nostalgic, emotional columns about his friend Chic Sale, his horse Dopey, his time at Kemper Military Academy, his silent pictures, and his vaudeville years. The latter topic came up during the filming of *Steamboat Round the Bend*, the last of the five films in a row and his third collaboration with John Ford, which started production in May. He played a snake-oil salesman turned steamboat captain, and the river scenes were shot on and near the Sacramento River. While the company was on location there, Will learned that his old vaudeville partner Buck McKee and his wife, Maude, were operating a riding company in the nearby town of Roseville. He went out to visit, and found a shady spot where they could escape the summer heat and talk about old times. "Buck looks fine, no older, and of course I am just practically a babe in arms yet," Will told his readers. Remembering the old days, the thought struck him that vaudeville was "the greatest form of entertainment ever conceived. Nothing in the world ever give the satisfaction of a good vaudeville show." And Buck: "He did look great when he come charging in on that stage with that beautiful brown pony."

In one scene in *Steamboat Round the Bend*, Will is the best man at the wedding of his late sister's son. It takes place in a jailhouse—the nephew is due to be executed on a trumped-up charge of murder—and a chorus of black prisoners sings softly in the background. At the point that the sheriff, played by Eugene Pallette, calls for the ring, Will was supposed to tell his nephew, "It belonged to your mother." But he was so choked with emotion that he couldn't say a word. Ford, seeing that something extraordinary was happening, kept the cameras rolling. Finally, Pallette ad-libbed a line: "It's mighty old-fashioned. Looks as if it might have belonged to your mother." Will nodded and managed to get out the faint words, "It was."*

WILEY POST was a great pilot. Of that, there is no doubt. On the day after he and Will crashed in Alaska, when questions were already being raised about whether the accident was a result of the aviator's poor judgment, Capt. Edward Rickenbacker, the great flying ace of World War I, gave an interview in which he enumerated four qualities that set Post apart from his peers. He was a natural flier—"a man born with as sensitive a touch as any aviator could develop." He had stamina—"he could take more punishment than any man I know and suffer less from it." He was fearless. And he had determination—"nothing could shake him from what he wanted to do, and he could become at will an irresistible force or an immovable object."

Born in Texas in 1899, Post moved to Oklahoma as a boy. He was working in an oil field when a man swinging a sledgehammer next to him sent a steel chip flying into his face. His eye became infected and had to be removed. (At first, he had a glass replacement, but, when he found that flying at high altitudes gave him a headache, he switched to the eye patch that became his trademark.) With the eighteen-hundred-dollar workmen's compensation money, he bought something he had wanted since he was a boy—an airplane. He painstakingly developed his depth perception, and became a barnstormer and commercial pilot. In 1931, he and a navigator, Harold Gatty, flew their plane, the *Winnie Mae*, around the world in just eight days—which beat the previous record by more than three weeks. Two years later, Post repeated the feat solo in the *Winnie Mae*, lopping almost a full day off the time. It was an astounding feat. No one made another round-the-world flight until 1938, when Howard Hughes and a crew of five did it in a little under four days. When asked how his flight compared with Post's, Hughes said, "Wiley

---

*Of all the tributes to Will after his death, John Ford's may have been the most eloquent. Route 66 was the route upon which the Dust Bowl Okies started their journeys to California, and in *The Grapes of Wrath*, Ford included a lingering close-up of a sign with the road's new name—Will Rogers Highway. It was a reminder of how much harsher the world had become, and how much it missed Will's presence.

Post's flight remains the most remarkable flight in history. It can never be duplicated. *He did it alone!* To make a trip of that kind is beyond comprehension. It's like pulling a rabbit out of a hat or sawing a woman in half."

After the solo flight, Post became interested in high-altitude flying. He unsuccessfully tried to break the altitude record of 47,000 feet, and he made four attempts at a transcontinental stratospheric flight. Although he was forced down each time, he was the first flyer to utilize the jet stream, and he developed a pressurized suit that was the direct ancestor of the suits used later by astronauts.

One day in 1925, Post was hanging around an Oklahoma City airfield with a barnstoming buddy named Burrell Tibbs when a phone call came in: Would Tibbs be able to fly someone to a nearby rodeo? The customer turned out to be Will Rogers, and, while Tibbs was preparing the plane, Will and Post got acquainted. Over the years, Will avidly followed the aviator's achievements, and became a friend; in 1931, he contributed the introduction to Post's and Gatty's book, *Around the World in Eight Days.* This despite the fact that, in all ways except his taciturnity, Post was the opposite of the princely Lindbergh. He was short, stocky, not particularly good-looking, and, because of his stubbornness, moodiness, and generally difficult temperament, not very well liked in the aviation community. An official of the National Aeronautic Association, which tracked aviation records, wrote to a colleague, "Wiley, as you no doubt have found out, is, we might say, a rather peculiar fellow when he gets the wrong idea of something. . . . In our experience we have found Wiley Post almost an impossible person to deal with."

"Wiley used to insist that the mechanics who worked on a plane go with him for a test ride," said Norman Blake, who helped construct both the *Winnie Mae* and the plane in which Post and Will made their Alaska trip. "We ran a check on the *Winnie Mae,* and we were just barely over the trees when the engine quit. It came back on just in time. When we were on the ground, Wiley said, 'I took off on an empty tank.' He wasn't too bright."

It was rumored that one of his transcontinental flights failed because a rival had put emery dust in the fuel tank. He finally gave up that quest in the spring and summer of 1935, and turned to a new project. He wanted to survey and establish a mail-and-passenger air route between the United States and Russia, by way of Alaska, and he had secured funding from one of the airlines for the trip. In a little hangar at the Lockheed Airport in Burbank, he put together a hybrid airplane, consisting of a Lockheed Orion fuselage, a custom-made, very long Lockheed wing, a 550-horsepower Wasp engine (145 pounds heavier than the original), the instrument panel from the *Winnie Mae,* a Hamilton propeller (fifty pounds heavier), and, in place of the original 160-gallon fuel tank, a tank that held 100 gallons more. Will was a frequent visitor. "Whenever Rogers had time," said director Henry King, who kept his own plane at Lockheed, "he'd run out to Burbank, and he'd sit there on the fence and crack jokes with Wiley, while Wiley was under the airplane or inside the airplane. . . . Once in a while Rogers would help him a little with something; he wouldn't know what he was doing, except hold something for Post." The plane was red and had a silver stripe across the side. Post declined the suggestion to name it after the craft in which he had circled the globe. "There was only one *Winnie Mae* and she has served her usefulness," he told a reporter. "This plane has a number. That's all that's necessary."

On June 28, Will took Post with him to a Salvation Army benefit in San Bernardino, California. Among the other performers were Leo Carillo, James Gleason, Buddy Rogers, Jane Withers, Ray Milland, dancer Rita Cansino (later to change her name to Rita Hayworth), Irvin S. Cobb, Alice Faye, and the Sons of the Pioneers. One of the members of that singing group, a young man named Leonard Slye, was so taken with Will that when, two years later, he was signed to a contract to make movie westerns, he took the name "Rogers." "Leroy" was suggested for a first name, but he didn't think it was manly enough, so he settled on "Roy."

On July 23, the Department of Commerce issued Post's plane a "restricted" license, meaning that it was not authorized to carry paying passengers, only a pilot plus a maximum of two crew members. Two days later, Post, his wife, and Will got on board and took off on a test flight, touring New Mexico and Colorado for four days. On July 31, Mr. and Mrs. Post left Los Angeles for Seattle, where more adjustments were made on the plane. Because of the conditions in Alaska, Post wanted floats, or pontoons, to be installed in place of normal landing gear. He had arranged for a loan of a set from Joe Crosson, an Alaskan pilot friend, but they had not yet arrived in Seattle and, impatient to get under way, he scavenged the pontoons from a Fokker trimotor plane. Since the Fokker was much larger than Post's hybrid, the addition aggravated an already-troubling tendency toward nose heaviness, caused by the new propeller, fuel tank, and engine.

Post originally intended to be accompanied by his wife and Fay Gillis Wells, a young aviatrix, who set out from New York to meet him in Seattle. But in Detroit, she got a call from her husband, journalist

Linton Wells, asking her to join him in covering the war in Ethiopia. "I thought for two seconds," she recalled, then she reversed her direction. Post asked Will to take her place—less for the pleasure of his company than because his original backer had backed out and he was desperate for money. The idea appealed to Will, who after his long siege of work was itching to get to the air. He and Betty had been talking about flying to Rio de Janeiro and then proceeding up the coast of Africa in a zeppelin. But Post's offer was tempting—Will had long been fascinated with Alaska, and had been frustrated the year before at not being able to see Siberia from the air. Even so, he apparently still had not decided by the time the Posts arrived in Seattle: In an interview they gave on Friday, August 2, there was no mention of any participation in the trip by Will. But the next day, Will and Betty each signed a one-page will, leaving all of their "property, both community and otherwise," to each other. He had made up his mind.

Will spent much of that Saturday with Will Hays, prowling around the countryside, looking at ranches. On the way back to town, out of the blue, he turned to Hays and said, "Bill, doggone it, Bill, I'm going to give you two horses." Hays made sounds of protest. "Yes, I am," Will insisted. "I'm going to give you two horses, and I know just which ones." That evening, Allene and Carol Stone came over for supper. All talk was about the upcoming trip. Will was so excited about it, Mrs. Stone said later, that "right then and there by the car, he danced a jig in the sand before we drove off."

"We took a long ride over the ranch the Sunday morning before he left," Betty wrote.

> We talked of some new trails he wanted made and of a few small things that were to be attended to. Then we turned off the bridle path, ducked our heads and rode through the brush to a hidden trail that led down into the canyon, where Will had built a little log cabin, just completed a few days before.
>
> We wound our way to the cabin, drew our horses up, dismounted and went in. I remember Will was sorry that he hadn't had a chance to stay there. The little wood cookstove was up and even the bunks and the mattresses were there. I tried to persuade him to postpone his trip for a few days. We'd take our bedrolls down and camp for the night, I told him. But he said, "No, let's wait till I get back.". . .
>
> In the early afternoon he packed two bags, discarding ninetenths of the things laid out for him to take. I walked in and out

of the room several times, and once he called me back. He had a characteristic, rather sheepish, small-boy look as he said, "Say, Blake, you know what I just did? I flipped a coin." When I said, "I hope it came tails," he laughed and held out his hand. "No, it didn't. It's heads. See, I win."

He saw part of a polo game at the Uplifters Club, then roped calves till suppertime. Bill, having graduated from Stanford that June, was at home. In the absence of other work prospects, Will had arranged with Oscar Lawler to get him a job on the Standard Oil tanker; it would ship out in a few days. (Jim had spent the summer working on Ewing Halsell's ranch with Jimmy Blake, and was about to head east to visit Mary, in her second summer with the Lakewood Players in Maine.) After eating, the three Rogerses piled in the car and went to the hospital to visit Emil Sandmeier, who had suffered a broken leg in an auto mishap. From there, they went to a rodeo at Gilmore Stadium. It was a cool evening, and Betty thought the idea of rodeo under the floodlights was incongruous. But Will enjoyed the show. He knew most of the contestants, and one by one they came over to shake his hand. Somebody gave him a little wood-and-paper puzzle. He toyed with it throughout the evening, and when they got up to leave he put it in his pocket. They drove to the airport, where Will was registered as Mr. McWilliams on the eleven o'clock flight to San Francisco. He picked up the next day's newspapers, said good-bye to his family, and got on board.

It was still by no means certain that Will would continue on to Siberia with Post. Betty had strongly communicated her preference that after seeing Alaska he join her, Mary, and Jim in Maine and then, just the two of them, take a motor tour of Cape Cod. But he wanted to leave all his options open. In San Francisco, he got his passport in order and met with the Soviet consul general, who arranged for the ambassador to send Will two letters—one indicating the course of his flight, the other requesting the cooperation of local postal and telegraph authorities. By late afternoon of the same day, he was in Seattle. When Will got a look at the plane, his first reaction was that the pontoons seemed awfully big; Post gruffly told him there was nothing to be concerned about. Still, the travelers wasted no time in taking off—possibly because Post feared a Department of Commerce inspection would conclude that the pontoons were too heavy. Mrs. Post was not with them. She later said that she backed out because she felt Will did not want her to have to suffer the hardships of wilderness traveling. Initial reports were that she would travel north by boat and join the two men in Alaska; in fact, she returned to Oklahoma.

Will described the next leg of the trip in his column: "Thousand-mile hop from Seattle to Juneau. Was going to stop at Ketchikan for lunch, but mist and rain and he just breezed through. Never over one hundred feet off the water, and talk about navigating, there is millions of channels and islands and bays and all look alike (to me), but this old boy turns up the right alley all the time. Nothing that I have ever seen is more beautiful than this inland passage (by either boat or plane) to Alaska."

An old friend turned up in Juneau. Rex Beach was reacquainting himself with Alaska that summer, and at the Gastineau Hotel, Will and Post had dinner with him and the famous Alaska bush pilot Joe Crosson, who had assisted Post when he had a forced landing in his round-the-world solo. After a horde of autograph hunters were obliged, Will told Beach and Crosson that he and Wiley had bought a couple of raincoats, an ax, and two cases of chili that day, so they considered themselves well equipped. (They already had the fishing tackle, hunting rifles, and eiderdown sleeping bags Wiley had loaded on the plane in Seattle.) Will was in superior form, Beach reported, and held forth long into the night—"until Wiley went to sleep with his head on his arms."

Will was completely taken with Alaska. And what was there not to love? By necessity, it was the most aviation-minded area in the country. And it was the final outpost of wilderness, the last place not yet conquered by so-called civilization. "This Alaska is a great country," he told his readers. "If they can just keep from being taken over by the U.S. they got a great future."

He was seeing it just the right way, too—prowling. "Was you ever driving around in a car and not know or caring where you went?" he asked in a daily dispatch. "Well, that's what Wiley and I are doing. We sure are having a great time. If we hear of whales or polar bears in the Arctic, or a big herd of caribou, we fly over and see it." From Juneau, they took off for Dawson, Yukon Territory, where they dined on moose steaks and caribou cutlets. Two days later, they went farther north, to Aklavik, Northwest Territory. On August 12, they flew to Fairbanks. Will holed up for a day in his hotel room, pounded out four weekly articles, and put them in the mail. The next day, Joe Crosson flew Will and Post south to the Matanuska Valley, where the government had established an agricultural colony for destitute farm families. The residents and administrators swarmed around the plane, and, as soon as Will stepped out, someone asked, "How do you feel, Mr. Rogers?"

"Why, uh, why—wait'll I get out, will you?" he said. "I came to look around, not to report on my health. . . . Where you boys from? Anybody here from Claremore?"

He and Post were driven on a quick tour of the colony, then returned to the plane, where a crowd was still gathered. "How do you think you'll like Russia?" somebody asked.

" 'Russia? Russia?' Will parried, feigning bewilderment," someone who was present wrote two days later. "Say, I saw a Communist here a minute ago." He wheeled and with pointing fingers singled out a transient whose full red beard reached down to the third button on his blue work shirt.

" 'There, there he is,' Rogers cried."

Just as Will was climbing back into the plane, the construction crew cook rushed up with a plate of six cookies. Will bit into one, wiped his mouth with his sleeve, and announced to the crowd, "They're good, but I'll toss them out if we can't get off the ground."

That same day, from Fairbanks, Will sent a telegram to Mary, who was appearing that week in a play called *Ceiling Zero,* playing a girl whose father dies in a plane crash: GREAT TRIP. WISH YOU WERE ALONG. HOW'S YOUR ACTING? YOU AND MAMMA WIRE ME ALL THE NEWS TO NOME. GOING TO POINT BARROW TODAY. FURTHEST POINT OF LAND NORTH ON WHOLE AMERICAN CONTINENT. DON'T WORRY. DAD. By that time, Betty had arrived in Maine, and, when she saw the wire, her heart sank. Nome was the point from which Wiley had planned to take off for Siberia. There would be no tour of Cape Cod.

Point Barrow was not on the way to Nome, and flying there meant a treacherous five-hundred-mile journey over the Endicott Mountains, but Will was determined to visit; the town's geographic distinction and the presence there of Charlie Brower, a legendary and venerable trader and trapper, would both provide superb journalistic fodder. Will was paying the bills, so Barrow it was. A Pacific Alaska Airlines representative checked the plane and declared everything in good order except for the generator. The engine could still be started by hand, however, and, after being informed that the generator couldn't be duplicated locally, Post refused the offer of a substitute. What really concerned him, he told Joe Crosson, was the excessive nose-heaviness of the plane. Especially on takeoff and landing, he had to keep reminding Will to stay in the rear of the cabin to provide balance. On the flight to Fairbanks, he said, his passenger had moved some luggage forward to make himself more comfortable, earning himself a stern reprimand.

They didn't leave on the fourteenth, most likely because of the vile weather Barrow had been having for weeks. Will bought magazines and chewing gum at Boots Noolin's drugstore and spent a few hours joking and shooting the breeze with the crew at the Pan American hangar. The next day, Will met Post and Crosson at a seaplane dock on the narrow, winding Chena River, two miles outside of town. The plan was to fill the fuel tanks only partially there, then fly to Lake Harding, fifty miles to the southeast, where there was more maneuvering room and it would be easier to take off with a full tank. They called Barrow for a weather report. At one o'clock, it still hadn't arrived. It was getting late. Post told Crosson it didn't really matter what the weather was. In all their Alaska travels, he had not flown in or above any cloud or fog bank. His plan that day was to proceed by "contact flying"—always keeping the ground in sight and turning back or landing if the weather became doubtful. When the plane took off, Crosson noticed that Post made a very steep climb. The weather report came in at 1:30. It read "Zero-Zero," meaning that the visibility and ceiling in Barrow were nil. Post had been told that he could phone from Lake Harding for the report. He did not do so. He took on his full load of fuel, and left at two o'clock.

The accepted air route from Fairbanks involved flying north by northwest, arriving at the Beaufort Sea and turning left, hugging the coast until Barrow. They arrived at the coast, made the turn, and got lost. Although the ceiling had increased to more than two hundred feet, Barrow was still hard to spot. A trapper crossing Smith Bay, sixty miles to the east of Barrow, reported hearing the sound of an airplane three different times. Post was circling, using up precious fuel. Will passed the time pounding away on his typewriter, working on a column; in short order, he was finished and, as was his custom, left the paper in his typewriter. Post eventually realized he was east of his destination and turned west, but he must have overshot his mark, because at about five o'clock, he touched down at a small lagoon right on the coast, fifteen miles southwest of Barrow, where a few Eskimo huts were visible. Will got out and, using pidgin English, asked a native named Clare Okpeaha the way to Barrow. After being told, he climbed back into the plane and Post took off. As he was banking to the right, the engine failed. Post couldn't recover in time and the nose-heavy plane dove straight down into the lagoon, tearing off its right wing and killing both men instantly.

Okpeaha walked to the wreck and called to the men. When he

heard no response, he began running to Barrow. Because the tundra was soaked with rain, it took him almost five hours to cover the fifteen miles. He communicated what had happened to Stanley Morgan, an army sergeant stationed there, and described the two men who had perished: one had a "rag on sore eye" and the other was a "big man with boots." With that, Morgan realized he was talking about Wiley Post and Will Rogers. He and Frank Daugherty, a schoolteacher, obtained a whaleboat and, with a crew of fourteen Eskimos, set out for the scene of the accident; Charlie Brower's son David went in a separate boat, pulling behind him a native umiak. "Dense fog with semidarkness gave upturned plane most ghostly appearance and our hearts chilled at thought of what we might find there," Morgan radioed to the War Department in his report the next day. Some natives had already removed Will's body and wrapped it in one of the sleeping bags; in his pockets were some cash, traveler's checks, a newspaper photo of Mary, a trick puzzle, a pocketknife, a pair of eyeglasses, a magnifying glass, and a two-dollar pocket watch that was still running. In order to extricate Post, David Brower had to rig up a tackle to rip off one of the pontoons. The flier's watch, which he kept at Oklahoma time, three hours later than Alaska time, had stopped at the moment of impact. It read 8:18. The men loaded the bodies on the umiak and started the long journey home.

"It is believed the natives felt the loss of these two great men as keenly as we," Morgan radioed, "and as we started our slow trip back to Barrow one of the Eskimo boys began to sing a hymn in Eskimo and soon all the voices joined in this singing and continued until our arrival at Barrow."

EPILOGUE

BETTY'S LIFE, in the years following Will's death, was busy (she wrote in a letter) "with inheritance tax attorneys pestering me, friends and a telephone, an adorable grandchild and the troubles of three grown children to listen to, besides the ranch, household help and social duties." As the first item in her list indicates, the family's finances were the biggest concern. Although Will left an estate of more than $2 million, he also left enormous mortgage and tax payments that had to be met every month. The family did not have the resources to do so, and, because of the Depression, could not sell land at an acceptable price. In exchange for tax relief, over the years Betty donated most of the land to the state of California.

A six-thousand-dollar fee was one reason, no doubt, that in 1938 she agreed to follow through on one of Will's unkept promises. He had never got around to writing his life story for *The Saturday Evening Post.* Wesley Stout, who became editor on George Horace Lorimer's retirement in 1936, asked her to take on the assignment, and she agreed. A professional writer was engaged, but Betty was not pleased with his work. "His writing is wordy and filled with unusual phrases," she complained to Stout. "My story must be told in a simple, intimate way—not bookish or literary." She ended up writing the articles herself. Simple, intimate, and insightful, they were published in the *Post* in 1940 under the title "Uncle Clem's Boy," and as a book, called *Will Rogers: His Wife's Story*, a year later.

Betty Blake Rogers died in 1944, at the age of sixty-five. She left the Pacific Palisades ranch to the state, with the understanding that the home and grounds would be preserved in the same condition as when the Rogers family lived there. Today, it constitutes the Will Rogers State Historical Park.

With some of his inheritance, Bill Rogers bought the Beverly Hills *Citizen,* a weekly newspaper, and for several years was its editor and publisher. In 1940, he was elected to Congress on the Democratic ticket, a development that would have provided his father considerable amusement and enormous pride. He enlisted in the army rather than seek re-election. In 1947, he ran and lost in California's Democratic primary for the U.S. Senate. He sold the *Citizen* in 1953 and moved to southern Arizona (a more congenial climate for his wife's asthma), working as an actor, commentator, and commercial spokesman. He died in 1993.

In the later 1930s and early 1940s, Jim Rogers acted in several cowboy pictures produced by his father's old boss Hal Roach. He liked the horses but not the cameras, and with some relief he bought a ranch near Bakersfield, California, where he still lives.

Mary appeared on Broadway in the fall of 1935 but subsequently gave up the stage. She had a brief, unhappy marriage in the early 1950s, and after that spent most of her time abroad. She died in 1990. According to several people who knew her well, she never got over her father's death.

Despite Betty's book, despite the park, and despite the Will Rogers Memorial (a museum and library opened in 1938 on some of the Rogers land overlooking Claremore, Oklahoma, and dedicated to preserving Will's legacy), Will's stature in the public mind diminished with the years. In part, this had to do with circumstance. For its first thirty-five years, the curator of the Memorial was Will's niece, Paula McSpadden Love, and her extremely protective attitude toward her uncle discouraged researchers from doing research and editors from disseminating his writing. Until the Oklahoma State University Press put out his collected works in the 1970s and 1980s, the most widely available edition was *The Autobiography of Will Rogers*, an inaccurately named pastiche in which an editor cut and pasted (and in many cases grossly rewrote) diverse pieces of Will's writing in the misguided attempt to offer the life story he had never gotten around to putting on paper.

Similarly hidden from view were his films, which in his later years made a bigger impact than anything else he did. Twentieth Century–Fox refrained from rereleasing any of them in the years following the crash, thinking that doing so would be seen as an unseemly attempt to cash in on tragedy. In the 1950s, when the movies of Will's contemporaries were starting to be shown on television, Fox was slow in marketing the Rogers films. The initial reason for this decision has been lost to history, but its result is clear: Young people didn't know Will had been the biggest movie star in the country, older people forgot, and eventually, even if someone at Fox had wanted to sell his films, there would have been no market for or interest in them.

There was another reason for the eclipse. Will's work in the newspapers, on the concert stage, and over the radio was tied to his times, to a degree that has never been true of any other commentator of his caliber. He was a human lyre through which the events of the day relentlessly blew, and the melody they made, wonderful and resonant as it was at the time, initially seem antique and quaint to a later generation.

This is especially true because, soon after he died, the tenor of the times changed so definitively and terribly. In the year of his death, Germany passed the Nuremberg Laws, which among other things deprived Jews of citizenship. Six years later, Japan attacked Pearl Harbor, and in 1945 the first atomic bomb was deployed. It's impossible to say what Will would have made of these developments (and the even more horrifying ones that were revealed in bits and pieces); they were harbingers of a world in which tragedy and evil were constant presences. In his day, Will was always able to scurry away from those twin horsemen; in ours, that is not an option. But it is not unreasonable to think that he might have risen to the occasion, just as he did when he saw so much suffering and fear in the early 1930s.

In 1991, a musical called *The Will Rogers Follies* opened on Broadway. The character of Will Rogers in it basically exists to provide some gags and rope tricks between production numbers. But late in the show, the actor playing Will steps up and delivers the radio unemployment speech he gave in 1931, the one where he said, "There is not an unemployed man in the country that hasn't contributed to the wealth of every millionaire in America." At the Democratic convention held in New York in the summer of 1992, Mac Davis, the star of *The Will Rogers Follies* at the time, walked to the microphone and gave the speech, word for word.

A few weeks later, a veteran journalist, someone for whom Will Rogers was just a name carrying some vague associations, was still struck by what she had heard. "It was," she said, "the best speech anyone gave at the whole convention."

ACKNOWLEDGMENTS

Years after Will Rogers's death, his friend Joel McCrea said of him, "He had an influence on everything that he touched. And the key word is 'glory.' He glorified everything." The time I have spent in Rogers's company, researching and writing this book, has given me an inkling of what McCrea meant. Part of it, for me, has been the chance to work with some remarkable people, and I welcome the opportunity to offer my appreciation for the help they gave me.

The book simply could not have been written without the cooperation and assistance of two groups of people. The first consists of the sons of Will Rogers: William Vann Rogers and James Blake Rogers. (His daughter, Mary, died shortly after I began work on the book.) In his capacity as president of the Rogers Company, Jim Rogers gave me permission to quote from the published and unpublished work of his father and mother. But he and Bill Rogers also provided wonderful reminiscences, insight, encouragement, and, most important of all, living proof of their father's legacy of spirit, vitality, and humor.

I owe almost as large a debt to the staff of the Will Rogers Memorial and Library in Claremore, Oklahoma. Shortly after I started my research, Joseph H. Carter was named director. One of his first acts was to tell me that he and the Memorial would offer me whatever assistance I required, and never ask for editorial oversight, much less control. He proved as good as his word: To enumerate all the kind and helpful acts of Carter and the Memorial would require a chapter, not a paragraph. His most valuable resource, at least as far as researchers are concerned, is Pat Lowe, librarian extraordinaire, who always answers the phone with an aural smile and is always ready to track down an obscure fact, date, or quotation. Curator Greg Malak and Director Emeritus Reba Collins also provided substantial assistance.

Great thanks are also due to the scholars and researchers whose labors provided an important foundation for this book. Foremost among them are Bryan Sterling, who, when he began his research on Will Rogers in the early 1970s, perceived and responded to the need to interview many of Rogers's surviving friends and associates, and who compiled a definitive Rogers filmography; James Smallwood, Steven K. Gragert, and the other editors of Oklahoma State

University Press's twenty-one-volume edition of the writings of Will Rogers, the starting point for any Rogers student; Reba Collins, whose ground-breaking work on genealogy and Rogers's literary career was indispensable; Peter Rollins, whose *Will Rogers: A Bio-Bibliography* was never more than one arm's length away as I wrote; and Elwyn Isaacs, indefatigable compiler of Rogersiana and the chief author of the extraordinary day-by-day Will Rogers chronology at Claremore. I would also like to express my appreciation to David Milsten, who interviewed Eddie Cantor, Lucille Mulhall, and Tom Mix; to Kathryn Stansbury, who unearthed many facts about the Mulhall family; and to Pam Ruffeto, who in the employ of the state of California has compiled a great deal of information pertaining to the Rogers ranch in Pacific Palisades.

There are not many people still around who knew Will Rogers, so I am grateful that I was able to have the direct testimony of Morey Amsterdam, Lina Basquette, Ray Bell, Betsy Rees Bevan, Norman Blake, J. J. Cohn, Douglas Fairbanks, Jr., B. K. Johnson, Keith Lummis, Paul Mellon, Muriel Merrill, Charlton Ogburn, Roy Rogers, Emil Sandmeier, Patricia Ziegfeld Stevenson, Doris Eaton Travis, Fay Gillis Wells, and Lucille Layton Zinman. Thanks to you all.

Conversation and correspondence with numerous scholars immeasurably contributed to my understanding of Rogers and his times. At the head of this particular line stands John Lukacs, who encouraged me from the beginning, whose editorial pencil greatly improved Chapter 12 and who has always provided for me an inspiring example of the possibility of combining literary eloquence, scholarly rigor, and bracing ideation. Kevin Brownlow, also in my pantheon of most-admired historians, helped me put Rogers's silent-film career in context. I will always be grateful to Arthur Wertheim, currently engaged in the herculean task of collecting all of Rogers's published and unpublished writing, for leading me to, among other things, the Buck McKee Papers. Murray Murphey helped me place Rogers in the political context of the 1920s and 1930s. Richard Ziegfeld was an enormously helpful font of all things Ziegfeldian. Rennard Strickland explained class distinctions within the Cherokee Nation. Barry Paris shared his insights into the peculiar demands of biography-writing. Vince Bruce, of *The Will Rogers Follies,* showed me how a rope is thrown. Thanks also to Scott Berg, Walter Boyne, James Card, Jan Cohn, Tom Dardis, Larry Dietz, Hervé Dumont, Hildegarde Dwane, Carol Felsenthal, Ronald Fields, Jerry Flemmons, Herbert Goldman, Chris Hodenfield, Larry May, Greg Mitchell, Doris L. Rich, Carrie Rickey, Marion Rodgers, Andrew Sarris, Arthur Schlesinger, Jr., Aubrey Solomon, Charles Stein, Gore Vidal, and Randy Young.

I have relied on the assistance (and sometimes kindness) of many librarians and archivists. Some went beyond the call of duty, and I would like to give them special thanks: Alexa Luberski, of the Parks and Recreation Department of the state of California; Charles Silver, of the Film Study Center at the Museum of Modern Art; Sam Gill, of the Academy of Motion Picture Arts and

Sciences' Margaret Herrick Library; Ned Comstock and Leith Adams, of the Archives of the Performing Arts at USC; the late Harold Potter, of Movietone News; Heather Smith, of the Western Manuscripts Collection at the University of Missouri, Columbia; Mary Jackson and her staff at the Interlibrary Loan Department of Van Pelt Library at the University of Pennsylvania; Jane Colihan of *American Heritage*; and Sandi Smith of the Oklahoma Historical Society. Strauss Zelnick, president of Twentieth Century–Fox Film Corporation, gave the order that I should be given access to legal and story records involving Will Rogers; Carol Bua made sure that it was done. Donnis DeCamp and Marc Selvaggio, proprietors of Schoyer's Books in Pittsburgh, not only tracked down every out-of-print volume I asked them to find but sent along some bonus prizes, too.

Stuart Krichevsky of the Sterling Lord Literistic Agency has been continuously available for sympathetically intelligent counsel. I thank Jonathan Segal of Alfred A. Knopf, first, for his initial interest in the book and, second, for helping to make it considerably better than it would otherwise have been. Also at Knopf, Melvin Rosenthal's careful eye saved me from many errors and stylistic infelicities.

In the early stages of the project, Verlyn Klinkenborg and David Black provided very welcome enthusiasm about what seemed to others like an iffy idea. Bill Stempel and David Smith, like the good friends they are, always were (or acted) interested in talking about Will Rogers. Bruce Beans, John Grossmann, Sam Hughes, Margaret Kirk, Mike Sokolove, and Tim Whitaker constituted a support group any freelancer would envy. Jonathan Schull is my gracious computer guru, and I thank him yet again.

Even closer to home, I'm indebted to my mother-in-law, Margaret Y. Simeone, whose frequent stays in our household made it possible for me to establish a home away from home in Oklahoma, and who has been my main source for Hollywood lore. My mother, Harriet Yagoda, has always been enthusiastic and supportive about my endeavors; she outdid herself this time. There's no one I'd rather have in my corner. More than likely, what drew me to write about a good man was having a good man for a father. Louis Yagoda didn't live to see the book completed, but he encouraged me from the start, and I like to think he would have approved of the results.

Gigi Simeone listened to my laments, steadied my sails, and—along with Elizabeth and Maria—made it all worthwhile.

NOTES

ABBREVIATIONS

BOOKS

DT 1   *Will Rogers' Daily Telegrams: The Coolidge Years, 1926–1929,* James M. Smallwood, ed. Stillwater: Oklahoma State University Press, 1978.

DT 2   *Will Rogers' Daily Telegrams: The Hoover Years, 1929–1931,* James M. Smallwood, ed. Stillwater: Oklahoma State University Press, 1978.

DT 3   *Will Rogers' Daily Telegrams: The Hoover Years, 1931–1933,.* James M. Smallwood, ed. Stillwater: Oklahoma State University Press, 1979.

DT 4   *Will Rogers' Daily Telegrams: The Roosevelt Years, 1933–1935.* James M. Smallwood, ed. Stillwater: Oklahoma State University Press, 1979.

WA 1   *Will Rogers' Weekly Articles: The Harding/Coolidge Years, 1922–1925,* James M. Smallwood, ed. Stillwater: Oklahoma State University Press, 1980.

WA 2   *Will Rogers' Weekly Articles: The Coolidge Years, 1925–1927,* James M. Smallwood, ed. Stillwater: Oklahoma State University Press, 1981.

WA 3   *Will Rogers' Weekly Articles: The Coolidge Years, 1927–1929,* James M. Smallwood, ed. Stillwater: Oklahoma State University Press, 1981.

WA 4   *Will Rogers' Weekly Articles: The Hoover Years, 1929–1931,* Steven K. Gragert, ed. Stillwater: Oklahoma State University Press, 1981.

WA 5   *Will Rogers' Weekly Articles: The Hoover Years, 1931–1933,* Steven K. Gragert, ed. Stillwater: Oklahoma State University Press, 1982.

WA 6   *Will Rogers' Weekly Articles: The Roosevelt Years, 1933–1935,* Steven K. Gragert, ed. Stillwater: Oklahoma State University Press, 1982.

RB   *Radio Broadcasts of Will Rogers,* Steven K. Gragert, ed. Stillwater: Oklahoma State University Press, 1983.

CA   *Convention Articles of Will Rogers,* Joseph A. Stout, Jr., ed. Stillwater: Oklahoma State University Press, 1976.

Letters   Will Rogers, *Letters of a Self-Made Diplomat to His President.* New York: Albert and Charles Boni, 1926; reprinted, Stillwater: Oklahoma State University Press, 1977.

WR:HWS   Betty Blake Rogers, *Will Rogers: His Wife's Story,* 2d ed. Norman: University of Oklahoma Press, 1979.

OWR   Homer Croy, *Our Will Rogers,* New York: Duell, Sloan and Pearce, 1953.

MANUSCRIPT

Sime   Will Rogers, undated, untitled handwritten manuscript, collec-
manuscript tion of Will Rogers, Jr.

COLLECTIONS

WRM   Will Rogers Memorial and Library, Claremore, Oklahoma.
FLPTC   Theater Collection, Free Library of Philadelphia.
MOMA   Film Study Center, Museum of Modern Art, New York.
NYTA   *The New York Times* Archives, New York.
BRTC   Billy Rose Theater Collection, New York Public Library for the Performing Arts, New York.
AMPAS   Margaret Herrick Library, Academy of Motion Picture Arts and Sciences, Beverly Hills.
WRSHP   Will Rogers State Historic Park, Pacific Palisades, California.
HCP   Homer Croy Papers, Western Historical Manuscript Collection, University of Missouri, Columbia.
COHC   Columbia University Oral History Collection, New York.

INDIVIDUALS

WR   Will Rogers
BB   Betty Blake
BBR   Betty Blake Rogers
CVR   Clement Vann Rogers

WRJR Will Rogers Jr.
JR James Rogers
HC Homer Croy
BY Ben Yagoda

Note: Unless otherwise indicated, all letters to and from Will Rogers and his family are located in the Will Rogers Memorial and Library.

INTRODUCTION

xi "Why not *try* to test Ronald Reagan": Warner Brothers Archives, *The Story of Will Rogers* file, Archives of the Performing Arts, University of Southern California, Los Angeles.

"Will Rogers, probably": *Congressional Record,* August 16, 1935.

"I cannot talk about it": unidentified clipping, reproduced in Reba N. Collins, *Will Rogers & Wiley Post in Alaska: The Crash Felt 'Round the World.* (Claremore, Oklahoma: Will Rogers Heritage Press, 1984), 73.

In a store in Maine: WR:HWS, 311–312.

xiv "He built himself up": Homer Croy, *Country Cured* (New York: Harper & Brothers, 1943), 224.

CHAPTER 1

3 "a pioneer who was a statesman": unidentified clipping, Scrapbook A-II, WRM.

three-eighths Cherokee: Sallie's mother was definitely one-quarter Cherokee, but there is some uncertainty regarding her father, Avery Vann. Avery Vann's father, Clement Vann, was married to a full-blood Cherokee named Wa-Wli, but there is no definite record that Avery had Cherokee blood, and it is possible that he was Clement Vann's son by a white woman. In that case, Clem Rogers would have been three-sixteenths Cherokee and Will Rogers seven-thirty-seconds. See the discussion in Reba Neighbors Collins, *Roping Will Rogers Family Tree* (Claremore, Oklahoma: Will Rogers Heritage Press, 1982), 58–59.

6 "the ingrained tradition": Morris L. Wardell, *A Political History of the Cherokee Nation* (Norman, Oklahoma: University of Oklahoma Press, 1938), 52.

plausible local tradition: Stillwell [Oklahoma] *Democrat-Journal,* June 28, 1973; reproduced in Collins, *Roping Will Rogers,* 8.

"See that Clem": Kate Wolf to Sallie Rogers McSpadden, April 11, 1938; quoted in Harold Keith, "Clem Rogers and His Influence on Oklahoma History," M.A. thesis, University of Oklahoma, 1941, 5.

After one bitter quarrel: ibid., 9, 10.

His sister remembered: ibid., 4–5.

On May 15, 1855: Joseph B. Thoburn, and Muriel H. Wright, *Oklahoma A History of the State and Its People,* vol. 3 (New York: Lewis Historical Publishing Company, 1929), 244.

7   An early settler: Keith, "Clem Rogers," 12.

By the late 1850s: Leslie Hewes, *Occupying the Cherokee Country of Oklahoma* (Lincoln, Nebraska: University of Nebraska Press), 19.

8   "live much in the style": ibid., 21.

9   "Oh, our God": "The Diary of Hannah Hicks," *American Scene* magazine, Gilcrease Institute, Tulsa, vol. 13, no. 3 (1972), 8; quoted in Alvin M. Josephy Jr., *The Civil War in the American West* (New York: Alfred A. Knopf, 1991), 359.

"The brilliancy and completeness": Grace Steele Woodward, *The Cherokees* (Norman, Oklahoma: University of Oklahoma Press, 1963), 289.

10   The cabin: undated manuscript, Clem Rogers file, WRM.

10–11   economics of cattle business: Ellsworth Collings, *The Old Home Ranch: The Will Rogers Ranch in the Indian Territory* (Stillwater, Oklahoma: Redlands Press, 1964), 50, citing Walter Prescott Webb, *The Great Plains* (Boston: Ginn and Company, 1931), 216.

11   "My father": WA 6, 90.

"Take it from me": Collings, *The Old Home Ranch,* 39.

12   On either side of the front walk: WR:HWS, 40–41.

In the winter: Sallie McSpadden, "Sketch of the Early Life of Will Rogers," *The Ranchman* (December 1941).

"She was loved": Agnes Walker oral history, Oklahoma Historical Society, Oklahoma City.

She told Mary Newcomb: "Stories Related about Will Rogers by Mary Newcomb Nairn to Daughter, Etta," undated manuscript, WRM.

Mary once was showing: William Howard Payne, and Jake G. Lyons, eds., *Folks Say of Will Rogers: A Memorial Anecdotage* (New York: G. P. Putnam's Sons, 1936), 17.

In a letter: quoted in Keith, "Clem Rogers," 31.

"Aunt Mary always met you": ibid., 27.

13   "In a political unit": Angie Debo, *And Still the Waters Run* (Princeton, New Jersey: Princeton University Press, 1940), 10.

14   "Clem's wife is sick": Payne and Lyons, *Folks Say,* 14.

According to a neighbor: Collings, *The Old Home Ranch,* 31.

15   One time Willie decided: "Stories Related about Will Rogers," 2.

On another occasion: OWR, 18–19.

"Willie would ride": Collings, *The Old Home Ranch,* 42.

"We played horse": Croy, *Our Will Rogers,* 6–7.

Since he was mainly ridden: Collings, *The Old Home Ranch,* 42.

"I didn't exactly want": Harold Keith, *Boys' Life of Will Rogers* (New York: Thomas Y. Crowell Company, 1937), 46. Keith's book, though written for the juvenile market, contains material gathered through interviews with several dozen people, all since deceased, who had personal contact with Will Rogers.

16   His cousin Spi Trent: Spi M. Trent, *My Cousin Will Rogers* (New York: G. P. Putnam's Sons, 1938), 83, 87.

"Catch him!": Keith, *Boys' Life,* 40.

McSpadden was the son: Collins, *Roping Will Rogers,* 14.

17　"was a little one-room log cabin": WA 4, 67.

He drove his horse: Keith, *Boys Life,* 63.

"My mother told him": Gazelle "Scrap" Lane oral history, Tape T7-83—T7-076-D, WRM.

"My own mother died": RB, 28.

18　"He cried when he told me": WR:HWS, 41, 47.

<h2 style="text-align:center">CHAPTER 2</h2>

21　"really at heart I love ranching,": WA 2, 160–161.

22　"W. P. ROGERS, CATTLE DEALER": CVR to Col. C. J. Harris, October 10, 1894, Indian Archives Division, Oklahoma Historical Society, Oklahoma City.

was a coeducational counterpart: "From observation and experience we are taught to believe that boys and girls should be educated together," noted the catalog. "The leading universities of our country recognize this fact and have opened their doors to the girls. Both sexes need incentives and restraints, and no better ones can be had than the rivalry that exists between them." Willie Halsell catalog, WRM, 17–18.

Although he squeezed onto the honor roll: Vinita [Oklahoma] *Indian Chieftain,* December 29, 1892.

"we will miss all the roundups": WR to Charley McClellan, February 24, 1893.

"You ought to be up there": WR to Charley McClellan, March 28, 1893.

"Careful and thorough training": Willie Halsell catalog, WRM, 23.

"Willie Rogers was inimitable": Vinita [Oklahoma] *Indian Chieftain,* December 29, 1892.

23　Charley McClellan anecdotes: Harold Keith, *Boys' Life of Will Rogers* (New York: Thomas Y. Crowell Company, 1937), 73–76.

24　"Mr. Will Rogers appeared in full Indian costume": Claremore [Oklahoma] *Weekly Progress,* September 20, 1901.

"the centrifugal force of the loop": Chester Byers, *Roping: Trick and Fancy Rope Spinning* (New York: G.P. Putnam's Sons; 1928, 2d edition, Cambridge, Mass.: Applewood Books, undated), 4.

25　"my mother would not let me": Margaret N. Price to Homer Croy, undated (probably 1952), HCP. Mrs. Price told Croy, who was then researching his biography of Will, "it was quite 'wicked' for the boys to go out to this place. Probably all of them didn't drink a bottle—but my mother heard a tale of some of the boys getting too much and falling off their bicycles. . . . I've no objection to your using [Will's] note, but would not like to create the impression that Will drank too much."

"I know I drink": WR to Maggie Nay, undated.

25   "even the most sanguine": Keith, *Boys' Life*, 97.

building collapse: Buffalo *Courier Express*, August 17, 1935.

assassination of Matt Yocum: Vinita [Oklahoma] *Indian Chieftain*, December 17, 1896.

26   "the charge taking effect": Vinita [Oklahoma] *Indian Chieftain*, July 22, 1896.

"there is a clue": Vinita [Oklahoma] *Indian Chieftain*, July 29, 1897.

"Rogers' son, Bill Rogers": Kansas City *Journal*, July 18, 1897.

27   "continued generally": Vinita [Oklahoma] *Leader*, October 20, 1898.

27–8   Kemper anecdotes: Arthur Martin Hatch, *Will Rogers, Cadet: A Record of His Two Years as a Cadet at the Kemper Military School* (Boonville, Missouri: Kemper Military School, 1935).

28   "Once a classmate referred": ibid., 16–17.

"I was leary": Sime manuscript.

"Even the postmaster disapproved": Betty Staples, *Will Rogers, Cowboy Humorist* (Columbus, Ohio: Better Books Press, 1931), 9.

29   "Will's father was thoroughly miffed": OWR, 46.

he hadn't been working: Frank Ewing to HC, August 15, 1952, HCP.

"I'll never forget how Will could eat": Keith, *Boys' Life*, 132–134.

30   "They tell me you're a killer": ibid., 136.

31   one authority pinpoints 1887: Lonn Taylor and Ingrid Maas, *The American Cowboy* (New York: Harper & Row, 1983), 17.

"We was driving": WA 6, 139.

32   Only two other men: Croy, *Our Will Rogers*, 16.

As early as 1870: Wardell, *A Political History of the Cherokees*, 275–276.

the first range fence: Collings, *The Old Home Ranch: The Will Rogers Ranch in the Indian Territory* (Stillwater, Oklahoma: Redlands Press, 1964), 58.

By 1897, he was marketing: Claremore [Oklahoma] *Weekly Progress*, August 14, 1897.

"C. V. Rogers, the Oologah wheat king": Claremore [Oklahoma] *Weekly Progress*, July 27, 1895.

33   "Are we powerless?": Collings, *The Old Home Ranch*, 57.

"The Intruders are coming": CVR to Col. C. J. Harris, October 15, 1894, Indian Archives Division, Oklahoma Historical Society, Oklahoma City.

34   A study presented to Congress: Senate Documents, 54th Congress, 1 Sess., no. 182 (Washington: Government Printing Office, 1897), 8.

"The head chief told us": Angie Debo, *And Still the Waters Run* (Princeton: Princeton University Press, 1940), 21–22. Henry George (1839–1897) was the antimonopoly economist known for advocating a "single tax" on land.

35 "We can settle": Harold Keith, "Clem Rogers and His Influence on Oklahoma History," M.A. thesis, University of Oklahoma, 1941, 77–78.

36 "we had em 3 times a day": Spi Trent, *My Cousin Will Rogers* (New York: G. P. Putnam's Sons, 1938), 53. Trent's book (actually he was the grandson of Will's mother's half sister) is the source for much of the information on this period of Will's life. Aside from being written in an infuriating dialect, the book contains much demonstrably false material, so the rest has to be taken with a grain of salt. But Spi and Will did live in the cabin for a time.

"He wasn't used to": Collings, *The Old Home Ranch*, 93.

37 "the coon song craze": James H. Dormon, "Shaping the Popular Image of Post-Reconstruction Blacks: The 'Coon Song' Phenomenon of the Gilded Age," *American Quarterly* 40 (December 1988), 450–471.

The newspapers reported: Claremore [Oklahoma] *Weekly Progress*, March 30, 1901.

"Thinking I'd get rid of him": *A History of Oologah* (Oologah, Oklahoma: privately printed, 1990), 11.

37–8 One day in October 1900: Ed Sunday, "Willie Rogers of Oologah," *The Ranchman* (November 1942), 11; Vinita [Oklahoma] *Leader*, October 4, 1900.

38 "He was vaccinated": Jim Hopkins oral history, Tape T7-087-1, WRM.

"You never knew what he would say": Gazelle "Scrap" Lane oral history, Tape T7-083–T7-076-0 WRM.

"a laugh greeted me": Portland *Oregonian*, August 17, 1935.

39 "It was the only time": Jim Hopkins oral history, Tape T7-087-1, WRM.

"the greatest ladies man": ibid.

"The house was cold": WR:HWS, 18.

40 "My Dear Friend": WR to BB, January 5, 1900.

"My Dear Betty": WR to BB, March 14, 1900.

41 "he was in his war paint": Vinita [Oklahoma] *Leader*, September 6, 1900.

"I kept looking for him": WR: HWS, 21.

"Willie aint never goin to amount to nothin": Trent, *My Cousin Will Rogers*, 145.

"The Love I had": CVR to Eulson Bibles, May 31, 1900.

42 They thought about asking for work: JR interview with BY, December 10, 1989.

"That was just bull luck": Sime mansucript.

42   When he got back to Oologah: Croy, OWR, 72.

"contest with each other": quoted in Clifford P. Westermeier, *Man, Beast, Dust: The Story of Rodeo* (Lincoln, Nebraska: University of Nebraska Press, 1947; reprinted 1987), 34.

On July 4, 1899: Claremore [Oklahoma] *Courier*, July 7, 1899.

43   "had bad luck": quoted in Keith, *Boys' Life*, 150.

"with almost human intelligence": unidentified clipping, dateline San Antonio, January 16, 1905, WRM.

"that gave me a touch of 'Show business' ": WA 5, 6.

44   "He was active": Jim Hopkins oral history, Tape T7-087-1, WRM.

"so speedy that he could turn": Trent, *My Cousin Will Rogers*, 132.

named after a girl: Edwin P. Hicks to HC, October 16, 1952, HCP.

On May 10: Keith, *Boys Life*, 157.

45   Will let another cowboy: Jim Hopkins, "My Friend Will," unpublished, undated manuscript, WRM, 19.

47   When Will joined up: ibid. 21.

Mulhall told the seventy-one cowboys: Vinita [Oklahoma] *Leader*, October 17, 1901.

"There is positively nothing": Kathryn B. Stansbury, *Lucille Mulhall: Her Family—Her Life—Her Times,* no publication information, 1985, 19.

on the second day of the roping: Vinita [Oklahoma] *Leader*, October 17, 1901.

the troupe packed up: Stansbury, *Lucille Mulhall*, 21.

Tomkins anecdote: Charles H. Tomkins to Homer Croy, August 1, 1952, HCP.

Will finished eleventh: Keith, *Boys' Life*, 165.

"I had a little Pony": WA 2, 268.

CHAPTER 3

51   Will picked up thirteen hundred dollars: WR to CVR, March 13, 1902.

"Our baggage was searched": WR to sisters, March 25, 1902, printed Chelsea [Oklahoma] *Reporter*, April 25, 1902. Some of the original manuscripts of Will's letters to his family do not survive, and in these cases quotes are taken from the published version. Instances where both versions are available indicate that editorial changes involved wording more than substance: words like *nigger* and *bloke* became *negro* and *fellow*, and there's an occasional formulation ("am obliged to pen them under severe difficulties," for example) of which Will Rogers would probably not have been capable.

"I had no idea": W.R. to "sister," November 27, 1903, as published in *Claremore Weekly Progress,* January 23, 1904.

"There is no end of theaters": WR to sisters, April 13, 1902, as published in Chelsea [Oklahoma] *Reporter,* May 16, 1902.

"Every time We eat": WR to sisters, April 4, 1902, in Reba Collins, *Will Rogers: Courtship and Correspondence, 1900–1915* (Oklahoma City: Neighbors and Quaid, 1992), 31.

53 "oh, what a horrible place": WR to sisters, April 24, 1902, as published in Chelsea [Oklahoma] *Reporter,* May 30, 1902.

"the street cars": WR to Claremore *Weekly Progress,* July 7, 1902, published August 23, 1902.

Argentina background: David Rock, *Argentina 1516–1982: From Spanish Colonization to the Falklands War* (Berkeley: University of California Press, 1986), 139–140, 171.

"The government will give you": WR to Claremore [Oklahoma] *Weekly Progress,* July 7, 1902, published August 23, 1902.

"We can't begin to compete": WR to sisters, June 9, 1902, as published in Chelsea [Oklahoma] *Reporter,* August 1, 1902.

54 "I asked the boss": WR to Claremore [Oklahoma] *Weekly Progress,* July 7, 1902, published August 23, 1902.

"I consider them the best ropers": [Omaha] Sunday *World-Herald,* undated, Scrapbook A–2, WRM.

"Willie, I wish you and Dick": James Cleveland to WR, June 25, 1902.

"Old Comanche": Pearl Yocum to WR, June 25, 1902.

55 "I don't think there is much use": WR to CVR, June 17, 1902.

"Good crops": CVR to WR, June 17, 1902.

"He says, I dident ask": Spi Trent, *My Cousin Will Rogers* (New York: G. P. Putnam's Sons, 1938), 152.

"I never cared for money": WR to CVR, July 31, 1902.

56 "by far the most valuable": unidentified clipping, Scrapbook 559-1-5785, WRSHP.

"I soon found I couldn't rassle": Sime manuscript.

"I will mail you a special edition": WR to "Folks," October 5, 1902. Although in his later career as a humorist Will prided himself on using all-original material, at this point he was not above stealing a good line. A couple of weeks after he sailed, a Buenos Aires crony of his named E. B. Camp, apparently an Englishman, wrote him a chatty letter that not only proved this point but indicates the kind of profanely cosmopolitan crowd Will ran with in Argentina. Camp began by thanking him for the "Winchester and the trunk" and remarking, "You may not believe it, but I really am getting tired of life in dear old Buenos Aires, city of 'vino y putas.' " About Will's voyage, Camp joked, "Do you think that a well-preserved mixture of pony-piss and sheep-shit will ever become fashionable as a perfume? . . . I shall expect to receive very soon a poem by William P. Rogers, entitled—Twenty one days on a floating dung-hill, or the experiences of Don Guillermo as chambermaid to a flea-bitten mule." E. B. Camp to WR, August 19, 1902, WRM.

56   "more different kinds of odd jobs": WR to "Folks," October 5, 1902.

57   "a damsel of some twenty winters": ibid.

"thirteen collars": WR to sisters, November 17, 1902, as published in Chelsea [Oklahoma] *Reporter,* January 2, 1903.

58   Texas Jack background: Herschel C. Logan, *Buckskin and Satin: The Life of Texas Jack* (Harrisburg, Pennsylvania: Stackpole Co., 1954), 24–26; "Prominent People," unidentified publication, WRM.

In 1899, he toured England: C. van Niekerk to WRJR, May 31, 1940.

This, as the name implied: undated program, WRM.

59   "blood curdling scenes": WR to sisters, December 28, 1902, as published in Chelsea *Register,* February 27, 1903.

he put burnt cork: WR to "Home Folks," January 28, 1903.

"My appearance amused the natives": Butte [Montana] *Miner,* undated clipping, Scrapbook A–2, WRM.

"They don't use Ropes": WR to "Home Folks," January 28, 1903, as printed in Collins, *Will Rogers: Courtship and Correspondence, 1900–1915,* 64.

"astounding": undated clipping, WRM.

"I want about 100 feet": WR to CVR, March 22, 1903.

60   "Jack is the finest old boy": WR to sisters, December 15, 1902.

"I am going to learn things": ibid.

"I would give anything": Jim Rider to WR, September 2, 1902.

"You can certainly have your pick": Sallie McSpadden to WR, April 25, 1902.

"I think you know enough": Maud Lane to WR, November 24, 1902.

61   "Quite a nice Valentine": Kate Ellis to WR, February 15, 1903.

"Your 2 Poneys": CVR to WR, October 21, 1902.

death of Charley McClellan: Harold Keith, *Boys' Life of Will Rogers* (New York: Thomas Y. Crowell Company, 1937), 176–177.

romantic attention: May Stine to WR, October 4, 1903.

"My Dearest loving boy": Annie Greenslade to WR, June 6, 1903.

"Let us both us try & save": Mamie S. to WR, undated.

62   "I am getting homesick": WR to CVR, May 21, 1903, as published in Claremore [Oklahoma] *Weekly Progress,* June 27, 1903.

"I must see a bit more": WR to CVR, September 4, 1903.

"I have very great pleasure": undated, WRM.

death of Texas Jack: C. van Niekerk to WRJR, May 31, 1940.

63   "It is very amusing": WR to CVR, September 28, 1903.

64   "a gentleman from America": Auckland [New Zealand] *Star,* January 20, 1904, WRM.

Someone offered him: Sime manuscript.

"I couldn't see any luck": ibid.

CHAPTER 4

67   "Now I am making my own way": WR to BB, November 6, 1904.

Each Cherokee citizen: Morris Wardell, *A Political History of the Cherokee Nation* (Norman, Oklahoma: University of Oklahoma Press, 1938), 326.

68   "always be remembered": WA 5, 76.

"big, blue-gray eyes": Kathryn B. Stansbury, *Lucille Mulhall: Her Family— Her Life—Her Times,* no publishing information, 1985, 33.

"the only Girl": WA 5, 77–78.

Lucille's record: Stansbury, *Lucille Mulhall,* 31.

69   Spi Trent: Spi Trent, *My Cousin Will Rogers* (New York: G. P. Putnam's Sons, 1938), 160.

some of the hands: David Milsten, *Will Rogers—The Cherokee Kid* (Chicago: Glenheath Publishers, 1987), 50. This is a slighly revised edition of Milsten's 1935 biography, *An Appreciation of Will Rogers.*

"Lucille never dressed": WA 5, 76–77.

"I haven't had a girl": WR to BB, October 29, 1904.

Mix biography: Paul E. Mix, *The Life and Legend of Tom Mix* (Cranbury, New Jersey: A. S. Barnes & Co., 1972).

70   "sitting at the piano": Milsten, *Will Rogers,* 108–109.

A St. Louis professor: Robert Rydell, *All the World's a Fair: Visions of America at American International Expositions, 1876–1916.* (Chicago: University of Chicago Press, 1984), 155–157.

71   "not a jumble of nonsense": ibid., 178.

Cummins program: Scrapbook A–1, WRM.

"There were many other Indian tribes": Geronimo, *Geronimo's Story of His Life, Taken Down and Edited by S.M Barrett* (New York: Duffield & Company, 1906; reprinted Williamstown, Massachusetts: Corner House, 1973), 198. Geronimo, allowed to visit the fair's other attractions in the company of federal guards, gave this memorable account of a ride on the Ferris wheel: "One time the guards took me into a little house that had four windows. When we were seated the little house started to move along the ground. Then the guards called my attention to some curious things they had in their pockets. Finally they told me to look out, and when I did so I was scared, for our little house had gone high up in the air, and the people down in the Fair Grounds looked no larger than ants. The men laughed at me for being scared; then they gave me a glass to look through (I often had such glasses which I took from dead officers after battles in Mexico and elsewhere), and I could see rivers, lakes and mountains. But I had never been so high in the air, and I tried to look in the sky. There were no stars, and I could not look at the sun through this glass because the brightness hurt my eyes. Finally I put the glass down, and as they were all laughing at me, I too, began to laugh. Then they said, 'Get out!' and when I looked we were on the street again. After we were safe on the land I watched many of these little houses going up and down, but I cannot understand how they travel. They are very curious little houses."

The next year, Geronimo marched in Theodore Roosevelt's inaugural parade. He died at Fort Sill in 1909.

71   "suddenly he would fall": "My Friend Will," unpublished, undated manuscript, WRM, 27, 28.

72   "If you want him": WR to CVR, April 28, 1904.

"I wont sell him": WR to CVR, June 11, 1904.

Mullhall *Enterprise* account: quoted in Stansbury, *Lucille Mulhall*, 40–42.

"Both jerked their guns": Jim Hopkins oral history, Tape T7-087-1, WRM.

73   Will missed it all: ibid.

New York Times article: June 19, 1904. Bert Smith, a fifteen-year-old bucking-bronco rider with the show, was the closest eyewitness to the shooting. Minutes after it happened, he wrote to a friend fifty-five years later, "Two men came to me and told me to get my gear together, that the show had closed and they would pay my fare home plus 15 bucks . . . one of the cowboys came to me and told me 'kid, it's a must. You don't argue when there's been a gunfight.' " Bert Smith to "Dave," July 4, 1959, HCP.

"did not seem a bit perturbed": unidentified clipping, microfilm roll 1, WRSHP.

"indignation meeting": Claremore [Oklahoma] *Weekly Progress*, June 25, 1904.

"If he had only": WR to CVR, June 19, 1904.

brush with the law: Charles H. Tomkins to Homer Croy, October 16, 1953, HCP.

new world's record: unidentified clipping, Scrapbook A–1, WRM.

program: Scrapbook A–1, WRM.

74   "After circling around": quoted in Stansbury, *Lucille Mulhall,* 43.

"As a reward": unidentified clipping, Scrapbook A–1, WRM.

"To Whom It May Concern": WRM.

a week's engagement: Sime manuscript. This is a five-thousand-word manuscript, written by Will circa 1911, on stationery from the Hotel St. Francis on West Forty-seventh Street in New York. It begins, "Sime asked me to say how I got into show business and why I stayed"—the reference is to Sime Silverman, who founded the weekly show-business newspaper *Variety* in 1905—and is a jocular, slangy, not necessarily reliable account that takes Will from his birth to his first weeks on the vaudeville stage. It was never published in *Variety,* but Donald Day put it, in significantly edited form, into his so-called *Autobiography of Will Rogers.* It is now in the collection of Will Rogers, Jr.

    Will claimed that his Chicago engagement was canceled because of his failure to send photographs and his preferred billing in advance ("I didn't have any pictures and I didn't know what billing was"). Betty Rogers used the story in her biography of her husband, and it has been picked up by all subsequent biographers. But it wasn't true. In his scrapbook, Will saved a printed notice showing the "Coming Attractions" at the Chicago Opera House for the week of October 17, 1904. Listed, along with Charles Hawtrey ("The eminent English actor"), Carlin and Otto ("The Funny German Comedians"), and the Trolley Car Trio, was Will Rodgers. And, on the nineteenth, he reported on the engagement in a letter to Clem, stating, "I am doing all O.K."

    Will also gave an account of his second engagement in Chicago: "Well I was starting in to see a show at Cleveland's theater over Wabash Avenue and as I was buying my ticket he [the manager, presumably] was talking over the phone and wanted an act right now and I told him I did an act and he said, How long before you could get into doing it? I said, Just as long as it will take me to run to the hotel a few blocks away. Well in three minutes I was opening up his troupe."

"Instead of trying": Sime manuscript.

75   "The girls . . . made no secret": WR:HWS, 82.

"Dear old Pal": WR to BB, undated.

"He looked so funny": WR:HWS, 83.

76   This first full letter: WR to BB, October 29, 1904.

77   "I am deeply grieved": WR to BB, November 6, 1904.

The letters continued: WR to BB, November 20, 1904; WR to BB, November 30, 1904.

78   "I just sized you up": WR to BB, June 3, 1905.

79   "If you passed there on Sunday": OWR, 64.

"liked to eat": Mrs. P. N. Knotts 'to HC, April 19, 1952, HCP.

79   "The two vaudeville actresses": quoted in Rogers [Arkansas] *Daily News,*
July 1, 1950.

"she would be working in the back room": ibid.

80   " 'This is funny' ": *Puck,* November 11, 1908, reproduced in J. Dickson
Black, ed., "Short Stories and Wit of Tom P. Morgan" (Bentonville, Ark.:
Northwest Printing Co., undated), 8.

"The company proposes": reprinted in Rogers *Daily News,* May 28, 1981.
Morgan—who was born in Connecticut in 1864 and moved to Arkansas
as a young man—sent Will some material, but it came from a comic sensibility too alien to be of use to a man who once boasted that he never
told a "funny story" in his life. But possibly the example of Morgan as
a man who earned his living by writing humor, would eventually have
significance for Will. Morgan continued to publish his pieces, and for
many years wrote a daily column for the Kansas City *Star* under the
name Tennyson J. Daft. Will and Betty saw him whenever they visited
Rogers. He had several bouts of illness in the 1920s. During one of them,
Morgan's nurse recalled, "Mr. and Mrs. Rogers sent him daily letters or
telegrams and so many flowers that they filled the bath tubs. This amused
Mr. Morgan greatly. He said, 'Gee, that's what I call a friend, fill the
bath tubs with flowers so we don't have to take baths.' " (Vera Key,
"Memories of Tom P. Morgan," in J. Dickson Black, "Short Stories and
Wit of Tom P. Morgan," 5.)
    When Morgan died, in 1928, Will wrote about him: "He was a queer
Character. He wouldent leave there. We used to try and get him to come
east and visit us, or to California, but he stayed right there, wrote all his
stuff just from what he read and his local surroundings. But it was always
original, it was nobody's idea. An old Batchelor, he lived to himself. If he
had gotten out and mixed with people and had a chance to see all that
was going on with his queer way of describing things, he would have
raised quite a rumpus as a Writer. But he dident want to, and I don't
much blame him. . . . He died as a think he would have liked to. He saw
all he wanted to see. He did what he wanted to do. He had his life, he
had his laughs. He was satisfied, and when you are satisfied you are successful." WA 3, 187.

"kept up on show business": WA 3, 187.

"the most attractive girl": Virginia Blake Quisenberry oral history, Tape
T7-078, WRM.

81   "An old hammock": ibid.

"I am kinder foolish": WR to BB, November 20, 1904.

He had to delay the trip: WR to BB, November 30, 1904.

82   "Before the speakers were through": unidentified clipping, Scrapbook
A-1, WRM.

"Tom Rogers": ibid.

"perhaps the finest ropeman": undated, Scrapbook A–1, WRM.

Will and Jim palled around: Jim Minnick interview, undated, HCP.

program: Scrapbook A–1, WRM.

Mix explained: Milsten, *Will Rogers*, 51.

83　"Nights, after the show": Fred Gipson, *Fabulous Empire: Colonel Zack Miller's Story* (Boston: Houghton-Mifflin, 1946), 239.

polo game: Stansbury, *Lucille Mulhall*, 55.

Will and Mix: *The New York Times*, April 25, 1925, VIII, 5.

"He was distributing": unidentified clipping, Scrapbook A–1, WRM.

84　"the open-air flowers": ibid.

"Bill came to me": Milsten, *Will Rogers*, 51.

85　"women screamed": New York *World*, April 28, 1905.

"Over seats and down the stairs": New York *Herald*, April 28, 1905.

Yet another newspaper: unidentified clipping, Scrapbook A-1, WRM.

Mildred Mulhall: OWR, 347.

Minnick gave his account: Jim Minnick interview, HCP.

"I never did get to write you": WR to CVR, May 8, 1905.

86　There were about forty theaters: Michael M. Davis, Jr., *The Exploitation of Pleasure: A Study of Commercial Recreations in New York City* (New York: Russell Sage Foundation, 1911), 21.

"I sold Comanche": WR to Sallie McSpadden, June 3, 1905, in Reba Collins, *Will Rogers: Courtship and Correspondence, 1900–1915* (Oklahoma City: Neighbors and Quaid, 1992), 114.

receipt: Scrapbook A-III, WRM.

he'd gone on the stage: Gipson, *Fabulous Empire*, 241.

"I will stay here": WR to CVR, May 8, 1905, WRM.

87　Orange Horse Show: unidentified clipping, Scrapbook A–1, WRM.

"the undivided middle": Edward Milton Royle, "The Vaudeville Theatre," quoted in Charles Stein, *American Vaudeville as Seen by Its Contemporaries* (New York: Alfred A. Knopf, 1984), 31.

"Well about 6:30": Sime manuscript.

"Will Rogers made his debut": unidentified clipping, Scrapbook A–1, WRM.

CHAPTER 5

89   "I wish there was a vaudeville": WA 6, 124–125.

"you see it is the way": WR to sisters, July 5, 1905, in Reba Collins, *Will Rogers: Courtship and Correspondence, 1900–1915* (Oklahoma City: Neighbors and Quaid, 1992), 115.

minimum wage: According to a magazine article printed in 1907, the $75 Will was getting was precisely the low end of vaudeville salaries; the high was the $3,150 commanded by Lillian Russell. Most acts, according to the article, got between $250 and $500 a week. Hartley Davis, "The Business Side of Vaudeville," *Scribner's Magazine,* quoted in Charles Stein, *American Vaudeville as Seen by Its Contemporaries* (New York: Alfred A. Knopf, 1984), 114–115.

"puffed up there": Sime manuscript.

90   "the leading Vaudeville Theatre": WR to BB, December 5, 1906.

Willie Hammerstein: Stephen Burge Johnson, *The Roof Gardens of Broadway Theatres, 1883–1942* (Ann Arbor: UMI Research Press, 1985), 89–90.

91   Among the adjectives: assorted clippings, Scrapbook A–1, WRM.

once Will followed a comic-barber act: Homer Croy, OWR, 108.

"As I come off": Sime manuscript. "The wow finish is that finish of any vaudeville act which will lift roaring waves of applause to sweep toward the stage; a finish that Philadelphia and Phoenix, Montreal and Macon, Boston and Baton Rouge will respond to as certainly as New York. An added kick at the finish of an act . . . is the elusive little thing that every vaudevillian tries to capture for the completely comprehensible reason that its possession usually guarantees long routes and pleasant profits. . . . in building a new act or revamping an old one, more of thought, worry, anxiety and, later, experimentation are expended on the finish than upon the rest of it combined. Start to tell a vaudevillian the idea of a new act and he will interrupt you to ask, 'What's the finish?' " Walter De Leon, "The Wow Finish," *The Saturday Evening Post* 197 (February 14, 1925): 16 ff., quoted in Stein, *American Vaudeville as Seen by Its Contemporaries,* 194.

92   "he didn't talk on stage": Eddie Cantor, *My Life Is in Your Hands* (New York: Harper and Brothers, 1928), 104.

"a character with lots of character": Philadelphia *Item,* June 27, 1905, Scrapbook A–1, WRM.

"Sunday School Circuit": In all Keith's dressing rooms, the following "NOTICE TO PERFORMERS" was posted:
> You are hereby warned that your act must be free from all vulgarity and suggestiveness in words, action and costume, while playing in any of Mr. ———'s houses, and all vulgar, double-meaning and profane words and songs must be cut out of your act before the first

performance. If you are in doubt as to what is right or wrong, submit it to the resident manager at rehearsal.

"Such words as Liar, Slob, Son-of-a-Gun, Devil, Sucker, Damns, and all other words unfit for the ears of ladies and children, also any reference to questionable streets, resorts, localities, and barrooms, are prohibited under fine of instant discharge.

GENERAL MANAGER

Edwin Milton Royle, "The Vaudeville Theatre," *Scribner's Magazine* 26 (October 1899); quoted in Stein, *American Vaudeville as Seen By Its Contemporaries,* 24.

93   "I couldn't see where they come in": Sime manuscript.

"The most serious thing": Edward Milton Royle, "The Vaudeville Theatre," quoted in Stein, *American Vaudeville as Seen By Its Contemporaries,* 26.

"his plainsman 'talk' ": Boston *Globe,* July 4, 1905.

"Rogers himself": unidentified clipping, Scrapbook A–1, WRM.

"personal magnetism": the *Sunday Telegraph,* July 23, 1905.

"He laughs and talks wittily": unidentified clipping, Scrapbook A–1, WRM.

Once he was preceded: Oklahoma City *Times,* September 2, 1935.

94   two sheets of stationery: WRM.

95   "Next week": WR to CVR, September 5, 1906.

"You see the good part": WR to Maud Lane, as quoted in Collins, *Will Rogers: Courtship and Correspondence, 1900–1915,* 122.

Most of his fellow performers: Robert Snyder, *The Voice of the City: Vaudeville and Popular Culture in New York, 1880–1930* (New York: Oxford University Press), 1989, 41.

96   "as hardy and self-reliant": Theodore Roosevelt, *Ranch Life and the Hunting Trail* (New York: Century Co., 1888), 9–10.

97   "He talks and he acts": Rochester *Herald,* October 24, 1905.

"To meet Rogers": unidentified clipping, Scrapbook A–1, WRM.

"Yep, I read it": *Baltimore World,* December 6, 1906.

"The success of Rogers": *Sunday Telegraph,* November 12, 1905.

he arranged for . . . Fred Tejan: Fred Tejan to Homer Croy, September 9, 1952, HCP.

98   "Now I'll show you": unidentified clipping, Scrapbook A–1, WRM.

He got Teddy a blue blanket: WR:HWS, 93.

"they ask you a few questions": WR to Maud Lane, November 20, 1905, in Collins, *Will Rogers: Courtship and Correspondence, 1900–1915,* 124.

"I don't care for this vaudeville life": unidentified clipping, Scrapbook A–1, WRM.

98   "Like this theater work?": [Rochester] *Union and Advertiser,* October 26, 1905.

99   "Well its the same": WR to BB, August 10, 1905.

      "I dont know": WR to BB, October 17, 1905.

      Will had reinitiated: WR to BB, June 3, 1905.

      "This might sound like a joke": WR to BB, August 10, 1905.

      "I know it is foolish": WR to BB, October 17, 1905.

      At Christmastime: WR to BB, December 22, 1905.

100   *Variety* announced: Abel Green and Joe Laurie, Jr., *Show Biz from Vaude to Video* (Garden City, New York: Garden City Books, 1952), 80.

      "got a bite to eat": WR to BB, March 26, 1906.

      "Polly vue Francaise": ibid.

101   "It seems that it is a fact": WR to BB, April 17, 1906.

      "a fiery mustang": box number 3, WRM; translated by Emil Sandmeier.

      "He always salutes": WR to BB, April 17, 1906.

101-2 A second memorable occurrence: George Martin, "The Wit of Will Rogers," *American Magazine* (November 1919): 118; Fox press release, June 17, 1935, AMPAS.

102   This impression was heightened: C. van Niekerk to WRJR, May 31, 1940.

      The English papers: undated clippings, Scrapbook A–1, WRM.

104   "he never looked": WR:HWS, 96.

      Will is on the far right side: the photograph is in Scrapbook A–1, WRM.

      "from my point of view": WR:HWS, 97.

      "are the best paid": Hartley Davis, "In Vaudeville," *Everybody's Magazine* 13 (August 1905): 234.

105   "the lonesome time": WR to BB, April 26, 1909.

      "You must not worry": WR to BB, June 17, 1908.

      "yes, dear": WR to BB, October 27, 1908.

106   "He was a good ballplayer": unidentified clipping, microfilm reel 1, WRSHP.

      "played a good game": unidentified clipping, Scrapbook A–2, WRM.

      "had a fine breakfast": WR to BB, May 1, 1909.

      "They even had the Orchestra": WR to BB, June 12, 1908.

107   "got a bit stuck on me": WR to BB, December 5, 1906, WRM.

      "Am very glad you wrote": Nina to WR, undated.

      "Dear Carl": undated, WRM.

      "The Western Circuit": Scrapbook A–2, WRM.

      he didn't demand his salary: WR to BB, December 21, 1906.

108   "You are truly worthy": undated, WRM.

"Vaudeville wasn't just a career": June Havoc, "Old Vaudevillians, Where Are You Now?" *Horizon* 1 (July 1959): 113.

Other performers: William Howard Payne and Jake G. Lyons, eds., *Folks Say of Will Rogers: A Memorial Anecdotage* (New York: G. P. Putnam's Sons, 1936), 37.

Will had a large ring: WR:HWS, 98; WR to BB, November 20, 1908.

In December 1906; WR:HWS, 100.

"buy anything you see": WR to CVR, September 6, 1906.

"I want to get all that land": WR to CVR, September 19, 1909.

By 1910: New York *Telegraph*, May 29, 1910, Robinson Locke Collection, BRTC.

109   "No Money to be made here": WR to CVR, undated.

"Having no horses": unidentified clipping, Scrapbook A–2, WRM.

"A real American cowboy": Remininiscences of Rouben Mamoulian, COHC.

110   "It seems that I cant get west": WR to BB, February 6, 1908, WRM.

To lure performers: Green and Laurie, *Show Biz from Vaude to Video*, 87–88.

twenty-five-week contract: WRM.

"The man has temperament": Chicago *Journal*, September 2, 1907.

horoscope: Scrapbook A–2, WRM.

111   "Kid, I havent any *plans*": WR to BB, October 30, 1906.

"Well I wont write": WR to BB, June 15, 1905.

"Honest Kid": WR to BB, December 5, 1906.

"Now listen Kid": WR to BB, October 30, 1906.

"My Ideal Husband": reprinted in Rogers [Arkansas] *Daily News*, May 28, 1981.

112   "By the way": WR to BB, February 20, 1908.

"My Dearest": WR to BB, March 7, 1908.

113   "You are right": WR to BB, September 23, 1908. Elsewhere in the letter, Will wrote: "I know you thought from the way I wrote in the last letter that I loved the woman. No you were all wrong. I wrote that way cause I did not want to appear like I was *knocking* her after all that had happened." In the correspondence from Will that Betty saved, and that eventually found its way to the Will Rogers Memorial, the previous letter is dated July 5—two and a half months earlier—and makes no mention of any woman, indicating that Betty destroyed at least one letter. There is no evidence, in any case, of the identity of the woman or the details of "all that had happened."

Harvey's suicide: Beckley [West Virginia] *Post-Herald*, October 7, 1963.

114   "Oh Betty": WR to BB, November 12, 1908.

115   "I cannot remain silent": Cap Lane to BB, November 18, 1908.

"I am sure": Maud Lane to BB, November 18, 1908.

Betty's age on marriage license: Rogers [Arkansas] *Democrat,* November 26, 1908.

"dark traveling suit": WR to BB, November 24, 1908.

"Mr. Rogers and bride": Rogers [Arkansas] *Democrat,* November 26, 1908.

CHAPTER 6

117   "It was nice": WR: HWS, 103.

It drove them: WRJR, "Yours, Betty Rogers," Beverly Hills *Citizen,* November 28, 1941.

118   "We heard the bells": WR:HWS, 104–105.

"I remember Mrs. Harvey's": ibid., 105. Oscar "Battling" Nelson had recently been crowned lightweight champion of the world. The Metropole Cafe is still in business at 725 Seventh Avenue. If anything, its reputation has worsened over the years. In the mid-1960s, at the age of ten, the writer was struck that one could see nearly bare dancers through its doorway by slightly craning the neck. Mrs. Harvey had been separated from Coin and living in Chicago since 1901. She did not grant him a divorce, thus permitting him to marry his companion of nearly three decades, until 1929.

119   "His life had been full": ibid., 107.

"I never see Bill": Buck McKee to Maude McKee, February 24, 1909, box 1972, folder 21, Buck McKee Letters, Manuscript Collection, California State Library, Sacramento.

120   "a gentleman's gold watch": unidentified clipping, Scrapbook A–2, WRM.

her letters: BR to CVR, July 7, 1909; September 18, 1911; November 9, 1910; July 30, 1909.

"displayed more activity": unidentified clipping, WRM.

121   "I congratulate you": ibid.

"I got the coat allright": WR to CVR, January 13, 1906.

"Uncle Clem": William Howard Payne, and Jake G. Lyons, eds., *Folks Say of Will Rogers: A Memorial Anecdotage* (New York: G. P. Putnam's Sons, 1936), 54.

"I used to think": unidentified clipping, microfilm reel 1, WRSHP.

"we will just all go over": WR to CVR, January 5, 1911.

122 "Quite a number of friends": Chelsea [Oklahoma] *Reporter,* January 19, 1911.

"Billy wants a boy": BR to CVR, August 21, 1911.

Clem picked up the pace of his letters: CVR to WR, October 9, 1911; October 17, 1911; October 19, 1911.

123 "a pioneer who was a statesman": unidentified clipping, Scrapbook A–2, WRM.

the payroll alone: Scrapbook A–3, WRM.

"Do this": WR to CVR, undated, Mrs. John Pettyjohn Collection, Western History Collection, University of Oklahoma.

"He and I passed a fortune teller's booth": Herb McSpadden, transcript of interview with Paula M. Love, February 26, 1972, WRM.

124 "WILL ROGERS, The Droll Oklahoma Cowboy": Scrapbook A-2, WRM.

125 "I was sitting out at the stage door": Fred Stone, *Rolling Stone* (New York: Whittlesey House, 1945), 163–164.

"Every morning Will would come over": Bryan Sterling, *The Will Rogers Scrapbook* (New York: Grosset and Dunlap, 1976), 130–131.

126 "Houn' Dawg" song: Springfield [Massachusetts] *Union,* undated, Scrapbook A–2, WRM.

127 "Last winter I met a charming gentleman": I. and M. Ottenheimer, *New Vaudeville Jokebook* (Baltimore: I. and M. Ottenheimer, 1907); quoted in Charles Stein, *American Vaudeville as Seen By Its Contemporaries* (New York: Alfred A. Knopf, 1984), 189.

"While coming to the theater": *New Book of Monologues,* no. 1 of Wehman Bros.' Handy Series, p. 37; quoted in Albert F. McLean, *American Vaudeville as Ritual* (Lexington, Kentucky: University of Kentucky Press, 1965), 122–123.

"The peculiar thing about the cowboy act": Columbus [Ohio] *Sunday Dispatch,* October 8, 1911.

"stands alone and unique"; Cherry Sisters: unidentified clippings, Scrapbook A–3, WRM.

Milwaukee critic: ibid.

128 "Old Vaudeville Act": WRM.

129 She decided he would fit: Reminiscences of Blanche Ring, COHC.

"I knew it was all right": *Variety,* undated, Scrapbook A–2, WRM.

130 Max Hart took out: Scrapbook A–2, WRM.

"the most popular entertainer": New York *Post,* September 24, 1915, Ned Wayburn Scrapbooks, BRTC.

"The change in policy": unidentified clipping, Scrapbook A-2, WRM.

131   In his scrapbook copy: Scrapbook A–2, WRM.

"there is a perfectly delightful person": unidentified clipping, microfilm reel I, WRSHP.

"Will Rogers may be playing": Arkansas *Journal*, March 13, 1915, Robinson Locke Collection, BRTC.

Hands Up: Burns Mantle, "What's What in the Theatre," *The Green Book*, December 1916; "J. J. Shubert Tells the Story of Will Rogers," [New York] *Sunday Mirror*, July 29, 1934; WR:HWS, 126–127; Dorothy Stone Collins interview, in Sterling, *The Will Rogers Scrapbook*, 129.

132   Homer Croy: OWR, 134–135.

Town Topics: Ned Wayburn Scrapbooks, BRTC.

133   In an early version: Robert N. Smith, "Town Topics, A Review in Two Acts," copyrighted 1915, Theatre Collection, Museum of the City of New York.

"the most emphatic hit in the show": undated clipping, microfilm reel I, WRSHP.

Gene Buck: Buck gave numerous renditions of this incident over the years, the fullest appearing in the Oklahoma City *Times*, September 3, 1935. The quote comes from OWR, 137.

CHAPTER 7

135   "startling unaccountable phenomena": Charles Higham, *Ziegfeld* (Chicago: Regnery, 1972), 11.

136   On the way to California: WA 5, 79–80.

"I was muscularly exhausted": ibid., 41.

137   "that indefinable aroma of impropriety": Channing Pollock, "Our Follies—and Mr. Ziegfeld's," *The Green Book*, September 1918, 389.

"the peculiar frigidity and purity": Edmund Wilson, *The American Earthquake: A Documentary of the Twenties and Thirties* (Garden City, New York: Doubleday, 1958), 51.

139   "a fine looking, broad-shouldered man": November 3, 1915, quoted in Paula McSpadden Love, *The Will Rogers Book* (Waco, Texas: Texian Press, 1972), xiv.

On a Wednesday night: *The New York Times*, January 13, 1916.

140   "The reason Mr. Z keeps me here": "Gag Book," typed manuscript, WRM.

141   his first widely repeated topical joke: George Martin, "The Wit of Will Rogers," *American Magazine* (November 1919), 34.

There were two keys: Will Rogers, "The Extemporaneous Line," *Theatre* magazine (July 1917); reprinted in Steven K. Gragert, ed., *"How to Be*

Funny" and Other Writings of Will Rogers (Stillwater, Oklahoma: Oklahoma State University Press, 1982), 2–4.

142   "more newspaper extras": Kansas City *Star,* September 17, 1916, Robinson Locke Collection, BRTC.

"I guess I'm a couple editions": Detroit *News,* undated, Scrapbook A–3, WRM.

"I wish a few more nuts": New York *American,* undated, Scrapbook 20, WRM.

"chief source of entertainment": *The New York Times,* September 15, 1915.

Will was making more money: "Mr. Will Rogers, U.S. Income Tax, Sept. 16, 1916," WRM.

"By the time the last bit": *Evening Mail,* January 25, 1916. Ned Wayburn Scrapbooks, BRTC.

143   "I always go to all the first nights": Will Rogers, "The Extemporaneous Line," in Gragert, ed., *"How to Be Funny" and Other Writings of Will Rogers,* 4.

"A big shot": *Collier's,* April 13, 1956, Will Rogers file, BRTC.

"unless I know them personally": Will Rogers, "The Extemporaneous Line," in Gragert, ed., *"How to Be Funny" and Other Writings of Will Rogers,* 4.

"It's a hell of a time": Chicago *Herald,* March 14, 1917, Robinson Locke Collection, BRTC.

144   Eight years later: WA 1, 194–196.

146   "the President was pie": unidentified clipping, microfilm reel 2, WRSHP.

"I'd travel ten times that distance": Dedication of Will Rogers Memorial, November 4, 1938, as broadcast on NBC; Tape T7-023–T7-074, WRM.

He nervously parked: Rennold Wolf, unidentified clipping, microfilm reel 1, WRSHP.

Wilson's enjoyment: Martin, "The Wit of Will Rogers," 34; Heywood Broun, "Will Rogers," unidentified clipping [1918?], WRM.

"the happiest moments": WA 1, 196.

According to Betty: WR:HWS, 131.

The alternate version: unidentified clippings, Scrapbook A–3, WRM.

147   He earned $34,000: Will Rogers, 1917 and 1918 income tax returns, WRM.

"Mr. Rogers' name": *The New York Times,* June 10, 1917.

It was Edmund Wilson: Wilson, *The American Earthquake,* 51.

the *Times* likened him to Mark Twain: *The New York Times,* May 21, 1916.

147-8 *Everybody's Magazine:* (October 1917): 494–495.

148   "his comment on American life": Heywood Broun, undated clipping, Scrapbook 20, WRM.

"he deserves the attention": undated clipping, Scrapbook 20, WRM.

One day, readers were informed: New York *Herald,* August 16, 1917, Robinson Locke Collection, BRTC.

"Bryan says that he will go to war": New York *Telegraph,* May 16, 1917, Robinson Locke Collection, BRTC.

"headed straight for the glistening waters": New York *Sun,* May 6, 1916, Robinson Locke Collection, BRTC.

149   "roped them gently but firmly": New York *Sun,* September 10, 1917, Robinson Locke Collection, BRTC.

"They're all wool": Gladys Hall, "What the Follies Girls Have Done to Me," undated clipping, Scrapbook 20, WRM.

"I don't know why": WA 6, 179.

150   "the three musketeers": Eddie Cantor, "My Life Is in Your Hands," *The Saturday Evening Post* (October 1928): 42.

"He was of the family": WA 6, 179–180.

"Now Eddie": Eddie Cantor, *Take My Life* (Garden City, New York: Doubleday, 1957), 106.

"Rogers was my grammar school": ibid., 104–105.

151   the ground-floor star dressing room: Louise Brooks, *Lulu in Hollywood* (New York: Alfred A. Knopf, 1982), 76.

"little third-floor dressing room": WR:HWS, 137–138.

"Isn't he a wonderful man?": Robert Lewis Taylor, *W. C. Fields: His Follies and Fortune* (New York: New American Library, 1967), 91. See also Ronald J. Fields, ed., *W. C. Fields by Himself* (Englewood Cliffs, New Jersey: Prentic-Hall, 1973), 476.

He received a one-thousand-dollar insurance payment: Will Rogers, 1917 income tax return, WRM.

152   "Rogers bit on that gag": Cantor, *Take My Life,* 106.

Once, Fields came into Will's dressing room: Cantor, "My Life Is in Your Hands," 44.

Decades later: JR interview with BY, December 10, 1989.

153   "She is the eternal type": Mayme Ober Peak, "Mrs. Rogers and Will, and 'The House that Jokes Built,' " Kansas City *Star Magazine,* August 22, 1926.

Long Island was still undeveloped: WRJR, interview with BY, August 18, 1991.

One of Will Rogers, Jr.'s earliest: ibid.

154 "loap up to your camp": Charles M. Russell to Ed Borein, February 13, 1918; reproduced in *Good Medicine: Memories of the Real West* (Garden City, New York: Garden City Publishing Company, 1930), 49.

"I am not only going to": Notebook 003, WRM.

"I wish they would let me": WR to Karl Schmidt, undated, Special Collections Department, UCLA.

155 Ziegfeld had told him: Plans for the show were announced in *Variety,* January 18, 1918; *The New York Times,* January 20, 1918.

Will responded: WR to Florenz Ziegfeld, undated.

156 Sitting at a table: New York *Herald,* April 26, 1918, Ned Wayburn Scrapbooks, BRTC.

CHAPTER 8

159 "Straight on": WA 6, 199.

Will apologized: New York *Globe,* April 26, 1918, Ned Wayburn Scrapbooks, BRTC.

The first to score: New York *Herald,* April 26, 1918, Ned Wayburn Scrapbooks, BRTC.

160 "the old ladies' home": A. Scott Berg, *Goldwyn: A Biography* (New York: Alfred A. Knopf, 1989), 71.

161 One night, he left Manhattan: unidentified clipping, August 18, 1918, Robinson Locke Collection, BRTC.

One day, a reporter: ibid.

"The Director says": Will Rogers "Breaking in the Movies," typed manuscript, "MVN 3" file, WRM.

162 "a new star to filmdom": *Variety,* September 27, 1918.

"pervaded the piece": New York *Evening Post,* June 19, 1918.

"The life of the evening": Dorothy Parker, *Vanity Fair,* August 1918, Robinson Locke Collection, BRTC.

"Rogers can't seem to do much": Heywood Broun, New York *Tribune,* June 19, 1918.

162–3 Goldwyn contract: WRM.

163 "Everything I don't like they buy": unidentified clipping, May 25, 1919, Robinson Locke Collection, BRTC.

"The more I think about it": William H. Briggs to WR, May 1, 1919.

164 "I . . . will make you": Pell Mitchell to WR, December 13, 1918.

"attracting Oklahomans by the trainload": Kansas City *Times,* March 10, 1919. Ned Wayburn Scrapbooks, BRTC.

"in his derby hat": Kansas City *Star*, March 11, 1919. Robinson Locke Collection, BRTC.

Ziegfeld presented him: WR:HWS, 137.

"to fling a few parting shots": *The New York Times*, June 8, 1919.

"on Board Cal Limited": Kansas City *Star*, June 15, 1919, WRM.

165   "all dolled up": unidentified clipping, Scrapbook 20, WRM.

sales of book: Emily Dugdale, Harper and Brothers, to E. P. Alworth, quoted in Alworth, "The Humor of Will Rogers," Ph.D. dissertation, University of Missouri, 1958, 33.

Goldwyn studio: Berg, *Goldwyn*, 86.

So Goldwyn assigned: Clarence Badger, "Reminiscences," quoted in Bryan B. Sterling and Frances N. Sterling, *Will Rogers in Hollywood* (New York: Crown Publishers, 1984), 8–9.

166   "Vot good did it do you": unidentified clipping, February 27, 1921, Will Rogers file, BRTC.

"If he wanted me": Oakland *Tribune*, June 21, 1964; quoted in Harold G. Davidson, *Edward Borein: Cowboy Artist* (Garden City, New York: Doubleday, 1974), 99.

"This is a very fair": WRM.

"The Goldwyn people had engaged him": Grace Kingsley, "A High-Geared, Non-Stop Kidder," *Photoplay*, June 1920, AMPAS.

167   "He makes you forget": New York *Morning Telegraph*, review of *The Strange Boarder*, April 25, 1920, Scrapbook 20, WRM

von Stroheim: *The New York Times*, August 25, 1923.

One day, the Goldwyn publicity office: *The New York Times*, February 27, 1921.

draft of an advertisement: movie notes, WRM.

"In fact, until the coming": Clarence Badger, "Reminiscences," in Sterling and Sterling, *Will Rogers in Hollywood*, 12.

168   "THOUGHT I WAS SUPPOSED TO BE": WR to Samuel Goldwyn, October 7, 1919.

170   The critics recognized: *Variety*, October 28, 1921; *The New York Times*, October 24, 1921.

"without wrapping around": Arthur Mayer, *Merely Colossal* (New York: Simon and Schuster, 1953), 35.

Another Goldwyn salesman: illegible correspondent to WR, February 23, 1921.

Will went out and got a haircut: Irene Rich interview, Sterling and Sterling, *Will Rogers in Hollywood*, 26.

171 "Don't you think it distracting": Frederick James Smith, "An Actor Who Hates Closeups," *Motion Picture Classics* (November 1918), AMPAS.

"We are very delighted": BR to Maud Lane, undated [1919].

172 In 1919, he saw a painting: Frederic G. Renner, *Charles M. Russell* (New York: Harry N. Abrams, rev. ed., 1971), 239.

"We wont be able to": Charles M. Russell, *Good Medicine: Memories of the Real West* (Garden City, New York: Garden City Publishing Co., 1930), 27.

Will had met: WR to Charles F. Lummis, December 8, 1908, Braun Research Library, Southwest Museum, Los Angeles.

173 "The ignorant, hopelessly un-American": quoted in Kevin Starr, *Inventing the Dream: California Through the Progressive Era* (New York: Oxford University Press, 1985), 89.

"Out West is anywhere": Charles F. Lummis, *Out West,* vol. XV, no. 1 (January 1902): 60; quoted in Turbese Fisk and Keith Lummis, *Charles F. Lummis: The Man and His West* (Norman, Oklahoma: University of Oklahoma Press, 1975), 111.

"we had the usual official supper": ibid., 163.

174 Sometimes Charley Russell would be there: ibid.

"There isn't a man alive": Charles F. Lummis to BBR, July 2, 1927, Braun Research Library, Southwest Museum, Los Angeles.

175 cowboys streamed into Los Angeles: Kevin Brownlow, *The War, the West and the Wilderness* (New York: Alfred A. Knopf, 1979), 290.

"Bill would come in and say": J. J. Cohn interview with BY, December 10, 1989.

Ray Bell took them to the local men's store: Ray Bell interview with BY, June 5, 1990.

176 When Will's sister Maud: WR:HWS, 148.

"We used to saddle up in the morning": Ray Bell interview.

177 By 1923, he was making payments: "REAL ESTATE PAYMENTS," WRM.

"one day I was driving": Ray Bell interview.

"at least fifteen original sayings": Marion H. Kohn to WR, February 18, 1920.

178 "FAMOUS OKLAHOMA COWBOY HUMORIST": CA, 5.

"Mexico don't know how": CA, 8.

"I said: 'What makes the delegates": ibid., 18.

179 Goldwyn financial problems: Berg, *Goldwyn,* 102.

"so-called wise guys": Sterling and Sterling, *Will Rogers in Hollywood,* 48.

180 The script: NO STORY AT ALL, WRM.

"There is more genuine entertainment": *The New York Times,* January 15, 1923.

181   $45,135.07: Will Rogers, 1921 income tax return, WRM.

Will Rogers, Jr.: WRJR interview with BY, December 13, 1989.

CHAPTER 9

183   "We are living": DT 3, 45.

184   "It seems that before the war come along": WA 3, 94–95.

186   "In case this is not": movie notes, WRM.

Arbuckle's salary: Andy Edmonds, *Frame-up!: The Untold Story of Roscoe "Fatty" Arbuckle* (New York: William Morrow and Company, 1991), 136.

excellent reviews: *Variety,* February 3, 1922; *The New York Times,* January 20, 1922.

187   "OKAY THREE WEEKS": Max Hart to WR, October 18, 1921.

Shubert press release: WILL ROGERS TO PLAY THREE WEEKS ONLY IN SHUBERT VAUDEVILLE, November 5, 1921, FLPTC.

1922 *Frolic:* script at the Archives of the Performing Arts, University Library, University of Southern California, Los Angeles.

"Well, I never saw a man": Reminiscences of Eddie Dowling, COHC.

188   "In the afternoon": Betsy Rees Bevan to BY, February 21, 1990.

"Roy Rosenbaum was the show manager": Lucille Zinman interview with BY, March 13, 1990.

In a later edition of the *Follies:* Lina Basquette interview with BY, February 1, 1990.

189   "great factor": Albert D. Lasker to Owen D. Young and Eddie Rickenbacker, October 11, 1935, WRM.

"Well Hays the minute he spied me": undated manuscript, collection of Will Rogers, Jr.

According to Gene Buck: Oklahoma City *Times,* September 3, 1935.

190   "a road company on tour": WR:HWS, 167.

"In fact, it sounded like one of the best speeches": unidentified clipping, datelined February 16 [1922], Scrapbook 20, WRM.

in his syndicated column: WA 1, 111.

191   *Herald* review: New York *Herald,* June 6, 1922.

by the second night: *The New York Times,* June 11, 1922.

"we are all surprised": Florenz Ziegfeld to WR, June 2, 1923.

191–2 Carl Clancy information: Carl Clancy, undated, untitled manuscript, HCP.

192   "it totaled $19,583.20": Will Rogers, 1921 income tax return, WRM.

"since this was still cheaper": Rudy Behlmer, ed., *Memo from David O. Selznick* (New York: Viking, 1972), 4.

"Nobody can refuse a Roosevelt": Speeches 006–6, WRM.

193   "the alert and incalculable Mr. Will Rogers": *The New York Times*, October 28, 1922.

194   "You gentlemen shape the world": Speech 006–24, WRM.

"I was fortified": WA 1, 84.

at least one installment: WRM.

195   "I read the ones you used": WR to Mr. Shipman, undated.

what sold Will on the idea: OWR, 173.

The *Times* paid the syndicate: Carr Van Anda to V. V. McNitt, December 27, 1922, NYTA.

"It seems THE TIMES": WA 1, 1.

196   "ME IN YOUR MARK TWAIN EDITION": WR to Hannibal [Missouri] *Courier*, February 27, 1925, WRM.

"When Henry gets his hands": WA 2, 98.

197   "I believe that the stuff": V. V. McNitt to Carr Van Anda, December 22, 1922, NYTA.

198   "Borrowing money": WA 1, 40–41.

199   It's easy to pick out comments: WA 1, 325; WA 2, 49; WA 2, 48; WA 1, 308.

200   "Now Mr. Gary": WA 1, 94.

201   "The only one you never hear mentioned": WA 2, 216–217.

202   "That's why I can never take": WA 1, 369.

"Everything nowadays": WA 2, 15–17.

203   "He was just a big overgrown Kid": WA 1, 19.

"Today, as I write this": WA 2, 33–34.

204   "I bet you hadent been up there three days": original mansucript, WRM.

205   Roach went to the *Midnight Frolic:* Victor Shapiro, autobiographical manuscript, Special Collections Department, UCLA.

"after the Follies closes": New York *Tribune*, February 25, 1923, MOMA.

guaranteed salary of two thousand dollars: 1922 ledger, Hal Roach Studio Archives, Archives of the Performing Arts, USC, Los Angeles.

Years later, Roach recalled: Bryan Sterling, *The Will Rogers Scrapbook* (New York: Grosset and Dunlap, 1976), 141.

206   "All I ever do" Bryan B. Sterling and Frances N. Sterling, *Will Rogers in Hollywood* (New York: Crown Publishers, 1984), 56.

"It is as funny": *The New York Times,* January 27, 1924.

206–7   "I like the snaps": Shapiro manuscript, UCLA.

207   it posted a total loss: Hal Roach Studio Archives, USC.

"I took the matter up": unsigned memorandum, November 5, 1923, WRM.

"back on the gold standard": JR interview, undated, WRSHP.

Will signed an agreement: WRM.

208   "There is no way we can keep them": Art [last name not given] to WR, April 19, 1925.

"From then on": Ray Bell interview with BY, June 5, 1990.

209   "how to get up the West Hill": WR to Lee Adamson, undated [1925].

"This Hundred Dollars": WR to Florenz Ziegfeld, undated, WRM.

"Mr. Speaker": *Congressional Record*, May 29, 1924.

"turned a fiery red": *The New York Times*, May 30, 1924.

"My old fighting friend Jim Reed": WA 1, 246–247.

210   "All my life": CA, 34–35.

"the thrill of my entire life": ibid., 36–38.

211   "We heard nothing": ibid., 56.

"Well, I saw something": ibid., 59–61.

"WE WANT AL SMITH": WR to William Jennings Bryan, July 3, 1924, WRM.

"Papa called us all": CA, 83.

212   "A big political leader": ibid., 67–68.

213   "DONT FEEL BADLY": William G. McAdoo to WR, July 11, 1924.

"I have heard of plays": Follies Notes, WRM.

"My moment of delight": Barry Paris, *Louise Brooks* (New York: Alfred A. Knopf, 1989), 87–88.

214   "No you never did": Reba N. Collins, "Will Rogers: Writer and Journalist," Ed.D. dissertation, Oklahoma State University, 1967, 248.

"I have known Mr. Rogers": Will Rogers, *The Illiterate Digest* (New York: Albert and Charles Boni, 1924; reprinted, Stillwater: Oklahoma State University Press, 1974), 7.

215   "Like Mark Twain": *The Saturday Review of Literature*, February 21, 1925, 540.

"You can switch that around": original manuscript, WS 2, WRM.

"People were amused": WR:HWS, 187.

216   "claims that an Englishman": original manuscript, WS 8, WRM.

"HOWEVER THE LONGER I LIVE": WR to George Horace Lorimer, Stout Collection, Library of Congress, Washington, D.C.

That same July: clippings in Scrapbook 25, WRM.

217   "Are the Prince and I": WA 1, 223.

"even worked it up": WA 1, 292.

"Why say, I couldn't": Frances Donaldson, *Edward VIII* (London: Weidenfeld & Nicolson, 1974), 136.

218   "The Prince of Wales": typed manuscript, WRM.

"There is something wrong with a Party": WA 2, 322.

"as agreeable as an Insurance Agent": ibid., 24–25.

CHAPTER   10

221   "A truck ran over me": unidentified clipping, Scrapbook 9, WRM.

222   "All I used to know": WA 2, 95.

"we were getting into towns": Bruce Quisenberry to Homer Croy, undated [1952], HCP.

"problem changed": Charles L. Wagner, *Seeing Stars* (New York: G. P. Putnam's Sons, 1940), 315.

"twenty years of doubt": WA 2, 108.

224   "Instead of allowing the reporter": Birmingham [Alabama] *Age-Herald,* undated clipping, Scrapbook 25, WRM.

"I think I enjoyed that meal": Robert Ranord to WRJR, May 27, 1952.

225   "We jumped back and forth": Bruce Quisenberry to Homer Croy, undated [1952], HCP.

"I never saw": OWR, 194.

"YOU KNOW WHAT DAY": WR to BR, November 25, 1925, collection of Will Rogers, Jr.

226   "the Old Blue Serge": WA 2, 189.

description of lecture: LECTURE ROUTINE, SEASON: 1925–26, typed manuscript, WRM.

He had a whole speech: VARIOUS STUFF FOR LECTURE, typed manuscript, WRM.

"Hey, bub": Interview with Bruce Quisenberry, unidentified newspaper, WRM.

227   "You know how scared": WR to WRJR, October 12, 1926, WRM.

"gassing and gossipping": Quisenberry interview, WRM.

228   "It was a Rogers house": *The New York Times,* May 12, 1926.

"still is on": WR to George Horace Lorimer, undated, Stout Collection, Library of Congress, Washington, D.C.

Letters of introduction: WRM.

229   "The strike was carried on": Letters, 31–32.

"The start is a running one": George Horace Lorimer to WR, May 26, 1926, Stout Collection.

229 "There is only one fault": George Horace Lorimer to WR, October 27, 1926, Stout Collection.

230 "He explained to Lloyd George": Letters, 27.

"Boy, where did you": ibid., 28.

"a cocktail of a woman": Michael Holroyd, *Bernard Shaw: The Search for Fantasy, 1918–1950* (New York: Random House, 1991), 102.

"Well Lady Astor whispered": Letters, 22.

" 'just renewing old acquaintanceship' ": ibid., 49, 51.

231 "I am, I bet you": ibid., 72. Herbert Johnson was the illustrator for Will's *Post* articles.

Mussolini interview: ibid., 58–64.

233 "A very nice Spanish Chap": ibid., 96.

"This will introduce you": Edwin James to Walter Duranty, June 19, 1926, WRM.

"It was piloted": Will Rogers, *There's Not a Bathing Suit in Russia & Other Bare Facts* (New York: Albert and Charles Boni, 1927; reprinted, Stillwater: Oklahoma State University Press, 1973), 25.

"The real fellow": ibid., 53. Andrew Mellon was Coolidge's secretary of the treasury, Senator William Butler a close ally of the President.

234 "I bet you": ibid., 52.

"When I die": Boston *Globe,* June 16, 1930.

"Well, young man": Pinky Tomlin, *The Object of My Affection* (Norman: University of Oklahoma Press, 1981), 59.

235 "Naturally, we of the audience": unidentified clipping, Scrapbook 21, WRM.

236 "the largest fee": *The New York Times,* August 18, 1926.

"came over especially from Paris": quoted in WR:HWS, 198.

"arranged matters with Lipton": Sir Thomas Dewar to WR, July 21, 1926, WRM.

237 "Nancy Astor": DT 1, 1.

"Hughes was reluctant": New York *Telegram,* undated clipping, Scrapbook 21, WRM.

238 "If that gentleman is not kidding me": WR to Everett Sanders, undated.

"This is what I call": Irwin Hoover, *Forty-Two Years in the White House* (Boston: Houghton Mifflin, 1934), 152–154.

Will's account: reprinted in Steven K. Gragert, ed., *More Letters of a Self-Made Diplomat* (Stillwater: Oklahoma State University Press, 1982), 10–16.

240 "I thought the matter of rather small consequence": Calvin Coolidge to WR, January 11, 1925.

"it is expected to make advertising": unidentified clipping, Scrapbook A–1, WRM.

241 "could afford to go out": WR to WRJR, October 12, 1926.

"We have seated them": WR to WRJR, March 14, 1927.

"I ALWAYS WAS WORRIED": Florenz Ziegfeld to WR, June 15, 1927.

presents: WRJR interview, tape T7–062-A3, WRM.

242 eighteen printings: Reba N. Collins, "Will Rogers: Writer and Journalist," Ed.D. dissertaion, Oklahoma State University, 1967, 240.

"It is wonderful": BBR to Maud Lane, undated [1924].

"He talked to himself": Jim Hopkins oral history, Tape T7–087–1, WRM.

"roam over the country": *The New York Times*, August 28, 1927.

Douglas Fairbanks, Jr.: interview with BY.

243 "He is the one man": DT 1, 129.

According to Betty: WR:HWS, 200. There is also an undated clipping from the New York *Telegraph* that probably predates 1915 and purports to be an account of his first flight. When it was over, he was quoted as saying to the pilot, "Try anything once. Try some things oftener; when you goin' up again?" Robinson Locke Collection, BRTC.

"I have always heard": WA 2, 28.

He tried to slip undetected: *The New York Times*, December 12, 1925.

"Mitchell later said": Ruth Mitchell, *My Brother Bill* (New York: Harcourt Brace and Co., 1953), 330.

"Here I am": Rogers, *There's Not a Bathing Suit in Russia*, 27.

244 aviator Nathan Browne: Reminiscences of Nathan Browne, COHC.

by the time of his death: Doris L. Rich, *Amelia Earhart: A Biography* (Washington, D.C.: Smithsonian Institution Press, 1989), 209.

"Paint has been put down": DT 1, 210.

245 "They just had their first snow": WA 5, 96.

"Other places": Mark Twain, *Adventures of Huckleberry Finn* (New York: Library of America, 1982), 739.

"slim, tall, smiling": DT 1, 90.

"picked him up": WRJR interview with BY, December 12, 1992.

"passed some pretty uneasy moments": OWR, 22.

"Didn't you see the way?": RB, 9.

246 "He eats, sleeps and drinks": WA 3, 89.

"I was kinder disappointed": Steven K. Gragert, ed. *"How to Be Funny" and Other Writings of Will Rogers* (Stillwater: Oklahoma State University Press, 1983), 65.

insisted that the aviatrix Blanche Noyes: Reminiscences of Blanche Noyes, COHC.

246 the worst coming in 1929: WR:HWS, 201–202.

"For the first time in my life": DT 1, 146.

247 "Bolshevist threat": quoted in Kenneth Davis, *The Hero, Charles A. Lindbergh: The Man and the Legend* (London: Longmans, 1960), 253.

"He was all over the place": Reminiscences of George Rublee, COHC.

"Any other aviator": DT 1, 158.

248 "There wasn't even as much as a sandwich": "Talk at Montclair High School, April 16, 1928," typed transcription, WRM.

"The throng on the field": Elizabeth Morrow diary, December 14, 1927, Sophia Smith Collection Smith College, Northampton, Massachusetts. Of the embassy dinner the night before, Mrs. Morrow had written, "Will R. very amusing—the President delighted."

"In France and America": DT 1, 158.

"Smile, Lindy, smile": *The New York Times,* December 15, 1927.

"I saw all Mexico": DT 1, 159.

"got an overdose of stimulants": *Mencken & Sara: A Life in Letters,* Marion Elizabeth Rodgers, ed. (New York: Anchor Books, 1992), 377.

249 best-paid columnist: V. V. McNitt to Adolph Ochs, May 16, 1930, NYTA.

"Please do not correct": F. T. Birchall memorandum, May 19, 1930, NYTA.

A visitor to Will's house: Homer Croy, "The Will Rogers Nobody Knows," unidentified publication, movie file, WRM.

"I think Mr. Coolidge's statement": DT 1, 115.

250 "No attempt at jokes": ibid., 90.

"had his father's blonde curly hair": DT 3, 137.

"Did you ever see such a day": ibid., 138

251 "Col. Will Rogers": "Congressional Record—House," January 9, 1928, 1198.

"When that was done as a joke": DT 1, 177.

"the Republican elephant": Steven K. Gragert, ed., *"He Chews to Run": Will Rogers' Life Magazine Articles 1928* (Stillwater: Oklahoma State University Press, 1982).

252 "The author of this article": ibid., 101.

"We had one hell of a time": Robert Sherwood to Homer Croy, March 17, 1952, HCP.

Still others saw both: Gragert, ed., *"He Chews to Run,"* 26, 27; Dorothy Van Doren, "Will Rogers, the Bunkless Candidate," The *Nation,* vol. 127, no. 3300 (October 3, 1928): 314.

"It was impossible to check": Robert Sherwood to Homer Croy, March 17, 1952, HCP.

253   For his last flight: Fred Stone, *Rolling Stone* (New York: Whittlesey House, 1945), 235–236.

"If he ever made that offer": Wagner, *Seeing Stars*, 319.

254   "If you sue": ibid., 322.

"Dorothy, I have news for you": Sterling, *The Will Rogers Scrapbook*, 133.

"When they brought him in": Bryan Sterling, *The Will Rogers Scrapbook* (New York: Grosset and Dunlap, 1976), 132.

255   "Mr. Rogers made havoc": New York *Tribune*, October 16, 1928.

"YOU GAVE ME SUCH A GRAND EVENING": Noel Coward to WR, November 2, 1928.

"The whole business out here": WA 3, 171.

256   "You meet an actor or girl": WA 4, 36.

257   "If Winnie Sheehan": Will Rogers contract, March 14, 1929, Twentieth Century–Fox Archives, UCLA.

CHAPTER 11

259   "Up betimes and at my stint": WA 5, 187. This passage, part of a column written in September 1932, was Will's attempt to "do like those New York columnists do"—especially O. O. McIntyre, whose pieces combined homey personal details with non sequitur observations. The "betimes" and "not one whit" were courtesy of the man Will had previously referred to as "some old writer called Pepy [*sic*], and all he did was just write what he did." WA 4, 227.

"Will Rogers is the man": Ken Taylor, unidentified review of *They Had to See Paris*, Scrapbook 9, WRM.

"Will Rogers sent a nifty Cadillac Roadster": Will and Ariel Durant, *A Dual Autobiography* (New York: Simon and Schuster, 1977), 183–184.

260   The company signed him to a new contract: Will Rogers contract, October 27, 1930, Twentieth Century–Fox Archives, UCLA.

261   "I'm not going to change": George C. Pratt, "In Search of the 'Natural': An Interview with Frank Borzage," *Cinema Journal* 28 (Spring 1989): 38.

"Mr. Rogers has an original way": *The New York Times*, July 28, 1929.

"I figured I better": WA 4, 69.

"My picture had opened": ibid., 72–73.

"best screen role": *The New York Times*, October 20, 1929.

262   "I don't remember": Samuel Goldwyn to WR, October 3, 1929.

262 profit of $700,000: Jack Lait, *Our Will Rogers* (New York: Greenberg, 1935), 23. This quickie biography, by a reporter and press agent who knew Will for more than two decades, is not particularly reliable, but the information on Will's movie career came directly from Winfield Sheehan, also a longtime friend of Lait's.

263 "I don't think he ever read": Bryan B. Sterling and Frances N. Sterling, *Will Rogers in Hollywood* (New York: Crown Publishers, 1984), 151.

"listening for cues": Rochelle Hudson, "On the set with Will Rogers," unidentified publication, movie file, WRM.

"I just wait and hear": Thornton Sargent, "Will Outwits the Sexy Fellows," unidentified publication, movie file, WRM. The actress quoted was Peggy Wood.

script for *In Old Kentucky*: Twentieth Century–Fox Screenplay Collection, Archives of the Performing Arts, USC, Los Angeles.

264 "His relaxed attitude": Sterling and Sterling, *Will Rogers in Hollywood*, 129.

"Will nudged me": ibid., 111.

"He got a five-ton truck": Bryan Sterling, *The Will Rogers Scrapbook* (New York: Grosset and Dunlap, 1976), 122.

265 "was visited by": undated, Will Rogers file, AMPAS.

" 'O.K. Now comes the window shot' ": Sterling Holloway interview, Sterling, *The Will Rogers Scrapbook*, 163.

"not really a ranch": WA 5, 48.

266 "Now look out we got a big Idea": WR to Lee Adamson, undated, WRSHP.

"as though a bird's-eye view": *Palisadian*, July 13, 1927.

267 "They stayed till they died": JR, undated interview, WRSHP.

"They wouldn't run": WRJR interview, March 18, 1976, WRSHP.

One time, William G. McAdoo: Jim Hopkins oral history, tape T7–087–1, WRM.

"I am no polo player": WR to Internal Revenue Service, undated, WRM.

268 "Will Rogers was the only polo player": Robert Stack, *Straight Shooting* (New York: Macmillan, 1980), 19.

"the puzzle figure of polo": Harry Carr, undated, unidentified clipping, Scrapbook 9, WRM.

269 "She took one golf club": JR interview, March 8, 1976, WRSHP.

Once, he picked up Big Boy Williams: Joel McCrea interview, Sterling, *The Will Rogers Scrapbook*, 121.

When he was traveling in Shanghai: unidentified clipping, WR file, AMPAS.

"There is no more fun now": WR to WRJR, March 14, 1927.

"a beautiful home": Los Angeles *Times,* January 23, 1927.

He engaged another architect: Frederick "Ken" Reese, "My Experiences with Will Rogers When Working for Him as a Young Architect," 1988 transcription of 1978 tape-recorded interview, WRSHP.

270   "it takes 'em so long": WA 4, 21–22.

271   "That's what makes a good Cow outfit": WA 5, 94.

"followed the children around": WR:HWS, 269. Sarah Kleberg's husband died in 1931, leaving a two-year-old son, Belton Dandy Kleberg Johnson, and Will wrote the baby a letter that testifies to the loyalty and care he lavished on his friends:

> Dear Sir,
>   I never met you, but I know you through some mutual friends. One is a particular friend of mine, and a casual friend of yours. Her name is Sarah Johnson. While you know her now, in after years you will know her better, and this is a kind of letter of introduction about her, that you can use in years to come, for she is liable to cross your trail many times in the future. Course you being a fine young man you might not be interested in older Women. But this one is unusual. She was always unusual. You know what she was as a Girl? Well, this might interest you (for being a young fellow raised up on a ranch like you, why stories connected with ranch life will always make you lend an ear).
>   Well this Sarah, she was just a Girl then. She grew up on a Big, Big, oh ever so Big Ranch, and her folks sent her to schools, fine ones in the east, and they thought naturally she would grow up and go in Society, and spend her summers with friends in the east, and come to the ranch occasionally, to visit her folks. But listen here Mr Belton, she dident do that, no, she just stuck around home. . . . She grew up with the Boys and the Cattle, and she got so she could work with em, not just go out and be in the way, but actually do 'Cow work.' She was a dandy rider. Oh you ought to have lived those days and seen her ride. . . .
>   This ranch that I am telling you about Mr. Johnson, was one of the noted places in our whole United States, and folks from even foreign Countries were tickled to death to get an invitation to visit there, and to maby go hunting, and let me tell you something about this Girl, and her hunting. She used to give these Dudes the first shot at a Coyote, or a Deer, and after they had missed him and he was going in behind a Mesquite Bush, she would up with her rifle and bump him off. Say Kid it would have done your heart good to see this girl.
>   Well I must get on with my story. She becomes famous for her riding and shooting, but for her graciousness, her personality, and

her consideration for others. Well the Ranch was known all over the world, and she was known by everyone that visited the ranch, and that was many, and they all wondered why she dident get married, for every young man that come her way would have offered his hand. But she just dident seem to Cotton to all these rich fellows. Well this kept along for quite awhile. Say I'm not bothering you with all this am I? I dident think I was for young fellows like you always like a romantic story. Well Sir just when it looked like she wasent going to ever fall in love with anyone, why a Boy right near home that she had known for a long time. He was a very fine young man, everyone liked him, and everyone was so pleased when they fell in love, it was a real love match.

But all great love stories in plays and in Literature must have drama. Well this was more sudden, for this healthy strong young fellow had an illness. It was of a long lingering nature, and he had to be taken to a hospital, so they chose the most famous in America, and this Girl went right with him, and they had famous Doctors who performed operation after operation, and she never lost hope, she just stayed right there not only week after week, but year after year. Her devotion was the talk of her friends. They all prayed that such love would be rewarded, and it was, not in the way they had prayed for at first, for this fine young sweetheart of hers was taken from her in the very honeymoon of their wonderful lives. But God works in mysterious ways, he repays us all in some way for the good or the bad that we do, and he repayed this wonderful Girl for her constant care, love, and devotion to her Lover. Before he passed on, he brought her the sweetest thing in life, a Baby, a Baby Boy, so that all her life she would have the offspring from their wonderful love. So she went back to the ranch, this tremendous big place, where she had rode as the Girl with no thought or care of the future. She come back among her loved ones, who loved her more than ever now that they knew the stuff she was made of. Her dreams are shattered, she dont come back with her Husband, but she does come back with her husbands Boy, and Her Boy.

Now aint that a sweet love story Mr Belton Dandy? But its not ended yet. We got another Chapter, another Act that has to be put on. This Baby, this Boy, this fulfillment of this love match, we have to make him grow up, and we must make him see the kind of Mother and Father he had. We must tell him that every day of his life he must do something that will make his Mothers sorrow easier to corry. He must try and be the reincarnation of his Father, he must know what a wonderful Mother he has, how brave she was, and how she carried on and raised him up to where he must carry on and care for her.

Now Mr. Belton dont you think that little fellow has a lot to live for, and a lot to be proud of? I think he is a pretty lucky little fellow after all to share all this love all to himself.

Well thats about all to my story. But you will, as I say, run into these folks from time to time, thats what will make this story interesting to you, and you see if this Woman aint like I tell you. And I bet the Boy will make her proud like I said too.

You would if you was him wouldent you Mr Belton Dandy Kleberg Johnson? Sure you would.

This is just the wanderings of an old Actor, that your family was nice to.

> Your friend always.
> Will Rogers.

WR to Belton Johnson, undated.

Sarah Johnson (on whom the character played by Mercedes McCambridge in the film *Giant* was based) died in a car accident in 1942. Her son eventually sold his interest in the King Ranch and became a prominent independent rancher in South Texas. For many years he owned the Fairmount and Hyatt Regency hotels in San Antonio; he sold the Fairmount in 1992. "I've lived by those letters for fifty years," B. K. Johnson said in 1993, referring to what Will wrote to him and to his mother. "I took them to Korea with me and I carry a copy of them in my briefcase wherever I go." (Interview with BY, April 26, 1993.)

271 a guest of William Randolph Hearst's: WRJR interview with BY, December 12, 1989.

"He would call to me": WR:HWS, 272.

"He loved the ranches": JR interview, March 8, 1976, WRSHP.

272 "I am going to get a regular slip": WR to WRJR, undated.

"seventh heaven": JR, interview with BY, December 10, 1989.

"She was in the romantic stage": ibid.

Once, Jim was in a school speaking contest: ibid.

"What are you trying to do": ibid.

273 "I would rather have you give up that Latin": WR to WRJR, November 23, 1926.

"You'd be sitting on a horse": JR, interview with BY, December 10, 1989.

274 "He not only adored Betty": unidentified clipping, Will Rogers file, FLPTC.

"left something on earth": WA 3, 189.

275 "A mighty narrow road": WA 6, 118.

"I swear": Elisabeth Cobb, *My Wayward Parent: A Book About Irvin S. Cobb* (Indianapolis: Bobbs-Merrill, 1945; reprinted, Westport, Connecticut: Greenwood Press, 1971), 203

"said he dident": WA 6, 118.

One day, he drove the young actor home: Sterling, *The Will Rogers Scrapbook*, 122.

276   Once, McCrea took Mary out: ibid., 118.

"Open all the cans": DT 3, 54.

"His jaws snap": quoted in CA, 105.

he kept rubbing the lenses: Hal Roach interview in Sterling, *The Will Rogers Scrapbook*, 141–142.

"fiddle-footed": JR interview, undated, WRSHP.

277   "That evening he came to my hotel": New York *Post*, August 26, 1935.

"I got one little old soft flat red grip": WA 6, 147.

"When I finally brought the two men": Charles Graves, *The Cochran Story* (London: W. H. Allen, undated), 136. In 1926, an English newspaper had reported that Shaw was a guest at a dinner for Will in London, and said upon being introduced to him, "Why, they told me you were a red Indian—I don't see any feathers." The article went on to quote Shaw as saying that Will had given him "more pleasure than any other American since Mark Twain lunched with him during his last visit to England." In 1944, a researcher sent Shaw a copy of the article and received the following reply: "This is completely fabulous. I saw Will Rogers once, at my own house in London when he called on me with a friend [Graves, presumably]. I had never read a line of his, nor even heard of his existence; and was no wiser when he left after a pleasant chat (he was to me only a likeable stranger) that lasted perhaps twenty minutes," George Bernard Shaw to ?, March 5, 1944, WRM.

"The old cowman": William Howard Payne and Jake G. Lyons, *Folks Say of Will Rogers: A Memorial Anecdotage* (New York: G. P. Putnam's Sons, 1936), 136–137.

278   "TO SEE WHAT THIS WARS ALL ABOUT": WR to Adolph Ochs, November 18, 1931, NYTA.

"China owns the lot": WA 4, 213.

"America could hunt all over the world": DT 3, 108.

279   "About all I do": WA 5, 53–54.

280   "He was rather diffident": Oscar Lawler: Los Angeles Attorney, Oral History Project, UCLA, 1962, copyright, regents of the University of California.

"He was the most sensitive": undated clipping, Will Rogers file, FLPTC.

"Beyond this hail-fellow-well-met personality": OWR.

"I'll come out there": ibid., 277–278.

"Your name is Corey Ford": WR to Corey Ford, undated.

"Now who cares": undated clipping, Will Rogers file, AMPAS.

281   "Then, suddenly": Ben Dixon McNeil, quoted in Payne and Lyons, *Folks Say,* 116.

One night, Goldberg was shocked: Peter C. Marzio, *Rube Goldberg: His Life and Work* (New York: Harper & Row, 1973), 92–93.

"What all of us know together": WA 5, 45–46. Presumably, Will meant to type "lose *it*" in the final sentence.

CHAPTER 12

285   "No nation in the history of the world": DT 1, 251–252.

286   "Coolidge went in": Rob Wagner's *Beverly Hills Script,* vol. 1, no. 18 (June 15, 1929): 4.

"Talking about Prohibition": RB, 53.

287   "long winded editorial": OWR, 278.

"early training at Eton and Oxford": quoted in DT 3, 298.

"Look at the man": St. Louis *Post-Dispatch,* June 11, 1928.

288   "Don't you think Will Rogers": Sulzberger to Ochs, January 17, 1927, NYTA.

"It has been our idea": January 17, 1933, NYTA. The *Times,* in fact, made an offer to Lippmann in 1931, but there was no swap involved. Ronald Steel, *Walter Lippmann and the American Century* (Boston: Atlantic-Little, Brown, 1980), 275.

"AM SURE YOU SHARE OUR HOPE": Ochs to WR, January 21, 1930, NYTA.

289   "It should be remembered": Ochs to WR, November 18, 1931, NYTA.

"WE DID NOT USE YOUR PIECE": February 1, 1933.

"One message of three words": DT 3, 238–239.

290   "destructive obscurantism": *The New York Times,* November 28, 1932. Ogburn went on to work for the U.S. State Department, rising to the position of chief of the division of research for the Near East, South Asia, and Africa. In 1957, he wrote a novel, *The Marauders,* about his World War II experience with a semiguerrilla regiment in Burma. The sale of the book to Warner Brothers enabled him to retire from the government and concentrate on writing, which he has done ever since, lately developing an expertise in alternative identities for Shakespeare.

"The Reconstruction Finance Corporation": DT 3, 271.

"Frank Phillips, of oil fame": DT 4, 52.

"No answer to this tonight": McCaw to James, undated, NYTA.

"HE MADE ME MAD JIMMIE": WR to Edwin L. James, November 29, 1930, NYTA.

It was followed by eleven letters: *The New York Times,* November 30, 1932.

290   "I would like to state": DT 3, 247.

291   "Well if they would just stop to think": WA 5, 212–213.

292   "You can never have another war": Jerome Beatty, "Betty Holds the Reins," *American Magazine* (October 1930).

Vice President Garner: Edwin A. Halsey to WR, June 9, 1933.

"All I have to say": Cleveland *Plain Dealer,* November 23, 1930.

293   "He never again had": Reminiscences of Horace M. Albright, COHC.

"Wait four years": Reminiscences of Jonah J. Goldstein, COHC.

"The Democrats nominated their President": DT 2, 233.

"I remember Young saying": Reminiscences of Frederick Trubee Davison, COHC.

294   "and talk to me of cabbages and kings": Franklin D. Roosevelt to WR, April 3, 1931.

"Oh it was a great game": WA 4, 87–88.

"It's really not depression": WA 5, 82.

"You know this darn thing": ibid., 132.

295   "Our rich is getting richer": WA 4, 216.

"Mr. Coolidge and Wall Street": DT 2, 64.

"If you live under a Government": WA 4, 224–226.

"barricades in the street": Robert S. McElvaine, *The Great Depression: America 1929–1941* (New York: Times Books, 1984), 90.

296   "Will Rogers likes to pose": quoted in Croy, *Our Will Rogers,* 279.

He gave two names: Joe Klein, *Woody Guthrie: A Life* (New York: Alfred A. Knopf, 1980; paperback edition, New York: Ballantine Books, 1986), 126.

his son Bill: WRJR, interviews with BY, December 12, 1989, and November 3, 1991.

On Washington's Birthday: DT 2, 274.

"Well, I believe if I was unemployed": DT 3, 67.

"Had a long talk": DT 2, 158.

297   "Now we read the papers": RB, 66.

"flying over great stretches of GOD's earth": *The New York Times,* April 23, 1931.

"My sober and considered judgment": McElvaine, *The Great Depression,* 79.

298   "it is beginning to look": Jackson [Kentucky] *Times,* July 3, 1931.

Governor James Ferguson: unidentified clipping, Scrapbook 9, WRM.

"Little did we realize": *Home Friend* magazine (May 1932), Scrapbook 9, WRM.

some of the responses: "Excerpts From Letters of Home Friend Readers Who Approve the Idea of Will Rogers being Nominated for the Presidency," typewritten manuscript, WRM.

He was surprised to find: Elsie Janis, "What I Know About Will Rogers," *Liberty* magazine, March 11, 1933.

"Don't forget": Franklin D. Roosevelt to WR, June 1, 1932.

299   "Will you do me one favor": DT 3, 46.

"I couldn't be a politician": WR to James Davenport, undated.

Will made an impromptu speech: articles quoted in CA, 133.

300   "that sterling citizen": ibid., 134.

"This is the biggest audience": WR:HWS, 278.

"I dident wire you": WR to Franklin D. Roosevelt, undated night letter.

302   "America hasn't been as happy": DT 4, 1.

"It just shows you what a country can do": ibid., 4.

303   "That bird has done more for us": RB, 73.

"He swallowed our depression": quoted in Peter C. Rollins, *Will Rogers: A Bio-Bibliography* (Westport, Connecticut: Greenwood Press, 1984), 211.

the White House phoned NBC: Arthur Frank Wertheim, *Radio Comedy* (New York: Oxford University Press, 1979), 80.

"Some people are wondering": Rollins, *Will Rogers*, 223.

CHAPTER   13

305   "I am glad": WRM.

"That Post": WA 5, 49.

"A fellow can't afford": WA 6, 237.

Real estate dealings: James Blake to Oscar Lawler, May 23, 1931; "Financial Statement of Will P. Rogers," May 1, 1928; schedule of interest payments, 1928—all, WRM.

306   "I looked at him and said": Bernard Baruch, *Baruch: The Public Years* (New York: Holt, Rinehart and Winston, 1960), 223.

His per-picture fee dropping: WR contracts, July 21, 1932; December 30, 1933—both, Twentieth Century–Fox Archives, UCLA.

he still made $324,314: Philadelphia *Bulletin*, undated clipping, Will Rogers file, Temple Urban Archives, Temple University, Philadelphia. Watson earned $364,432.

almost as much: *The New York Times*, March 30, 1930.

"Ziegfeld's Follies of the Air": Detroit *Free Press*, August 17, 1935.

Fox finances: Aubrey Solomon, *Twentieth Century–Fox: A Corporate and Financial History* (Metuchen, New Jersey, and London: Scarecrow Press, 1988), 13, 24.

307   "When that alarm goes off": "Good Gulf Show," May 17, 1933, quoted in Peter C. Rollins, *Will Rogers: A Bio-Biography* (Westport, Connecticut: Greenwood Press, 1984), 10.

"On the stage when you tell anything": WA 3, 127.

"laugh at the serious parts": RB, 97.

308   "Mr. Rogers said, 'Since you're here": Emil Sandmeier, interview with BY, June 8, 1990.

J. Frank Drake: "Statement of J. Frank Drake," typewritten manunscript, WRM.

"Our record with the Indians": RB, 18.

309   he *should* have been censored: "Good Gulf Show," January 21, 1934; January 28, 1934; quoted in Rollins, *Will Rogers*, 217.

the anecdotal evidence: unidentified clippings, Scrapbook 9, WRM.

"reverted to the word": WR to Mr. Tobias, undated, WRM.

310   Fox's first production: Solomon, *Twentieth Century–Fox*, 16.

"divorced from the necessity": New York *Herald Tribune*, January 27, 1933.

consistently brought in rentals of over a million dollars: This statement is based on figures provided by Twentieth Century–Fox to the author of a master's thesis about Lamar Trotti, who wrote or co-wrote three late Rogers pictures: *Judge Priest* (rentals of $1,222,600), *Life Begins at Forty* ($1,329,800), and *Steamboat Round the Bend* ($1,568,300); Maynard Tereba Smith, "A Survey of the Screenplays Written by Lamar Trotti with Emphasis on Their Acceptance by Professional and Non-professional Groups," master's thesis, University of Southern California, June 1953, 264.

"They give a comfortable feeling": New York *Sun*, April 5, 1935, quoted in Bryan B. Sterling and Frances N. Sterling, *Will Rogers in Hollywood* (New York: Crown Publishers, 1984), 156.

311   "At a time when the American farmer": Dwight Macdonald, "Notes on Directors," *Symposium 1933*, Will Rogers file, AMPAS.

"Rogers' philosophy was reactionary": David Thomson, *A Biographical Dictionary of Film* (New York: William Morrow and Company, 1976), 487.

312   "Paht of the time he suhprises me": unidentified clipping, February 24, 1935, Will Rogers file, MOMA.

313   which Ford late in his life: Sterling and Sterling, *Will Rogers in Hollywood*, 151.

"fine, shrewd, humorous": Eugene O'Neill, *Ah Wilderness!* in *The Plays of Eugene O'Neill*, vol. II (New York: Random House, 1982), 188.

"THERE IS ROOM IN THE LEGIT": quoted in WA 6, 123.

314   Alexander Dean: Alexander Dean to Mary Rogers, May 30, 1934.

"It is, perhaps, news": undated clipping, Mary Rogers Scrapbook, WRM.

"with a simple sincerity": *The New York Times,* May 1, 1934.

Variety reported: *Variety,* July 3, 1934.

"for some reason": unidentified clipping, Will Rogers file, MOMA.

Eddie Cantor, who wrote: Eddie Cantor, *As I Remember Them* (New York: Duell, Sloan and Pearce, 1963), 143.

"desires of the flesh": O'Neill, *Ah, Wilderness!* 295.

315   his copy of the script: WRM.

"Well, after I finish": WA 6, 240.

"With that proverbial outburst of laughter": quoted in OWR, 290.

Hearst newsreel: Videotape VA 4185M: "Hearst Newsreel Footage Will Rogers III," UCLA Film Archive.

Jim Rogers had armed himself: JR interview with BY, December 10, 1989.

"So for six days": WR:HWS, 303.

316   "it's a great trip": DT 4, 211. Carnera, the Italian heavyweight champion of the world, was known as the "Amblin' Alp."

"Perhaps Charles and I": Anne Morrow Lindbergh to WR and BR, September 27, 1934.

317   "He is sho chockful of personality": WA 6, 198.

"There ain't been nobody like Will": Robert Gregory, *Diz: The Story of Dizzy Dean and Baseball During the Great Depression* (New York: Viking Press, 1992), 6.

On October 3: ibid., 5.

"I believe I am the only fellow": DT 4, 226.

"a darn nice fellow": WA 6, 135.

318   "the battle is between": Greg Mitchell, *The Campaign of the Century* (New York: Random House, 1992), 389.

"There's some pretty smart birds": ibid., 347.

Once Long was in the middle of a filibuster: statement of Howard B. McLellan, handwritten manuscript, undated, WRM.

Long asked Will to see: Amon Carter, [Reminiscences of Will Rogers], typewritten manuscript, Amon Carter Archives, Amon Carter Museum, Fort Worth, Texas, 10–11.

Three days later: T. Harry Williams, *Huey Long* (New York: Alfred A. Knopf, 1970), 836.

319   "Well the old year will be passing": DT 4, 258.

On the last day of January: telegram, Sid to Winny Sheehan, January 31, 1935, Twentieth Century–Fox Archives, UCLA.

"one of the oldest cattle ranches": W. C. Denny to WR, February 23, 1935, WRM.

319   "There ain't any unemployed": WA 6, 251.

Baton Rouge trip: Baton Rouge *State Times,* August 16, 1935, microfilm reel 1, WRSHP.

320   Spi Trent: Spi Trent to WR, August 15, 1933.

"I am a young man": WA 6, 26–27. Milsten's book, *An Appreciation of Will Rogers,* was published in 1935, a revised edition, *Will Rogers—the Cherokee Kid,* in 1987. Tinney began researching his book in Oologah, where he lived. Realizing that he needed a way to gain access to Will, whom he didn't know, he convinced Will's old roping buddy Jim Rider to go out to California with him. Will was so happy to see his friend that he let Tinney stick around for a week. Tinney became a newspaper columnist and radio commentator with a style whose similarities to Will's were not completely unintended. *"Town and Country* published a picture of me and identified me as a cousin of Will Rogers," Tinney said in a 1990 interview with the author. "When I was back in Oologah, Will sent me a message through Herb McSpadden—'You don't get ahead in show business by being like somebody else.' " In his column about biographers, Will was referring to Tinney when he wrote, "One of these budding young biographers blew into my old country from Lord knows where, but he happened to land near the old ranch where I was on. He heard a couple of stories about my early day cavortings, so he goes so far as to get a fountain pen, and from then on he was my Boswell. Being some sort of Northerner by trade, he even works himself up into my semi-southern dialect, hits New York as 'The Voice of Rogers.' By that time he has become a brother cowpuncher who was born and raised right next to me and gradually works himself up into a cousin.

"Well, a progressive minded fellow like that writing your biography is liable to turn out in his story to be my father. In other words there is just too much imagination there to work on another fellow's life. There is a fellow ought to take his own life. With two more fountain pens he could work himself up into a Lincoln." WA 6, 26–27.

According to Tinney, he got word to Will through Homer Croy, an acquaintance, that the *Town and Country* caption was not his doing. By the time Croy was working on his biography, in the early 1950s, Tinney had still not gotten very far on his own book, so he let Croy use the notes for the interviews he had already done. As late as 1989, Tinney was impersonating Will in one-man shows in Tulsa.

"John D. Rockefeller's son-in-law": WA 6, 196. Will was referring to John D. Rockefeller, Jr.'s daughter, Abby, and her husband, David Milton.

321 Harry Truman: David McCullough, *Truman* (New York: Simon & Schuster, 1992), 214.

One day he was roping: Tulsa *Daily World*, July 9, 1935

He would take the newspapers: WA 6, 214.

Morey Amsterdam: BY interview with Morey Amsterdam, April 4, 1992. Amsterdam met Will in 1931, when the younger man was sixteen years old and playing the cello in a Los Angeles theater where Will was doing a charity engagement. "There was one bathroom that all the performers with dressing rooms on a floor had to share," Amsterdam recalled. "The toilet was incredibly loud, so I had the stage manager print up a sign that said, 'If you're constipated, just flush the toilet. It'll scare the shit out of you.' When Will saw the sign, he called over the stage manager and said, 'Who wrote this?' He told him that I did. Will called me over and said, 'Kid, that's the funniest thing I ever heard.' " During the engagement, according to Amsterdam, Will would read him his daily column and ask for suggestions; thereafter, he would occasionally contribute gags. To his knowledge, Amsterdam said, he was the only person who ever wrote material for Will.

"Buck looks fine": WA 6, 228.

In one scene in *Steamboat*: Fox press release, undated, WR file, AMPAS.

322 "a man born with as sensitive a touch": unidentified clipping, reproduced in Reba N. Collins, *Will Rogers & Wiley Post in Alaska: The Crash Felt 'Round the World* (Claremore: Oklahoma: Will Rogers Heritage Press, 1984), 47.

"Wiley Post's flight remains": John Keats, *Howard Hughes* (New York: Random House, 1966), 117.

323 One day in 1925: Burrell Tibbs, undated handwritten manuscript, Burrell Tibbs Collection, History of Aviation Collection, University of Texas at Dallas.

"Wiley, as you no doubt have found out": William R. Enyart to Joseph Nikrent, July 29, 1935, Wiley Post file, National Air and Space Museum, Washington, D.C.

"Wiley used to insist": Norman Blake, interview with BY, July 30, 1990.

It was rumored: unidentified clipping, reproduced in Collins, *Will Rogers & Wiley Post in Alaska*, 41.

hybrid airplane: Memo to Assistant Secretary of Commerce Johnson, Record Group 237, Civil Aeronautics Administration, file 835, box 373, National Archives, Washington, D.C. The superstitious will not be surprised to learn that some of the parts had unhappy pasts. The plane of which the Orion fuselage was a part had been in an accident. The wing had been part of a Lockheed Explorer, the *Blue Flash*, which aviator Roy Ammel had flown nonstop from New York City to the Canal Zone in 1930. As it was taking off from there, the plane skidded and crashed on its back; Ammel had to be chopped out with axes. Stanley R. Mohler and Bobby H. Johnson, *Wiley Post, His Winnie Mae, and the World's First Pressure Suit.* Smithsonian Annals of Flight No. 8. (Washington, D.C.: Smithsonian Institution Press, 1971), 107.

324   "Whenever Rogers had time" Bryan Sterling, *The Will Rogers Scrapbook* (New York: Grosset and Dunlap, 1976), 172.

"There was only one Winnie Mae": unidentified clipping, reproduced in Collins, *Will Rogers & Wiley Post in Alaska,* 6.

Leonard Slye: interview with BY, January 6, 1993.

precise provenance of the floats: In *Wiley Post* (p. 111), Stanley R. Mohler and Bobby H. Johnson, citing Will D. Cooper, say that Post scavenged a set of floats (much too heavy for his hybrid) from a Fokker trimotor plane. In a letter written in 1985, however, Lloyd R. Jarman asserted that Post used Edo floats, of appropriate weight, taken from a plane in which Jarman himself had flown. (Lloyd R. Jarman to Reba Collins, December 8, 1985, WRM.) This jibes with the August 30, 1935, Department of Commerce memo on the plane.

325   "I thought for two seconds": Fay Gillis Wells interview with BY, May 18, 1992.

In an interview: unidentified clipping, reproduced in Collins, *Will Rogers & Wiley Post in Alaska,* 7.

one-page will: August 3, 1935, WRM. The witnesses were Ewing Halsell and Eddie Vail.

Will spent much of that Saturday: Will Hays, *The Memoirs of Will Hays* (New York: Doubleday and Company, 1955), 474–475. Hays wrote that five or six weeks later, while he was in New York, he got a phone call from the man supervising the construction of his new California house. "The Rogers ranch truck just brought over two of the prettiest horses you ever saw," the foreman said.

"right then and there": unidentified clipping, Will Rogers file, FLPTC.

"We took a long ride": WR:HWS, 304.

326   met with the Soviet consul general: M. G. Galkovitch to WR, August 5, 1935.

his first reaction: WA 6, 251.

She later said that she backed out: Mohler and Johnson, *Wiley Post,* 111.

327   "Thousand-mile hop": DT 4, 344.

Rex Beach was reacquainting himself: Rex Beach, "Will Had All Alaska Laughing, Then Came Crash, Leaving Sourdoughs Stunned," unidentified clipping, reproduced in Collins, *Will Rogers & Wiley Post in Alaska,* 27.

"This Alaska is a great country": DT 4, 347.

"Was you ever driving around": ibid., 346.

moose steaks and caribou cutlets: undated clipping, [Vancouver] *Daily Province,* WRM.

visit to Matanuska Valley: *The New York Times,* August 17, 1935.

328 "GREAT TRIP": WR to Mary Rogers, August 14, 1935.

departure for Barrow: the fullest account is in a four-page memo from Director of Air Commerce Eugene L. Vidal to the secretary of commerce, August 30, 1935, Record Group 237, Civil Aeronautics Administration, file 835, box 373, National Archives, Washington, D.C.

329 Will bought magazines: Gene Fields, "The Last Goodby," undated manuscript, WRM.

When the plane took off: telegram, Murray Hall to Col. J. Carroll Cone, August 19, 1935, in Record Group 237, Civil Aeronautics Administration, file 835, box 373, National Archives, Washington D.C.

330 He communicated what had happened to Stanley Morgan: "Sergeant's Graphic Story Of Crash of Post and Rogers and Removal of Their Bodies," unidentified clipping, reproduced in Collins, *Will Rogers & Wiley Post in Alaska,* 32.

EPILOGUE

333 "with inheritance tax attorneys": BBR to Wesley Stout, June 17, 1940, Wesley Stout Papers, Library of Congress, Washington, D.C.

size of estate: OWR, 315.

"His writing is wordy": BBR to Wesley Stout, December 11, 1939, Wesley Stout Papers.

INDEX